HOWARD
GARDNER
Under Fire

The Under Fire™ Series

General Editor: Jeffrey A. Schaler

HOWARD GARDNER

Under Fire

The Rebel Psychologist
Faces His Critics

EDITED BY

JEFFREY A. SCHALER

OPEN COURT
Chicago and La Salle, Illinois

Volume 2 in the series, Under Fire™

To order books from Open Court, call toll-free 1-800-815-2280, or visit our website at www.opencourtbooks.com.

Open Court Publishing Company is a division of Carus Publishing Company.

Library of Congress Cataloging-in-Publication Data

Howard Gardner under fire : the rebel psychologist faces his critics / edited by Jeffrey A. Schaler.
    p. cm. — (The under fire series ; v. 2)
    Summary: "Thirteen essays criticize Howard Gardner's theories of Multiple
    Intelligence, ability traits, U-shaped curves in development, and other
psychological concepts of spirituality, creativity, and leadership; Gardner
responds to each" — Provided by publisher.
    Includes bibliographical references and index.
    ISBN-13: 978-0-8126-9604-2 (trade paper : alk. paper)
    ISBN-10: 0-8126-9604-2 (trade paper : alk. paper)
    1. Psychology — Philosophy. 2. Gardner, Howard. I. Schaler, Jeffrey A. II.
Gardner, Howard.
    BF38.H67 2006
    150.92 — dc22   2006022995

To Samara Orli

Being no Michelangelo or Mozart does not condemn one to be uncreative. . . . The best solution is to find a project that will benefit humanity, in line with your limited talents, and to make the most of your situation.

— WALTER KAUFMANN (1973)

To us mind must remain forever a realm of its own which we can know only through directly experiencing it, but which we shall never be able fully to explain or to 'reduce' to something else.

— F.A. HAYEK (1952)

Contents

About the Authors

SUSAN M. BARNETT is currently a Visiting Scholar in the Faculty of Education at Cambridge University and a member of Wolfson College. Her research and writing focuses on issues regarding intelligence, expertise, and transfer of learning. She has a Ph.D. and M.A. in Developmental Psychology from Cornell, an M.B.A. from Harvard, and a B.A. and M.A. in Experimental Psychology from Cambridge. Dr. Barnett was the recipient of a National Science Foundation Graduate Research Fellowship from 1994 to 1997. She has written articles and chapters for a variety of publications, including *Psychological Bulletin*, and is a member of both the American Psychological Association and the British Psychological Society.

NATHAN BRODY is Professor Emeritus of Psychology at Wesleyan University. He is Past President of the International Society for Individual Differences and was a member of the American Psychological Association's Taskforce on Intelligence. As well as scholarly articles highly respected by scientific psychologists, his books include *Personality: Research and Theory* (1972), *Intelligence* (1976, second edition 1992), *Human Motivation: Commentary on Goal-Directed Action* (1983), *Personality: In Search of Individuality* (1988), and *Personality Psychology: Science of Individuality* (with Howard Ehrlichman, 1997).

STEPHEN J. CECI holds a lifetime endowed chair in developmental psychology at Cornell University. He has written over three hundred articles and chapters, and given hundreds of invited addresses around the world. His past honors and awards include the Lifetime Distinguished Contribution Award of the American Psychological Association (2003, shared with Elizabeth F. Loftus), and the American Psychological

Society's James McKeen Cattell Award (2005, shared with E. Mavis Hetherington). Ceci is also the recipient of the American Academy of Forensic Psychology's Lifetime Achievement Award (2001), the Division of Developmental Psychology's Bronfenbrenner Award, and the Society for Research in Child Development's Science and Policy Award. His 1995 book (co-authored by Maggie Bruck), *Jeopardy in the Courtroom: A Scientific Analysis of Children's Testimony*, is an American Psychological Association bestseller and winner of the 2000 William James Award for Excellence in Psychology, and his 1996 book, *On Intelligence: A Bioecological Treatise on Intellectual Development* won critical acclaim.

ANNA CRAFT is Professor of Education at the University of Exeter and Visiting Scholar at Harvard University. Her twelve books include *Creativity Across the Primary Curriculum* (2000), *Creativity in Early Years Education: A Lifewide Foundation* (2002), and *Creativity in Schools: Tensions and Dilemmas* (2005). She is co-founder and joint convenor of the British Educational Research Association Special Interest Group, Creativity in Education.

HOWARD GARDNER is the John H. and Elisabeth A. Hobbs Professor of Cognition and Education at the Harvard Graduate School of Education. He also holds positions as Adjunct Professor of Psychology at Harvard University, Adjunct Professor of Neurology at the Boston University School of Medicine, and Senior Director of Harvard Project Zero. The author of over twenty books translated into twenty-six languages, and several hundred articles, Gardner is best known in educational circles for his theory of multiple intelligences (MI), a critique of the notion that there exists but a single human intelligence that can be assessed by standard psychometric methods. His recent books, available in paperback, are *The Disciplined Mind: Beyond Facts and Standardized Tests*, the K–12 *Education that Every Child Deserves* (2000) and *Intelligence Reframed: Multiple Intelligences for the 21st Century* (1999). In 2004, two new books were published: *Changing Minds: The Art and Science of Changing our Own and Other People's Minds* and *Making Good: How Young People Cope with Moral Dilemmas at Work* (with Wendy Fischman, Becca Solomon, and Deborah Greenspan).

DEANNA KUHN is Professor of Psychology and Education at Teachers College, Columbia University. She holds a Ph.D. in developmental psychology from the University of California, Berkeley, and was previously on the faculty at the Graduate School of Education at Harvard University. She is a fellow of the American Psychological Society and a board member of the Cognitive Development Society, as well as a member of numerous other organizations in psychology and education. She is former editor of the journal *Human Development* and is co-editor of the *Cognition, Perception, and Language* volume of the *Handbook of Child Psychology*, fifth edition, and the forthcoming sixth edition. She has published widely in the fields of psychology and education in outlets ranging from *Psychological Science* and *Psychological Review* to *Harvard Educational Review* and *Liberal Education*. She is co-author of *The Development of Scientific Thinking Skills* and author of *The Skills of Argument*. Her *Education for Thinking* (2005), seeks to identify the thinking skills that we can justify as objectives of education.

TANYA LUHRMANN is the Max Palevsky Professor in the Committee on Human Development. She trained at the University of Cambridge (Ph.D., 1986), taught for many years at the University of California San Diego, and joined the University of Chicago faculty in 2000. Her work focuses on the social construction of psychological experience, and the way that social practice alters psychological mechanism, particularly in the domain of what some would call the 'irrational'. She is an anthropologist, and uses primarily ethnographic methods to identify the salient features of the social context. Her books include *Persuasions of the Witch's Craft* 1989), *The Good Parsi* (1996), and *Of Two Minds* (2000). She is a director of the Clinical Ethnography project in the Department of Comparative Human Development.

DAVID R. OLSON is Professor of Applied Cognitive Science at the Ontario Institute for Studies in Education, University of Toronto, and University Professor Emeritus of the University of Toronto. He is author or editor of numerous articles and books including *The World on Paper* (1994) and co-editor with Nancy Torrance of *The Making of Literate Societies* (2001) and author of *Psychological Theory and Educational Reform* (2003). Olson is a Fellow of the Royal Society of Canada and the U.S. National Academy of Education. He was a Fellow at the Harvard Center for Cognitive Studies in the 1960s where he first met and became friends with Howard Gardner.

DAVID PARISER is a Professor of Art Education, in the Fine Arts Faculty at Concordia University, Montreal. He has taught art in the public schools in Massachusetts and Illinois. A Fellow of the American

Psychological Association, he has published reviews, essays and research articles in *Leonardo, Studies in Art Education, Poetics, Visual Arts Research*, and the *American Journal of Education*. He is the author of several book chapters and encyclopedia entries. His interests include: the study of juvenile work of great artists; emerging models of graphic development; cross-cultural models of aesthetic development, and the study of life in classrooms. He is the director of the teaching internship program in Art Education.

MARK RUNCO earned his M.A. and Ph.D. (Cognitive Psychology) at the Claremont Graduate School. He soon earned the Young Scholar Award from the National Association for Gifted Children. A few years ago he earned the E. Paul Torrance Lifetime Achievement Award from the same Association. He is Past President of the American Psychological Association's Division 10 (Psychology and the Arts) and founding Editor of the *Creativity Research Journal*. He co-edited the *Encyclopedia of Creativity* (1999). Currently he is Professor at the California State University at Fullerton at the Norwegian School of Economics and Business Administration in Bergen.

JEFFREY A. SCHALER is General Editor of the *Under Fire* Series and Executive Editor of *Current Psychology: Developmental, Learning, Personality, Social*. Schaler taught psychology at Johns Hopkins University's Peabody Conservatory of Music from 1993 to 2003, and is now professor in the Department of Justice, Law, and Society at American University's School of Public Affairs. He is the author of *Addiction Is a Choice* (2000), and has edited or co-edited several books, including *Drugs: Should We Legalize, Decriminalize, or Deregulate?* (1998), *Smoking: Who Has the Right?* (with Magda E. Schaler-Haynes, 1998), and *Szasz Under Fire: The Psychiatric Abolitionist Faces His Critics* (2004). In 1999 the Center for Independent Thought awarded him the Thomas Szasz Award for Outstanding Contributions to the Cause of Civil Liberties.

DEAN KEITH SIMONTON is Distinguished Professor of Psychology at the University of California, Davis. He has authored more than three hundred articles and chapters, plus nine books, including *Scientific Genius*; *Greatness, Genius, and Creativity*; *Origins of Genius*; *Great Psychologists and Their Times*; and *Creativity in Science*. He has received the Sir Francis Galton Award for Outstanding Contributions to the Study of Creativity, the Rudolf Arnheim Award for Outstanding

Achievement in Psychology and the Arts, the William James Book Award, the Theoretical Innovation Prize in Personality and Social Psychology, and the George A. Miller Outstanding Article Award. He is Fellow of several professional organizations, including the American Association for the Advancement of Science, American Psychological Society, and American Psychological Association.

ROBERT M. SPILLANE is Professor of Management at the Macquarie Graduate School of Management, Macquarie University, Sydney, and was Dean of the School from 1989 to 1991. He has been a Visiting Scholar at the London Business School, the University of Stockholm, and the Abcor Institute in Frankfurt. From 2003 to 2005 he delivered a highly acclaimed series of lectures for the Art Gallery Society, New South Wales. He has published nine books, more than 120 scholarly articles, and the play, *Entertaining Executives*, first performed at the Mermaid Theatre, London, in 2006. His recent books include *The Mind's Eye: An Introduction to Philosophy* (2004), *Questionable Behavior: An Introduction to Psychology* (2005), and *The Management Contradictionary* (with B. Marks and R. Marks, 2006).

GRAEME SULLIVAN is Chair of the Department of Arts and Humanities and Associate Professor of Art Education, Teachers College, Columbia University. His research involves the investigation of critical-reflexive thinking processes and research practices in the visual arts, described in his book *Art Practice as Research: Inquiry in the Visual Arts*. Sullivan has published widely in the field of art education and in 1990 he was awarded the Manual Barkan Memorial Award from the National Art Education Association for his scholarly writing. He maintains an active art practice; his *Streetworks* continue to be created and installed in different cities and sites (www.streetworksart.com).

CARLOS E. VASCO, M.Sc. (Physics), Ph.D. (Mathematics), is now Professor Emeritus of the National University of Colombia at Bogota. In 1985–86 he was Distinguished Schumann Fellow and Lecturer in Education at the Harvard Graduate School of Education in Cambridge, Massachusetts, where he has often been appointed Visiting Scholar during the last twenty years. Dr. Vasco was awarded a Guggenheim Fellowship in 1989. He was Advisor to the Ministry of Education from 1978 to 1993 in charge of the mathematics syllabus design. In 1993 he was selected by the President of Colombia to co-ordinate the Presidential Commission on Science, Education, and Development, and he published the seven-volume series of documents of the Commission. Now he teaches part-time and directs doctoral dissertations in cognitive development and in mathematics-and-science education in two doctoral programs at the Universidad de Manizales in Manizales and the Universidad del Valle in Cali, Colombia.

JOHN WHITE is Emeritus Professor of Philosophy of Education at the Institute of Education University of London, where he has worked since 1965, before which time he taught in secondary schools and colleges in Britain and France. His interests are in interrelationships among educational aims and applications to school curricula, especially in the areas of the arts, history, and personal and social education. His books include *Towards a Compulsory Curriculum* (1973), *Philosophers as Educational Reformers* (with Peter Gordon, 1979), *The Aims of Education Restated* (1982), *Education and the Good Life: Beyond the National Curriculum* (1990), *A National Curriculum for All: Laying the Foundations for Success* (with Philip O'Hear, 1991), *The Arts 5–16: Changing the Agenda* (1992), *Education and the End of Work: A New Philosophy of Work and Learning* (1997), *Do Howard Gardner's Multiple Intelligences Add Up?* (1998), *Will the New National Curriculum Live Up to Its Aims?* (with Steve Bramall, 2000), and *The Child's Mind* (2002).

WENDY M. WILLIAMS is a Professor in the Department of Human Development at Cornell University, where she studies the development, assessment, training, and societal implications of intelligence and related abilities. She holds Ph.D. and Master's degrees in psychology from Yale University, a Master's in physical anthropology from Yale, and a B.A. in English and biology from Columbia University. In the fall of 2001, Williams became co-founder and co-director of the Cornell Institute for Research on Children (CIRC), funded for $2.5 million by the National Science Foundation. In addition to dozens of articles and chapters on her research, Williams has authored eight books and edited four volumes. She is a Fellow of the American Psychological Society and four divisions of the American Psychological Association. She received the 1996 Early Career Contribution Award from Division 15 (educational psychology) of APA, and the 1997, 1999, and 2002 Mensa Awards for Excellence in Research to a Senior Investigator.

Acknowledgments

For her help with many facets of preparing this manuscript for publication, I thank Lindsay Pettingill. I also thank Mindy Kornhaber, Seana Moran, and Ellen Winner for useful suggestions about my responses. Editor Jeffrey Schaler has been a great help throughout the planning and execution of the volume.

H.G.

Many years of conversation with my friend Ernest H. Bradley contributed significantly to my thinking on these and related matters. I appreciate Howard Gardner for trusting me. David Ramsay Steele continues to be a great Editorial Director.

J.A.S.

Introduction

JEFFREY A. SCHALER

Howard Gardner, a name to conjure with among today's public intellectuals, is most celebrated for his conception and development of the theory of Multiple Intelligences, which has revolutionized educational thinking. But Gardner has also made outstanding original contributions to the study of leadership, of creativity, of child development, and humanly-fulfilling work. All of these topics are explored in this volume, by way of a debate between Gardner and his critics.

It's in the theory of intelligence that Howard Gardner has made the biggest splash. Intelligence is an area charged with emotion. In the deep conflicts it stirs up, a test of intelligence is more like a test for HIV than a test of blood pressure. I have frequently encountered people whose problems-in-living were bound up with their perceptions of their own intelligence and its assessment. I will mention here a couple of cases out of many.

Years ago, an undergraduate student of mine was about to graduate and he looked somewhat down. I asked "aren't you happy you're going to graduate in a few days?" He said "I'm not happy at all." I asked him why. He explained "I've hated college for the past four years and it's only since I've taken the last few courses with you that I've been excited about what I'm actually learning. Now that I'm finally excited, college is over. I was just beginning to enjoy college."

I was touched and decided to talk to him more about why he was so unhappy in other classes. He told me that he was bored. His grades were always among the highest in the class. I noticed that he didn't seem to study much for exams in my courses and still wrote outstanding answers to exam questions. At one point he told me how much he hated the exams. When I questioned him about this, it came out that he had several times, in high school and college, been falsely accused by his teachers of cheating.

His family was poor. He had grown up in a rural area of New England. His parents had separated and at times he and his mother and siblings lived out of their car. He was asked to come to school on Saturdays. He despised doing so, but his mother and the school administrators insisted. I asked him why and he explained this was because of his scores on a certain test. "What test?" I remembered asking him. He said he didn't like to talk about it because people thought of him differently when they knew about his scores on this test. To make a long story short, he had scored 170 on an IQ test. What was odd, too, was that his physical dress and appearance—back then, punk-rock style with a black belt full of chrome skulls—was nothing like one might expect of someone we might consider, with an IQ so high, well into the genius category. What is being "highly intelligent" here? What does it look like?

A second story comes to mind. A man in his forties came to me many years ago for counseling. He was very depressed. It seemed clear to both of us that if he went back to college and got a master's degree, he could improve his prospects as a teacher. I'd suggested Johns Hopkins University, if for no other reason than that it had a good master's program available for adults who already had jobs. Since he'd been out of school for so long, apparently the admissions department at Hopkins insisted that he take a few courses to see how well he performed before they formally admitted him into their graduate program. I discovered that he was taking two courses more than those required during the probation period. He received A's in all those graduate courses.

He continued to see me in what evolved into analysis while he worked on his master's degree. He would weep in each of our sessions, saying over and over again how he couldn't do well in class and couldn't do what was necessary to complete the master's degree successfully. He was especially upset over one course in particular. He was convinced he could not pass this course. I looked at the work required, and told him that I thought it was difficult, but emphasized that I also thought he was clearly "smart enough"; what he needed to do was put in more energy studying and less energy whining.

One day several weeks later he told me that he was ending his analysis with me. I asked why and he explained that he had visited an "educational psychologist" who told him that his distress at not being able to do well in school was a symptom that he should not be tackling strongly intellectual work, but should be focusing his educational training on vocational skills, skills that did not require much intellectual effort. He was apparently "traumatizing" himself. She recommended he go for an IQ test.

I told him I thought this was the last thing he should do. He asked me why. I asked him, "What if you find that your IQ score is below average? Is that proof that you're not smart? And if your IQ score is higher than average, what will that mean to you?" I asked him to consider how his problem was not that he was dumb, but that he *believed* he was dumb. He said his mind was made up, we shook hands and said goodbye. As he was walking out the door of my office, I asked "How did you do in that one course you were so upset about." He paused and said rather sheepishly "I got an 'A'."

I expected never to hear from him again. About a year later, I found a message on my phone machine: "Jeff, this is X, I just want you to know that I received my master's degree from Hopkins, I have a new position of teaching responsibility I said I could never achieve, and I want to thank you for everything you taught me." To me, his story was a perfect example of someone whose belief about his ability had more to do with success and failure than his ability itself.

Gardner and Multiple Intelligences

Prior to Gardner's *Frames of Mind*, there was little sustained theoretical opposition to the reigning paradigm of IQ, in which it is supposed that intelligence is a single concept known as 'g', exhibiting itself in scholastic attainment and detectable by a narrow range of puzzle-solving tests. Gardner transformed the discussion of intelligence and education by making a powerful case that there are several different forms of intelligence, some of which express themselves in activities not traditionally considered strictly academic.

Using eight criteria to demarcate separate 'intelligences', Gardner at first identified seven:

1. linguistic intelligence;
2. logico-mathematical intelligence;
3. musical intelligence;
4. bodily-kinesthetic intelligence;
5. spatial intelligence;
6. interpersonal intelligence;
7. intrapersonal intelligence.

Because Gardner sees individual humans as combining these intelligences in differing magnitudes, the multiple-intelligences (MI) approach leads to a greater appreciation of individual uniqueness. It views individual humans in a multidimensional, rather than unidimensional, way. And this, I believe, is definitely for the better, especially when we consider the self-perpetuating and self-reinforcing quality of assessments of 'intelligence'. Schools teach courses emphasizing that students solve certain kinds of problems and think in certain ways. People who do well in activities thus conceived tend to get college places and promotions, and to have more of a voice in how others will be evaluated. Rich rewards accrue to the individuals Herrnstein and Murray termed "the cognitive elite," while those talented in other ways may find themselves unrecognized and unvalidated.

MI theory quickly became very popular with educationists, less so with theoretical psychologists. It has been disputed whether all seven are really separate intelligences, or (from a contrary viewpoint) whether the list could easily be extended. Suggestions for other kinds of intelligence include naturalist intelligence, spiritual intelligence, existential intelligence, and moral intelligence. Howard has accepted naturalist intelligence, but still has his reservations about the others.

Intelligence is useful, it seems, only in terms of what people can and can't do with their lives. The demands a society places on a person to become a producer may require certain skills and not others. The task of growing up is to develop a marketable skill. This is something that is not achieved through intelligence, *per se*, but through a combination of many different factors. First and foremost, it seems to me, are effort and discipline. When we teach people that they have a limited ability called intelligence, they seek to live up to this label or identity. In this sense, believing what a person can do seems to have much more to do with motivation and success in life than intelligence or luck. If one doesn't have the will to act on one's intelligence, it seems that intelligence, whether singular or plural, loses its effectiveness. Howard has written on the importance of creativity, and I agree with him here for the most part. In my own work as a therapist, professor, and writer for over thirty-three years, I find that motivation and "meaning-making" are more the keys to leading a good life, a rewarding life, and ultimately the "intelligent" life.

Multiple Accomplishments

When I first met Howard Gardner, I remember, as we were planning this book, and planning whom to invite to contribute to it, that Howard did not strike me as the kind of person who thought there were two kinds of people in the world at all—for instance, those who went to Harvard and those who went to college somewhere else. I remember a few remarks we exchanged as we ate lunch together. People think they're special because they went to a certain school, much like people think they're special because they've scored well on an intelligence test. However we view it, intelligence is something highly valued throughout the world, much like going to Harvard and teaching at Harvard will always be. People like to find ways to make themselves feel important.

Howard Gardner has moved on from his multiple writings on multiple intelligences, and MI is certainly not the only contribution he will be remembered for. While his other achievements are described more fully in this volume, we should especially note his theoretical work on creativity, leadership, and personal development.

Just to touch on a few of Gardner's contributions:

In *Creating Minds* (1993), Gardner provoked a Gestalt switch in public understanding of creative genius. He analyzed the lives and achievements of seven diverse personalities (Freud, Einstein, Stravinsky, Eliot, Martha Graham, Picasso, and Gandhi) each of whom founded "a new system of meaning," and each of whom sacrificed some personal fulfillment in pursuit of their revolutionary missions.

In Project Zero, inspired and launched by the late Nelson Goodman, Gardner has conducted and directed research into children's artistic development, yielding many controversial conclusions and providing new ideas for educators.

The GoodWork Project, begun in 1995, is a broad empirical investigation of the experiences of professional workers in a range of occupations. Its ongoing research seeks individuals and institutions most conducive to work which is good both ethically and technically, as well as engaging for the workers. The Project seems ideologically motivated by a pronounced hostility to economic freedom, which I cannot share.

In *Changing Minds* (2004), Gardner made a popular application of findings in cognitive psychology to explain how people's deep-rooted convictions can be changed. He catchily identified seven elements necessary for intellectual transformation: reason, resonance, redescriptions, research, real-world events, resources, and resistance. The book has been found highly stimulating by a wide range of readers, from business leaders to social psychologists.

In the varied endeavors he has undertaken, Howard Gardner has combined broad erudition and a concern for rigorous research with an unpretentious formulation which immediately engages the interest of practical people going about their everyday lives. His conclusions have always been hotly debated, and many of the debates around Howard's work are still heating up. He is therefore perfectly suited for the *Under Fire* format, in which a leading controversial thinker is confronted by leading critics, and gets to have the last word—at least within the covers of this volume.

A Blessing of Influences

HOWARD GARDNER

Searching for the Right Theme

The familiar last movement of Beethoven's Ninth Symphony begins with a series of short musical motifs. In a conversation that the composer is having with himself, as much as with his eavesdropping audience, Beethoven rejects one theme after another until he finally arrives at a motif appropriate for the climactic finale.

A scholar who attempts an autobiography is likely to find himself in an analogous position. Over the years I have written various autobiographical accounts. As I embark on the present scholarly autobiography, several potential openers—some already used, some devised for this occasion—occur to me:

- Trying to envision my childhood, I see myself seated at the piano, usually next to my mother, playing a Bach invention.

- Two events that were long hidden from me—the accidental death of my older brother and my family's losses in the Holocaust—came to dominate my childhood.

- To all intents and purposes, my involvement with the life of the mind began when I arrived in Cambridge, Massachusetts in September 1961 to attend Harvard College as a freshman.

- My family has always been the most important thing in my life. As a child, I thought about both of my parents every hour, and now I think about my wife, my four children, and my grandchild with equal regularity.

- I see my research and writing as having four phases. First I studied how minds developed. Then I studied how minds break down. Third, I studied how minds are organized. Now I study how minds change.

- Three crucial personal encounters in the 1960s transformed my intellectual development: I remember vividly my first meetings with the psychologist Jerome Bruner, the philosopher Nelson Goodman, and the neurologist Norman Geschwind.

I don't know whether the Beethoven symphony would have achieved equal fame had the composer chosen another motif. I've come to realize that each of these openings—and a dozen more that I could easily contrive—could serve as reasonable points of departure for the present essay. Such openings, after all, are simply convenient clothing racks on which I can hang the crucial names, numbers, and experiences—and, if I so choose—highlight certain perspectives, hide others, pay debts, and settle scores.

In my sixty-three years I have been extraordinarily lucky: lucky in the parents I chose (as I like to put it), lucky with the rest of my family, lucky with my place of birth, lucky with my academic and artistic educations, lucky with my friends and colleagues, lucky with my supporters (and perhaps even my detractors), lucky with the course of my work. Of course, not everything has worked out in my personal and professional lives—and a full account should chronicle failures, mistakes, and losses. But I have chosen to organize this autobiographical account around the many, mostly highly positive influences that have combined to create a good scholarly life and a good personal life. I delineate the ways I was influenced by these various individuals and forces. And, because this volume is focused on critiques, I include a brief discussion of the influence that I have had, and the influences that I would like to have. My reactions to the critiques, organized according to five themes, appear toward the end of this book.

My Contributions

I view myself as a psychologist-scholar who has tried to understand the human mind in its full richness and complexity; I seek to share my conclusions both with other scholars concerned with the mind and with the broader educated public.

This self-characterization requires a bit of unpacking. All psychologists and many other social scientists are interested in the mind, and properly so. My focus has fallen not on the basic processes of perception, memory, learning, and the like but rather on 'high end' cognition—intelligence, creativity, leadership, artistry. Many scholars hope to have a wide readership, but most psychologists devote their efforts to authoring articles that appear in peer-reviewed technical journals. Indeed during the first fifteen years of my scholarly life, I wrote dozens of such articles. Unlike most colleagues I have always written books as well, and now the bulk of my writing is either in book form or in articles intended for a wider audience. Such technical writing as I still do is almost always in collaboration with students, who require training in scientific writing.

My obituary is likely to read "The Father (or, less respectfully, 'The Guru') of Multiple Intelligences." From one angle that appellation is appropriate: I am best known as the individual who, in the early 1980s, argued that human beings are better described as having several relatively autonomous intellectual capacities than as having a single all-purpose intelligence (technically, 'g'). At least half the communications and half the invitations that I receive continue to focus on "MI" theory; and it would have been easy to load this volume of critique with dissections of the theory.

The hypothetical one-line obituary does not align with my self-concept. To begin with, I see myself as a social scientist or social commentator, and, at times, as a public intellectual. Unlike many social observers and public intellectuals—but like my teacher Jerome Bruner—I approach societal issues from the perspective of cognitive or developmental psychology.

Expanding on one of the trial motifs cited above, I see my career as having had several ordered but overlapping phases:

1. I began my career with a focus on how the mind develops, with particular reference to the development of symbol-using capacities in the arts. I came to construe artistic development as more complex—less linear—than scientific development; in some ways, the child of five is more akin to the mature artist than is the child of 10 or 15.

2. Shortly thereafter, I began to study how mental processes break down under conditions of brain damage, again with a particular focus on higher-order thought processes in the arts and other symbol-using realms. I discovered that the right cerebral hemisphere makes many important contributions to artistic thinking, even in the supposedly 'left hemisphere' realms of language (metaphor, irony, humor, comprehension of narrative all rely crucially on the nondominant hemisphere). As I put it, it is the right hemisphere that 'gets the point'.

3. These two lines of work culminated in the positing of the theory of multiple intelligences. The dual lines of training, along with considerable firsthand experience with normal and gifted children and with brain-damaged adults, led to the conclusion that all human beings possess linguistic, logical-mathematical, musical, spatial, bodily-kinesthetic, naturalistic, interpersonal and intrapersonal intelligence.

The unexpectedly enormous response to MI theory, particularly among educators, led to two further career milestones:

4. I began to focus more directly on educational issues. I pondered the educational implications of MI theory. I embarked on several collaborative projects designed to explore how multiple intelligences could affect assessment, curriculum, and pedagogy.

I also began to consider the nature of the unschooled mind; the importance (and the difficulty) of mastering disciplinary ways of thinking; the even greater challenges involved in interdisciplinary thinking; the desirability of alternative, performance-based forms of assessment; and the centrality of deep understanding in any educational endeavor.

5. If MI theory were even approximately correct, this state of affairs entailed implications for the understanding of other human capacities. Exploring human creativity through case studies of individuals who exhibited different intellectual profiles, I discovered as well a variety of forms—ranging from problem solving and problem finding to the creation of works in a genre and the execution of high-stake performances. I confirmed the importance of non-intellectual factors (personality, temperament, choice of domain, influence of powerful gate-keepers and institutions) in creative achievement.

Turning to leadership, I carried out case studies of individuals who led institutions or populations of various sorts; and I delineated the contributions of story-telling capacities in effective leaders. The focus on leadership has led, in turn, to a more general consideration of what it takes to change minds: as leaders, creators, teachers and trainers, therapists, family members, and individuals who consider ourselves open to change.

6. Since the middle 1990s, I have been carrying out collaborative studies with my close colleagues Mihaly Csikszentmihalyi and William Damon. We have sought to understand the nature of GoodWork®—work that is at once excellent in its technical aspects, ethically responsible, and personally engaging. The Good Worker takes seriously the implications of his or her work for the broader society in which it takes place. Our study has entailed extensive interviews and data analyses with over twelve hundred professionals in various domains. We have identified both the difficulties of carrying out good work at a time of vastly powerful market forces, and the particular individual, domain, and organizational features that influence the incidence of good work.

7. Finally, in the recent past, I have begun to think about the kinds of minds that will be needed in the future for our increasingly interconnected and intimate global society. I use the term 'needed' in two sens-

es: what our young people will need to compete effectively in this new, multiply interconnected world; what our world will need to survive and to thrive. My current list includes the disciplined mind; the synthesizing mind; the creative mind; the respectful mind; and the ethical mind (see Gardner 2007).

Examined from the top of the mountain (so to speak), I discern this sequence:

A. How minds develop;
B. How minds break down;
C. How minds are organized;
D. How to change minds in general;
E. How to change minds in ways that are productive for the society and the planet.

Childhood

Recently I received an unexpected, massive packet from Michael Rich and David Neustaedter, two individuals unknown to me. These distant relatives in Ohio sent me an eighty-page tree from the Gardner/Goldsmith (Gaertner/Goldschmidt) side of my family. Scanning this document, I learned about the names of relatives dating back three hundred years. And I discovered that I am related to all manner of persons ranging from the Sulzburgers of the *New York Times* to the Freud family. Presumably, an analogous family tree from my mother's (Seidenberger/Weilheimer) side would reveal other surprising and intriguing connections.

Still, from personal testimonial knowledge, my lineage dates back only to the latter years of the nineteenth century in the Bavarian city of Nuremberg and its suburbs. The Gardners were in the stove business. My father Ralph was born in 1908. When his father Siegfried died unexpectedly in 1925, my father left school and went into the family business—making and selling stoves. He met my mother Hilde Weilheimer in 1930, and they got married in January 1932, when Hilde was but twenty. The Weilheimer family were in the 'hops' futures business (a career which my uncle Harry has continued till this day).

I would describe both sides of this German family tree as comfortable but not affluent. They were successful in business but not titans. They did not have higher education—in fact, I am probably the first person on either side of the family to have had a full college education. They were not intellectuals, but they read easily and widely, and were interested in music and other arts. Having been born before the First World War and reared in Weimar Germany, they knew conflict, chaos, runaway inflation, and even hunger. Yet they were completely unprepared for the rise of the Nazis and the consequent disasters of the Second World War and the Holocaust.

My parents were eminently sensible persons—they thought ahead and displayed good judgment in abundance. As early as 1934, they moved to Italy to get away from Hitler; and when Hitler and Mussolini signed a non-aggression pact, they moved back to Germany and my father began a series of trips to the United States in an attempt to emigrate. In the absence of rich patrons (which my parents lacked), admission to the United States was not easy to achieve. But both my parents were very determined individuals. Not only did they manage to escape Germany in 1938, arriving in the U.S. on the infamous Kristallnacht of November 9th, but during the following years, they operated like leaders of a small military unit, tracing the emigration of members of their far flung kin, helping in whatever way they could (I cannot count the number of kin who stayed with us at various times in our tiny apartment), and serving as central figures—cynosures—for dozens of relatives on both sides of the family.

In 1935, Erich (anglicized as Eric) Gardner was born. From all reports he was an unusually bright and sensitive boy. With my parents, he sailed to New York and then moved to Scranton, Pennsylvania (where my parents remained for fifty-two years). My parents had lost their country and had no money. Eric was the one bright spot in their lives—indeed, knowing no English on his arrival, he had nonetheless skipped second grade. In January 1943, when my mother was three months pregnant with me, Eric was in a fatal sleigh riding accident witnessed by my mother with her own eyes. My parents told me subsequently that if my mother had not been pregnant with me, they would probably have killed themselves. The death of their only son was so painful for my parents that they refrained from telling me about it for a full decade. At some level, I must have known about their loss. I am skirting psychoanalytic interpretations in this essay—but I am sure that the loss of this child placed a heavy psychic burden on survivors in my family, including me.

Following my unproblematic birth on July 11th, 1943, I spent the first decade and a half of my life in a middle-sized declining coal-mining city in northeastern Pennsylvania. I was joined by my sister Marion, born on March 9th, 1946. Professionally, my father did quite well. Joining forces with his cousins (as he had also done in Europe) he first built up an automotive supply business and then shifted to the binding and sale of children's books. My father was a gifted salesman with good financial sense. He was able to sell the business, retire comfortably at the age of fifty-eight, and spend the next thirty-three years playing the stock market, reading, eating out with his friends (who dubbed him "the baron"), and enjoying his family. I don't think that he ever recovered from the death of my brother and he would have preferred if he had never had to leave German-speaking Europe.

My mother, still alive and active at the age of ninety-four, is a remarkable woman. Deprived of a higher education, and spending her early adult years dealing with personal and national tragedy, she became a much admired leader of the volunteer community in Scranton. People instinctively warm to my mother, and she displays a comfortable and supportive manner to individuals of diverse backgrounds and stations. For decades, indeed generations, she has served as "zero degree of separation" for hundreds of individuals all over the world. Without having to take notes, she maintains a mental catalogue of what everyone has been doing and feeling and makes optimum use of these data in all communications—including not a little gossip! Like my father, she has common sense in abundance; and she complemented his wisdom about political and business matters with wisdom about personal matters. She was much more involved than my father in childrearing. She sat alongside me nearly every day for years as I practiced the piano. And she exhibited that involvement in scouting, schooling, and synagogue that signaled to Marion and me that what we did was important.

I consider my childhood to have been unremarkable in a positive sense. I was a good student, who loved to read, and stood comfortably at the head of my class. I liked to play the piano and was quite good at it, though I ceased formal lessons before adolescence when it became clear that I would have to practice much more if I wanted to move from amateur to professional status. (In the succeeding five decades, I have continued to enjoy music, I play the piano when possible, and—for a number of years—I supplemented my income with one or two piano students). I am not a natural athlete; and because of my brother's death I was sheltered from anything that seemed physically risky. I always had friends though, until high school, I would not have been considered popular. I was a cub and boy scout for seven years and eventually attained the rank of Eagle Scout. I did not love scouting but it was part of 'the program' and, ever the good young German-American, I therefore marched through the ranks without protest. Though awkward, I turned out to be an excellent driller! Like other first generation families, my extended family was quite close. The Gardners spent more time with our relatives in Scranton, New York, and elsewhere, than with any other people. I consider this immersion in family to have been a very positive experience.

As I think about influences in my childhood, I would unhesitatingly place my family—nuclear and extended—first. My interests, values, style of interaction all draw on the few dozen Gardners, Weilheimers, and Seidenbergers with whom I spent much of my spare time. I was comfortable with peers and teachers but was rarely stretched by them. Indeed, it was the conclusion—reluctantly reached—that I had more knowledge than some of my high-school teachers that convinced me I should finish secondary school at a local independent school rather than at Scranton Central High School. At nearby Wyoming Seminary, I was for the first time challenged by a few teachers and a few peers. I began to learn the difference between reading and reading deeply; between writing the way one speaks and writing to express a point of view precisely, elegantly, and persuasively. And for the first time, I became a leader in campus organizations and in social life.

If you had seen me at age sixteen or seventeen, I would have appeared like the prototypical Jewish boy who hated the sight of blood. Most people, including me, expected that I would become a lawyer—or, just possibly, a journalist. I had the typical teenage boy's interests in popular music, spectator sports, the mass media, social life, and girls. Scrantonian Mark Harris, the peer whom I most admired, had gone to Wyoming Seminary and Harvard College—and so that is what I wanted to do as well.

Cambridge

In September 1961, I journeyed to Cambridge, Massachusetts, to begin my undergraduate years at Harvard College. I had no inkling at the time that I would end up spending the next forty-plus years within a few miles of Harvard Square. Like any proverbial 'big fish in the small pond', I had certain apprehensions about whether I could 'make it' in what had now become a highly competitive national, if not international institution. Unlike those who had attended independent schools like Phillips Exeter or Andover, I knew no one else in the Freshman Class. And while I had thought I was a good pianist, one stroll past the practice rooms in the basement of the Harvard Union demonstrated that I was but one of dozens with some talent at the keyboard. A few early papers and exams reminded me that I could no longer assume that I would be the best in the class. Nonetheless, it would be misleading to say that I was overwhelmed by Harvard. I found that I was good at the academic enterprise, and indeed received high grades as a freshman and throughout my undergraduate career.

Let me put it more strongly. I loved Harvard and I loved Cambridge. For the first time in my life, I could talk and argue with individuals who were my peers—and, in not a few cases, my superiors— in every sense. Almost everyone was interested in ideas, and conversation about significant political, economic, and cultural matters was the unspoken rule. I took the classes that I wanted to take in all manner of subjects and may well have set a record for the number of courses audited for a full term. The surroundings also excited me. Boston was a lively city and Cambridge had an amazing number of inviting bookstores, restaurants, cafés, artistic performance centers, and comfortable places to talk, read, write, and reflect. It was thrilling to walk the streets and inhabit the building associated with such legendary names as Ralph Waldo Emerson, Henry David Thorcau, and William James. At Commencement, I routinely walked by individuals like the journalist Walter Lippmann (Class of 1910), the pioneering television newsman Lawrence Spivak (Class of 1921), and two distinguished historians of the United States, each sporting bowties—Professor Arthur M. Schlesinger Senior, and his son Professor Arthur M. Schlesinger Junior, Class of 1938, then on loan to John F. Kennedy, class of 1940. I also saw John Kennedy at the annual Harvard-Dartmouth football game, as well as many other members of his entourage.

During my undergraduate education, I shifted course in a number of ways. Academics was not just something that I tolerated or even enjoyed; I began to realize that I wanted to spend my life in the academy. I had started as a history major, and have continued to enjoy history, but I came to realize that I was more interested in the social sciences, and so I shifted my major to Social Relations—an idiosyncratic (and regrettably short-lived) amalgam of psychology, sociology, and anthropology. I had previously enjoyed journalistic writing but began to write like a budding scholar. With everyone else in my family, I had thought that I would become some kind of a professional and, to prove that I could have, I took pre-law and pre-medical courses. When I did well in those courses, I felt 'liberated' to embark on an academic track.

I was attracted most to professors in the social sciences, as well as those professors in the humanities or the natural sciences who had a very broad set of interests. Often, though not invariably, these professors were Jewish and some came from the same kind of European background as my parents. I could mention dozens but I will single out two who became friends: the psychoanalyst Erik Erikson, scholar of human development and the 'identity crisis', who became my tutor for two years: and the lawyer-turned-sociologist architect David Riesman, who achieved fame for his study of American's 'lonely crowd', who read many of my papers, commented at length on them, and took a personal interest in my development. I was also privileged to take or audit courses with political scientist Henry Kissinger, already a legend in pre-Nixon times; the legal scholar Paul Freund, who was the outstanding scholar of constitutional law; the Nobel Prize winning biologist George Wald, who introduced generations of undergraduates to the discoveries of the new DNA science; the historian H. Stuart Hughes, who helped me to understand the European intellectual heritage that I had unconsciously absorbed from my family; the literary scholar Walter Jackson Bate (who personified Samuel Johnson for hundreds of American students); and the literary historian Perry Miller, who charted the New England mind of the seventeenth century and who died tragically during the fall of 1963 when I was auditing his course.

I drop these names not because they will necessarily be well known to readers, nor to pay homage to them, but rather to underscore a crucial point. The untutored undergraduate is essentially a blank slate when it comes to the world of scholarship. Each of these men—and I could provide additional names, also men—represented a whole universe of thought. They introduced me not only to their subject but to a distinctive way of thinking and creating, one that (in the happiest cases) I have been able to internalize in some way. Erik Erikson, for example, showed me how one could 'read' a novel or a film for deep knowledge of the experiences of the protagonist; Stuart Hughes revealed how thinkers consciously and unconsciously build upon and revise (even 'rewrite') their predecessors; Paul Freund illustrated how the law, an inherently conservative institution, can nonetheless adjust to take into account unanticipated events and trends.

That is what is most special about Harvard and Cambridge. During the period I have lived there I have had the privilege of encountering literally dozens of individuals who have created a new area of scholarship and in many cases I have had the opportunity to absorb at least something of their powerful if sometimes idiosyncratic ways of thinking. And there were others whom I did not meet but who also affected me deeply: literary critic-journalist Edmund Wilson, whose sketches of historical and literary figures from the past century were finely wrought; philosopher Susanne Langer, who first revealed to me the power of different kinds of symbol systems, including those featured in the arts; ethologist

Konrad Lorenz, who documented the stimuli and processes in the natural environment that unlocked instinctual patterns of behavior—just to name a few. As I look at the development of my own thinking and writing, I can actually see in operation some of the lessons learned from these and other comparable intellectual giants.

Had I not hitched a ride to Ann Arbor, Michigan, in the spring of 1965, I would in all likelihood not have had two life-altering experiences. I met the distinguished pioneering cognitive psychologist Jerome Bruner, who hired me to work that summer as a researcher on an innovative new elementary school curriculum in social studies called *Man: A Course of Study*; and working for Bruner, in turn, I met and fell in love with Judy Krieger, an age-mate and kindred spirit from Long Island, whom I married in London in June of 1966 and with whom I had three children: Kerith (1969), Jay (1971), and Andrew (1976).

Judy and I got married in London because I had won a Knox Fellowship to study at the London School of Economics. I did not do much formal study—London in the era of the Beatles and Twiggy was much too exciting a place, even for a committed student. The year was very important. I did a tremendous amount of undisciplined reading, a good deal of traveling, immersed myself in what was then considered 'modernism' in the arts, and (inspired by my intensive stint the previous summer with Bruner) decided to pursue a graduate career in developmental and cognitive psychology at Harvard.

Professional Development and Professional Angst

While I loved my undergraduate years as much as anyone I know, I did not like graduate school. In fact, after the first few months, I seriously considered quitting. I resented the seemingly irrelevant hoops through which I was expected to jump, I rejected the hierarchy of student and professor, and I was not sure that I cared enough about academic psychology to devote my life to it. I remained in part because everyone (including my fellow doctoral student Judy Gardner) expected me to remain and because I was able to convince myself that the pros outweighed the cons.

As soon as I negotiated the initial hoops, and made my peace with the dystopic aspects of graduate education, the angst dissipated. And indeed, I made important personal and intellectual connections during the late 1960s. In Roger Brown, a gifted social psychologist with special interests in language and music, I found a wonderfully supportive adviser, who helped me with writing, and counseled me with career dilemmas and (unlike the standard adviser of the time) did not pressure me to join his 'lab'. Allowing me to go my own way—in the face of counter-pressures from much of the rest of the professionally-oriented faculty—was an enormous gift: one that I have in turn tried to pass on to my own students. To this day, I remain the faculty adviser of choice for doctoral students who are pursuing unconventional topics.

In Nelson Goodman, a brilliant and iconoclastic philosopher, I found a person with kindred interests in the arts who was also an intimidating model of precise thinking and writing. In the post-Sputnik era, where much money had been invested in scientific and technological education, the Graduate School of Education at Harvard received a grant to study arts education. The beneficiaries had the foresight to approach Goodman, and he agreed to head an initiative that he christened Project Zero "because no one knows anything systematic about arts education." As fate had it, in 1967, I became a charter member of Project Zero, the research organization with which I have been affiliated for almost forty years.

Toward the end of my graduate years, I met the acclaimed behavioral neurologist Norman Geschwind. Geschwind was a scholarly polymath and a spellbinding lecturer, who introduced a whole generation to the fascinating intellectual and personality profiles exhibited by individuals who had the misfortune to suffer from brain damage. Geschwind kindled my interest in the brain and helped me to see that I could better understand the nature of artistry if I were to study how artists fare under conditions of brain damage; I enjoyed over a decade of extremely stimulating interactions with this intellectually generous man before his untimely death in 1984.

I also took or audited courses in several art forms: poetry with Robert Lowell, musical composition with Leon Kirchner, and visual arts with Rudolf Arnheim. Probably the most enduring influence came from Bruner, whose conceptualization of cognitive psychology, commitment to education, and infectious mode of interaction with his younger associates in the aforementioned school curriculum and in the fabled Center of Cognitive Studies were all tremendously important. It says something about memory—or at least my memory—that I was unable for several years to recognize the strength of my 'identification' with Bruner. Perhaps the fact that he had been a somewhat prickly adviser to Judy Gardner contributed to this selective amnesia.

There were also influences beyond Harvard and Cambridge. As a budding social scientist, I had already immersed myself in the writings of Freud, Marx, Weber, Durkheim, and other founding social scientists. During my fertile year in London I traveled to Russia and learned for the first time about the distinctive developmental psychological approach of Lev Vygotsky and Alexander Luria; and, of symbolic importance, Judy Gardner and I spent our first night as a married couple in Geneva, visiting the great developmental psychologist Jean Piaget the following morning. These thinkers, along with Bruner, convinced me that the area of social science on which I should focus was human cognitive development—and that remains today my central discipline.

As a young developmental psychologist, I could not help but be tremendously influenced by Piaget's brilliant investigations and conceptualizations. Bruner had also introduced me to the work in structural anthropology of Claude Lévi-Strauss and the revolutionary approach to linguistics of MIT's Noam Chomsky. I read extensively in the works of all three of these individuals and wrote a book about the then-new social scientific approach called structuralism—*The Quest for Mind*, published in 1973. I became increasingly interested in the study of artistic symbolization undertaken by Susanne Langer, as well as other philosophers like Ernst Cassirer. These thinkers underscore the extent to which human thought is pervaded—indeed constituted—by symbols and, paralleling work undertaken by my mentor Goodman, also delineated the features that differentiated various kinds of artistic symbols—musical, literary, dance—from one another and from symbols foregrounded in mathematics and the sciences.

By the time that I received my doctoral degree in developmental psychology in June 1971, I had already embarked on a somewhat unusual career course. While officially a psychologist, I still identified more with the broad social scientists of my undergraduate years—Erikson, Riesman, Bruner and their ilk—than with paradigmatic psychologists of the B.F. Skinner-S.S. Stevens-George Miller stripe. (The latter were in the Psychology department, the former had all been affiliated with the Social Relations department). I had already completed three books: a textbook in social psychology (embarrassingly entitled *Man and Men*) that appeared in 1970; the study of structuralism (*The Quest for Mind*) that was published in 1973; and an ambitious and contentious treatise in developmental psychology called *The Arts and Human Development*, also published in 1973. Reflecting their own training most developmentalists construed cognition as culminating in the mind of a scientist; in contrast, I argued in the latter book that the apogee of human development is better construed as "participation in the artistic process." As an author of books (rather than only of technical articles), I was already embarked on a course different from my psychology peers at Harvard and other institutions.

My work with Nelson Goodman, and my reading of Piaget and Bruner, had convinced me that it was worth investigating the development in children of various artistic capacities. Piaget had explored the development in children of the capacities needed to think in a logical and scientific manner. For my doctoral thesis, I investigated the emergence in children of sensitivity to painting style. And in the years immediately following completion of my doctoral studies, my colleagues and I undertook studies of the origins of capacities central to the arts—creation and understanding of metaphor, creation and understanding of stories, sensitivity to style in other art forms, and the mastery of other forms of artistic sensitivity, such as appreciation of balance, expressivity, and composition in various art forms. More directly paralleling Piaget, I also embarked on a study of the development in a cohort of nine children of the gamut of human symbol using capacities. Whereas Piaget looked at the development in his nine children of the Kantian concepts of time, space, number, and object, my colleagues and I examined early competences in narrative, figurative language, two-dimensional depiction, three-dimensional depiction, numerical competence, gestural and bodily expressiveness, and musical perception and production.

While I applied for a teaching position, I was pleased and relieved to receive three years of postdoctoral support to work directly with Norman Geschwind and his colleagues at the Boston Veterans Administration Medical Center. I was—and remain to this day—an avid student; and here was my chance to learn about neurology, neuropsychology, and the brain (I used to do a 'mean' neurological examination from the neck up). I found fascinating the phenomena of brain damage—the peculiar variety of competences and incompetences that may result from a stroke (and that have since been made famous by Oliver Sacks). The puzzle of how symbol-using capacities develop and break down fascinated me and became the throughline for my empirical and theoretical work for the next decade. And indeed, without having planned it that way, I embarked on fifteen years of full-time research at Project Zero and at the Boston VAMC. This decade and a half was a gift. It not only enabled me to focus on thinking, research, and writing during a period when I was intellectually fertile; but it also freed me to pursue the lines of synthesis that ultimately yielded MI theory. I did not miss for a minute the life of the untenured professor.

But I am getting ahead of my story. In 1971, I was a developmental psychologist oriented toward the arts and creativity. I had not yet learned much about the brain, and I had not thought much about education. I had written books but I still saw myself principally as a contributor to the peer-reviewed, empirically-oriented journals in developmental psychology. I was beginning to raise a family. Though I read *The New York Times*, I did not subscribe to a local newspaper, because I did not have the faintest inkling that I was destined to spend the rest of my career walking and jogging along the same Cantabridgian streets that I had inhabited for the past decade. But without realizing it, I had probably accumulated the intellectual capital on which I would draw for the remainder of my scholarly life.

From Chronology to Topics

In describing the first part of my life, I have favored a chronological account. For the last thirty-five years, my professional life has consisted largely of a number of research projects, carried out and written up one after another. That strange but essential document—a curriculum vitae—serves as the most reliable record of the issues on which my colleagues and I were working and the findings that we were obtaining. Accordingly, for the remainder of this essay on influences, I shift to a topical or thematic perspective.

The *Zeitgeist*

While it is possible to give an account of my scholarly life that is largely propelled by internal forces, such an account is misleading. In several instances, it seems clear, at least in retrospect, that I (and others) were responding to larger social, cultural, and intellectual factors. To begin with, my decision to enter the academy occurred at a time when a young scholar could readily advance through the ranks and lead a comfortable—though not affluent—life. I am being candid when I say that, in the late 1960s, I had no inkling that I would one day be a well-known scholar, let alone the subject of a collection like this. And yet at the same time, I blithely assumed that I would one day be teaching at a major institution like Harvard, Yale, or Princeton. The reason for this (in retrospect grandiose) assumption is that, during a period of unprecedented growth in American universities, just about all of the young graduates and tutors whom I knew were getting jobs at flagship universities—even if they were humanists! Had I been in college forty years earlier, or forty years later, I can readily see that I might have chosen another, more obviously lucrative career, like that of lawyer.

Mid century was also a growth period for the behavioral sciences. Launched only a few decades before, there was much optimism abroad that psychology and other social sciences would advance as quickly as biology had in the previous century. This confidence now seems misplaced. But in the late 1960s, developmental psychology was clearly a 'growth stock' because of the quality of the most senior individuals (Piaget), the current faculty at Harvard and elsewhere, and several of the students.

When I told my teachers that I wanted to spend some years learning about neurology, they were skeptical. In mainstream psychology this was still the time of the 'black box', when the nature and functioning of the gray matter between the ears seemed to be someone else's concern. However, as it has turned out, the biological sciences, rather than the social sciences, have continued to ascend. Now just about everyone interested in the mind acknowledges vital discoveries emerging from neuro-imaging, fundamental neuroscience, and eventually if not tomorrow, genetics. Psychology departments are morphing into cognitive neuroscience departments. I now spend as much time scanning the neuroscientific and genetics literature as I do perusing the literature of cognitive development. And when my colleagues and I on the GoodWork® project decided to study professions, I enthusiastically took on the task of monitoring trends in genetics.

While housed at the Harvard Graduate School of Education since 1967, Project Zero was essentially an autonomous agency. We paid lip service to issues of education (and monetary overhead to the University). This stance changed quite markedly in the 1980s, again thanks to the *Zeitgeist*. In 1983 (by coincidence, the same year that *Frames of Mind* was published), the U.S. National Commission on Excellence in Education issued its now famous "wake-up" report *A Nation at Risk*. Abandoning its position on the perennial backburner, pre-collegiate education became an increasingly important part of the nation's domestic agenda. No doubt buoyed by the considerable interest in MI theory displayed by educators in the United States and abroad, my own interests veered sharply toward education, and they have retained that orientation to this day.

In recent years, my own work has taken further turns and, once again, I see these as influenced by broader trends. The GoodWork Project focuses on the fate of professions in American society today; our anxiety about the durability of the professions undoubtedly results from the increasingly pervasive and unchecked role of market forces in the United States and elsewhere. The Project is also concerned with issues of value: not only have these been much debated in the United States of late, but a concern with values is more likely to emerge during the later years of life (and the three principal investigators are indisputably at that chronological point). Finally, the emergence of globalization as a major theme—perhaps the defining theme—of our time has led me to think of how precollegiate education ought to be rethought in the twenty-first century.

To be sure, I might have pursued these ideas even if they had not been in the 'air'. I might well have followed alternative paths had, for example, there been no reaction among educators to MI theory, or I had not encountered discussions of globalization amongst a particular network of colleagues. But my guess is that, the further removed we are from the current moment, the easier it will be to see my work (and that of my contemporaries) as reactions to broader (if currently less transparent) forces.

Peers, Near-Peers, and Students

By far, the biggest influence on my intellectual trajectory over the last three and one half decades has been exerted by the individuals with whom I have been privileged to work at Project Zero. Initially, Project Zero was a small, deliberately heterogeneous group of Boston-area scholars, who shared an interest in the nature of artistic thinking and education and were sympathetic to rigorous philosophical and empirical investigations of artistic cognition. With his scintillating intellect and fascinating research agenda on the nature of artistic thinking, Nelson Goodman was undoubtedly the central intellectual figure. But from early on, I learned a great deal from founding members, including philosophers Israel Scheffler and Vernon Howard, who sharpened our conceptualization of artistic practice; experimental psychologist Paul Kolers, who showed us how to study key perceptual and linguistic capacities in the laboratory; musician-turned -psychologist Jeanne Bamberger, who illustrated how a musically-informed Piaget might have studied the development of musical capacities; and my long-term colleague David Perkins, who has brought the rigors of cognitive science to such elusive topics as artistic problem solving and human creativity. We met regularly alone or with visitors, we debated, argued, designed studies, wrote about them, and felt that we were part of a group of innovators—now unknown, one day to be acknowledged. When Nelson Goodman retired in the early 1970s, he gave Perkins and me the opportunity to continue Project Zero, which we did until 2000, when we turned over the reins to our long-time associate Steve Seidel.

Over the years Project Zero grew steadily in size, scope, and influence. Grounded in philosophical and psychological investigation, we incorporated other disciplines. Focussed initially on the arts, we came to consider the range of cognitive (as well as some non-cognitive) capacities. Reflecting the *Zeitgeist* of the 1980s and 1990s, we became far more engaged in educational issues. And Perkins and I were able to attract a group of talented somewhat younger peers who carried out important lines of research: in my case, Dennie Wolf, who co-directed the study of early symbolization in seven different symbol systems; Laurie Krasny Brown, who studied the effects on cognition of media like television and storybooks; and artist-turned psychologist Ellen Winner, who carried out pioneering studies of how children understand and produce figurative language. After we had worked together for awhile, Ellen and I fell in love with each other. More on that later.

Second in influence to Project Zero was the group of investigators at the Boston Veterans Administration Medical Center and the Boston University School of Medicine, where for twenty years I conducted empirical research on the cognitive effects of brain injury. Norman Geschwind (the other NG in my life) had attracted a group of brilliant colleagues, including Harold Goodglass and Edith Kaplan. From these redoubtable clinicans, I learned how to examine patients, how to observe changes in behavior from one day or week to the next, and how to put together disparate lines of evidence to arrive at a diagnosis and regimen of treatment for victims of brain injury. In turn Geschwind, Goodglass, and Kaplan had assembled a set of wonderful contemporaries of mine, chief among them Edgar Zurif, a talented psycholinguist from Canada. For close to twenty years Edgar and I co-directed a laboratory that focussed on the breakdown, under conditions of brain-damage, of linguistic and other cognitive and symbol using capacities. Edgar provided powerful theoretical insights, many of them from Chomskian linguistics, as well as considerable experimental ingenuity; I was the observer of intriguing clinical phenomena and the writer who wove together our sometimes disparate lines of research. From day one, we had pleasurable intellectual and personal relations, perhaps because there was just the right degree of distance from one another in terms of background and interests. Once again, as rising young investigators, we were able to attract a very talented set of younger persons, most prominent among them Hiram Brownell, who has continued several lines our work, sometimes in collaboration with Ellen Winner.

Working for twenty-plus years on a daily basis with such talented colleagues is a rare privilege. None of us can say for sure which conceptual ideas or methodological innovations came from whom, at what time, or in what way. Nor does it matter, except possibly to historians of

Project Zero, the Boston VAMC, or behavioral science in the latter years of the twentieth century. Science is a communal effort and nearly everything that was discovered by one person would have been discovered sooner or later by others. It is important to say that, like many aging investigators, I look back on these times, when we could pursue our own interests without undue attention to careerist opportunities and senior-scholar obligations, as unforgettably special.

Pleased to report, there were other catalytic groups as well. As early as the middle 1970s, with the support of the Spencer Foundation, psychologist-educators David Olson from Toronto, Gavriel Salomon from Israel, David Feldman from Boston, and I began to meet regularly, to discuss the role of symbolization in the development of human cognition. These meetings were important for me. We were a group of young investigators, all influenced by Piaget, but all cognizant that Piaget had ignored issues of media, symbol systems, and education. Discovering common links and a common cause, we began a series of informal contacts and collaborations that have endured. From the middle 1970s, I also had regular encounters with leaders in the area of arts education, such as Elliot Eisner from Stanford (with a special expertise in visual art), Maxine Greene from Teachers College, Columbia University (literary and performing arts), and Bennett Reimer, from Northwestern University (music). Not only did these personal associations connect me to other Centers that were carrying out work analogous to our Project Zero efforts: but their expertise in different art forms complemented my own artistic profile.

In the late 1970s, a Dutch Foundation, the Bernard Van Leer Foundation, awarded a large grant to Harvard for a study of 'the nature and realization of human potential.' This grant gave me exposure to another set of valued colleagues in Cambridge and elsewhere. As one of the leaders of the project, I also had the invaluable opportunity to synthesize my own and others' works on human cognition, an opportunity that led, ultimately, to the positing of the theory of multiple intelligences. The Project on Human Potential included collaborations with individuals abroad. I made several trips to Western Europe, and also initial trips to Latin America and Africa, and intellectually-more-crucial trips to Japan and China.

By the 1980s, I was regularly attending a number of national and international forums, and benefiting from the colleagues encountered there, not to mention the intriguing places that academics choose as meeting sites. For over a decade I attended the annual meetings of the Europe-based International Neuropsychological Symposium. Not only did I meet spectacular colleagues; but I learned that even in science, the kinds of issues approached and the ways in which they are framed typically reflect distinct cultural styles. For example, my interest in artistic and other forms of symbolization proved closest to that of Italian colleagues with whom I ended up forming valued ties. During the same decade, I played a central role in a committee of the Social Science Research Council focused on the development of human talents. I continued my relation with David Feldman and entered into fruitful collegial relations with Anne Colby, Mihaly Csikszentmihalyi, William Damon, Howard Gruber, and Helen Haste. This group, which also continues its informal links, helped to effect a number of important shifts in the understanding of giftedness, talent, and creativity. These phenomena came to be seen as processes that develop, rather than as traits with which individuals are born; and instead of being construed as properties of a single human psyche, they came to be seen as phenomena that jointly involve an individual, the particular domain or discipline in which she works, and the judgments of quality and originality rendered by a group of knowledgeable experts.

By the 1990s, I had ceased attending most of these regularly-scheduled professional 'initialized' meetings (APA, SRCD, INS): they were getting too large and I no longer enjoyed the mélange of disparate talks and incessant networking. Unlike many of my colleagues, I had no interest in leading these groups: I sought neither the power, the prestige, nor the responsibilities that attend the presidency of a scholarly group. Instead, more of my work centered around meetings with close associates on common research interests. As a direct consequence of a year at the Stanford Center for Advanced Study in the Behavioral Science (1994–95), I began the longest and deepest collaboration of my scholarly life—the GoodWork Project, in association with fellow Fellows Bill Damon and Mihaly Csikszentmihalyi. Since the three of us did not have funds for regularly scheduled meetings once we had returned to our respective campuses, we became extremely opportunistic. Whenever we received invitations 'in the neighborhood', we found ways to spend face-to-face time together. And thanks to telephone, fax, and e-mail, it has proved possible to collaborate even over vast differences in space and time. While there is no substitute for being together in the same locale, long-distance collaboration has become infinitely easier in the last few decades.

Until the middle 1980s, the younger persons with whom I worked were paid research assistants, many of whom also turned out to be fantastic colleagues and persons (For example, Dennie Wolf, Ellen Winner, and Laurie Brown all started out as researchers on specific Project Zero strands of research). By the middle 1980s I had accepted a teaching position at the Harvard Graduate School of Education, and I began to have regular students as well. Difficult as it is to single out peers by name, it is even more problematic to single out a few students. With the understanding that they stand out for a much larger cohort, I will mention Mindy Kornhaber, who has carried out important studies of multiple intelligences, with special attention to policies directed towards underserved populations; Veronica Boix-Mansilla, who has been a valued partner in studies of disciplinary and interdisciplinary knowledge; and Tom Hatch, who approached the most complex issues of school reform with rigor, skepticism, and hope. And, from a different category altogether, I mention Marcelo Suarez-Orozco, an expert on the educational effects of immigration on succeeding generations of students, the younger colleague from whom I have learned the most in recent years. Indeed, catalytic conversations with Marcelo led to my current interest in the agendas of education and globalization.

True Angels

Only in America, and only in the last fifty years, could a research-oriented young social scientist carry out numerous lines of research in developmental psychology, neuropsychology, and education. I have never done the math, but it is clear that I would be a very wealthy man if I could have kept all of the funds that have been awarded to nonprofit institutions (Harvard, the Boston Veterans Administration Medical Center, Boston University School of Medicine) for the support of our research. And while I have been critical of philanthropies in various ways, I must express my unalloyed gratitude to those funding agencies that have allowed us to carry out our work. Over the years I have been fortunate enough to have received grants from three dozen separate funding agencies.

The shifting sources of that funding tell a revealing story. During the first fifteen years of my career (roughly, the middle 1960s to the early 1980s), most of my funding came from the government: NIH, NSF, NIE and the Veterans Administration. Once the Reagan administration had assumed office, social science came under suspicion (apparently Reagan actually conflated sociology with socialism!) and it became far more difficult to secure funds from federal sources unless one pursued the current political agenda. For the next fifteen years, my funding came largely from the large private foundations. In recent years, I have been the beneficiary of support from individuals of means, who have been interested in various lines of our work. And as I have been able to attract honoraria for writings and talks, I contribute an ever larger proportion of my income to the support of my own research. I believe that this is appropriate. I also believe—and I hope that readers will take this in the right spirit—that it makes most sense for me to invest excess income not in the stock market, real estate, or luxury items but in my own scholarly enterprises. Still, our work requires hundreds of thousands of dollars each year, and my own contributions would need an extra zero or two to make the crucial difference.

With thirty-some funders, dozens of collaborators, and nearly a hundred separate projects, I once again have an embarrassment of riches. It is not possible to mention every funder. I must single out the Chicago-based Spencer Foundation which supported my work for nearly thirty years—at which point I joined the Board and can no longer receive funds. I must also mention the Hewlett Foundation which was the first to see merit in the GoodWork Project and funded it for a decade. And I owe an unbelievably large debt to the Atlantic Philanthropies who for over a decade supported both Project Zero as an entity and several lines of my own work. When it first began funding us, the Atlantic Philanthropic Services (as it was then called) was an anonymous donor and we respected the anonymity of "AP" even conferring the pseudonyms Rex Harrison and Agatha Christie on our program officers Ray Handlan and Angela Covert. AP actually pioneered some of the currently touted practices of venture philanthropy—such as the strengthening of the infrastructure of organizations through long term institutional support—but did so gracefully and behind the scenes.

On a personal level, I benefited enormously from the awarding in 1981 of a MacArthur Prize Fellowship. Not only did this award provide me with five years of security during a fragile time (when the government had stopped supporting my lines of research and I had no academic position); but it was also the first unambiguous vote of confidence that I had received from the wider community. (My parents could still not say 'my son the lawyer' but they could now say 'my son, the genius' [sic]). And it is with deep gratitude that I mention several other wonderful persons who have shown exemplary generosity both in the amounts that they have given me and in the flexibility with which those funds have been administered: John Bryant and Patricia Bauman, Jeffrey Epstein, Julie Kidd, Louise and Claude Rosenberg, Courtney S. Ross, Elisabeth and John Hobbs (who funded my professorial chair), and my college roommate Tom Lee (with his wife Ann Tenenbaum).

Catalytic Trips

As scholars become better known, we have the opportunity to travel. And while we may not be able to afford five-star hotels, we have a special privilege; no matter where we venture, we can find colleagues with shared interests (and, if we are lucky enough to speak English, colleagues with whom we can easily converse).

At least three trips have influenced my scholarship and thinking in a significant way. In 1980, I had the chance to visit Matsumoto, a small city in Japan, and observe lessons in the Suzuki method of Talent Education. While the trip was brief, it had an important effect on my thinking. Before that time, I had assumed that talented young string players had special innate gifts. Exposure to Shinichi Suzuki and his philosophy demonstrated to me that, if genius was involved in young musicianship, it inhered in the method of teaching. The Japanese fiddlers were ordinary kids; Suzuki and the teachers whom he had trained made the difference.

Around the same time, I made the first of a series of trips to China. While I had spent much time in Europe, China was the first radically different culture that I had visited and it made a deep impression on me. Not only was China a major civilization that had existed in uninterrupted form for millennia; but it had just gone through the incredible trauma of the Cultural Revolution. I was deeply attracted to much of Chinese culture even as I was—and continue to be—repelled by the totalitarian aspects of the current regime. But after visiting dozens of classrooms over a seven-year period, sometimes accompanied by my wife Ellen, I also revised many of my thoughts about the nature of creativity. It is not necessary, as I had thought, for young individuals to begin with a period of unfettered Dewey-Piaget playful exploration. Strict skill-building is an appropriate initial regimen, so long as it is eventually balanced with 'progressive' periods of flexibility and imaginative leaps. I expanded on these thoughts in a 1989 book *To Open Minds: Chinese Clues to the Dilemma of Contemporary Education*, which includes an earlier effort at autobiography.

Also, in the early 1980s, with my wife Ellen, I made the first of a series of trips to Reggio Emilia, a small city in northern Italy. The preschools in that part of the world were beginning to become well known and we were fortunate enough to receive an invitation from Loris Malaguzzi, one of the few geniuses in twentieth-century education. Japan had shown me the importance of excellent methods of instruction; China had revealed the different routes to creativity. In Reggio I enlarged my views of what is possible in the education of children during the first six years of life. Given committed and properly trained teachers, community support, and a powerful philosophy of pedagogy, it is possible to combine exploration and discipline in exemplary fashion. The youngsters in Reggio schools carry out projects of beauty and originality; through these projects, that often take weeks or even months to execute, they express themselves in 'one hundred languages' and achieve deep understanding of key concepts and phenomena. In collaboration with Mara Krechevsky and Steve Seidel, I have had the chance to carry out studies of the Reggio approach and contribute to a collaborative book (*Making Learning Visible, 2001*). That volume details our early conclusions about the learning that takes place in groups and about the scrupulous documentation of learning that occurs on a daily basis in Reggio.

When Reggio teachers are asked what happens to their young graduates, they give the disarmingly simple response "Just look at our community." And indeed, if the rest of the world worked as well as this region of Northern Italy, it would be a far better place. My experiences in Reggio have convinced even a hidebound psychologist of the importance of the surrounding community. No wonder my revered teacher Jerome Bruner spends a month in Reggio each year.

I want to mention one other form of catalytic voyage: the regular meetings of groups of individuals who gather without a rigid agenda and just 'mix' for a few days. I have been privileged to receive invitations to gatherings of the MacArthur fellows; the yearly Renaissance Weekend, where families celebrate a holiday weekend and all attendees give talks on issues of personal or political interest; and the somewhat more formal World Economic Forum, where, as a 'Fellow,' I have been part of the 'entertainment' for political and business leaders. The very flexibility of these formats gives participants a chance to meet many persons of diverse backgrounds with whom one would not ordinarily rub shoulders. I realize how lucky I am to have these opportunities and only wish that more persons could participate. As sociologist Mark Granovetter has suggested, our modern world is marked by the increased importance of many 'weak' ties among individuals, rather than the more traditional reliance on a small number of 'strong ties'. Though my small-town and European background inclines me to favor strong ties, I realize that the 'weak ties' engendered by such forums has been of great benefit to me, my students, and even my family.

Disappointments, Duds, and Dead Ends

Soon after Ellen Winner began to work at Project Zero, she took on a key role in our constant efforts to raise funds. She set up three folders: rejections (by far the largest file); acceptances (always slender); and the intriguingly entitled 'ray of hope'. Anyone involved in science, anyone involved in fund raising, knows that rejection and failure are part of the daily routine. If every application is being accepted, if every hypothesis is being confirmed, it is likely that you are not taking enough chances, or that you are the chosen 'one in a million'.

As a father, I make a special point to share with my children my disappointments, rejections and failures. This is important—and it is important in an account like this—because otherwise readers may draw the erroneous conclusion that everything always goes well. I can assure you that has *not* been the case with me. I have had countless rejections of initiatives to funders and foundations. I have had far more rejections of scholarly and popular articles than I have had acceptances. And while I have been extremely fortunate in my collaborations, a number of them have not worked out well.

In 1984, barely a year after the publication of *Frames of Mind*, I was approached by a producer at the British Broadcasting Company. With an assist from my friend Helen Haste, Martin Freeth had been introduced to the idea of multiple intelligences; and he proposed a seven-part television series, each episode devoted to the explication of a specific intelligence. For all the obvious reasons, I was attracted to this idea: I cleared my calendar of other obligations and prepared to spend a year or two working in collaboration with the BBC team. And, indeed, for a solid year, we worked effectively together, researching the intelligences and lining up 'the talents' to appear on the program. At that point, however, a new 'head of department' entered the scene. This man and I did not get along; and whether as cause or effect, he began to change the program's concept and my role in it. We had a series of increasingly unproductive exchanges and I finally decided to withdraw. This decision on my part came as a shock to the BBC; and several people sought to persuade me to reconsider this rejection. ("One does not withdraw from a BBC series" I was informed in solemn tones). I believe that I made the right decision. But I learned two lessons: 1) Television is a tricky enterprise over which one has much less control than is the case with writing; 2) Dedication of a full year to a project, without any guarantee of success or even a product that one can circulate elsewhere, is a decision that one should not take lightly.

In addition to the synergistic collaborations alluded to above, I have had several collaborations that have been disappointing. In general, these collaborations were ones that had been strongly encouraged by funders, and I was loath to second guess a goose who had offered a golden egg. Nor do I blame my collaborators—I may well have been at least an equal partner in the less-than-sterling interactions. But in retrospect, I am not sure how much was gained by joining forces with Robert Sternberg, to create a curriculum on 'practical intelligence for school'; with Educational Testing Service to create alternative performance-based assessments in the arts; and with the Lincoln Center Institute, to create tasks that document the value of aesthetic education. The ATLAS collaboration (between Project Zero and three other school reform organizations) to create a new "break the mold" model of schooling was personally rewarding, but neither I, nor the other leaders of the key organizations, devoted enough time to this collaboration; and those whom we asked to carry the ball in our absence, did not do so with the requisite expertise, enthusiasm, and dedication. For a research-practice collaboration to be effective, many diverse elements have to fall into place. Unless both personal and intellectual chemistry obtains among the principal players, the effort rarely succeeds.

I have also personal disappointments in collaborators. In some cases, I believe that the other collaborator did not share in the work, and after a while I got tired of being the individual who does eighty percent of the work. In one case, the collaborator not only failed to deliver but always put the blame on me. I created the neologism 'blame-arang'—a person who is culpable but who manages predictably to hurl the blame back at you. With age, I take ever greater care in the selection of collaborators.

And also of assistants. In general, I have been tremendously lucky with the younger individuals who have aided me with research and other scholarly work. For example, Lisa Bromer gave me eight years of wonderful service; and other valued assistants have gone on to distinguished careers at Project Zero and elsewhere. But once I made the mistake of not asking enough questions of referees and of myself, and I ended up hiring a nationally-known con man. The discovery of this fact (by our vigilant human resources director Shana Waldman) constituted the greatest shock of my professional career. Fortunately, while he committed some misdeeds during his months as my assistant, the con man did not do major damage, except to confidence in my own judgment.

Let me mention some other things that did not work out. During my post-college year abroad, I wrote a novel of over a thousand pages. It was terrible. Fortunately, I knew that it was terrible and thus saved myself a long and painful set of rejections. As a graduate student, I made at least feeble efforts to write computer programs, to master electrical equipment, and to carry out studies in the neuro-biological 'wet' lab; I soon discovered that such scientific abilities as I had lay in conceptualization, writing, and decidedly 'dry' experiments with human beings. As a young author, I was lucky enough to be published by Knopf, deservedly the most prestigious of New York trade publishers. However, my work came to be seen as a bit too academic and insular for Knopf and so editor Bob Gottlieb referred me to Basic Books, a less sparkling publisher which—in the face of many ups and downs—nonetheless has published more than a dozen of my books. Various book projects have been still born: these range from a 1976 manuscript *Kinds of Minds* (an early effort to work out notions that later evolved into multiple intelligences) to a study of Mozart to a book about Carleton Gajdusek, a brilliant Nobel laureate in Medicine or Physiology who had become a friend. Unfortunately, as I was working on his biography, Gajdusek was arrested and subsequently convicted of pedophilia. I have not been able to return to this project.

Most people assume that I have had many job offers over the years but this is not true. I failed to get a job at Yale while in my last year as a graduate student; since then, as far as I can recall, I have never applied for any job except for my present position at Harvard. No point in speculating about the lack of job offers; but if I had wanted to 'play' one offer off another, I have never had that opportunity. I have had a few offers to apply for administrative jobs at Harvard and elsewhere but have never been tempted. I don't think I have the talents to be a good administrator, except possibly of my own projects; and in any event, the best administrators focus full time on their job, something which I as a committed researcher-writer would not have been prepared to do. For similar reasons, I have never been involved in electoral politics nor even in testifying for legislative bodies. Again, I don't think I have much talent for these pursuits and am not prepared to devote time to them; my observations of political life in America is that a part-timer virtually never wins when one's opponent is devoted fulltime to the opposite mission. Recently, while being interviewed on public radio, I had occasion to call the President's scientific adviser a 'prostitute'. I soon regretted that term but learned that, if one wants to get publicity, name-calling provides an easy way to accomplish that end.

I have had some success as a public intellectual (in 2005 I was even selected by two magazines as one of the hundred leading public intellectuals in the world) but not as much as I would have liked. How heavenly it would be to send a letter or op ed to *The New York Times* with a high success rate. Talk about rejections! Or to be asked at least occasionally to write for the *Atlantic Monthly*, *New Yorker*, or *New York Times Sunday Magazine*. This has not happened. I have enough self confidence to believe that I could have written for one of these publications, just as I believe that I could have been a reasonable composer of Broadway show music. But I was not good enough to do either of these things 'on the side' and not prepared to take the risks and the challenges of attempting to be a free-lance author like my hero Edmund Wilson or a full-time composer like George Gershwin or Stephen Sondheim (not that I believe for a nanosecond that I could have attained what any of these three individuals did).

I have been far more blessed with mentors than with anti-mentors or tormentors. (My colleague David Feldman suggests that I have a talent for attracting effective mentors—if so, I thank my lucky stars). Nelson Goodman succeeded in playing a role as both mentor and most stringent critic, and I thank him for filling both roles. Probably the closest to an anti-mentor was the brilliant social psychologist Stanley Milgram. When I was a student in a pro-seminar in social psychology in 1966, I dared to voice a criticism of Milgram's famous 'obedience to authority' studies. In front of my peers as well as another senior social psychologist who was co-teaching the course, Milgram attacked me vociferously. I was stunned by the attack—even more stunned that no one, not even the other senior scholar, came to my defense during that painful hour. I learned—or relearned—that one cannot count on others in such a pinch, one has to rely on one's own defensive and offensive skills. (As I tell my students and my children, one must always be prepared to step in the limelight, willingly or not). Thereafter, neither Milgram nor I ever mentioned the incident, and we became reasonably close colleagues. To this day I do not know whether Milgram was really furious at me or just doing one of his signature 'social psychology' experiments on an unsuspecting student-victim.

At last, personal disappointments. By far the greatest one was the dissolution of my marriage to Judy Gardner. We fell in love almost at first sight; and even though we adhered to our parents' admonitions not to marry right away, I got married at twenty-two, a young age for my cohort. We were extremely well-matched superficially, and we respected one another. We also shared many values, including the most important ones regarding childrearing. But fundamentally, we were—or grew to be—very different kinds of persons. When I fell in love with Ellen Winner in the middle 1970s, I realized that I could not be happy with

Judy Gardner and I made the painful decision to seek a separation and then a divorce. This created an awful situation for everyone—children, parents, friends, Judy, and—from a different angle—for Ellen and me. I know that the divorce also caused enormous anguish for Judy and the children, and I will always carry guilt for the hurt that I caused. Judy continued to be a wonderful mother, picked up the pieces of her life, and she, Ellen, and I eventually reconciled. I was completely unprepared for Judy's sudden collapse from an aneurysm and subsequent tragic death in 1994. It seemed right at the time—and it still seems right in retrospect— to dedicate my next book to Judy's memory and to the memory of Erik Erikson, two individuals who had played such a vital role in my earlier years. I did so. Since then Ellen and I have been able to constitute a wonderful new family, which incorporates our four children, a grandchild, and all of the grandparents including Judy's surviving mother.

Beyond Influences: Going My Own Way

So much of my life as a scholar can be explained in terms of strong, benevolent influences. In reflecting on these influences, however, I realize that I did not just accept these influences passively. In fact, like many ambitious young persons, I also was capable of moving away from these influences.

First the movement was geographical: later, it involved shifting interests. At age fifteen I left the comfort of Scranton Pennsylvania and my extended family—attending a boarding school fairly close to my home; and then, at age eighteen, moving permanently to Massachusetts. Beginning college, I expected to be a lawyer, but then I elected to pursue a life of scholarship. I shifted from clinical psychology to developmental psychology, then to neuropsychology, then to educational studies, and now to broad based social science research and commentary on public issues. Within my chosen fields, I also was capable of rejecting the orthodoxy. Most cognitive developmentalists focused on scientific development, while I targeted the development of artistic capacities and skills. Most psychologists endorse the picture of intelligence as a single faculty, but I rejected that perspective. Most of my peers remained as laboratory experimentalists publishing primarily in technical journals, but I undertook case studies, qualitative analyses, syntheses, and lots of books. Clearly, though I feel myself to be traditional and conservative, it does not look that way from the outside.

The greatest intellectual influence in my life was Jean Piaget, a brilliant scholar whom I met only a few times. But I can see much of my

career as a struggle with Piaget's major ideas. Piaget saw all development as of a piece and foregrounded scientific development. I looked at
development from the perspective of artistry and came to see human
intelligence as multi-faceted. These 'lovers' disputes' did not in the least
lessen my regard for Piaget, because it is he who posed the fundamental
questions in my area of study.

I can tally my differences with the other scholars who exerted enormous influence on me. Erik Erikson seduced me into the study of psychology—but I came to see rather soon that the questions that most
engaged me were cognitive in nature, rather than questions of personality, affect, trauma, or therapy. Also, I was more interested in understanding people than in helping them. Nelson Goodman showed me the
consequences of following a line of thinking to its logical conclusion.
But I came to realize that human psychology is not always logical, and
that empirical findings can—and often do—trump an analysis which
seems impeccable on rational grounds. Norman Geschwind opened my
mind to the complex, often non-rational ways in which the human brain
makes sense of experience. But Geschwind paid too little attention to the
role of different kinds of tools and media in human cognition and also—
despite his cosmopolitan bearing—did not factor cultural influences into
his account of cognition. My eyes were opened to these neglected factors by my studies of the writings of Lev Vygotsky, Alexander Luria,
Clifford Geertz, and my decades-long interaction with Jerome Bruner.
My modest disagreements with Bruner have to do with educational matters. Like John Dewey, Bruner underestimates the power of the early theories espoused by children and the educational challenge involved in
overthrowing those misconceptions in favor of more adequate explanations. Bruner famously asserted that one can teach any idea to any child
at any age in a form that is intellectually honest. I would respond that
almost every person is filled with ideas that are attractive but false, and
that successful teaching must grapple with these already extant ideas.

Friends

While I do not have that gift of friendship on which my mother holds the
patent, I have been fortunate to have had good friends throughout my
life. And though it is not always possible to do so, I have sought to retain
relations with friends from my earliest years in Scranton, secondary
school at Wyoming Seminary, and especially my roommates and closest
associates at Harvard College. (Recently I spent a memorable day with
ten of my closest friends from College). The latter is the easiest to do

because almost everyone who attended Harvard returns at least periodically to visit, and those of us with offices within a stone's throw of Harvard Square indeed occupy a 'window on the world'. Not only do I get unequalled personal gratification from these early friends; they keep me in touch with a world beyond my immediate professional circle and often are called upon to fill the role of imagined conversationalists when I am trying to explain my incipient ideas to a wider world. Though I am not by nature a host (I am too introverted and I cannot boil an egg), Ellen and I try to mark visits from friends from out of town by hosting meals of various sizes, including an annual brunch. Given the hectic lives that so many of us lead, it is far preferably to see both personal and professional friends at least once a year, rather than leaving reconnection to chance. And at such social events we make every effort to involve individuals of widely different ages; for many years, my close friends included the noted psychologist Henry A. Murray and his wife Nina, though "Harry" was fifty years older than I was; and David Riesman, the sociologist, who was thirty-five years my senior, along with his wife Evey.

Most of our friends share at least some common professional interests—friendships are easiest to maintain when they involve overlapping worlds. But sometimes the connections evolve out of strange coincidences. Both Mark Wolf, District Court Justice in Boston, and James Freedman, also a distinguished lawyer and the former President of University of Iowa and Dartmouth College, live close by.[1] And yet we might well not have become friends if we had not met at a Renaissance Weekend a decade ago. And so now two of my closest friends happen to be lawyers—and we often get together with another friend, the redoubtable Alan Dershowitz. By coincidence I had breakfast with that trio the morning after the con man-assistant was discovered. Just think of what it would have cost to assemble the legal talent that happened to be gathered around that table at the Charles Hotel that December morning in 2003.

I cannot always specify how friends affect my work, though I know that they do in important ways. And I know that they affect my psychic health, certainly important influences in being able to work and play productively.

Family and Families

As we grow older, it is probably inevitable that we think much about our families—what went well, what went poorly, what formed us, and how

---

[1] Alas, Jim Freedman died in March 2006.

we may be forming others. I have made clear the enormous influence of my family on my early development and the importance that family continues to play every hour of my life. It is up to others to say what kind of a son, brother, cousin, husband, uncle, grandfather, and father I have been. But it is my happy lot to affirm how important these individuals have been and continue to be in my life. Their influence has been incredible and almost entirely benign.

But we live at a time when we have not only families of relatives but also 'families' of friends, colleagues, and students. I am not being precious here; I really feel as if the individuals who worked at Project Zero and at the Boston VAMC, the colleagues with whom I have worked on other projects, my friends in Boston and beyond, and my students, are each part of my extended family—some circles discrete, some overlapping. Usually, they mix well, but when not, that is okay as well. I even feel that those individuals who are critical of my work—including those represented in these pages—are part of an important family: colleagues who share a scholarly orientation and can disagree in a civil manner. I believe it is vital to pass this legacy on, just as one passes on valued beliefs and traits to one's direct descendants. I conclude an essay that has focussed on 'influences' by expressing the hope that I will one day be seen as having been a benevolent influence on the various families to which I have been privileged to belong.

1

What Develops (and How?)

DEANNA KUHN

Whether their concerns are personal or professional, Howard Gardner has without doubt done many people a great service in expanding conceptions of what it means to be intelligent. This is no small achievement, and this is especially so in an era of debate as to what human capabilities it is the mission of education to instill. If, as Gardner has taught us, we can observe intelligence in aesthetic or kinesthetic or socio-emotional realms, it becomes less convincing to define the educated person in terms of achievements within a narrower spectrum of what humans are able to do.

Gardner's contributions by no means resolve the question of what it means to be educated, but they have certainly served to raise it, in a deeper, more profound way than would be likely, absent his work. In today's information age, it has become decreasingly feasible to define the educated person in terms of mastery of any specific, prescribed body of knowledge, even if one regards such mastery as the goal of education. If instead, we seek a definition along the lines of an individual's having learned to use his or her mind, or intelligence, well, then it becomes paramount to understand the nature and scope of that intelligence.

As a developmental psychologist, I bring to my reading of Gardner's work a longstanding interest in how the intellect develops—its pathways, endpoints, and mechanisms of transformation. The questions I raise are therefore these developmental ones. But I am also deeply concerned with education, and even partial answers to these developmental questions I believe are central to the challenge we face as a society of identifying sound purposes and goals, as well as practices, for the education of our youth.

It is perhaps not entirely surprising, then, that in reflecting on Gardner's ideas, and appreciating all of their insight, what I find missing is deep engagement with the question, "What develops?" Gardner presents the multiple intelligences—linguistic, logical-mathematical, musical, kinesthetic, naturalistic, intrapersonal, interpersonal, and existential—as alternative pathways for intellectual development. They do not themselves tell us what it is that is developing. Gardner (1999, p. 72) defines them as different kinds of mental representations. In other words, each is a medium for conveying meaning, not the meaning itself. What is being represented remains to be specified, and Gardner emphasizes that the same meaning is capable of being addressed in each representational medium.

For his vision of what meanings educators should help students to achieve, Gardner (1999) turns to the traditional subject disciplines. Here he makes a strong case for depth over breadth within each discipline. But if, as he emphasizes, one Mozart opera versus another or one Dicken's novel versus another may suit a teacher's instructional purposes equally well and can be expected to yield comparable educational benefits, then both operas (or novels) must be serving some further purpose, distinguishable from what is derived from study of either one itself. We involve students with some body of knowledge not as an end in itself (since we could as well have employed another), but because we hope they will acquire something further from the experience. It is critical that we be able to specify very clearly what this something is. It is here, then, that I seek answers to the question of what the intellectual competencies are that we are seeking to develop.

Gardner turns to the disciplines themselves—history, science, and music—for answers. He stresses that each has its own methods as well as content and students must become familiar with both. Students must "learn to think like scientists." To master historical thinking they must "become familiar with the circumstances of a particular historical era and then acquire the tools to evaluate rival accounts of its causes and consequences" (1999, p. 218). He does not trivialize the task. These "disciplinary habits of mind," he says, "may be deeply counterintuitive" (2004, p. 138). And ". . . it is necessary to confront directly the many misconceptions (literally, wrong concepts) that youngsters hold . . . by . . . regular and systematic confrontation of their 'natural' but typically inadequate modes and conclusions of thought" (2004, p. 139).

Gardner says little about the nature of these discipline-specific methods of inquiry, and here it would be unfair to fault him. I suspect he is well aware that he would have to tread delicately indeed to characterize in non-expert terms how experts in history or physics or biology do business and what epistemological foundations and standards of truth are accepted within each of their disciplines.

There is another kind of knowledge, however, that I see as highly relevant to the task at hand and that is knowledge about the set of intellectual competencies that children bring to the task. Children have their own ways of knowing and these are the ones we must make contact with, come to know and respect, and seek to develop. And, it follows directly, we need to know all we can about how they develop—the sequences and pathways and mechanisms in terms of which more mature understandings are achieved. Gardner acknowledges children's "inadequate modes" of thought but suggests only that they need to be "confronted" (see the passages quoted above) and replaced by the proper discipline-informed epistemologies.

More is involved, I would claim, in the process of intellectual development. Educators need to serve as guides and collaborators as students traverse paths that involve multiple transformations in ways of knowing and resulting understandings. Some of these sequences and pathways and mechanisms we have learned a fair amount about. One foundational sequence, for example, is the progression in children's broad understandings of what knowing and knowledge consist of (both across and within disciplines)—a sequence that progresses from knowledge as uncontestable *facts*, to unchallengeable *opinions*, and ultimately, if all goes well, to *judgments* supported by argument and evidence (Hofer and Pintrich 2002). Or, to take another example, we also know something about sequences, pathways, and mechanisms with respect to inferential "tools to evaluate rival accounts of causes and consequences," to use Gardner's words cited above. Even in these cases we still have much more to learn (Kuhn and Franklin, 2006), and in other areas we know still less.

But my argument is that it is here—with the child's mind, as much as or more than the nature of the discipline, that we must start. Not to do so is to lead without having taken the pains to learn whom we are leading and what they have to contribute to the journey. This knowledge, moreover, is clearly prerequisite to devising the most effective pedagogical methods. In a pedagogical vein, Gardner (quoted above) refers to "regular and systematic confrontation" of the child's "inadequate modes of thought." In addition to knowing as much as we can about these evolving "inadequate modes"—they are a moving target—we need to develop a repertoire of methods for fostering change in both processes and products of knowing. "Systematic confrontation" is not enough, and Gardner offers no further suggestions, seemingly focused instead on the destination—what it is we want the child to come to understand and appreciate—rather than the journey. New methods and interest have led to a wave of progress in understanding mechanisms of change in the process of knowledge construction (Bereiter 2002; Kuhn 1995: Siegler 2006) and this, in my view, is where much of our attention should now be focused.

What contribution might the idea of multiple intelligences make here? The potential is great, the idea of individual developmental pathways having assumed increasing prominence in developmental psychology. Unfortunately, however, key information is not yet available that would enhance the contribution that MI theory stands to make. Some of this is readily obtainable empirical data. Gardner notes that "the configuration of intelligences, and relationships among them, will shift over time, in response to people's experiences" (1999, p. 72), but, despite the widespread interest in MI theory, no one appears to have collected longitudinal data on the stability of profiles over time or how they respond to experience. In what ways do multiple intelligence profiles develop? Without these basic data, MI theory cannot assume the role it might in the study of intellectual development.

The underlying theory and pedagogical implications of the MI approach also seem to me to need further specification if its contribution is to achieve its full potential. Even based on a child's profile at a single point in time, it is not clear what individualized educational prescription follows. Education should be personalized, Gardner recommends, to take account of a child's individual profile. But how, exactly?

On the one hand, he recommends, "one should try as much as possible to develop the idiosyncratic strengths of each [child]" (1999, p. 104). In close conjunction with this recommendation, however, he says, "children are encouraged to interact with all the materials, and thus to exercise their range of intelligences" (1999, p. 104) and "families receive a . . . profile that . . . describes a child's strengths and weaknesses and suggests activities that could be undertaken at home or in the wider community to encourage the child's personal development along various pathways" (p. 104). To put the question succinctly, is the developmental goal to make a child's individual profile more uniform (by strengthening weaker modalities) or less uniform (by concentrating learning experiences in favored modalities)?

In the end, however, it is not the individualization suggested by MI theory, but the universality of "the disciplines" that provide Gardner his vision of where education should be headed. All students should come to appreciate the universals of truth, beauty, and goodness, as instantiated in the traditional subject-matter disciplines. I would comment here only that as appealing and hard to object to as this vision is, it is a vision rooted in Gardner's discipline-based perspective and not the only possible vision of what education should seek to achieve. Rather than focus on the end product, aspiring to instill the wisdom contained in the disciplines, one might focus on process and begin at the beginning, seeking to develop to their fullest the intellectual powers the child brings to education. In my own thinking about the topic, I have defined the educated person as one capable of certain kinds of activities of an intellectual nature—notably, inquiry and argument—and who values these activities as worth engaging in because they are seen as sound paths to achieving goals, solving problems, and maximizing welfare (Kuhn 2005). These are goals having to do not with what students have come to know but rather with what they have come to know how to do in pursuit of their own knowledge goals. I am not suggesting that Gardner would not be sympathetic to the latter conception. Indeed, he makes it clear that he is: "Youngsters ought to be reared so that they enjoy learning, develop wide-ranging interests, and want to nourish their minds for the remainder of their lives" (1999, p. 52). But he also notes that these goals are not easy to achieve. Seeking to achieve them demands a great deal of knowledge about the ways in which children's thinking and learning develop (Kuhn and Franklin 2006; Kuhn and Pease 2006), and it is this knowledge that we should continue to seek.

REFERENCES

Bereiter, C. 2002. *Education and Mind in the Knowledge Age.* Mahwah: Erlbaum.

Gardner, H. 1999. *The Disciplined Mind.* New York: Simon and Schuster.

———. 2004. *Changing Minds: The Art and Science of Changing Our Own and Other People's Minds.* Boston: Harvard Business School Press.

Hofer, B., and Pintrich, P., eds. 2002. *Epistemology: The Psychology of Beliefs about Knowledge and Knowing.* Mahwah: Erlbaum.

Kuhn, D. 1995. Microgenetic Study of Change: What Has It Told Us? *Psychological Science* 6, pp. 133–39.

————. 2005. *Education for Thinking.* Cambridge Massachusetts: Harvard University Press.

Kuhn, D., and Franklin, S. 2006. The Second Decade: What Develops (and How)? In D. Kuhn and R. Siegler, eds., (W. Damon and R. Lerner, series eds.), *Handbook of Child Psychology: Volume 2. Cognition, Perception, and Language.* Sixth edition. Hoboken: Wiley.

Kuhn, D., and Pease, M. 2006. Do Children and Adults Learn Differently? *Journal of Cognition and Development.*

Siegler, R. 2006. Microgenetic Studies of Learning. In D. Kuhn and R. Siegler, eds., (W. Damon and R. Lerner, series eds.), *Handbook of Child Psychology: Volume 2. Cognition, Perception, and Language.* Sixth edition. Hoboken: Wiley.

2

Becoming Responsible for Who We Are: The Trouble with Traits

DAVID R. OLSON

It is a moot question whether the science of psychology has any use for ability concepts at all, any more than advanced chemistry (unlike applied geology) needs to talk about minerals. . . . It is very possible that problems of know-how [skills]will eventually see resolution in much the same fashion as have past problems in the theory of demonic possession, namely, by our becomeing sufficientl sophisticated in alternative interpretations of the phenomena at issue that older conceptions thereof simply fade into the myths of our prescientific past. (Rozeboom 1972, p. 32)

Dispositions, as Wittgenstein emphasized, have no normative force. (Davidson 1994, p. 24)

The very concept of character was founded on errors that modern psychology has exposed. (McEwan, I., *Atonement,* p. 281)

Ironically, Howard Gardner is held in highest esteem by educators for the very views from which many cognitive psychologists are at pains to distance themselves. Gardner (1983; 1999) has championed the existence of basic dispositions, traits or abilities that, he suggests, provide access to adult forms of knowledge and that could, ideally, inform pedagogical practices. Yet, his cognitive science colleagues have, in large part, abandoned cognitive dispositions, traits and abilities, including mental abilities, as explanations. Rather, they have launched a program of analyzing these putative abilities as cognitive structures organized in terms of rules and representations. The explanatory value of dispositions is either denied completely, as in the epigram to this chapter, or else turned into the problem by recognizing that dispositions, unlike action and intention, lack normative force, as in the second epigram to this chapter.

Admittedly, Gardner has attempted to distance himself from the venerable tradition of intelligence testing by placing equal emphasis on products of cognition in the arts and sciences including mathematics, architecture, music and philosophy. By examining the criteria for evaluating such products and processes he at least approaches issues of normativity (Gardner, Csikszentmihalyi, and Damon 2001). Yet, for Gardner, intelligence, even when pluralized, remains a dispositional trait. And dispositional traits, as Rozeboom (1972) argued, have yielded pride of place to a psychology of knowledge. Like all trait theorists, Gardner sees ability traits as enduring properties of individuals to account for their interests, efforts, and competencies and in this he joins the tradition that leads back to Spearman, Terman, and Thorndike. But in so doing he has slipped past or failed to confront a major issue in the cognitive and educational sciences, the relation between cognitive dispositions and forms of knowledge he valorizes. Consequently, it may be useful to examine the place of disposition accounts in a cognitive psychology and to point out more clearly just why dispositional accounts are limiited and, in important contexts such as education, misleading.

The roots of the problem lie in the fact that Gardner, as a psychologist, is largely committed to psychology as a natural science. As a science, psychology attempts to elucidate the "laws" of the mind through the discovery of the causes of behavior. These laws, like the laws of all the natural sciences describe the regularities to be found in a domain in terms of its underlying the causal structure. Dispositions are such causal structures that are offered as explanations of subsequent learning and development. Importantly, the natural sciences advert only to such causes.

The laws of man, on the other hand, are social and have "normative" force. Unlike the laws of nature, the laws of man can be obeyed or disobeyed. They may be good or bad, fair or unfair, judged true or false, appropriate or inappropriate. We hold ourselves responsible and accountable in terms of these laws and norms. "Normative" means having a norm or authoritative standard in terms of which actions may be judged. The social sciences differ from the natural sciences on just this dimension, the former being an examination of normative rules and laws, the latter of the natural causes of events. Psychology, and in particular the science of mind, lies precariously along the border between these two. Some days psychologists seem to be searching for the causal processes of cognition, on other days for whether or not the mind is honoring or violating a specific rule or injunction. Once can be held accountable for violating a rule as in failing to raise one's hand before speaking, but one cannot be held accountable for one's genetic predispositions any more than one can be held responsible for sneezing or throwing up. Explanations of behavior, as even modern novelists such as McEwan have noted, cannot be explained simply in terms of traits.

Here is where traits and dispositions become problematic. "Dispositions, as Wittgenstein emphasized, have no normative force" (Davidson 1994, p. 24). What Davidson is asserting is that dispositions are taken to be natural properties of individuals, presumably dictated by one's genes. This is not to deny their existence but rather to say they are not subject to normative standards or judgments. Mental states, on the other hand, such as beliefs and intentions and actions are subject to normative standards. Beliefs, for example, may be judged as true or false; actions may be judged good or bad; moves in chess may be judged correct or incorrect. Furthermore, we can be held accountable, that is held responsible, for our mental states and our actions. Normativity and responsibility are interdependent.

The importance of the normative rises from the fact that because we are responsible for our beliefs and actions we may revise them on the basis of those judgments and in this way come to meet a common standard for a community. In a sense, one joins a community by learning a language and by learning to play by the rules. Dispositions and traits lack this normative dimension. For this reason, cognitivists such as Rozeboom and Davidson doubt that dispositions have a role to play in a mature cognitive psychology. Habits, such as toilet training, lie in the middle ground. Rules may become second nature and therefor habit-like (Harré 2001). Conversely, habits may become subject to norms as when one complies with a no-smoking sign but the habit itself is not changed by judgment but by what the behaviorists called extinction.

Once we grant the importance of normativity to mental life, we may find a way to address the problem of dispositions more productively. Traits and dispositions can take on a normative property when they become subject to moral or other standards. As Goldie (2004) recently pointed out, a personality trait when subject to a moral standard becomes a character trait. A character trait is one for which we are responsible or as he says is "reason-responsive". Kindness can be a character trait because we have reasons for being kind and those reasons underlie our acts of kindness. Rationality is a matter of behaving in particular ways for good reasons. As abilities and dispositions, intellectual or otherwise, lack this normative force we neither control them nor are we responsible for them. Responsibilities arise when one uses whatever resources are at hand to take on and meet the norms and standards for any activity whether doing mathematics or painting a picture.

The normative dimension becomes critical when one approaches educational theory. In school, behavior becomes increasing subject to normative standards, that is, to rules and norms for thinking and acting. Behavior becomes "reason-responsive". One acquires competencies as one takes on responsibility for meeting certain standards. In meeting a standard one thereby earns a credit. Traits and dispositions, on the other hand, have no normative force, and displaying them neither earns credit or blame. One is not responsible for mere dispositions; as argued earlier, dispositions are causes of action not reasons for acting. A theory of education has to spell out how children come to take on responsibilities for learning and how one, whether teacher or learner, goes about judging whether those responsibilities have been met[1].

Unexamined application of theories of traits and dispositions lead to inappropriate educational practice and policy. In most developed countries, considerations of justice have led to the guarantee that all children have equal access to an education. Once general access is granted, further access to educational resources or privileges is justified, correctly in my view, by saying that one has earned a privilege by meeting a standard or that one needs further resources in order to meet that standard. One earns access to an advanced level of study by meeting a certain standard at an entry level. That is, one earns a privilege by meeting a normative standard. However, teachers and policy makers subvert this practice on the basis of unwarranted claims about dispositions whether intelligence or other aspects of behavior. Thus, teachers are notoriously disposed to explain children's success and failure in terms of putative abilities and learning styles rather than on the conditions that make learning easy or difficult. In regard to educational policy in some states, children are granted special educational resources on the basis of dispositions, such as a high IQ score or a putative talent rather than on achievement or merit. Such access is not earned but rather a gift. "Giftedness" classes, then, are one case of such unearned privilege

---

[1] This was the burden of Olson 2003.

based on unexamined assumptions about dispositions. Such "gifted-ness" programs are in sharp contrast with "accelerated" programs in which participants earned the privilege by taking on and meeting or exceeding the standard. Not *ability* but *responsibility* is the key.

The issue of dispositions also raises the problem of what to do with students who fail to meet or even attempt to meet a standard. Children's behavior in such cases is presumably a product of the dispositions and habits that lack normative force—that is, on factors for which they are not responsible. The central task of education and socialization general-ly is to help children transform such habits and dispositions into inten-tional actions for which they can take responsibility. Education's first task, then, is to encourage and allow children to take on responsibilities, that is, to attempt to meet the standards or norms for what they decide to believe and decide to do. And the school's responsibility is to hold them accountable to those standards.

Even if Gardner fails to trace a route from the dispositional accounts of personality theory to the theories of intention and reason-informed character, his attempt to interpret traits in terms of the symbol systems of a society may be read as an attempt to come to terms with normative standards. Any symbol system embodies a set of rules as to what is appropriate or inappropriate, apposite or inapposite, correct or incorrect, pleasing or boring, and so on. That is, action in a symbol system is sub-ject to judgment and something for which one can be held responsible. In fact, the fledgling attempts to draw or model or express something provide the occasion for the child's own judgment; meeting those stan-dards gives the child a feeling of success as well as earning the appro-bation of teachers and peers. Intentional action and judgment bring agency and responsibility to the actor. The development of character is a matter of premising action not on one's predispositions but on the basis of one's reasons and judgments. In this way agency, intentionality and responsibility could become the central features of a psychology that has special relevance for education. Abilities, traits and dispositions can be either left to find a new place in the natural sciences or else relegated to the dust-bin of history.

REFERENCES

Davidson, D. 1994. The Social Aspect of Language. In Davidson, *Seeing through Language* (Town: Publisher), pp. 15–27.
Goldie, P. 2004. *On Personality.* London: Routledge.

Gardner, Howard. 1983. *Frames of Mind.* New York: Basic Books.

———. 1999. *Intelligence Reframed.* New York: Basic Books.

Gardner, H., M. Csikszentmihalyi, and W. Damon. 2001. *Good Work.* New York: Basic Books.

Harré, R. 2001. Norms in Life. In D. Bakhurst and S. Shanker, eds., *Jerome Bruner: Language, Culture, Self* (London: Sage), pp. 150–166.

McEwan, Ian. 2003. *Atonement.* New York: Knopf.

Olson, David R. 2003. *Psychological Theory and Educational Reform.* New York: Cambridge University Press, 2003).

Rozeboom, W.W. 1972. Problems in the Psycho-philosophy of Knowledge. In J.R. Royce and W.W. Rozeboom, eds., *The Psychology of Knowing* (New York: Gordon and Beach), pp. 25–109.

3

Multiple Invalidities

JOHN WHITE

The theory of multiple intelligences (MI) has been influential in school reform across the world. In England, for instance, it is widely used to back the idea that pupils have preferred 'learning styles': some make better progress if they can involve their musical or interpersonal or other strengths in their learning than if they have to be dependent on language ability alone.

But does MI theory hold water?

Everything turns on the claim that there are a few relatively discrete intelligences: linguistic, musical, logico-mathematical, spatial, bodily-kinaesthetic, intrapersonal and interpersonal, to which have now been added naturalist and possibly existential intelligences. One reason for the popularity of MI theory is its rejection of the unitary general intelligence associated with IQ testing. Children who have been seen, or have seen themselves, as dim are recognized to have other strengths. This is an important thought. But it could be true and MI theory false. Long ago the philosopher Gilbert Ryle (1949, p. 48) reminded us that "the boxer, the surgeon, the poet and the salesman" engage in their own kinds of intelligent operation, applying "their special criteria to the performance of their special tasks." On his view, intelligent action has to do with flexible adaptation of means in pursuit of one's goals. This means that there are as many types of human intelligence as there are types of human goal. Gardner has corralled this variousness into a small number of categories. Is this justified?

Everything turns on how the intelligences are identified. The basic text here is Gardner 1983, Chapter 4. He writes

> First of all, what are the prerequisites for an intelligence: that is, what are the general desiderata to which a set of intellectual skills ought to conform before that set is worth consideration in the master list of intellectual competences? Second, what are the actual criteria by which we can judge whether a candidate competence, which has passed the "first cut", ought to be invited to join our charmed circle of intelligences? (p. 60)

Identifying an intelligence is thus a two-stage process.

Prerequisities

The first stage is, in a way, the more important. If a candidate fails here, it stands no chance. So what Gardner says about prerequisites is crucial. He tells us (1983, pp. 60–61) that

> A human intellectual competence must entail a set of skills of problem-solving . . . and must also entail the potential for finding or creating problems—thereby laying the groundwork for the acquisition of new knowledge. These prerequisites represent my effort to focus on those intellectual strengths that prove of some importance within a cultural context.

He goes on to say (p. 62) that

> a prerequisite for a theory of multiple intelligences, as a whole, is that it captures a reasonably complete gamut of the kinds of abilities valued by human cultures.

Failing candidates

Which candidates fail and which pass the test? Among failures, Gardner includes the "ability to recognize faces" and the "abilities used by a scientist, a religious leader, or a politician" (p. 61). The former "does not seem highly valued by cultures." The latter abilities *are* of great importance,

> yet, because these cultural roles can (by hypothesis) be broken down into collections of particular intellectual competences, they do not themselves qualify as intelligences. (*Ibid.*)

Is it true that the ability to recognize faces is not valued by cultures? This seems counterintuitive. For if most of us could not recognize the faces of our relatives, friends, colleagues, or political leaders, it is hard to see how social life would be possible.

How can one tell whether an ability is culturally important? Gardner writes as if there are clear tests at this first of the two filters. Yet his very first example of a failure is disputable.

His treatment of the "abilities used by a scientist, a religious leader, or a politician" shows that not only does an ability have to be valued within cultures: it has also not to be breakable-down into more basic intellectual abilities. Presumably Gardner has in mind some or all of the seven intelligences which he goes on to describe.

But this is also problematic. In what sense is being a political leader breakable down into some or all of these seven? "Breaking down" could hardly refer to sufficient, as distinct from necessary, conditions. No combination of the intelligences is sufficient to produce competence in political leadership, for otherwise those many of us who possess all the seven (or so) intelligences to some degree would also possess this competence—and not all of us do.

But if it is necessary conditions that are intended, while it is true that one cannot be a political leader without linguistic competence or interpersonal understanding, it is also true that one could not have logico-mathematical abilities without having some linguistic abilities. This would cause a problem for Gardner, because if an intelligence cannot be broken down—in the present sense—into other more basic abilities, then logico-mathematical intelligence fails at the first hurdle, just like political competence.

Passing Candidates

I turn now to those candidates which pass the first test. In Gardner 1983 these must include the seven intelligences. They must have all been picked out for their problem-solving and problem-creating skills important in human cultures.

Why these areas? It seems an odd list. For one thing, many of the items seem to be logically interrelated—and this casts in doubt that these are "relatively autonomous" competences (1983, p. 8). Mathematical abilities are, to a large extent, a specialized kind of linguistic ability. One could not understand oneself and identify others, as the personal competences require, unless one had some linguistic abilities. Logical abilities are not necessarily tied to mathematical abilities, but *are* required by linguistic ability. There could be no linguistic abilities unless people by and large possessed the spatial ability of "perceiving the visual world accurately" (1983, p. 173). And so on.

Secondly, if one asks "what kinds of problem-solving and problem-creating competences are valued in human societies?", what sort of answer might be expected? There would need to be more precision about the range of societies in question. Are we talking about all of them, most, or only some of them? Gardner is not clear on this. On the one hand he says:

> The prerequisites are a way of ensuring that a human intelligence must be genuinely useful and important, at least in certain cultural settings. (1983, p. 61)

On the other, *Frames of Mind*, like the wider Harvard Project of which it was the first fruit, is a study of 'human potential' *tout court*, not human potential within certain cultures. In a later work, Gardner has written:

> The theory is an account of human cognition in its fullness—I put forth the intelligences as a new definition of human nature, cognitively speaking. (Gardner 1999a, p. 44)

This would seem to suggest that the first filtering must be based on what all—or at least virtually all—human societies value. How would we find out what this might be? We have historical evidence stretching back a few millennia; and very patchy archeological evidence taking us back another few. From these sources, and from what we know of the kinds of creatures we are, it is reasonable to suppose that all, or nearly all human societies have attached importance to linguistic ability, to some degree of interpersonal understanding, to using parts of the body, to accurate visual perception (I am taking for granted the logical interconnexions here). Have counting skills also been universally important? Probably. About musical skills, we have less reason to be confident: even if all known societies have prized these, what can we say about unknown ones? About intrapersonal skills, we have every reason to be skeptical. These have to do with "access to one's own feeling life" (1983, p. 239). We know this has been valued in certain civilizations, for example in Athens, in Taoism, in the individualistic world of post-Renaissance times. But we have no grounds to expect to find it prized in the hypertraditional societies that have been so prominent among known human cultures.

So the "first cut" selection of the seven original intelligences looks as though it may have been based on something other than a study of skills which all or nearly all human societies have valued. I will come back to this later. In addition, there are other skills, not included among the intelligences, which have as much *prima facie* plausibility for this title as many so included: food-producing skills, for instance, shelter-building skills, medical skills, child-rearing skills. Has Gardner considered these, but rejected them at the 'second cut', that is, at the criteria stage?

It could be that he did not consider them at all, since he tells us that he understands human intelligences as "human *intellectual* competences" (my italics) and the skills just mentioned are practical rather than intellectual. On the other hand, it is uncertain what his term 'intellectual' covers. Gardner aside, in one common usage it has to do with activities concerned with the pursuit of truth, like history, science, philosophy. More broadly, it can also include artistic pursuits and perhaps the application of academic thinking to such fields as politics and medicine. Gardner's usage seems to go even wider. His bodily-kinaesthetic intelligence covers the abilities of artisans, ball-players and instrumentalists "who are able to manipulate objects with finesse." On this definition, good plumbers, electricians, tilers, bricklayers come out as intellectuals.

On such a wide definition, perhaps human-wide skills to do with food-producing and with shelter-building *would* be covered by Gardner's scheme. It is not clear. All we can say is that Gardner does not approach his "first cut" via a comprehensive consideration of what the valued problem-solving skills in any human society might be, drawing on whatever empirical data is available. I will say more later about the approach he *does* adopt. Meanwhile, I will leave problems thrown up by the "prerequisites" condition, and turn to the "criteria."

Criteria

Once a candidate intelligence has satisfied the prerequisites, it has to meet various criteria. These comprise (1983:62-9):

- potential isolation of the area by brain damage
- the existence in it of idiots savants, prodigies and other exceptional individuals

- an identifiable core operation/set of operations
- a distinctive developmental history, along with a definable set of expert 'end-state' performances
- an evolutionary history and evolutionary plausibility
- support from experimental psychological tasks
- support from psychometric findings
- susceptibility to encoding in a symbol system.

There are problems about several of these items taken individually; as well as more general problems about the identification and application of the criteria. I begin with specific items. For convenience, I begin with two of them taken together.

"an identifiable core operation/set of operations"

"a distinctive developmental history, along with a definable set of expert 'end-state' performances"

The interconnectedness of these two can be illustrated by reference to linguistic intelligence. This has as its "core operations" a sensitivity to the meaning of words, to order among words, to the sounds and rhythms of words, and to the different functions of language (1983, p. 77). These core operations are seen at work "with special clarity" in the work of the poet.

Linguistic intelligence also possesses a distinctive developmental history, culminating in expert 'end-state' performances like those of the poet. Syntactical and phonological processes lie close to the core, since they unfold "with relatively scant need for support from environmental factors" (1983, pp. 80–81). Other intelligences illustrate the same point. Musical intelligence involves, as core operations, pitch, rhythm, and timbre (1983, pp. 104–05). It begins in infancy with rudimentary singing (p. 108) and develops towards end-states exemplified this time by composers. Spatial intelligence develops from such core abilities as perceiving the visual world accurately, performing transformations on one's visual experience, and recreating aspects of the latter (p. 173). The expert end-state performances are painting, sculpture and the sciences. Similar claims are made about the remaining intelligences.

Gardner's theory of intelligence is developmentalist. Developmentalism is the theory that the biological unfolding between two poles from seed through to mature specimen that we find in the physical world—for example of plants, or human bodies—is also found in the mental world.

In his criteria, Gardner acknowledges the two poles in the mental case. At one end, there are allegedly genetically given capacities common to human beings like visual perception, innate knowledge of the rules of language (following Chomsky, p. 80), the ability to move our bodies in different ways, and so forth. At the other end is the mature state, the "definable set of expert 'end-state' performances" mentioned among the criteria. We have already seen examples in the highest flights of poetry, music, painting, sculpture, and science. Intrapersonal intelligence, whose core capacity or mental seed is "access to one's own feeling life," finds its full development in the work of a novelist like Proust or the patient or therapist "who comes to attain a deep knowledge of his feeling life" (1983, p. 239). Interpersonal intelligence, arising out of the primitive "ability to notice and make distinctions among other individuals" generates its "highly developed forms . . . in political and religious leaders (a Mahatma Gandhi or a Lyndon Johnson, in skilled parents and teachers," and so forth (*Ibid.*).

Problems in Developmentalism

Gardner's theory faces an objection besetting all forms of developmentalism. This theory is based on the assumption that the unfolding, familiar in the biological realm, is also found in the mental. There are two problems about this, one for each of the two poles, problems we see illustrated in Gardner's own writings.

i. First the seed, or initial state. What is characteristic of biological seeds, including the union of sperm and egg at the beginning of human development, is that *they have within them the power to unfold* into more complex stages, given appropriate environmental conditions like air, light and water in the growth of a plant. To locate a parallel initial state in the mental case it is not enough to pick out innately given capacities. There is no doubt that such capacities exist. We are all born with the power to see and hear things, to move our bodies, to desire food and drink, to feel certain basic emotions like fear, to feel pain and pleasurable sensations. But we should not assume that any of the abilities just mentioned have within them the power to *unfold* into more complex forms of the same thing. I have italicized the word "unfold" advisedly. For there is equally no doubt that many of the primitive capacities just mentioned do *change* into more sophisticated versions: the desire for food, for instance, becomes differentiated into desires for hamburgers and ice-cream; the brute ability to move one's limbs becomes specified into, for instance, the ability to run half-marathons or to tango. The changes wrought in these capacities are cultural products: people are socialized into them. This social shaping cannot be characterized, as a defence of developmentalism might urge, as environmental conditions which have to be satisfied for natural processes of growth to occur—the mental equivalents of air, light and water in the growth of plants. For in the latter case air, light and water are *causally* necessary for the innate propensities to unfold from within, while the cultural induction required in the case of learning language and other skills dependent on this is *logically* necessary. Linguistic concepts cannot conceivably be acquired on one's own, since one could not know what would count as correct or incorrect instantiations of them. They can only be learnt from those already adept in their use and aware of these norms (Hamlyn 1978, pp. 58–60).

ii. The second problem concerns the other pole, the mature state—Gardner's "end-state." We understand this notion well enough in physical contexts like fully-grown hollyhocks or human bodies. A fully-grown human body is one which can grow no further: it has reached the limits of its development. The same is true of delphiniums and oak trees. Like these, the human body can certainly go on *changing,* but the changes are to do with the maintenance and deterioration of the system, not with its further growth. If we apply these ideas to the mind, do we want to say that all human beings have mental ceilings—for example, in each of Gardner's intelligences—beyond which they cannot progress? This goes against the grain for many of us. We like to think of our intellectual life as expandable, and deepenable in principle, in all sorts of directions. True, psychologists like Cyril Burt have built the notion of mental ceilings into their notion of intelligence, but their views have been rightly criticized. The claim that we all have individually differing intellectual limits is both unverifiable and unfalsifiable. As such, it is a metaphysical claim, on a par with the claims that all historical events are predetermined, or that a personal deity exists. It is not a scientific claim at all (White 1998a, pp. 29–32).

One answer to this might be that the development of intelligence is unlike physical development in that here there are no ceilings, simply the potential for endless growth. Grounds would have to be provided for this claim—which is tantamount to saying that mental development fails to manifest a feature found in biological development. But if we leave this on one side, the claim still includes the idea of growth towards states of relative maturity, even if ceilings are not to be found. It is not clear whether Gardner would embrace this claim. On the one hand he writes of "end-state" performances (1983, p. 64), which suggests finality; on the other, he describes the process of development as leading to "exceedingly high levels of competence," which does not.

Whichever view he takes, he still has to say *what counts* as maturity in the case of the intelligences. With the oak tree and the human body, we know through the use of our senses when maturity has occurred: over time we can *see* that a person is fully grown, physically speaking, or that an oak tree has reached its full dimensions. What equivalent is there in the mental realm? How do we know either that people have reached their mental ceiling or, on the ceiling-less view, that they are more mentally mature than they were?

We do not just use our senses. We cannot see a person's intellectual maturity as we can see that he or she is physically fully grown. So how *do* we tell?

In ordinary life we make all sorts of judgments about people's intellectual or moral maturity. These judgments tend to be controversial. Some people would understand intellectual maturity in quiz show terms, as being able to marshal and remember heaps of facts; others would emphasize depth of understanding; yet others a synoptic grasp of connexions between different fields; and so on. In moral understanding, what counts as maturity is similarly contentious. Candidates here might be: having seen the need to conform to certain absolute rules; sensitivity to others' needs; a philosophical understanding of what morality is all about; an awareness of the great plurality of moral values and the need to strike sensitive balances among them.

Judgments of mental or moral maturity lack the consensus found in judgments about fully grown pine trees or badgers. This is because we are in the realm of value judgments rather than of observable facts: different people apply their own intellectual or moral values.

Gardner's examples of high levels of development in the intelligences seem to reflect his own value judgments about what kinds of qualities are important. He starts from problem-solving skills which are useful and important within a cultural context. He has in mind the achievements of outstanding poets, composers, religious leaders, politicians, scientists, novelists, and so on. Would everyone agree with him, for instance, that the poet is the best example of a person whose sensitivity to the meanings and other features of words has reached a high degree of perfection? Why not the philosopher or propagandist?

In his introduction to the second (1993) edition of *Frames of Mind,* Gardner backs off from using only ethically acceptable persons to illustrate the higher realms of the intelligences. He writes:

> intelligences by themselves are neither pro-social nor antisocial. Goethe used his linguistic intelligence for positive ends, Goebbels his for destructive ones; Stalin and Gandhi both understood other individuals, but put their interpersonal intelligences to diverse uses. (1993, p. xxvi)

This may cast doubt on whether "end-states" are always achievements highly valued within a culture. But the more central point is that in the earlier 1983 version of MI theory (repeated in the 1993 main text) the "end states" are identified not by observation of what happens in nature, as with plants or bodies, but by what is held—by Gardner—to be socially valuable. It is his value judgments, not his empirical discoveries as a scientist, that are his starting point.

I have tried to show that whether we look towards the beginning or towards the end of the development process, towards the seed or towards the full flowering, we find apparently insuperable problems in identifying mental counterparts to physical growth. Since developmentalist assumptions are central to Gardner's MI theory, the latter is seriously undermined.

"susceptibility to encoding in a symbol system"

Gardner writes:

> following my mentor Nelson Goodman and other authorities, I conceive of a symbol as any entity (material or abstract) that can denote or refer to any other entity. On this definition, words, pictures, diagrams, numbers, and a host of other entities are readily considered symbols. (1983, p. 301)

It is important to see how wide the range of Gardner's symbols is. They include not only obvious ones like words and mathematical symbols, but also paintings, symphonies, plays, dances and poems. It is because works of art are symbols in his view that he can connect many of his intelligences with their own kind of symbolic entities. For instance, it is not only words which are the symbols associated with linguistic intelligence: this also contains such symbols as poems.

Gardner states that "it may be possible for an intelligence to proceed without its own symbol system" (1983, p. 66). He may be thinking here of the personal intelligences (see also p. 242). But these, he argues, are dependent on "a symbolic code supplied by the culture" (*ibid.*), presumably linguistic symbols. Or he may be thinking of bodily-kinaesthetic intelligence. Although, if works of art can be symbols and mime and dance are symbols associated with this intelligence, what is one to say about the achievements of the swimmer, the boxer or the athlete? Are these symbolic insofar as they incorporate aesthetic elements? Or are they not symbolic entities at all? Gardner does not tell us.

A controversial feature of Gardner's position is his extension of the notion of a "symbol" to works of art. He writes:

> In addition to denoting or representing, symbols convey meanings in another equally important but less often appreciated way. A symbol can convey some mood, feeling or tone . . . Thus a painting, whether abstract or representational, can convey moods of sadness, triumph, anger, or 'blueness' (even if the painting itself is red!). By including this important expressive function within the armament of a symbol, we are able to talk about the full range of artistic symbols, from symphonies to square dances, from sculpture to squiggles, all of which have potential for expressing such connotative meanings. (1983, p. 301)

It looks as if Gardner is saying that not all symbols are like words. A word is a symbol in that it stands for something outside itself. The English word 'cat' and the French word 'chat' refer to the same kind of thing in the world, namely cats. But some symbols—some works of art—do not denote or represent: they convey or express feelings.

The difficulty with this is that while works of art can be expressive of emotion, it is hard to see why they should be called 'symbols' for that reason. What are they symbolizing? One can understand the notion readily enough when talking about words, flags, or communion wine. In each of these cases one can draw a distinction between the symbol and what it is a symbol of: cats, America, the blood of Christ. If a song is a symbol in the same way, what is the thing symbolized which lies outside it? Suppose it expresses sadness. Is sadness what it is symbolizing?

Gardner does not say so. It would be hard, in any case, to argue that it is symbolizing this—or, indeed, that works of art symbolize anything—even though some of them, portraits, for instance, *represent* something outside themselves. We can understand symbolizing well enough by reference to words and flags. Here a symbol not only picks out something else. It is also replaceable by equivalent symbols, those with the same function. Words are translatable into other languages; a flag is replaceable by a statue. But a Rembrandt portrait or Mozart piano concerto cannot be replaced by symbols with an equivalent function: works of art are unique. If they are said to be symbols, we cannot understand what this means by reference to what we know of symbols in uncomplicated cases. The use of the term in Gardner is obscure. If in an artistic context 'symbolising' means no more than 'expressing feeling', the term is redundant. In addition, 'symbol' now comes to have a different meaning in the arts from what it has in language and in mathematical thinking. On the other hand, if Gardner's 'symbolizing' is *not* equivalent to 'expressing feeling', it is difficult to see what sense can be attached to it. We do not know what a work is supposed to symbolize or in what way its being a symbol is like or unlike symbolism in the unproblematic sense. The term—and the theory of MI that depends on it—become radically obscure.

Without going through all the other criteria, a word about two of them.

"the potential isolation of the area by brain damage"

The criteria to do with development and with symbol are central items on Gardner's list. This can be seen if one tries to imagine their absence. I shall come back to the centrality of the symbol criterion later. Meanwhile let us imagine the exclusion of the development criterion. Suppose we take what appears to be the weightiest of the other criteria: "the potential isolation of the area by brain damage." And let us take it that there are localized areas of function within the brain. If one part of the brain is damaged, one's sight is impaired, if another, one's ability to move one's left hand, or feel pain, or talk, or understand speech. What this shows is that certain physiological necessary conditions of exercizing these capacities are absent. It does not help to indicate the existence of separate 'intelligences'. It is well known that language ability is impaired through brain injury to parts of the left hemisphere of the cerebral cortex. But the injury could in principle impair wired-in abilities implicated not only in language use but in all sorts of other things as well; and there does indeed seem to be empirical evidence that this is the case (Richardson 1999, pp. 85–88). The capacities in question are not those of a language module but of "much more general and lower-grade functions" (p. 87).

Given his developmentalism, one can understand why Gardner should look to brain localization in order to identify intelligences, for he has to provide an account of the 'seed' which is to unfold into its mature form, and this seed has to be part of our original, biologically given, constitution. But the kinds of function picked out by brain localization research do not have the power, as far as I can see, to grow into more developed forms. I am indeed born with the power of vision or the power to move my thumbs, but although various forms of socialization are built on these abilities, the latter do not themselves *unfold* into maturer versions of themselves.

"the existence, in an area, of idiots savants, prodigies, and other exceptional individuals"

Gardner invokes the existence of *idiots savants* to support his theory, but what I know of them does not lead me to think of them as intelligent. Well known recent examples include an eleven-year-old London boy who can draw complicated buildings perfectly having just seen them; a twenty-three-year-old man who can play piano pieces perfectly having heard them only three times; and a young man who can tell you the day of the week of any date presented to him. All these cases are of subnormal mental ability. What they all have in common is a *mechanical* facility, one which lacks the flexibility of adapting means to ends found in intelligent behavior.

Prodigies only support Gardner's case if there is good evidence that their talents are innate. But the evidence there is seems to point to acquired abilities (Howe 1997, pp. 131–32).

Conclusion

It would be natural to think that the 'criteria' against which one measures candidate intelligences that have survived the first cut are all straightforwardly applicable—in the sense that it is an empirical task (although perhaps a complicated one) to look at the relevant facts and come to a judgment. But this is not so. The criteria to do with development and with symbols presuppose the truth of *theories*—one in psychology, the other in aesthetics—which, once subjected to philosophical critique, turn out to be untenable. And this undermines the viability of MI theory as a whole.

How are the criteria to be applied?

How does one use the criteria to pick out intelligences? If they are all necessary conditions, each has to be met before we can say that an intelligence exists. Although some of them seem to be necessary—to judge by remarks like "an intelligence must also be susceptible to encoding in a symbol system" (Gardner 1990, p. 933), in his original work Gardner makes it clear that not all have to be satisfied (Gardner, 1983, p. 62). In places, the demand is more stringent. In his 1990 discussion of how he came to pick out his intelligences, he writes that "only those candidate intelligences that satisfied all or a majority of the criteria were selected as *bona fide* intelligences" (Gardner 1990, p. 932). If this is to be taken literally, then if five or more of the eight criteria listed are met, a candidate automatically passes the test. But *Frames of Mind* states that there is no "algorithm for the selection of an intelligence, such that any trained researcher could determine whether a candidate intelligence met the appropriate criteria" (p. 63). Rather, Gardner goes on:

> At present, however, it must be admitted that the selection (or rejection) of a candidate intelligence is reminiscent more of an artistic judgment than of a scientific assessment. (p. 63)

The identification of intelligences appears, then to be a subjective matter, depending on the particular weightings that Gardner gives to different criteria in different cases.

It is worth dwelling on this point. Gardner sees it as a special virtue of his theory, which differentiates it from rival accounts, that it is *scientifically* based. He writes:

> There have, of course, been many efforts to nominate and detail essential intelligences, ranging from the medieval trivium and quadrivium to the psychologist Larry Gross's list of five modes of communication (lexical, social-gestural, iconic, logico-mathematical, and musical), the philosopher Paul Hirst's list of seven forms of knowledge (mathematics, physical sciences, interpersonal understanding, religion, literature and the fine arts, morals, and philosophy). On an *a priori* basis, there is nothing wrong with these classifications; and, indeed, they may prove critical for certain purposes. The very difficulty with these lists, however, is that they are *a priori*—an effort by a reflective individual (or a culture) to devise meaningful distinctions among types of knowledge. What I am calling for are sets of intelligences which meet certain biological and psychological specifications. In the end, the search for an empirically grounded set of faculties may fail; and then we may have to rely once more on *a priori* schemes, such as Hirst's. But the effort should be made to find a firmer foundation for our favourite faculties. (1983, pp. 61–62)

In saying that selecting intelligences is more like making an artistic judgment than making a scientific assessment, Gardner thus seems to be contradicting himself. The non-empirical nature of his theory has also been shown above. We have seen how the 'first cut' selection of the intelligences is not based on empirical investigation of what different societies have held to be valuable; and that the 'criteria' depend on theories in psychology and aesthetics which themselves are not empirically founded.

Gardner has replied to the charge I made originally in White 1998b, based on the same quotation about artistic judgment, that his choice of intelligences is subjective. He wrote

> White correctly notes that my original list depended on the judgment of a single analyst, who made his data available to others. However, White is naïve if he believes that science begins in any other way. (Gardner 1998)

What he may have in mind is the Popperian point that science begins with conjectures. But not all conjectures eventuate in science. Some may be empirically untestable—the conjecture, for instance, that every event is predetermined. A fundamental question about MI theory is whether it is empirically testable. Because it is not clear when a candidate intelligence passes or does not pass the 'criteria' test, it is uncertain under what conditions it might be refuted. Empirically refuted, that is. If I am right in what I said about development and symbols, it may be that MI theory is refutable on philosophical grounds. But Gardner needs not *a priori*, but empirical, refutability.

Why These Criteria?

A further—and surely fundamental—question is: how does Gardner justify using the particular criteria he lists to pick out intelligences?

I have not been able to find any answer in his writings. Whenever he introduces the criteria, they are each spelt out in some detail, but there is no account of why these ones have been employed and not others. In a properly scientific theory one would expect a rationale for this.

MI Theory in Biographical Perspective

That is not to say that no explanation can be given. I believe there *is* a reason. But it is not a reason in the sense Gardner needs. What one can do is tell a plausible historical story about how he came to put weight on the criteria. This would be an explanation of how they have come about, but not a justification of them. And it is a justification that Gardner needs to make good his claim that his is an objective, scientific theory. In what follows I shall concentrate on the same two major criteria examined above—to do with development and with symbol systems. As we shall see, the historical discussion will throw light not only on the criteria, but more broadly on MI theory as a whole. It will help to make sense of it. It will also bring us back to the vital importance of Gardner's 'first cut'.

As far as I can judge, the historical story runs like this. In the 1960s Gardner began his career as a developmental psychologist, profoundly influenced by Piaget as well as by structuralist thinkers in other fields, notably Lévi-Strauss in anthropology.

> The structuralists are distinguished first and foremost by their ardent, powerfully held conviction that there is a structure underlying all human behavior and mental functioning . . . (1972, p. 10)

The young Gardner was also "a serious pianist and enthusiastically involved with other arts as well" (2003, p. 1).

> No surprise, then, that when I first began to study developmental psychology, I was soon struck by certain limitations in the field. The child was seen by nearly all researchers as an exclusively rational creature, a problem-solver—in fact, a scientist in knickers. . . . While a first-year graduate student, I elected to direct my own research toward a developmental psychology of the arts. (1982, p. xii)

He goes on

> The structuralist approach to the mind has limitations. . . . Though creative thought has not escaped their attention, each of the major cognitive structuralists views the options of human thought as in some way preordained, limited in advance. This makes their work especially problematic for a study of the mind where the major focus falls on innovation and creation, as in the fashioning of original works of art.
>
> To my mind the limitation implicit in the standard structuralist stance can be circumscribed by a recognition of one special feature of human thought—its ability to create and sponsor commerce through the use of various kinds of symbol systems. These symbol systems—these codes of meaning—are the vehicles through which thought takes place: by their very nature they are creative, open systems. Through the use of symbols the

human mind, operating according to structuralist principles, can revise, transform and re-create wholly fresh products, systems, and even worlds of meaning. (*Op. cit.*, pp. 4–5)

These various quotations indicate the centrality of theories of development and of symbol systems in Gardner's pre-1983 thinking. Much of his published work in this period was about the application of developmental psychology to the arts. He describes his 1973 book *The Arts and Human Development* as

> fleshing out the picture of development proposed by Piaget, extending it to the vast majority of people who are not scientists . . . but who nonetheless participate in a significant way in complex intellectual activities. (1973, p. vii)

Key to this extension of Piagetian ideas to the arts is the notion of a 'symbol'. Here Gardner was influenced by the aesthetician Nelson Goodman, co-founder with himself of Project Zero at Harvard Graduate School of Education in 1967. Goodman, in the tradition of Ernst Cassirer and Suzanne Langer, saw works of art as a whole as symbols and also as containing symbols within themselves. Different arts, he held, have their own symbol schemes—hence the title of his *Languages of Art* (Goodman 1968). Sometimes artistic symbols have a denoting function, as words do, in that they stand for something outside themselves. In fact words constitute some works of art; other denoting symbols are portraits and drawings from nature. Other artistic symbols 'exemplify' rather than denote. Just as a sample of household paint exemplifies the properties of the paint itself, so a piece of music, in its sad qualities, exemplifies sadness generally—not literally but metaphorically. Understanding a work of art is not a matter of appreciation or aesthetic experience, but of interpreting correctly what and how it symbolizes. The arts, for Goodman, are forms of knowledge.

Gardner's early intellectual biography throws light on his *Frames of Mind*, especially the first five intelligences: linguistic, musical, logico-mathematical, spatial, and bodily-kinaesthetic. Of these, logico-mathematical intelligence is related particularly to mathematics and science and its treatment follows Piaget's scheme quite closely. The other four intelligences reflect Gardner's work in extending Piagetian developmentalism into the arts: poetry is prominent in the chapter on linguistic intelligence, music in that the musical chapter, the visual arts in the spatial, mime and dance in the bodily-kinaesthetic.

Piaget's and Goodman's theories are examples of developmentalism and the symbol theory of art respectively, both of which were criticized above. In addition, there are further conceptual problems damaging to these two theories taken specifically. These have been explored by David Hamlyn in the case of Piaget (Hamlyn 1967; 1978) and Roger Scruton in the case of Goodman (Scruton 1974).

Until 1979 Gardner's work extended Piagetian thinking into the arts. By 1983 it broadened again, now into an overall theory of human intelligences.

I shall explore why in the next section. In this present section I have argued that if we ask why he used the criteria he did, we look in vain for a justification from Gardner himself, but find a likely explanation in the historical progress of his ideas. I have explored this for the criteria to do with symbols and development.

The van Leer Project

A crucial turning point for Gardner came in 1979, when he moved from his long-standing project on the development of artistic competences to an all-embracing theory of intellectual development. Why?

The answer, as he indicates in Gardner 2003, has to do with the Harvard Project on Human Potential funded by the Bernard van Leer Foundation in 1979. The Foundation

> asked the Harvard Graduate School of Education to assess the state of scientific knowledge concerning human potential and its realization and to summarize the findings in a form that would assist educational policy and practice throughout the world. (Gardner 1983, p. x)

Gardner's task in the interdisciplinary team was to look at psychological, as distinct from philosophical and anthropological, considerations. *Frames of Mind* was the first publication from the team. Unlike the second volume, *Of Human Potential*, Israel Scheffler's (1985) philosophical investigation of this notion, Gardner's book did not look globally at the topic, since it focused on 'human *intellectual* potential' (1983, p. x; my italics).

As suggested above, the first five intelligences in this book drew on Gardner's pre-1979 work in the Piagetian and Goodmanian traditions and areas of interest. The other two were the personal intelligences. It is understandable that Gardner should wish to include other areas of interest than mathematics, science and the arts. The van Leer remit wanted something more comprehensive. Strictly, a general study of human potential—insofar as one can attach a defensible sense to the notion (White 1986)—is unrestricted by subject-matter. Human beings can possess capabilities of innumerable sorts, not only intellectual ones connected with the pursuit of knowledge, but also practical ones to do with threading needles, cutting one's toenails, running merchant banks. Gardner did not take on this whole gamut. He restricted himself to intellectual areas, in the sense of those concerned with the pursuit of knowledge. (I bypass his inclusion of artisans and others in his discussion of bodily-kinaesthetic intelligence—see above). Having agreed, as his contribution to the van Leer project, to look at human intellectual potential, he had to determine what further intellectual areas should be considered beyond the sciences, mathematics and the arts. The result was the two personal intelligences—those to do with understanding oneself and understanding other people.

In answer to his own question "why have I incorporated personal intelligences in my survey?", Gardner says

> Chiefly because I feel that these forms of knowledge are of tremendous importance in many, if not all, societies in the world—forms that have, however, tended to be ignored or minimized by nearly all students of cognition. (1983, p. 241)

This is revealing. It shows him making another 'first cut'. The personal intelligences pass this test because of their huge social importance. Gardner then sees how far they pass the second, 'criteria', test. In one way, the first test is sufficient. If you are reviewing the full range of forms of understanding, and so far your work has included only scientific, mathematical and artistic understanding, it will not take long to light on self-understanding and understanding of others as further significant areas, given, as Gardner says, their importance in human life.

He may reply, perhaps, that his task was not to identify forms of knowledge in an *a priori* way—after all, Paul Hirst and others had done that. He needed empirical evidence for them. This meant seeing how well the personal intelligences meet the second-cut criteria.

Contra Gardner, they do not meet them very well. He devotes a section to 'the development of the personal intelligences' from infancy through to maturity (1983, pp. 243–253). The evidence he produces is of *changes* in understanding—which becomes more sophisticated and discriminating in various ways. It is not evidence of change which is also an unfolding. As Gardner for the most part treats "the development of personal knowledge as a relatively natural process" (1983, p. 253), he radically underplays the role of young children's mentors, especially their parents, in inducting them into the language, experiences, ethical involvement, and folk-psychological insight necessary for this kind of understanding. Gardner's preconception that development *must* occur appears to blind him to what most people would see as an obvious explanation.

The symbol test does no better. Gardner admits that "one does not ordinarily think of forms of personal knowledge as being encoded in public symbol systems," and falls back on the true, but lame, thought that these forms of knowledge depend on "a symbolic code supplied by the culture" (1983, p. 242)—presumably he means everyday words in the language. Since a person could hardly be said to possess *any* intellectual competence unless he or she were a language-user, Gardner's point cuts little ice.

In addition, what he says about brain lesion evidence points to changes in *mood and emotion*, for example depression, following injury to the frontal lobes, but not, as far as I can see, to changes in self- or other *understanding*. He himself says that positive evidence is sparse with regard to the criteria to do with evolutionary evidence, exceptional individuals, experimental psychology and psychological testing (1983, p. 242). Despite all this discouraging news, the two intelligences get their diplomas.

This prompts the thought: once they were past the first cut, were they not going to get them anyway? Gardner has always emphasized that little turned for him during the van Leer Project on calling his multiple competences 'intelligences'.

> I don't remember when it happened but at a certain moment, I decided to call these faculties "multiple intelligences" rather than abilities or gifts. This seemingly minor lexical substitution proved very important; I am quite confident that if I had written a book called "Seven Talents" it would not have received the attention that *Frames of Mind* received. (2003, p. 4)

Another synonym in play at that time was 'forms of knowledge':

> nothing much turns on the particular use of this term ['intelligences'], and I would be satisfied to substitute such phrases as 'intellectual competences', 'thought processes', 'cognitive capacities', 'cognitive skills', 'forms of knowledge', or any other cognate mentalistic terminology. (1983, p. 284)

We saw above that Gardner's reason for including the personal intelligences was that

> I feel that these forms of knowledge are of tremendous importance in many, if not all, societies in the world . . . (1983, p. 241)

We also saw that he included Paul Hirst's list of seven forms of knowledge among the "many efforts to nominate and detail essential intelligences" and that if his own empirical approach to demarcating intelligences should fail, "then we may have to rely once more on *a priori* schemes, such as Hirst's" (1983, pp. 61–62).

Once Gardner saw that the personal competences were tremendously important forms of knowledge (intelligences), it is hard to see how they could be excluded from his final list. On this line of thinking, the 'first cut' looks to be the crucial one.

A further question arises here about how Gardner conceived his project in this 1979–83 period. If his intelligences are in the same ball park as Hirst's forms of knowledge—and indeed as "the medieval trivium and quadrivium" (*ibid.*), can they still be equated with abilities or talents? From the former point of view, they come out as ways of categorizing the realm of intellectual phenomena; from the latter, as ways of categorizing individuals' intellectual competences. The first classification is extra-individual: it is of epistemological phenomena in the social world. The second is intra-individual—of attributes of persons.

For Gardner at this time the two ways of classifying were linked. He saw his theory as bridging the—bio-psychological—world of individual nervous systems and the—epistemological or anthropological—world of social forms. Symbols have a central role in this.

> . . . there is no ready way to build a bridge directly between these two bodies of information [biology and anthropology], their vocabularies, their frames of reference are too disparate. . . . The domain of symbols, as it has been constituted by scholars, is ideally suited to help span the gap between the aforementioned entities. (1983, p. 300)

Outside Gardner's theory, the two classifications can be kept apart. Paul Hirst, for instance, saw himself as doing epistemology, not psychology. His theory is about how knowledge is to be logically carved up, not about the kinds of intellectual abilities belonging to individuals.

For Gardner, the two spheres are inseparably connected. This is implicit in his developmentalism and his symbol theory: abilities unfold

from seeds within the nervous system towards mature end-states found
in different intellectual activities; and it is through the acquisition of
symbols that these end-states are those of the highest flights of creative
activity. Because of this inseparable connection, studying one pole of the
process throws light on steps leading to the other. The bio-psychological
study of individuals is a key to the social-epistemological world of the
disciplines; and *vice versa*.

Conclusion

It has become clear that the requirements of the van Leer project allowed
Gardner to expand from the limited theory of artistic development on
which he had previously concentrated to a fuller account of the development of human intellectual competences as a whole. In doing so, he
was able to retain the master-ambition which had motivated his work
from his earliest days as a structuralist, bringing Piagetian insights into
harmony with those of Lévi-Strauss: the desire to link biology and
anthropology, to show that they are part of the same system.

MI Since 1983

Since 1983 there have been several modifications of MI theory.

a. The original seven intelligences have now been extended to
include 'the naturalist intelligence' and—possibly—'existential intelligence' (1999a, Chapter 4). Naturalist intelligence is picked out by reference to a valued social role found across many cultures: people expert
in recognizing and classifying the varieties of plants and animals in their
environment. This is the 'first cut'. Naturalist intelligence is then shown
to satisfy all or most of the 'criteria'.

There are by now familiar points to be made about how well the criteria are met, not least those to do with development and with symbols.
But a prior question is why the new naturalist intelligence came to be
proposed in the first place. Gardner tells us that 'those valued human
cognitions that I previously had to ignore or smuggle in under spatial or
logico-mathematical intelligence deserve to be gathered under a single,
recognized rubric' (1999a, p. 52). This seems to imply that, having
reviewed the full gamut of intellectual activities, he realized that the tax-
onomic aspects of biology had been given short shrift in his original
scheme.

This thought is reinforced by what he says in the same chapter on
possible forms of spiritual intelligence and of existential intelligence—

to do with 'big questions' about one's place in the cosmos, the significance of life and death, the experience of personal love and of artistic experience—as the strongest candidate among these (pp. 53–65). Religious and philosophical thinking are also parts of the intellectual world; and these, too, were ill-represented in the 1983 scheme.

All this lends strength to the suggestion that what powers MI theory is the attempt to identify all major divisions of the intellectual life (taking the arts as always to be forms of knowledge). Crucial to the theory, as we have seen, is the 'first cut'.

b. Since 1983, too, Gardner has become bolder about the significance of MI theory. What began as a response to an external funder's request—the extension of a pre-existing interest in development in the arts as well as in Piagetian areas into a more global survey of 'human potential'—has generated

> a new definition of human nature, cognitively speaking. Whereas Socrates saw man as the rational animal and Freud stressed the irrationality of human beings, I (with due tentativeness) have described human beings as those organisms who possess a basic set of seven, eight, or a dozen intelligences. (1999a, p. 44)

This, it seems to me, is to write a prescription about desirable intellectual attainments into a description of human nature as a whole. In any case, why make *intellectual* activity the defining characteristic of our human nature? Human beings are into all sorts of things other than the pursuit of knowledge and the arts. So why highlight these?

c. A third—related—departure since 1983 has been Gardner's distinction between 'intelligence' and 'domain' (1999a, p. 82). The former is 'a biopsychological potential that is ours by virtue of our species membership'. The latter is a "socially constructed human endeavor," for example "physics, cooking, chess, constitutional law, and rap music." It is "characterized by a specific symbol system." Gardner says he could have made this distinction more carefully in 1983. Readers would then have seen more clearly that several intelligences can be applied in the same domain, and the same intelligence in many domains.

This move detaches from each other the two dimensions—the biological and the social—which Gardner tried to hold together through his career. It makes MI theory unintelligible. For it has always been part of the concept of an intelligence that it is an ability that develops from a physiological origin towards an end-state belonging to a valued social activity. Poetry, music, the visual arts, dance, mathematics, logic, sport—the loci of the 1983 end-states—are all social constructions. Similarly, the idea of an intelligence was originally founded partly on the thought that symbols are bridges between the biological and the social. The 1999 version separates the previously inseparable and puts symbols and end-states firmly on the side of the social—as attached to *domains* rather than intelligences. At the same time, the 'criteria', which remain unchanged from 1983, include reference to both symbols and end-states among the distinguishing features of *intelligences*. This is why the 1999 version of MI theory is unintelligible.

MI and Education

Until the van Leer project Gardner was a psychologist, not an educationalist. But he had to adhere to the van Leer request that the Harvard team summarize its findings about human potential "in a form that would assist educational policy and practice throughout the world" (Gardner 1983, p. x). This was because the van Leer Foundation was an international non-profit-making institution dedicated to helping disadvantaged children to realize their potential (Scheffler 1985, p. ix). In *Frames of Mind* Gardner

> touched on some educational implications of the theory in the concluding chapters. This decision turned out to be another crucial point because it was educators, rather than psychologists, who found the theory of most interest. (2003, p. 4)

Since 1983 MI theory has had a huge influence on educational reform, especially school improvement, across the world. It has affected its views about pupils and their aptitudes, methods of learning and teaching, and curriculum content. If the argument of this essay is correct, all this has been built on flaky theory.

a. Gardner holds that while nearly all children possess all the intelligences to some degree, some of them have particular aptitudes in one or more of them. "My own belief is that one could assess an individual's intellectual potentials quite early in life, perhaps even in infancy" (1983, p. 385).

It is not surprising that ideas like these have—not intentionally—encouraged educational policies and practices to do with selection, specialisation, individualisation of learning, and assessment. But if the intelligences are not part of human nature but wobbly constructions on the part of their author, educators should treat them with caution. There may or may not be good grounds for personalised learning and other policies, but if they exist they must come from elsewhere. That teachers often need to vary the way they teach according to what best motivates particular pupils has been part of pedagogy for centuries; there is no good reason for confining this notion within the 'intelligences' framework.

b. There is abundant evidence that MI theory has been influential in reducing the low self-esteem of pupils who see themselves as stupid or thick, where this kind of judgment derives from conventional ideas of general intelligence based on IQ. The idea that intelligence is not necessarily tied to prowess in logical, mathematical and linguistic tasks but can be displayed across a variety of fields is true—as our opening quotation from Gilbert Ryle illustrates. But the idea is not necessarily tied to MI theory (White 1998a, pp. 3–4).

c. One reason why MI theory has been so influential may be its basis in supposedly discrete forms of intellectual activity—in Gardner's broad use of the term to embrace not only disciplines based on the pursuit of truth like biology and mathematics, but also the arts and athletics. With some exceptions, the areas it covers are close to those in a traditional so-called 'liberal education' based mainly on initiation into all the main areas of knowledge, to be pursued largely for their own sake. The addition of naturalist intelligence and (possibly) existential intelligence have made the fit even closer, seeing the affinities of these areas with biology and with work of a philosophical or religious sort.

On the whole, Gardner has refrained from deriving curricular consequences from MI theory. His writings on what the content of education should be show that the type of schooling he favors is in the 'liberal education' tradition.

> Education in our time should provide the basis for enhanced understanding of our several worlds—the physical world, the biological world, the world of human beings, the world of human artifacts, and the world of the self. (1999b, p.158)

He also thinks this understanding should be largely for intrinsic ends. "I favor . . . the pursuit of knowledge for its own sake over the obeisance to utility" (1999b, p. 39). This locates him firmly within the 'liberal education' camp, along with—in Britain—(the early) Paul Hirst, Richard Peters, Roger Scruton and others.

It is not surprising that Gardner's curricular ideas dovetail with his ideas of the intelligences, even if this was not his original intention. For the 'liberal education' tradition and MI theory share the same starting point. They both assume the importance in human life of intellectual activities pursued largely for their own sake.

It is not surprising that educators reacting against recent utilitarian tendencies in schooling and looking for a more humane alternative have been attracted by MI theory, given its closeness to traditional 'liberal education'. But the latter idea is not necessarily tied to MI. Hirst, Peters, and others have argued for it on quite other grounds (Hirst 1974; Peters 1966,Chapter 5).

What is more, 'liberal education'—in this sense of intellectual learning for its own sake—itself needs justification. The reasons I have seen in favor of this do not hold water (White 1982, Chapter 2). There is a danger that in basing children's schooling on it we are imposing a life ideal on them—to do with the pursuit of truth and beauty for their own sake—which *we*, as intellectually inclined people, may find personally appealing, but which, after all, is only one of many possible life ideals. There is a good case for a broader view of educational aims that, while celebrating intrinsic intellectual aims, also embraces other perspectives on a worthwhile human life, thus leaving young people less confined in deciding the paths they wish to take.[1]

REFERENCES

Gardner, H. 1972. *The Quest for Mind.* London: Coventure.

———. 1973. *The Arts and Human Development.* New York: Wiley.

———. 1982. *Art, Mind, and Brain.* New York: Basic Books.

———. 1983. *Frames of Mind: The Theory of Multiple Intelligences.* London: Heinemann.

———. 1990. The Theory of Multiple Intelligences. In N. Entwistle, ed., *Handbook of Educational Ideas and Practices* (London: Routledge).

———. 1993. *Frames of Mind: The Theory of Multiple Intelligences.* Second edition (London: Heinemann).

———. 1998. An Intelligent Way to Progress. *The Independent* (19th March).

———. 1999a. Intelligence Reframed: Multiple Intelligences for the 21st Century. New York: Basic Books.

---

[1] I am most grateful to the following UK teachers for information about how MI theory has been applied in their schools: Margaret Grant, Deputy Headteacher of Broughton Hall School, Liverpool, and James McAleese, of Richard Hale School, Hertford.

————. 1999b. *The Disciplined Mind*. New York: Simon and Shuster.

————. 2003. Multiple Intelligences after Twenty Years. Paper presented at the American Educational Research Association, Chicago (21st April, 2003) http://www.pz.harvard.edu/PIs/HG_MI_after_20_years.pdf.

Goodman, N. 1968. *Languages of Art*. Indianapolis: Hackett.

Hamlyn, D. 1967. Logical and Psychological Aspects of Learning. In R.S. Peters, ed., *The Concept of Education* (London: Routledge).

————. 1978. *Experience and the Growth of Understanding*. London: Routledge.

Hirst, P.H. 1974. Liberal Education and the Nature of Knowledge. In Hirst, *Knowledge and the Curriculum*. (London: Routledge).

Howe, M.J.A. 1997. *The IQ in Question*. London: Sage.

Peters, R.S. 1966. *Ethics and Education*. London: Allen and Unwin.

Richardson, K. 1999. *The Making of Intelligence*. London: Weidenfeld and Nicolson.

Ryle, G. 1949. *The Concept of Mind*. London: Hutchinson.

Scheffler, I. 1985. *Of Human Potential*. London: Routledge.

Scruton, R. 1974. *Art and Imagination*. London: Methuen.

White, J. 1982. *The Aims of Education Restated*. London: Routledge.

————. 1986. On Reconstructing the Notion of Human Potential. *Journal of Philosophy of Education* 20:1.

————. 1998a. *Do Howard Gardner's Multiple Intelligences Add Up?* London: Institute of Education, University of London.

————. 1998b. Intelligence Guru on a Sticky Wicket. *The Independent* (19th February).

4

Geocentric Theory:
A Valid Alternative to Gardner's
Theory of Intelligence

NATHAN BRODY

This chapter is being written in the centennial of the publication of Spearman's paper outlining the theory of general intelligence (g) (Spearman 1904). Gardner's theory may be considered as an alternative to g theory. g may be defined as the common element present in diverse measures of intellect. Geocentric theorists believe that g is more important than any other component of intelligence. In this chapter I want to review some of the research that supports g theory and explain why what we know about g contradicts Gardner's view of intelligence.

The Positive Manifold and Its Foundation

Psychologists have devised thousands of short tests of different intellectual abilities measuring such characteristics as memory, spatial abilities, quantitative reasoning and verbal abilities. There are thousands of studies in the literature in which a group of subjects is presented with a battery of tests of intellectual ability. It is possible to measure relationships among measures in such a battery of tests by computing correlations between all possible pairs of tests. (A correlation is a statistical measure of the degree of relationship between two variables ranging from +1.00 to –1.00. The square of the value of the correlation is taken as a measure of the degree of predictability between measures—i.e. the percent of variance in one measure predicted by the scores on the other measure.)

A remarkable finding in this extensive literature is that the correlations form a positive manifold—that is, all of the correlations in the battery tend to be positive. This implies that individuals who excel on any one measure of intellectual ability are likely to excel on any other measure. This does not imply that people perform in an equivalent manner on all measures of intellectual ability. Individuals exhibit profiles of strengths and weaknesses on different measures. An individual may do better on tests of verbal ability than on tests of spatial ability. Carroll (1993) summarized and integrated the results of several hundred studies in which a battery of tests of intellectual abilities is presented to a group of individuals. Carroll's analysis supports a hierarchical theory of intelligence in which g occupies a position at the apex of the hierarchy and special abilities are arrayed at subordinate strata of the hierarchy. Carroll's analysis permits one to decompose any test of intellectual ability into a g component and one or more components that are independent of g. The amount of variance attributable to g in any measure of intellect varies. On average, g accounts for close to 50% of the variance among measures of intelligence. The g factor accounts for far more variance among measures of intellect than any other component of intelligence.

Gardner's Explanation

Three of the abilities originally postulated by Gardner in his theory of multiple intelligences are included in the analysis of relationships among several measures of abilities—linguistic intelligence, logical-mathematical intelligence, and spatial intelligence (Gardner 1993). And, there is no doubt that measures of these intelligences are related to one another and that they each contain a g component that accounts for a substantial source of variance.

Gardner accepts the evidence supporting relationships among these measures but he does not accept these correlations at face value. Gardner expresses his reservations about these results by noting, "Nearly all current tests are so devised as to call principally on linguistic and logical faculties. . . . Accordingly, a person with the skills important for success on such instruments is likely to do relatively well even in tests of musical or spatial abilities, while one who is not especially facile linguistically or logically is likely to be impaired on such standard tests even if one has skills in the areas that are allegedly being tested" (Gardner 1993, p. xx).

Basic Information Processing and Complex Abilities

Gardner's assumptions about the role of linguistic and logical faculties in the measurement of intelligence are contradicted by studies indicating that relatively simple laboratory based measures of speed or accuracy of information processing are substantially related to measures of intelligence.

Consider studies of inspection time, reaction time, and "oddball" tasks. Visual inspection time tasks present subjects with a stimulus consisting of two lines clearly different in length. The lines are followed at relatively brief intervals by the presentation of two dense black lines that occlude the original stimulus. The subject's task is to indicate which of the two lines is longer. A threshold measure is obtained of the minimal time required for exposure to the stimulus prior to the onset of the mask in order to judge line lengths accurately. Performance on this task is related to performance on tests of intelligence. High-IQ individuals are able to detect differences in line length at shorter exposures than low-IQ subjects. A summary of a relatively large number of studies of inspection time and IQ relationships indicates that inspection time measures account for approximately 25% of the variance in IQ (Grudnick and Kranzler 2001).

Deary, Der, and Ford (2001) administered a test of reaction time to a representative sample of middle-aged Scottish subjects. The reaction-time measure they used required subjects to respond as quickly as possible to the onset of one of several lights. This choice reaction time measure correlated with IQ –.49. High IQ subjects have faster reaction times than low IQ subjects.

Stelmack and his colleagues have investigated the relationship between IQ tests and performance on an "auditory oddball task." In this task subjects are required to identify whether a tone is one of a series of more frequently occurring tones that have a probability of occurrence of .85 or a less frequently occurring tone. The task is rendered difficult by the use of a backward masking tone that follows the onset of the target tone and makes it difficult to determine whether the tone heard by the subject is an oddball tone. Beauchamp (2004), working in Stelmack's laboratory, obtained a correlation of .53 between the probability of correct identification of the tone and IQ in a sample of 58 undergraduates. He also obtained measures of a brain wave, P-300, that is indicative of the detection of a stimulus. The amplitude of P-300 responses to the stimulus correlated .54 with IQ. In another condition of the experiment subjects were asked to ignore the tones and read a book. The subjects reported that they were not aware of variations in the tones presented to them. Mismatch negativity wave functions were obtained from brain waves in this condition. This is a brain wave difference in responses to frequent and infrequently presented tones that is thought to indicate the initial pre-attentive encoding of auditory stimuli. The latency of the function was inversely related to IQ ($r = -.40$). These results indicate that differences in brain wave responses to stimuli that subjects are not required to respond to are predictive of IQ. The correlations obtained in the oddball study are substantial. They are obtained from a sample of high-IQ individuals which reduces their magnitude. An index combining brain wave measures and behavioral responses would probably account for more than fifty percent of the variance in IQ.

The results of the experiments using inspection time, reaction time, and auditory oddball responses indicate that it is possible to measure general intelligence using tasks that do not require linguistic or logical reasoning faculties. Although all of these tasks may be used to predict differences in intellectual ability in college students they may be administered to elementary school children who have no difficulty in understanding and performing these tasks. These results suggest that g is related to basic information processing abilities. Luo and Petrill (1999) explored the relationship between performance on a battery of information processing tasks and a battery of tests of intelligence. They obtained separate g factors for their standard measures of intelligence and their basic information processing battery of tasks. Each of these g factors is a measure of the common component present in each of the tests in the set. Thus the g factor for the information processing battery of tests is an index of the common component in this set of tasks. The g factors derived from each of these batteries had a correlation of .58. They also attempted to predict performance on tests of academic achievement using these measures. They found that a comprehensive g factor based on performance on psychometric tests of intelligence and tests of basic information processing abilities provided a better prediction of academic achievement than a g factor based solely on a battery of psychometric tests. This result may be interpreted as indicating that g is an abstract construct that is partially independent of performance on psychometric tests that call on linguistic and logical faculties.

It is also the case that the best measures of g are not invariably those that are based on linguistic and logical faculties. Condon and Schroeder (2004) analyzed data obtained from a sample of 60,000 subjects given the

Johnson O'Connor battery of twenty-two tests of intelligence. The best measure of g in the battery was a memory for designs test. This test presents subjects with a design consisting of a meaningless set of straight lines. Subjects are required to observe the design for ten seconds and then attempt to reproduce it. The test was the best single measure of g in the battery of twenty-two tests used. The variance on the test may be partitioned into a g component and components related to spatial and memory abilities. Note that it does not have a linguistic or reasoning component. Nevertheless the test is the best measure of the common component in a large battery of tests that do tap verbal and logical faculties.

Genetic Influences on Relationships among Measures

Relationships among different psychometric tests and between psychometric tests and basic information processing abilities may be understood in terms of genetic linkages among these measures. Behavioral genetic methods may be used to study the degree to which a particular phenotype (such as IQ or height) is determined by variations in a genotype in a particular population. These methods may also be used to ascertain the role of genetic and environmental influences on the relationship between phenotypes.

Two correlated phenotypes could in principle be heritable (influenced by genotypes) and the relationship between them could be entirely determined by environmental influences. The behavioral genetic methods used to ascertain the genetic and environmental influences on the relationship between different phenotypes are similar to those used to determine genetic and environmental influences on a single phenotype. If MZ twins exhibit higher correlations for a phenotype than DZ twins it is possible to infer that the phenotype is heritable. So too, in a behavioral genetic analysis of relationships between phenotypes, if the correlation between phenotypes is stronger among MZ twin pairs than DZ twin pairs it is possible to infer that both phenotypes are influenced by the same genes.

Luciano and her colleagues analyzed relationships among inspection time, choice reaction time and IQ in a sample of twins (Luciano et al. 2003). They found that phenotypic relationships among these measures were accounted for by a single latent trait (i.e. a trait that combined these measures). Ninety-two percent of the shared variance on the latent trait was attributable to genetic influences. The remaining shared variance was attributable to unique environmental influences that lead individuals reared in the same family to differ from one another. These results indicate that the relationships between these two relatively simple information processing measures and IQ derive from genetic influences that are common to all of these measures.

The relationships among different psychometric tests may also be analyzed by behavioral genetic methods. Petrill (2002) summarized studies dealing with genetic and environmental influences on the relationships among different ability measures. The literature he summarizes includes both twin studies and adoption studies using diverse samples and measures and supports three generalizations about genetic influences among different measures of abilities.

First, analyses of continuities in scores on tests of intelligence in longitudinal studies indicate that genetic factors are largely responsible for continuity in intelligence and unique environmental factors contribute to change in intelligence. Second, genetic influences increase from childhood to adulthood. Third and most relevant to the present discussion, relationships between different intellectual abilities are primarily influenced by genetic factors after early childhood. Petrill's summary of the relevant data indicates that relationships among different intellectual abilities are increasingly determined by shared genetic influences as these influences become more important determinants of the phenotypes for different intellectual abilities. If, as Gardner argues, the relationships among different intelligences are influenced by linguistic and logical faculties these results suggest that genetic influences on these faculties contribute to their ability to create correlations between abilities. And, if the genetic relationships among diverse abilities are related to genetic influences on basic information processing measures, the common genetic pathways are not those that uniquely determine variations in logical and linguistic abilities. g is more general than Gardner assumes and the genetic influences that contribute to relationships among components of g are similarly more general than those that influence logical and linguistic abilities.

Can We Measure Abilities that Are Unrelated to g?

Gardner has not developed tests of his independent intelligences. Thus it is not possible to ascertain whether or not proposed tests of these intelligences would be related to g. Gardner has advocated wider use of portfolios and the use of assessment center methods that are based on performance on tasks that are highly relevant to the tasks which an individual will be asked to perform in an employment or academic setting.

There are several difficulties with the use of such methods as a way of selecting individuals for various roles. The assessments are expensive and time consuming. It is difficult to obtain reliable scoring of an individual's performance. Such methods often require one to judge performance using the aggregate judgments of several skilled evaluators. And, such methods often yield results that are not substantially different from those obtained by the use of standard tests of intelligence. Sackett and his colleagues reviewed the use of these methods as a means of reducing the adverse impact of cognitive ability tests (Sackett et al. 2001). African-Americans score approximately one standard deviation (15 IQ points) lower on tests of cognitive ability than White Americans. Therefore, the use of cognitive ability tests for selection will have adverse impact. The use of such tests will decrease the probability of selecting African-Americans unless different standards of selection are used for African-American applicants and White applicants—a procedure ruled constitutional by the Supreme Court in a recent decision dealing with the admission procedures used at the University of Michigan.

Sackett and his colleagues review studies comparing Black-White differences in performance on task relevant assessments and on conventional ability tests. In studies comparing assessments on such tasks as legal skills and teaching skills he finds that Black-White differences on the assessment tasks are comparable to those obtained on multiple choice intelligence tests when test differences are corrected for differences in the reliability of assessment. They find that the use of assessment procedures based on actual task performance tends to yield comparable results if the assessments deal with the ability to perform cognitively complex tasks. The methods advocated by Gardner do not overcome the adverse impact associated with the use of cognitive ability tests.

Sternberg's Theory

Gardner is not the only psychologist who has argued for the expansion of the assessment of cognitive abilities using different methods. In this section I want to briefly consider research on Sternberg's Triarchic Abilities Test and the Mayer, Salovey, and Caruso Test of Emotional Intelligence (MSCEIT)—two of the most prominent efforts to measure intellectual abilities that are assumed to be relatively independent of g.

Sternberg accepts the evidence for the importance of g (Sternberg et al. 2000). He has one major criticism of this research. He believes that the standard methods of assessing intelligence that give rise to the positive manifold are in part derived from the use of tests that fail to sample the entire range of human abilities. He argues that standard test batteries fail to assess practical knowledge which he defines as the ability to adapt to, shape, and select everyday environments. Sternberg also developed a triarchic theory of intelligence that assumes that there are three fundamental abilities—analytical ability which is analogous to the ability measured by conventional tests and is best defined as g, practical intelligence, and creative intelligence. The latter two intelligences are believed to be relatively independent of g. Sternberg believes that standard assessment may be supplemented by measures of creative and practical intelligence that are as predictive as general intelligence of educational and occupational achievement.

Sternberg developed the Triarchic Abilities Test to assess the three independent abilities he postulates. I reviewed the studies he cites and concluded that the Sternberg Triarchic Abilities Test (STAT) is primarily a measure of g (Brody 2003a; 2003b). Each of the abilities measured by STAT is correlated with scores on the Cattell Culture Fair Test of ability—a standard measure of g. Sternberg and Clinkenbeard (1995) obtained disattenuated correlations (correlations corrected for measurement error) between the three abilities measured by STAT and the Cattell test of .68 for analytical ability, .78 for creative ability, and .51 for practical ability. Contrary to the triarchic theory, the correlation between g and these abilities was not limited to analytical ability. Not only are these abilities related to a measure of g, they are also related to each other. The disattenuated correlations among these abilities ranged from .62 to .75. These data indicate that STAT does not measure abilities that are substantially independent of g.

Sternberg developed a new test of triarchic abilities that includes a wider range of items and formats. Relatively little research using this test has been published. In one of the few published studies Henry, Sternberg, and Grigorenko (in press) used the expanded test to predict school grades. They found that the best single predictor in their battery was a score on a briefly administered multiple-choice test of creative ability used in the original version of STAT. It accounted for 14.4% of the variance. Note that this subtest was the subtest with the highest correlation with the Cattell test of g. The entire expanded battery of measures designed to more fully assess triarchic abilities accounted for 16.3% of the variance in grades. These data suggest that the new assessment of triarchic abilities has limited incremental predictive validity for academic achievement over and above the predictability obtained by measures of general intelligence.

Sternberg and his colleagues also developed various measures of tacit knowledge that are analogous to situational judgment tests in which individuals are asked to evaluate various job related scenarios and indicate their preferences for courses of action. Tacit knowledge tests are assumed to measure practical intelligence. Gottfredson (2003) analyzed the research cited by Sternberg and his colleagues in support of the validity of these tests. She notes that the validity data deal with two different kinds of criteria careerist, referring to such characteristics as job prestige and salary level and non-careerist referring to ratings of performance or objective data relevant to performance such as sales volumes.

Her analysis indicates that the mean validity coefficient (weighted by sample size) for careerist indices is .28 and the comparable correlation for non-careerist indices is .12. These data are consistent with a meta-analysis (a statistical integration of all of the relevant data) of situational judgment tests performed by McDaniel, Hartman, and Gruber (2003). They obtained a meta-analytic correlation of .27 for measures of tacit knowledge and work related indices based on studies in which both measures are obtained concurrently. They found when situational judgment tests were used to predict subsequent work related performance the validity coefficient was .14. McDaniel et al. (2001) obtained a correlation of .46 in a meta-analysis of the relationship between g and performance on situational judgment tests. These data indicate that tacit knowledge measures of practical intelligence are correlated with g. The data reviewed above are compatible with the assertion that tacit knowledge tests, particularly when used as predictors of subsequent performance in occupational settings, may have only a small incremental validity over g.

Emotional Intelligence

Goleman (1995) argued that individual differences in emotional intelligence were as important as individual differences in cognitive intelligence in determining success in our society. Academic researchers have developed tests of emotional intelligence. Tests such as the Mayer, Salovey, and Caruso Emotional Intelligence Test (MSCEIT) are assumed to measure abilities that are largely independent of g but nevertheless are related to important socially relevant outcomes. Thus, the use of the MSCEIT is assumed to provide incremental predictive validity to predictions of various social outcomes when used in conjunction with measures of g.

Schulte, Ree, and Caretta (2004) note that the evidence for the relationship between g and the MSCEIT is derived from studies using verbal intelligence measures. They used the Wonderlic Test—a brief measure of general intelligence that correlates .92 with the full scale Wechsler test score to assess general intelligence. They obtained a correlation between the Wonderlic and the MSCEIT of .45 (disattenuated r = .50). This correlation suggests that ability-based definitions of emotional-intelligence are likely to show the same sort of positive manifold as is shown by all other cognitive abilities, meaning that emotional intelligence should be positively correlated with other cognitive abilities and with g. Thus, for example, it is reasonable to believe that people who are good at spatial visualization tasks will also tend to be good at working with emotional information (much in the same way that people good at spatial visualization also tend to be good at paragraph comprehension). g is the factor that ultimately ties all other cognitive abilities together, and it is very likely that g will play the same role in abilities that are part of emotional intelligence. Emotional intelligence is likely to be one component of g, not a substitute for g.

Schulte, Ree, and Carretta also noted that scores on the MSCEIT correlated with scores on a measure of five basic personality traits. They obtained a disattenuated multiple correlation between the Wonderlic, personality measures and sex of participants and the MSCEIT of .81—implying that the MSCEIT was primarily a measure of g and of standard personality traits.

Mayer, Salovey and Caruso (2004) summarized the evidence for the validity of the MSCEIT in a target article published in *Psychological Inquiry*. I wrote a commentary on this article. I noted that some of the studies they cite control for intelligence, some control for personality, and some control for neither of these traits. If emotional intelligence is to be construed as a new ability it is important to demonstrate that a test of emotional intelligence measures something other than intelligence and standard personality traits. Few of these studies control for both personality and intelligence. Some of these studies, including those indicating that the MSCEIT is related to occupational performance, are not published in peer-reviewed journals that are easily accessible for review. The MSCEIT yields five scores—a general factor score and a score for each of four branches of emotional intelligence. Validity correlations are sometimes reported for a general score and sometimes for one of the branch scores. The use of five measures with selective reporting of a single measure inflates the probability of wrongly obtaining a significant result. This is compounded by the use of multiple dependent variables in some of the studies and a tendency to selectively report significant results without noting that most of the correlations obtained between the MSCEIT and the dependent variables were non-significant. Most of the significant correlations between the MSCEIT and dependent variables were relatively low. I concluded my review of Mayer, Salovey, and Caruso's review of validity studies as follows: "There is not a single study reported that indicates that EI has nontrivial incremental validity for a socially important outcome variable after controlling for intelligence and personality" (Brody 2004, p. 237).

The MSCEIT is a test that has a strong conceptual relationship to the personal intelligences postulated by Gardner. The analysis presented above indicates that the test measures abilities that are related to g. The review of research on MSCEIT and STAT leads to more general conclusions about the efforts to develop tests that assess important components of intelligence that are independent of g. It is easy to argue that the standard test batteries that yield positive manifolds omit important dimensions of ability. When attempts are made to develop measures of these allegedly independent types of intelligence the results indicate that the measures are substantially related to g. They do not provide evidence for the restricted nature of the positive manifold that provides the foundation for the g construct. Rather, the evidence merely expands the evidence for the ubiquitous nature of g.

What Does g Predict?

Gardner claims that intelligence tests rarely assess skill in assimilating new information or in solving new problems. This assertion is contradicted by extensive studies documenting relationships between performance on tests of intelligence and performance in various real world settings.

Performance of High-ability Individuals

The predictive relationship between IQ and creative accomplishments is supported by analyses of pupils selected to participate in the Johns Hopkins study of gifted adolescents. Children are selected for this project at age thirteen solely on the basis of their performance on the SAT. The subset of these children with the highest scores falling at or above a ratio of 1 in 10,000 are not only likely to excel in formal educational settings—many go on to receive graduate degrees—but are also likely to make contributions to knowledge by publishing in scientific journals, patenting inventions and in original writing. A twenty year follow-up of this group of individuals indicates that 18% of the males have obtained patents for inventions by the time they are 33 years old (Lubinski et al. 2004). The lifetime base rate for securing a patent for a male in the United States is approximately one percent. Seven percent of the total group have secured tenure track positions in one of America's top fifty universities and twenty-two percent of these academics are full Professors before they are thirty-three.

A meta-analysis of relationship between the Miller Analogies Test and measures of success in graduate school indicates that the test's validity for predicting graduate school comprehensive examination results is .58. The validity correlation for predicting ratings of creativity by graduate school professors is .36 (Kuncel, Hezlett, and Ones 2004). These results contradict Gardner's assertions about the lack of relationship between tests of cognitive ability and the ability to solve novel problems.

g and Academic Performance

The relationship between tests of cognitive ability and performance in various academic settings is ubiquitous. There are thousands of studies indicating that g is invariably related to academic performance. One of the most comprehensive studies of the relationship between g and academic performance has recently been completed by Deary (2004). He analyzed the relationship between performance on tests of intelligence at age eleven and performance on twenty-five tests of achievement that constitute the required assessment of academic competence of students finishing their compulsory education in England at age sixteen for a representative sample of 70,000 British students. The tests represent all of the subjects taught in British secondary schools. Students typically take a subset of these tests—usually about eight, in order to obtain evidence of their academic qualifications. These qualifications are used to secure employment and admission to universities.

The correlation between his measure of g obtained at age eleven and the total score of academic qualifications obtained by a student at age sixteen was .69. The academic qualifications measures include tests of knowledge of English, History, Foreign languages, Mathematics, Sciences, Social Sciences and tests of a number of more applied achievements including workshop skills in such fields as metal working and woodworking, and artistic design and tests of work with textiles. g predicted performance on each of the twenty-five tests of knowledge. The lowest correlation between g and a measure of performance was for a test of art ($r = .42$) and the highest was for the math test ($r = .77$). Deary also performed a latent trait analysis for these data. In this analysis the relationship between hypothetical error-free composites is analyzed. He analyzed a composite g measure based on performance on IQ tests at age eleven and a composite based on performance on five of the most frequently selected academic qualification tests taken at age sixteen—English, Math, Science, Geography, and French. The hypothetical correlation between the latent traits was .81. Deary's results indicate that a single measure of g obtained prior to the start of secondary school is highly predictive of a comprehensive assessment of the total academic achievement of students at the end of secondary school.

Deary also analyzed differences in the performance of students attending schools supported by local school authorities and schools that were not under the direct control of local authorities. The latter schools are thought to be superior to the former schools—pupils attending locally supported secondary schools obtain lower achievement test scores than pupils attending non-locally supported schools. When Deary analyzed differences in school performance after adjusting for differences in the cognitive ability of students entering these schools there was no difference in school performance for students attending these two types of schools. Deary's results imply that differences in academic achievement among different schools are determined by differences in the cognitive ability of pupils entering the school (see Jencks 1972 for a comparable analysis for American schools).

g and Performance in the Workplace

There is an extensive body of meta-analytic research indicating that g is related to performance in virtually every work setting (Ones Viswesvaran and Dilchert in press). Tests of cognitive ability predict the acquisition of job-related knowledge and job related knowledge is related to job performance. Gardner notes that he is aware of this extensive literature but he notes that the "correlations are typically between test scores and supervisors' ratings" (Gardner 1995, p. 939). This is correct. Gardner's assertion fails to note that there is now an extensive body of literature indicating that tests of cognitive ability predict a variety of measures of job performance other than supervisor ratings. There are work sample tests for several jobs and performance on these actual measures of work are predicted by performance on tests of intelligence. The validity of tests of intelligence for predicting work-related performance varies with the complexity of the job. In one analysis reported by Hunter (1986), the validity was .23 for low complexity jobs (such as cannery worker) and .58 for high complexity job (such as game warden). Complex jobs involve the integration of diverse bodies of knowledge to solve novel problems.

Mortality

IQ tests are also related to a number of other significant social outcomes. Among these is an influence on mortality. Deary and his colleagues obtained a relationship between mortality at age seventy-six and IQ at age eleven in an analysis based on IQ test scores derived from the entire population of eleven-year-old children tested on the same day in Scotland (Deary et al. 2000). A one standard deviation decrease in IQ (a decrease of fifteen IQ points) was associated with a 21% decrease in the probability of surviving to age 76; a two standard deviation decrease in IQ was associated with a 37% decrease in the probability of surviving to age 76.

It is plausible to assume that the effects of childhood IQ on mortality are mediated by the influence of IQ on education and occupational status. Individuals with high IQ are likely to hold good jobs, to work in safer occupational settings, to have been reared in families with high social status, and to have better access to medical care. Although this explanation for the relationship between childhood IQ and mortality is plausible, it is not correct. Deary and Der (in press) obtained IQ scores for a representative sample of Scottish adults in 1988 when they were fifty-six years old. They obtained mortality data for these subjects in 2002 when they were seventy years old. They found the relationship between IQ and mortality was comparable to that obtained in their earlier studies using age eleven IQ as a predictor of mortality. They also analyzed the effects of IQ on mortality after controlling for occupational status, smoking behavior, and number of years of education attained. The relationship between IQ and mortality was not appreciably diminished after controlling for these variables. Variations in educational background and parental and adult occupational status do not explain the relationship between IQ and mortality.

There are two plausible possible explanations for the relationship between IQ and mortality: 1. IQ is related to health-related knowledge.

Beier and Ackerman (2003) developed a comprehensive measure of health knowledge. They obtained a correlation between their health-knowledge questionnaire and their measure of general intelligence of .88. Superior knowledge of health may be associated with a tendency to live a healthier life style. Gottfredson (2004) argues that the adequate care of one's health is a cognitively demanding task. It requires the ability to follow medical directions and to be knowledgeable about the appropriate actions to be taken in response to various medical emergencies. She argues that high-IQ individuals are likely to perform health related tasks in a superior manner to low-IQ individuals and are as a result likely to have better health. 2. The genes that influence IQ may be related to the genes that influence mortality. Whatever the reason for the relationship between general intelligence and mortality, the relationship provides further evidence for an important social outcome related to scores on tests of intelligence. Indeed, it is hard to imagine a more consequential socially relevant outcome variable than mortality. These results certainly indicate that IQ tests measure something more than school-related abilities.

Intelligence, Class, and Family Background

Gardner views performance on tests of intelligence as being determined by class and educational opportunities. He writes, "Much of the information probed for in intelligence tests reflects knowledge gained from living in a specific social and educational milieu. For instance, the ability to define *tort* or to identify the author of the *Iliad* is highly reflective of the school one attends or the tastes of one's family." (Gardner 1993, p. 18). This assertion is contradicted by the results of behavioral genetic analyses of the IQ phenotype. Family background (called shared environmental influences in behavioral genetic analyses) is related to performance on IQ tests in childhood. But this influence declines after early childhood. This assertion is supported by two of the most informative behavioral genetic analyses in the contemporary literature—the Swedish study of twins reared together and apart and the Colorado longitudinal study of adoption. Pedersen and her colleagues obtained correlations of .78 for MZ twins reared apart, .80 for MZ twins reared together, .32 for DZ twins reared apart and .22 for DZ twins reared together on measures of g for a systematically ascertained sample of older Swedish twins (Pederson et al. 1992). Note that in this study twins reared apart are as similar to one another as twins reared in the same family. It should be noted that the twins reared apart may have been reared in similar social circumstances. The degree of similarity of social class background in the rearing of separated twins did not, however, influence their degree of similarity in scores on IQ tests in this study. And, separated DZ twins were reared in separate families that were as similar in social class as separated MZ twins. The Swedish study indicates that similarity of g in older adult twins is not dependent on the influence of shared family environments. Rather, this similarity is observed equivalently among MZ twins reared together or apart. And, MZ twins exhibit greater similarity than DZ twins as older adults whether they are reared together or apart.

Plomin, Fulker, Corley and DeFries (1997) repeatedly administered intelligence tests to adopted children for the first sixteen years of life in a longitudinal study. Their study also included a control sample of children reared in the same community by their natural parents who had similar social backgrounds and IQs as the biological and adoptive parents of the adopted children. They obtained correlations between the IQs of the biological parents and the IQs of their adopted-away children at different ages. These correlations were compared to correlations between the IQs of the adoptive parents of these children and the IQs of their adopted children. In addition, correlations were obtained between the IQs of the biological parents in the control families who were rearing their natural children and the IQs of their children at comparable ages. The correlations between biological parents and children are quite similar for the biological parents who are rearing their children and for the biological parents whose children have been adopted-away and who have limited post-natal contact with their biological parents. Both sets of correlations indicate increasing relationships between the IQ of biological parents and the IQ of their children as they grow older. At age sixteen, the oldest age tested, the correlations are slightly higher for biological parents whose children have been adopted-away shortly after birth than the correlations for natural parents rearing their own children. The correlations between adopted parents and their adopted children are close to zero. These results again indicate that the cultural environment of the family in which a child is reared is not, contrary to Gardner's assertion, a major determinant of performance on IQ tests after early childhood. (For evidence that this generalization may not be valid for individuals reared by parents who have less than eight years of formal education see Rowe 2003.)

There is considerable variation in IQ among individuals occupying similar social class backgrounds. Murray (1998) provided convincing evidence of the relationship between IQ and important social outcomes that is independent of the influence of family background. He analyzed sibling data from the National Longitudinal Survey of Youth—a fifteen-year longitudinal study of a representative sample of over 12,000 subjects. In this analysis he compared outcome data for biologically related siblings who were reared in the same family but who differed in IQ test score. This methodology controls for social class influences as well as for the effects of being reared in a particular family. There were 1,009 siblings in his sample whose IQs were between the twenty-fifth and seventy-fifth percentile. Of these, 19.6% received a bachelor's degree. There were 590 siblings of this group whose IQs were below the 25th percentile. Of these, 2.6% received a bachelor's degree. There were 419 siblings whose IQ was at or above the 75th percentile whose sibling had an IQ between the 25th and 74th percentile. 56.8 percent of these siblings received a bachelor's degree. The data on the IQs of these siblings were obtained prior to the age of college entry. These data indicate that biologically related siblings reared in the same family who differ in IQ also differ in the probability of obtaining a bachelor's degree. Differences between siblings who differ in intelligence in the amount of education obtained are also mirrored in corresponding differences in the prestige of their occupations and in earned income. These data clearly indicate that intelligence is a characteristic of persons that influences socially relevant outcome variables among individuals with comparable social backgrounds and even among individuals reared in the same family.

The Use of Tests

There are many educational settings where the use of tests of cognitive ability for selection is absurd. We would not ask a student violinist applying for a position in an orchestra to submit scores on an IQ test in support of her application; nor would we want to choose a story for a literary magazine by asking its author to submit an IQ test score. I share with Gardner a preference for a reduced use of the SAT as a basis for admission to selective colleges. Students who have attended excellent secondary schools should be judged on the basis of the knowledge that they have acquired rather than on a measure of their alleged aptitude to acquire knowledge. Scores on tests of achievement indicating knowledge of math, languages, history, and so forth are likely to be more indicative of academic aptitude than scores on the SAT. At the same time, I think that the use of the SAT and of cognitive ability tests is useful to judge the academic potential of students who have not had the opportunity to attend an excellent secondary school. It is unfair to compare the knowledge of calculus for a student who attends a secondary school that does not offer this subject with a student who is able to take the equivalent of an advanced calculus course in high school.

The use of tests of achievement as a basis of selection of students for colleges is unfair in the United States where the curriculum of different schools and the academic rigor of what is taught are variable. Good grades in a school where few of the students go on to attend selective colleges may not provide useful information about the ability of the student to compete with students who have had excellent secondary school educations. In such a situation, the SAT is probably the most informative index available to judge the academic potential of a student attending an inferior secondary school. Of course, in the best of all possible worlds, there would be no inferior secondary schools and no need to use the SAT to judge academic potential!

The use of achievement tests rather than aptitude or ability tests for selection is likely to be particularly unfair for African-American students, for two reasons. First, they are more likely to attend inferior secondary schools. Second, tests of academic achievement are, in a technical sense, biased. Bias is defined in this context in terms of the predictive relationship between tests and some outcome of interest. Although tests of cognitive ability tend to be roughly equivalent in predicting the academic performance of White and Black students, where differences exist they tend to favor White students. Black students with the same SAT test scores as White students tend to obtain lower scores on tests of achievement than White students (Jensen 1980). Note that this result when it obtains implies that Black students are advantaged relative to white students when data obtained from White students is used to predict performance for Black students.

I believe that tests of intelligence may be used to identify students from socially underprivileged backgrounds who have high academic ability. America's selective colleges have made some strides in diversifying their undergraduate student bodies with respect to race and ethnicity. They have been considerably less successful in attaining social class diversity. IQ tests given to elementary and secondary school students can be used to identify students with above average academic potential who are not socially privileged. Such students can be provided with opportunities for educational enrichment that will enhance their opportunity to attend selective colleges.

Gardner advocates the wider use of alternative assessments based on portfolio assessments. It is certainly reasonable to use portfolios reflecting a student's work on a project to provide feedback to a student. The use of portfolio assessments for high-stakes testing is, in my opinion, far more problematic. Such work may be difficult to judge in a reliable way. More critically, portfolios of actual educational accomplishments may be highly class-biased instruments. Accomplishments in music, dance, and art are strongly influenced by the provision of expensive private lessons. These lessons are not always available to less affluent children. Science projects may be more easily developed in secondary schools that have excellent laboratory facilities and teachers with the time and training to encourage individual projects. We do not escape class bias by using portfolios—indeed I suspect that we would enhance class bias by the use of such methods for selection.

The issue of class bias in testing and assessment is related to a broader concern I have about Gardner's approach to intelligence. The use of a single score on a test that is not easily manipulated may reduce the opportunity of parents to secure social privileges that they may have for their children. A model of multiple intelligences provides a wider range of opportunities to assume that a child is gifted in some way and to secure social privileges for that child. More generally, the shift to admissions criteria that are more opaque and more easily manipulated is a method for creating a social aristocracy. Consider some of the ways in which it is possible to enhance the admissions credentials of secondary school students. Parents can pay for lessons that will enable students to develop special talents in the arts. Students who receive financial support from their parents can use their summer vacations to volunteer and to travel abroad thus enhancing their ability to describe experiences that may appeal to college admissions officers. And, more nefariously, parents may hire skilled admissions counselors to edit or even write personal statements for secondary school students. Opaque admissions standards are class biased and are probably more class biased than tests of intelligence that are only weakly correlated with social class background.

Conclusion

In this chapter I have not presented a critique of Gardner's views directly. I have indicated that a voluminous literature based on an analysis of performance on tests of intelligence supports a geocentric theory of intelligence. Gardner does not deal with this literature. Either he ignores it or makes misleading assertions about what is known about g. g is a ubiquitous component of virtually all measures of cognitive ability. Individual differences in g probably derive from heritable differences in basic information processing capacities. These differences relate to the acquisition of knowledge in school and in work settings. Individual differences in IQ tests that provide estimates of g may be used to identify individuals who are likely to excel in many occupational and academic settings. Such tests may be used to identify students from lower social-class backgrounds who are likely to benefit from enhanced educational opportunities.

REFERENCES

Beauchamp, C.M. 2004. Mental Ability and Event-related Potentials in an Auditory Oddball Task with Backward Masking: From Description to Explanation. Unpublished doctoral dissertation submitted to the Faculty of Graduate Studies and Research, University of Ottawa.

Beier, M.E., and P.L. Ackerman. 2003. Determinants of Health Knowledge: An Investigation of Age, Gender, Abilities, Personality, and Interests. *Journal of Personality and Social Psychology* 84, pp. 439–447.

Brody, N. 2003a. Construct Validation of the Sternberg Triarchic Abilities Test (STAT): Comment and Reanalysis. *Intelligence* 31, pp. 319–329.

———. 2003b. What Sternberg Should Have Concluded. *Intelligence* 31, pp. 339–342.

———. 2004. What Cognitive Intelligence Is and What Emotional Intelligence Is Not. *Psychological Inquiry* 15, pp. 234–38.

Carroll, J.B. 1993. *Human Cognitive Abilities.* Cambridge: Cambridge University Press.

Condon, C.A., and D.H. Schroeder. 2004. Memory for Design: An Overlooked Mental Ability. Paper presented at the annual meeting of the International Society for Intelligence Research in New Orleans.

Deary, I.J. 2004. Spearman (1904) Revisited: General Intelligence and Educational Achievement. Paper presented at the annual meeting of the International Society for Intelligence Research in New Orleans.

Deary, I.J., and G. Der. In press. Reaction Time Explains the IQ Association with Mortality. *Psychological Science*, forthcoming.

Deary, I.J., G. Der, and C. Ford. 2001. Reaction Time and Intelligence Differences: A Population Based Cohort Study. *Intelligence* 29, pp. 389–399.

Gardner, H. 1993. *Frames of Mind* (tenth anniversary edition). New York: Basic Books.

———. 1995. A Response on Four Fronts. *American Psychologist* 40, pp. 938–39.

Goleman, D. 1995. *Emotional Intelligence.* New York: Bantam.

Gottfredson, L.S. 2003. Dissecting Practical Intelligence Theory: Its claims and Evidence. *Intelligence* 31, pp. 343–397.

————. 2004. Intelligence: Is it the Epidemiologists' Elusive "Fundamental Cause" of Social Class Inequalities in Health? *Journal of Personality and Social Psychology* 86. pp. 174–199.

Grudnick, J.L., and J.H. Kranzler. 2001. Meta-Analysis of the Relationship between Intelligence and Inspection Time. *Intelligence* 29, pp. 523–535.

Henry, P.J., R.J. Sternberg, and E. Grigorenko. In press. Capturing Successful Intelligence through Measures of Analytic, Creative, and Practical Skills. In O. Wilhelm and R. Engle, eds., *Understanding and Measuring Intelligence* (London: Sage).

Hunter, J.E. 1986. Cognitive Ability, Cognitive Aptitudes, Job Knowledge, and Job Performance. *Journal of Vocational Behavior* 29, pp. 340–362.

Jencks, C. 1972. *Inequality: A Reassessment of the Effect of Family and Schooling in America.* New York: Basic Books.

Jensen, A.R. 1980. *Bias in Mental Testing.* New York: The Free Press.

Kuncel, N.R., S.A. Hezlett, and D.S. Ones. 2004. Academic Performance, Career Potential, Creativity, Job Performance: Can One Construct Predict Them All? *Journal of Personality and Social Psychology* 86, pp. 148–161.

Luciano, M., M.J. Wright, G.A. Smith, G.M. Geffen, L.B. Geffen, and N.G. Martin. 2003. Genetic Covariance between Processing Speed and IQ. In J.C. Plomin, J.C. DeFries, I.W. Craig, and P. McGuffin, eds., *Behavioral Genetics in the Postgenomic Era* (Washington, D.C.: American Psychological Association), pp. 163–181.

Luo, D., and S.A. Petrill. 1999. Elementary Cognitive Tasks and Their Roles in g Estimates. *Intelligence* 27, pp. 157–174.

Mayer, J.D., P. Salovey, and D.R. Caruso. 2004. Emotional Intelligence: Theory, Findings, and Implications. *Psychological Inquiry* 15, pp. 197–215.

McDaniel, M.A., N.S.Hartman, and W.L.Grubb III. 2003. *Situational Judgment Tests, Knowledge, Behavioral Tendency, and Validity: A Meta-Analysis.* Paper presented at the 18th Annual Conference of the Society for Industrial and Organizational Psychology, Orlando, Florida.

McDaniel, M.A., F.P. Morgeson, E.B. Finnegan, M.A. Campion, and E.P. Braverman. 2001. Use of Situational Judgment Tasks to Predict Job Performance: A Clarification of the Literature. *Journal of Applied Psychology* 86, pp. 730–740.

Murray, C. 1998. *Income, Inequality, and IQ.* Washington, DC: American Enterprise Institute.

Ones, D.S., C. Viswesvaran, and S. Dilchert. In press. Cognitive Ability in Selection Decisions. In O. Wilhelm and R. Engle, eds., *Understanding and Measuring Intelligence* (London: Sage).

Pedersen, N.L., R. Plomin, J.R. Nesselroade, and G.E. McClearn.1992. A Quantitative Genetic Analysis of Cognitive Abilities During the Second Half of the Life-Span. *Psychological Science,* 3, pp. 346–352.

Petrill, S.A. 2002. The Case for General Intelligence: A Behavioral Genetic Perspective. In R.J. Sternberg and E. Grigorenko, eds., *The General Factor of Intelligence: How General Is It?* (Mahwah: Erlbaum), pp. 281–298.

Plomin, R., D.W. Fulker, R. Corley, and J.C. DeFries. 1997. Nature, Nurture, and Cognitive Development from 1 to 16 Years: A Parent-Offspring Adoption Study. *Psychological Science* 8, pp. 442–47.

Rowe, D.C. 2003. Assessing Genotype-Environment Interactions in the Postgenomic Era. In R. Plomin, J.C. DeFries, I.W. Craig, and P. McGuffin, eds., *Behavioral Genetics in the Postgenomic Era* (Washington, DC: American Psychological Association), pp. 71–86.

Sackett, P.R., N. Schmitt, M. Kalin, and J.E. Ellingson. 2001. High-Stakes Testing in Employment, Credentialing, and Higher Education: Prospects in a Post-Affirmative Action World. *American Psychologist* 56, pp. 302–318.

Schulte, M.J., M.J. Ree, and T.R. Carretta. 2004. Emotional Intelligence: Not Much More than g and Personality. *Personality and Individual Differences* 37, pp. 1059–068.

Spearman, C. 1904. General Intelligence, Objectively Determined and Measured. *American Journal of Psychology* 15, pp. 201–292.

Sternberg, R.J., and P.R. Clinkenbeard.1995. The Triarchic Model Applied to Identifying and Teaching Gifted Children. *Roeper Review* 17, pp. 255–260.

Sternberg, R.J., G.B. Forsyth, J. Hedlund, J.A. Horvath, R.K. Wagner, W.M. Williams, S.A. Snook, and E.L. Grigorenko. 2000. *Practical Intelligence in Everyday Life.* Cambridge: Cambridge University Press.

Whalley, L.J., and I.J. Deary. 2001. Longitudinal Cohort Study of Childhood IQ and Survival up to Age 76. *British Medical Journal* 322, pp. 819–822.

5

Is the Ability to Make a Bacon Sandwich a Mark of Intelligence?, and Other Issues: Some Reflections on Gardner's Theory of Multiple Intelligences

SUSAN M. BARNETT,
STEPHEN J. CECI, AND
WENDY M. WILLIAMS

This chapter focuses on what is arguably Howard Gardner's most famous work—that on intelligence, beginning with his theory of multiple intelligences. Gardner has written numerous books and articles on this topic, starting with *Frames of Mind* in 1983. This work has been influential in education and has even become quite well known among the general populace.

Gardner's work has served the highly important and useful purpose of drawing broad societal attention to fundamental questions about what we mean by intelligent behavior and how we develop it in schools. He has offered what many would consider to be an optimistic perspective on the potential for all members of society to develop skill in some valued area of intellectual functioning. Gardner's views have motivated both teachers working with traditionally less-academically-successful students and those students themselves. His work has prompted educators to develop new approaches to teaching and testing which, whether or not they are all strictly derived from his theoretical work, have nevertheless often proved successful (Gardner 1991; 1993a; 1993b; 1999).

What Is Intelligence?

Rooted in his analysis of the literature in different areas (such as developmental psychology, neuroscience, and cross-cultural analyses), Gardner's original theory of multiple intelligences proposed seven largely independent, distinct kinds of intelligence. Three of the original group of seven intelligences—linguistic, logical-mathematical, and spatial—have been traditionally included in definitions of intelligence, and thus have not caused particular controversy.

However, Gardner's theory expands the usage of the term 'intelligence' to include skills or abilities that were not previously, and are still not normally, considered to be aspects of intelligence. For example, skill in music is a core aspect of what is termed 'musical intelligence', "the ability to use one's body in highly differentiated and skilled ways" becomes 'bodily-kinesthetic intelligence', and the ability to understand oneself and others and effectively use such understanding become intra- and inter-personal intelligence (Gardner 1983, p. 207). Naturalist intelligence, a particular understanding of the natural world, was added later, as was a possible existential intelligence, defined roughly as being exemplified by "individuals who exhibit the proclivity to pose (and ponder) questions about life, death, and ultimate realities," such as Aristotle, Confucius, Einstein, Emerson, Plato, and Socrates (Carlson-Pickering 1997). Much of the debate surrounding Gardner's theory concerns these new forms of intelligences.

As pointed out by Hunt (2004, p. 2), "Virtually everyone agrees that there are wide-ranging differences in these skills. But should they be called intelligences?" Halpern (2005) has suggested that, "If Gardner had called his theory multiple abilities or multiple talents it [*Frames of Mind*] might have long gone the way of other texts and be resting comfortably in some dark section of the library" (p. 4). Instead, it continues to exert considerable influence. Thus, the use of the label 'intelligence' is key.

What, precisely, is Gardner claiming by using this loaded word? He states, "If we are to encompass adequately the realm of human cognition, it is necessary to include a far wider and more universal set of competences than has ordinarily been considered . . . An *intelligence* is the ability to solve problems, or create products, that are valued within one or more cultural settings" (Gardner 1993, p. xiv). His stated intention is to "capture a reasonably complete gamut of the kinds of abilities valued by human culture" (1983, p. 62). This constitutes a very broad definition indeed, and one that implies that anything that is not part of intelligence is *not* valued, an implication that probably not even Gardner himself would agree with. Indeed, elsewhere he does specifically exclude valued attributes such as creativity and ethical behavior from the concept of intelligence. The suggestion that intelligence is the ability to create valuable products contrasts with typical dictionary definitions such as "the act or state of knowing; the exercise of the understanding" (Webster's Revised Unabridged Dictionary, p. 1913). Products seem inherently different from knowledge and understanding. Is the ability to make a bacon sandwich a mark of intelligence[1]?

Gardner offers eight more specific criteria to determine whether or not a skill qualifies as an intelligence. He claims that the application of these criteria provides an empirical foundation for his theory that makes it superior to others' *a priori* lists of intelligences. However, most of these criteria seem intended to distinguish *between* different intelligences, not to draw a boundary *around* the concept of intelligence. For example, the potential for isolation by brain damage and the existence of individuals who are highly expert in a particular area but not expert in other areas (for example *idiots savants*) are good reasons to consider certain skills to be separable from others. But they do not provide evidence for why these skills should be classified as aspects of intelligence. One criterion which might serve to establish what does and does not qualify as intelligence is the existence of basic information processing mechanisms for specific kinds of input. Gardner states, "One might go so far as to define a human intelligence as a neural mechanism or computational system which is genetically programmed to be activated or 'triggered' by certain kinds of internally or externally presented information" (1983, pp. 63–64). At first blush this sounds somewhat narrower than the 'all valued products' definition mentioned earlier. However, given that all human skills must have at their base some neural system for processing information, perhaps it does not narrow it down a great deal. When the neuropsychological findings are used to support the existence of multiple processing components, their usefulness is compromised by alternative interpretations because of the tricky logical issue of separating the brain's involvement in singular versus multiple intellectual performances. Demonstrations that brain regions control

---

[1] Note that, in this chapter, we focus on the use of the term 'intelligence' to describe individual differences between people rather than the sense in such questions as, 'Is there intelligent life on Mars?', where a different, lower, standard for intelligent behavior may be applied. This reflects the usage of the term in most of the discussions concerning Gardner's work.

specific forms of intellectual activities (spatial, verbal, musical, and so forth) do not rule out the presence of a singular mental processor that is necessary, albeit perhaps not sufficient, for all forms of intellectual activity. This is why the most impressive forms of evidence Gardner recruited to justify his multiple intelligences—neurological and clinical findings—fall short of the mark. Elsewhere, one of us has written:

> On logical grounds, it would seem that the use of neuropsychological findings to refute the singularity of (and support the modularity of) intelligence is problematic. Although the results of clinical studies are more congruent with a modular view of the mind, these studies can be explained in another manner, too. An analogy from athletics may be informative. Suppose that performances on various track and field events tend to be correlated, with running speed, javelin throwing, long jumping, and pole vaulting all tending to go together. In other words, athletes good at one event tend to be above average at the others, too. Some underlying general factor could be invoked to explain this positive manifold of correlations, perhaps physical strength. That is, it could be suggested that the reason all of these track and field performances tend to be correlated is because they all require some degree of physical strength.
>
> But this inference does not mean that other factors are not also involved in the track and field performances. Localized damage to the non-dominant hand might diminish pole vaulting, as both hands are needed in that sport, but leave the remaining track and field skills unimpaired. Or localized damage to the dominant hand might impair javelin throwing as well as pole vaulting, while leaving running and jumping unimpeded. And so on. The point of the analogy is simply that one could imagine a model that would postulate different neural bases for specific as well as general factors and damage to the former would tend to mask the existence of the latter, especially if the latter represented a necessary but not sufficient condition for some specific performance. Thus, neuropsychological results from patients with brain lesions may indicate only that the specific functions that are impaired are subserved in part by specific neuroanatomical systems—not that these functions are independent of some general neural factor. In short, that specific functions are lost as a result of localized brain insult is pretty clear; but that this implies the absence of a single biologically based cognitive factor (g) is not so clear, at least not until evidence is found that rules out the existence of some underlying cortical unit that performs a uniform operation but varies from region to region and area to area, according to extrinsic connections. So even when the neuropsychological findings are used to argue in favor of the hypothesis of multiple intellectual potentials (and against the singularity of intelligence), they can be problematic. (Ceci 1996, p. 104)

The most promising candidate for a defining criterion is the embodiment in a symbolic system. Is all symbolic processing intelligent and does all intelligence involve symbolic processing? The latter may be true, as it is hard to think of an example of intelligent behavior that does not involve symbolic processing using language or some other representational system. However, there might be examples of rather simple symbolic processing which we would be reluctant to credit with intelligence, which generally implies something about complexity as well. And it is by no means obvious that symbolic processing is a vital component of bodily-kinesthetic skills such as dancing, notwithstanding the fact that dance moves can be translated into a symbolic notation format if desired.

The apparent fruitlessness of this endeavor suggests a different approach may be required. In fact, one might argue that, if Gardner's boldest claim is to include in the notion of intelligence skills which others would not, then what he needs to focus on is why all these skills are similar rather than why they are separable. If the various skills he discusses are, in his mind, so clearly separable, why confuse matters by labelling them all with the same term? Why call them all apples if they truly are, in many ways, independent skills—that is, apples and oranges? This criticism is not unique to Gardner's theory; most traditional theories also draw on evidence for the separability of certain skills they term intelligence, such as 'fluid', 'crystallized', 'verbal', 'spatial', and so on. However, they typically draw on factor analyses showing the variance they share with so-called general intelligence, or g. Hence, traditional theories are tied together as part of a g-centric universe of mental life in a way that Gardner's multiple independent skills are not.

Part of Gardner's motivation in this enterprise seems to be a moral objection to the way Western society values traditional intelligence. Consider:

> In delineating a narrow definition of intelligence . . . one usually devalues those capacities that are not within that definition's purview: thus, dancers or chess players may be talented but they are not smart. In my view, it is fine to call music or spatial ability a talent, so long as one calls language or logic a talent as well. But I balk at the unwarranted assumption that certain human abilities can be arbitrarily singled out as qualifying as intelligence while others cannot. (Gardner 1993, p. xxiv)

Here we see a far more democratic, egalitarian view of human beings' intelligence than is apparent in traditional theories. Sure, one may refer to musical or bodily-kinesthetic proclivities as "abilities" or "talents", but if one does so, then one should be consistent and refer to mathematical reasoning or verbal fluency as talents, too. Gardner seems to say that singling out the skills that are tapped by traditional intelligence tests as the *sine qua non* of intelligence is unwarranted. However, such singling out is only unwarranted if one assumes the term 'intelligence' has no defined meaning.

The definition of intelligence has been a source of discussion since the inception of scientific thinking about intelligence (see the survey by the editors of the *Journal of Educational Psychology*, 1921 and the later survey by Sternberg and Detterman 1986). It is fair to say that there has been some overlap in modern and historical views of intelliegnce (a 0.5 correlation between the attributes listed by the 1921 scholars and the 1986 scholars), although there is clearly a great deal of disagreement about the nature and multiplicity of this construct. The question of whether there is one underlying form of intelligence or many forms is one that scholars have not agreed on. The resolution will probably have to await breakthroughs in genetics, radiology, and statistics. Having said this, the lack of consensus does not give license to pick and choose whatever behaviors we prefer as our personal candidates for intelligence. Candidates must be grounded in evidence and tied together in ways that makes their construct validation apparent. Gardner's multiple intelligences satisfy the first of these requirements, even if one were to quibble with their inclusion. However, the validation that these multiple types of behavior are forms of intelligence will require further work before we agree that these are the best way to parse the mind. Perhaps other vectors will be better, for example, "transferable skills" (Barnett and Ceci 2002) that allow some to take what they learned in one domain and transfer it to a distant domain, might emerge as a candidate. Obviously, one is limited only by her or his imagination in generating a list of competitors, and the challenge would be to show these competitor intelligences provide greater scientific leverage than those nominated by Gardner.

Gardner also points out that the traditional Western view of intelligence is parochial: "Some cultures do not even have a concept called intelligence, and others define intelligence in terms of traits that Westerners might consider odd—obedience or good listening skills or moral fiber, for example" (Gardner 1999, p. 19). However, just how we know it is appropriate for us to translate a term from another language as 'intelligence' when it refers to obedience or good listening skills or moral fiber is unclear. Who makes this judgment? Unless the label 'intelligence' is being used to refer to whatever is *most* valuable and important in society, an upgrading of the notion of intelligence from its current status, then what does it mean to say that members of another culture define intelligence as something else? Surely they don't mean that "obedience" or "moral fiber" are equivalent to "the act or state of knowing". This kind of logic gets dangerously close to being circular. Independent and defensible criteria are needed here, lest we wind up with the kitchen-sink definition of intelligence and literally hundreds of candidate intelligences.

Halpern (2005) suggests that "the greatest appeal of the theory of multiple intelligences is that it allows everyone to be intelligent 'in their own way'" and that, on the flip side, "detractors of Gardner's theory have called it a handbook for self-esteem enhancement." Books abound with titles such as, *You're Smarter than You Think: A Kid's Guide to Multiple Intelligences* (Armstrong 2003). This volume "introduces the theory, explains the eight intelligences, and describes ways to develop each one. [The author] tells young readers how to use all eight intelligences in school, build them at home, and draw on them to plan for the future."

There is nothing inherently wrong with something that has the potential to raise the self-esteem of otherwise dispirited students. That is a laudable goal and fruitful if it motivates otherwise disillusioned students to work hard in areas they are not naturally good at (though it can be argued that it is not so useful if it gives official sanction to giving up on domains that are difficult, providing the excuse that "I'm no good at that kind of intelligence"). Unfortunately, mere relabelling may not have a permanent curative effect. And, importantly, focusing on the label rather than on meaningful performances that demonstrate skill may lead children to become further disillusioned once the first blush passes. Educators must target skills, not feelings; research has shown that gang members have higher self esteem than do high school students earning all A's, and a recent meta-analysis showed that high self esteem is not the panacea some have thought (Baumeister *et al.* 2003). The focus must be on displaying meaningful skills and competencies, not simply on feeling that one is smart. Furthermore, expanding the use of the term 'intelligence' to include a wide variety of different skills merely invites the introduction of some new term, hopefully less unwieldy than 'traditional intelligence' or 'logical-mathematical/linguistic/spatial intelligence', to refer to what intelligence used to be used to mean. (And it shouldn't be IQ or 'psychometric intelligence', because that specifies not just a capability but also the means to measure it, something about which there is a considerable, though separate, debate.) Then, if history is any guide, that term would acquire status and therefore, presumably, its meaning would have to be expanded to include other skills, and so on.

An alternative approach is to confine intelligence to its traditional, narrow definition, whilst acknowledging that there is more to life than that. Music, dance and social skills can be important even if they are not specifically referred to as "intelligences"! Let us move past the issue of the appropriate scope of the label intelligence, and turn now to other aspects of Gardner's theory.

A criticism of virtually all multiple intelligence theories, including Gardner's, is that such theories fail to specify the details of the processes by which the hypothesized multiple intelligences operate to produce the expected benefits. All multiple-intelligence approaches share a macrolevel orientation (for example, focusing on holistic performances such as spatial reasoning skills and verbal fluency) that can be distinguished from theories that focus on microlevel processing (for example, encoding of information of various types). In other words, multiple-intelligence theories, regardless of the nature and number of their types of intelligence, usually are summarizations of macrolevel processes.

For example, suppose that a 'musical' factor emerges from an analysis of the neurological, clinical, cross-cultural, and developmental literature. What this means is that a set of performances on macrolevel musical tests were found to covary in certain ways. The nature of the musical processes that support these performances (for instance, re-auditorization) may or may not be revealed. Their discovery is a matter of chance, as is the discovery of the subprocesses that underpin these processes (for example, pitch encoding). Unlike other approaches that have the discovery of such subprocesses as their primary aim, in the multiple intelligence approach the level of reduction is a function of the type of tasks examined, thus the discovery of subprocesses can be chancy. Rabbitt (1988) has made the point most cogently:

> The observed degree of transfer from one such learned production to another will, likewise not depend on any intrinsic structure of the human cognitive system. . . . but rather on the structure of the particular tasks that we compare to obtain our data. . . . Thus, in all cases, the actual structure of the tasks that we compare will determine the nature of the inferences we draw about the structure of the human cognitive system. (Rabbitt 1988, p. 182)

In other words, in the absence of a detailed functional analysis of the tasks we use to infer the existence of a type of intelligence, multiple intelligence theories—including not only Gardner's but also psychometric models based on factor analytic techniques—may represent misleading ways of drawing inferences.

The testability of Gardner's theory is one issue that has stirred particular debate. In answer to the question of whether his theory is the sort of theory that one can test, or is rather more of a loose framework, Gardner (1999, p. 97) suggests it's somewhere in the middle: "There is no systematic set of propositions that could be voted up or down by a board of scientists, but the theory is not simply a set of notions that I dreamed up one day." He suggests that, as neurological and other evidence accummulates, the plausibility of aspects of his theory will be enhanced or reduced, as with other social science theories that are never wholly proven right or wrong. We think this is a reasonable position, one that entails some modesty and an avoidance of the 'presentism' that so obscures many of our theories. Gardner should not be held to a standard that prohibits him from sharing meaningful insights into human intellectual functioning and learning until he can document every aspect of the processes involved—no scientist should. The key is that findings and ruminations must be distinguished as such, and that people being influenced by the work must be appropriately informed of its limitations.

Finally, another criticism of Gardner's theory of multiple intelligences might be that with the benefit of hindsight, some of his ideas sound obvious. However, this is a criticism that could be leveled against most influential theories; it ignores the fact that they did not appear obvious until long after they became influential. Gardner's theory caused a stir in both the research and practice communities precisely because it seemed novel or because it provided the most cogent argument to date.

Implications for Teaching

Implications for teaching can be grouped into three types. First, if nontraditional intelligences are, or should be, just as important as traditional intelligences, then presumably their development should be given equal emphasis in schools. The question here is a societal one rather than a psychological one, and as such we will not attempt to answer it here. Note, however, that a redistribution of resources in schools would potentially short-change students if it was not matched by a redistribution of rewards for the application of various intelligences outside the academic environment. It might be considered unfair to children to shift educational resources away from developing their linguistic intelligence, for example, towards developing their bodily-kinesthetic intelligence, if this led to them being less employable upon leaving school. Of course, future employability would have to be weighed against other aspects of quality of life, which might be enhanced by such a change.

These are weighty societal and political issues which cannot be resolved here. It is one of Gardner's major contributions that this important issue is raised at all. One aspect of the writings of Gardner's critics that strikes us as unfortunate and short-sighted is their failure to acknowledge the substantial benefits of redefining the problems in an area and reframing the debate on these problems. Critics of Gardner offer valuable points, but at times they may fail to acknowledge the forest that has grown up around the trees on which they are focused. North American and European societies used to think about intelligence from a simplistic, reductionist perspective, and the educational practices of these societies reflected the limitations of these views. Although we can criticize Gardner for failing to provide adequate evidence for the physical and biological separability of his intelligences, we should also laud him for calling attention to the inadequacies of traditional thinking, regardless of whether he has or can solve every dilemma he raises. The fact that teachers and the general public think more broadly about intelligence today than they did twenty-five years ago is due in large part to the work of Gardner. Where we do not wish to see too much influence, however, is in the limiting of students' and schools' emphasis on the abilities our societies now demand. The debate about what our societies *should* demand has been opened by Gardner, and it behooves all of us and all educators to participate in it.

The second and third implications of Gardner's work on intelligence for the practice of teaching concern the ways in which traditional academic skills should be taught in schools, both across the board for all students and in tailoring the approaches used for individual students. Gardner suggests that, in addition to providing multiple end points for the educational endeavor, his multiple kinds of intelligence should be viewed as different ways for students to learn any given subject. That is, one could fruitfully teach standard academic material, or whatever else society deems worthy to learn, through multiple intelligences. More specifically, *all* students might benefit from being taught any given skill or knowledge through multiple approaches. Also, Gardner's work implies that *individual* students might benefit differentially from the different approaches, suggesting a tailoring of the portfolio of teaching approaches to individual students' strengths. One might teach science using music and dance, rather than paper and pencil problem-solving tasks combined with the traditional hands-on experiments. Gardner (1999) cites evidence that applying the theory of multiple intelligences to schools does work, at least in terms of improvements in standardized scores, parental involvment, and student discipline.

Also, research has shown that more active, hands-on learning helps. For example, one of us (Williams) co-authored an educational program based on Gardner's approach combined with the approach of Robert Sternberg, and in rigorous matched-control-group studies, the children taught the experimental program outperformed control children on various measures of reading, writing, and homework, and in test-taking abilities (Williams *et al.* 1996; Williams *et al.* 2002).

Halpern (2005, pp. 6–7) offers an example of what such an approach might look like: "I can imagine a lesson on molecules in which the standard material is augmented with the actual movement of students as though they were molecules in a chemical reaction, or the imagined movement is used as the inspiration for a dance class, or the children are asked to create a converstation among molecules as a project when learning how to use a cartoon computer program." However, she goes on to say, "I do not know whether any of these ideas for using MI [multiple intelligences] in middle-school science are necessarily MI-based, because they are all in the chapters I have written on encouraging creativity, and none of these chapters specifically called for the development of bodily kinesthetic or personal intelligences." This example makes clear that it is not enough to demonstrate that teaching approaches compatible with Gardner's thinking are beneficial, it is also necessary to show that these teaching approaches could not be equally well derived from other theories. Hunt (2004, p. 3) expresses a similar view: "A good TMI [Theory of Multiple Intelligences] school should respond to children's individual talents. Fine, I agree, and so do most educators . . . Gardner's recommendations are, for the most part, recommendations that any astute observer of our educational system would make, if there were time and money . . . Success of programs that implement his recommendations provides only weak evidence for TMI, because he is recommending what many other people recommend, for many other reasons."

For example, researchers from other methodological approaches such as Hatano (Hatano and Inagaki 1984), Brown (1989), Halpern (1998), and Chen and Klahr (1999), have separately suggested that variety in examples promotes deeper, more principled learning (see Barnett and Ceci, 2002) even if the variety does not involve multiple intelligences. In several of these studies, the investigators used multiple training contexts or transfer contexts.

Implications for Assessment

One of the factors driving Gardner's redefinition of intelligence appears to be his frustration with what Hunt (2004) describes as Drop In From the Sky testing (DIFS).[2] "Formal testing has moved much too far in the direction of assessing knowledge of questionable importance in ways that show little transportability" (Gardner 1991, p. 134). Many have criticized IQ testing as yielding an unrepresentative measure of human intellectual performance (see for instance Mackintosh 1998; Sternberg 2000; Sternberg and Pretz 2005). Gardner refers to Neisser's suggestion that "Academic knowledge is typically assessed with arbitrary problems that a student has little intrinsic interest in or motivation to answer, and performances on such instruments have little predictive power for performances outside of a scholastic environment" (Gardner 1991, p. 133). However, proponents claim it measures some sort of underlying potential (see, for example, Herrnstein and Murray 1994). We have argued elsewhere (Ceci 1996; Barnett and Ceci 2005a) that such testing, and indeed other forms of academic tests, are measures of developed expertise in the particular domain of such tests, rather than accessing a raw capacity. We have also argued (Ceci 1996; Barnett and Ceci 2005b) that performance on such tests is affected by the context of testing. Both imply that such tests may be unrepresentative to at least some of the situations to which they are to be generalized. In short, a test score measures more than just ability.

Gardner raises two potentially separable challenges to traditional psychometric testing. The first, which clearly follows from his broadening of the definition of intelligence, is that intelligence tests (assuming they can be done properly) should be testing multiple intelligences, rather than just the traditional linguistic, logical-mathematical, and spatial components. Clearly, this is correct if one accepts his definition of intelligence, and is not correct if one does not.

The second challenge concerns the method of testing. This issue is potentially of relevance to the design of measures of intelligence, whether or not one agrees with his broadening of the definition of intelligence itself. The argument, which has been around for a long time, is that IQ tests are 'artificial tests in artificial surroundings' (as mentioned earlier, based on Neisser 1976, 1979) and as such do not capture true capability. Gardner (1983, p. 387) suggests, "The general idea of finding intriguing puzzles and allowing children to 'take off' with them

---

[2] Hunt attributes the term to Robert Mislevy of the Educational Testing Service.

seems to offer a far more valid way of assessing profiles of individuals than the current favorites world-wide: standard measures designed to be given within a half-hour with the aid of paper and pencil . . . It should be possible to gain a reasonably accurate picture of an individual's intellectual profile—be he three or thirteen—in the course of a month or so, while that individual is involved in regular classroom activities. The total time spent might be five to ten hours of observing—a long time given current standards of intellectual testing, but a very short time in terms of the life of that student."

There are two problems with this. First, the simple question of resources—everyone would agree that a bigger snapshot of behaviour is likely to provide a more accurate indicator than a smaller shapshot, but the former takes time and money that may not be available. (Of course, one might counter that if you can't afford to do it right then don't do it at all!) Second is the question of objectivity. Many purposes to which testing is put—whether evaluating the performance of students or educational establishments—require comparability and therefore measures that are not open to potential bias. The rigid standardization of IQ tests and other similar measures is designed to minimize evaluator effects and maximize objectivity. It would be more difficult to do that in the course of naturalistic observation. Of course, one way to solve this problem would be to simply do away with the use of tests for these so-called 'high stakes' purposes. This would reduce the temptation to bias results. However, it could still leave the possibility for unintended bias due to teacher prejudice and so forth. ("Which student is my favorite? Who acts up more in class?"). The challenge, if one wants to test at all, is to devise reliable, but more meaningful and generalizable, tests.

The optimal solution here depends on the purpose to which the tests are being put—what skills are we trying to test and why are we trying to test them. As Gardner (1991, p. 145) says, "One cannot begin to evaluate the effectiveness of schools unless one makes clear one's ambitions for the school". IQ tests, and tests similar to them, have been used for a variety of purposes since the early 1900s. Binet and Simon (1916) originally devised them to identify children struggling at school who might benefit from extra academic help. IQ-like tests have also been used over the years to determine access to English grammar (selective secondary) schools and U.S. universities, as well as for programs offering gifted and remedial education. The current U.S. "No Child Left Behind Act" (U.S. Department of Education, 2002) and English SATs (Direct.Gov.UK 2005) both use subject-based achievement tests which, although not IQ tests in terms of the materials they intend to test, suffer from some of the same criticisms regarding the somewhat artificial and brief snapshot of performance that they provide. As we have argued elsewhere (Barnett and Ceci 2005b), most such tests assess so-called near transfer of learning, rather than far transfer (Barnett and Ceci 2002), though proponents of IQ tests might argue that this is not the case for traditional IQ tests. If far transfer—transfer of learning to new and different situations outside the school—is the goal of education, then tests that predict far transfer must be used. Gardner (1991) suggests that the goal of education is to yield greater understanding in students, significant not superficial understanding. For this, he suggests (Gardner 1991, p. 145), "New and unfamiliar problems, followed by open-ended clinical interviews or careful observations, provide the best way of establishing the degree of understanding that students have attained." Deeper understanding is generally considered to be conducive to greater transfer.

Traditional IQ tests, whether one likes them or not, have been shown to have predictive power in educational and occupational success, as well as in terms of future income (Schmidt and Hunter 1998; Gottfredson 1986; Hunt 1996). As far as we are aware, it is not yet known whether tests conducted in more naturalistic settings, as Gardner proposes, would deliver more predictive power. However, it may merit investigation, given the demonstrated effects of context on performance on at least some cognitive tasks (Ceci 1985). Before predictive power can be assessed, agreement needs to be reached regarding appropriate measures to predict. To do that, the goals of the educational process need to be defined, and agreed upon (Barnett and Ceci 2005b), not just in terms of understanding to be acquired, but also contexts to which transfer is desired.

Though IQ tests aim to be as knowledge-free and as culture-free as possible, all test are knowledge-intense in some ways. In the case of IQ tests, the knowledge is simply of a particular sort. Thus, knowledge needs to be equated or only relevant knowledge needs to be tested. But the sheer presence of knowledge-loading or culture-loading is not a bad thing. The job of predicting is also culture- and knowledge-loaded, that is, we want to predict success within a specific cultural context rather than in some abstract sense that fails to make contact with the culture.

One approach that is being developed to address this problem is Sternberg's dynamic testing. Here the idea is to use learning to assess potential for future learning. This approach avoids irrelevant bias due to differences in crystallized knowledge specific to the test questions, and attempts to measure the process of learning itself as a means of understanding competence. Sternberg's work has proven fruitful in this regard (see Sternberg and Grigorenko's 2002 description).

Another approach, also championed by Sternberg, is to assess so-called practical intelligence. Here, the emphasis is less on potential and more on crystallized, but generally more relevant, skills. The idea behind assessment of practical-thinking skills is that traditionally-academic skills may not be as important in some cultures—so, for example, Sternberg (Grigorenko, Meier, *et al.* 2004; Sternberg 2004) tests route-finding skills in Alaskan children who negotiate the wilderness to see if real-world instantiated tasks yield better measures of competence. Sternberg (Sternberg, Nokes, *et al.* 2001; Sternberg 2004) has also evaluated Kenyan youth's knowledge of folk remedies for diseases—again, a task with extraordinary real-world relevance—which he claims represents a better predictor of intelligence in this group than traditional measures of g. In many of his writings (see, for example, Sternberg 1997), Sternberg argues forcefully for the importance of both practical and creative abilities in school and life success.

As Gardner (1995, p. 939) proposes, we "should be looking at abilities that truly matter (like understanding the relations among numbers) rather than abilities that might correlate with abilities that we truly value." We wholeheartedly agree, not in the least because proxies always pose the risk of proving unreliable in unforseen circumstances. The challenge is to *identify* what truly matters, a task unfortunately rather oft neglected by both the educational and psychological communities!

Implications for Other Big issues in Intelligence Research

Although his main emphasis is on aspects of what he calls intelligence that are not so-called by other intelligence researchers, and are therefore not studied by them, Gardner does have something important to say about some of the current big issues in intelligence research.

One such issue is the question of biology: Are intelligences best viewed from the perspective of learning and context or from brain functioning. For Gardner, the answer seems to be: both. He readily acknowledges the key role of brain processing, as this is one of the forms of evidence he requires to call something an intelligence. But he also develops curricular interventions that have nothing to do with the direct alteration of brain functioning.

A related issue concerns the degree to which individual differences in intelligence are due to nature or nurture. This has been the source of great controversy over the years (see, for example, Herrnstein and Murray's, 1994 *The Bell Curve* or Neisser's 1996 APA task force report). Gardner's reliance on biological arguments for the existence of his various separate intelligences seems to have pushed him somewhat towards the nature camp on this issue, in that his theory suggests that individuals differ in their inherited profile of abilities in the different forms of intelligence. Thus he is at odds with expertise researchers such as Ericsson (Ericsson and Charness 1994) and Charness (1994) who suggest that extensive deliberate practice is what differentiates experts from non-experts in most domains. Although Gardner certainly appreciates the importance of practice and focus in bringing native talents to fruition, it seems he takes a harder view than expertise researchers, implying that not everyone has the needed biological substrate to excel in all forms of intelligence. There is a certain irony here: Gardner's theory is at once "soft" in the sense that it holds out the possibility that everyone can excel at something; but it is hard in the sense of implying that there are probably important biological differences that will render some unable to achieve highly.

Most researchers now agree that some combination of both nature and nurture plays a role in the development of intelligence (see Neisser *et al.* 1996), and, despite his belief in inherited capability differences, Gardner seems to be in line with this view. However, he suggests (1983, p. 318) that "nearly every normal individual can attain impressive competence in an intellectual or a symbolic domain," given enough support and hard work. This is probably more optimistic than most views would allow.

Another timely issue within the intelligence research community concerns the competence versus performance distinction. Here, Gardner seems to sit on the fence separating the extreme views of adherents on each side: "It seemed ill-advised and perhaps impossible, to attempt to measure 'raw' intelligence . . . Intelligences are always expressed in the context of specific tasks, domains, and disciplines. There is no 'pure' spatial intelligence: instead, there is spatial intelligence as expressed in a child's puzzle solutions, route finding, block building" (1993, p. xx). Recently Sternberg and Grigorenko (2004) expressed a similar view, and we suspect that Gardner may be joined by many if not most researchers. To his credit, he was known for this view before most, though not all (see the 1921 *Journal of Educational Psychology* symposium and Sternberg and Detterman 1986).

Postscript

Ultimately, it doesn't really matter what we call various human abilities. What matters is how effectively we can help young people learn skills that they will find useful in work and family life, which will help them to become good citizens and good friends, and which they will enjoy. As developmental psychologists our role is to research and understand how these skills develop and how we can influence their development. History will judge Howard Gardner not just by whether he was right, but also by the effects his work had on these processes. The thought-provoking and motivating influence his work has already had on educators, researchers, and parents will ensure his mark will endure, even if some of his specific ideas fail to receive empirical support.

REFERENCES

Armstrong, Thomas. 2003. *You're Smarter than You Think: A Kid's Guide to Multiple Intelligences.* Minneapolis: Free Spirit.

Barnett, S.M., and S.J. Ceci. 2002. When and Where Do We Apply What We Learn? A Taxonomy for Far Transfer. *Psychological Bulletin* 128: 4, pp. 612–637.

————. 2005a. The Role of Transferable Knowledge in Intelligence. In R.J. Sternberg and J. Pretz, eds., *Cognition and Intelligence: Identifying the Mechanisms of the Mind* (Cambridge: Cambridge University Press).

————. 2005b. Re-Framing the Evaluation of Education Using a Taxonomy of Transfer Context and Content. In J.P. Mestre, eds., *Transfer of Learning: Research and Perspectives* (Greenwich, Connecticut: Information Age).

Baumeister, R.F., J.D. Campbell, J.I. Krueger, and K.D. Vohs. 2003. Does High Self-Esteem Cause Better Performance, Interpersonal Success, Happiness, or Healthier Lifestyles? *Psychological Science in the Public Interest* 41, pp. 1–44.

Binet, A., and T. Simon. 1916. *The Development of Intelligence in Children.* Vineland: Publications of the Training School in Vineland.

Brown, A.L. 1989. Analogical Learning and Transfer: What Develops? In S. Vosniadou and A. Ortony, eds., *Similarity and Analogical Reasoning* (Cambridge, Massachusetts: Harvard University Press), pp. 369–412.

Carlson-Pickering, Jane. 1997. Existential Intelligence. www.chariho.K12.ri .us/cirriculum/MISmart/exist.htm. Retieved 17th July, 2006.

Ceci, S.J. 1996. *On Intelligence: A Bioecological Theory of Intellectual Development.* Cambridge, Massachusetts: Harvard University Press.

Ceci, S.J., and U. Bronfenbrenner. 1985. "Don't Forget to Take the Cupcakes out of the Oven": Prospective Memory, Strategic Time-monitoring, and Context. *Child Development* 56: 1, pp. 152–164.

Chen, Z., and D. Klahr. 1999. All Other Things Being Equal: Acquisition and Transfer of the Control of Variables Strategy. *Child Development* 70: 5, pp. 1098–1120.

Direct.Gov.UK. 2005. National Curriculum Key Stage Tests. From http://www.direct.gov.uk/EducationAndLearning/Schools/ExamsTestsAndTheCurriculum/ExamsTestsAndTheCurriculumArticles/fs/en?CONTENT_ID=10013041&chk=iP4twF.

Education, U. S. Department of. 2002. No Child Left Behind Act of 2001: Public Law, pp. 107–110.

Ericsson, K.A., and N. Charness. 1994. Expert Performance: Its Structure and Acquisition. *American Psychologist* 49: 8, pp. 725–747.

Gardner, Howard. 1993a. *Frames of Mind: The Theory of Multiple Intelligences.* Second edition. New York: Basic Books.

———. 1993b. *Multiple Intelligences: The Theory in Practice.* New York: Basic Books

———. 1995. A Response of Four Fronts [Response to *Review of Multiple Intelligences: The Theory in Practice*, by David Lubinski and Camilla Benbow]. *Contemporary Psychology: APA Review of Books* 40: 10, pp. 938–39.

———. 1999. *Intelligence Reframed: Multiple Intelligence in the 21st Century.* New York: Basic Books.

———. 1991. *The Unschooled Mind: How Children Think and How Schools Should Teach.* New York: Basic Books.

———. 1983. *Frames of Mind: The Theory of Multiple Intelligences.* New York: Basic Books.

Gottfredson, L. 1986. Societal Consequences of the g Factor in Employment. *Journal of Vocational Behavior* 29, pp. 379–410.

Grigorenko, E.L., E. Meier, *et al.* 2004. Academic and Pactical Intelligence: A Case Study of the Yup'ik in Alaska. *Learning and Individual Differences* 14: 4, pp. 183–207.

Halpern, D.F. 1998. Teaching Critical Thinking for Transfer Across Domains. *American Psychologist* 53: 4, pp. 449–455.

Halpern, Diane F. 2005. An Anniversary Celebration for Multiple Intelligences. [Review of *Frames of Mind: The Theory of Multiple Intelligences (1993)*, by Howard Gardner]. *PsycCritiques: Contemporary Psychology—APA Review of Books* 50: 12, Article 9.

Hatano, G. and K. Inagaki. 1984. Two Courses of Expertise. *Research and Clinical Center for Child Development* 83 (Annual Report), pp. 27–36.

Herrnstein, R., and C. Murray. 1994. *The Bell Curve.* New York: Free Press.

Hunt, Earl. 2004. Multiple Views of Multiple Intelligence [Review of *Intelligence Reframed: Multiple Intelligence in the 21st Century*, by

Howard Gardner]. *PsycCritiques: Contemporary Psychology—APA Review of Books*. Originally published in *Contemporary Psychology: APA Review of Books* 46: 1, pp. 5–7.

Hunt, E. 1995. Will We Be Smart Enough? New York: Russell Sage.

Intelligence and its Measurement: A Symposium. 1921. *Journal of Educational Psychology* 12, pp. 123–147, 195–216, 271–75.

Mackintosh, N.J. 1998. *IQ and Human Intelligence*. Oxford: Oxford University Press.

Neisser, U. 1976. General, Academic, and Artificial Intelligence. In L. Resnick, ed., *The Nature of Intelligence*. Hillsdale: Erlbaum.

Neisser, U. 1979. The Concept of Intelligence. *Intelligence* 3, pp. 217–227.

Neisser, U., G. Boodoo, T. Bouchard, N. Brody, S.J. Ceci, D. Halpern, J. Loehlin, R. Perloff, R.J. Sternberg, and S. Urbina. 1996. Intelligence: Knowns and Unknowns. *American Psychologist* 51, pp. 1–25.

Rabbitt, P. 1988. Does It Last? Is Speed a Basic Factor Determining Individual Differences in Memory? In M.M. Gruneberg, P. Morris, and P. Sykes, eds., *Practical Aspects of Memory* (London: Wiley), Volume 2, pp. 172-191.

Schmidt, F.L., and J.E. Hunter. 1998. The Validity and Utility of Selection Methods in Personnel Psychology: Practical and Theoretical Implications of 85 Years of Research Findings. *Psychological Bulletin* 124: 2, pp. 262–274.

Sternberg, R.J. 1997. Successful Intelligence: How Practical and Creative Intelligence Determines Success in Life. New York: Plume.

Sternberg, R.J., ed. 2000. *Handbook of Intelligence*, New York: Cambridge University Press.

———. 2004. Culture and Intelligence. *American Psychologist* 59: 5, pp. 325–338.

Sternberg, R.J., and E.L. Grigorenko. 2002. Dynamic Testing. New York: Cambridge University Press.

Sternberg, R.J., C. Nokes, *et al.* 2001. The Relationship between Academic and Practical Intelligence: A Case Study in Kenya. *Intelligence* 29(5), pp. 401–418.

Sternberg, R.J. and J.E. Pretz, eds. 2005. *Cognition and Intelligence: Identifying the Mechanisms of the Mind*. New York: Cambridge University Press.

Sternberg, R.J., and D.K. Detterman. 1986. *What Is Intelligence?* Norwood: Ablex.

Sternberg, R.J., and E.L. Grigorenko. 2004. Why Cultural Psychology Is Necessary and Not Just Nice. In R.J. Sternberg and E.L. Grigorenko, eds., *Culture and Cognition* (Washington, D.C.: APA Books), pp. 207–224.

Sternberg, R.J., and E.L. Grigorenko. 2002. Just Because We 'Know' It's True Doesn't Mean It's Really True: A Case Study in Kenya. *Psychological Science Agenda* 15: 2, pp. 8–10.

Webster's Revised Unabridged Dictionary, 1913

Williams, W.M., T. Blythe, N. White, J. Li, R.J. Sternberg, and H. Gardner. 1996. *Practical Intelligence for School*. New York: HarperCollins.
Williams, W.M., T. Blythe, N. White, J. Li, H. Gardner, and R.J. Sternberg. 2002. Practical Intelligence for School: Developing Metacognitive Sources of Achievement in Adolescence. *Developmental Review* 22, pp. 162–210.

6

On Spirituality

T.M. LUHRMANN

In his now classic *Frames of Mind*, Howard Gardner set out eight "signs" of what he calls an intelligence: potential isolation by brain damage; the existence of *idiot savants*, prodigies and other exceptional individuals; an identifiable core operation or set of operations; a distinctive developmental history, along with a definable set of expert 'end-state' performances; an evolutionary history and evolutionary plausibility; support from experimental psychological tasks; support from psychometric findings; and susceptibility to encoding in a symbolic system. In *Intelligence Reframed*, seemingly pressed from many sides on the question of whether there were more intelligences than the seven he had initially identified, and perhaps prodded specifically by the "fanatics and frauds who evoke spirituality as if it were a given, a known truth," Gardner turned to the question of whether there was a spiritual intelligence. The answer, he concluded, was "no." Spirituality was too complicated, too messy. One could not even be clear about what would count as the content of such an intelligence, the knowledge or skill that was unambiguously spiritual. He pointed out that spirituality could be described as a concern with cosmic or existential issues, or the achievement of a state of being, or an effect which some people had upon others. And yet he was ambivalent about dismissing so quickly an area of human endeavor that so many have called a way of knowing. He thought that existential intelligence—a concern with ultimate issues— was the most cognitive dimension of spirituality, and he hesitantly and tentatively suggested that perhaps existential intelligence might count as an intelligence.

Howard and I would argue about this when we were fellows at the Center for Advanced Study in the Behavioral Sciences in Palo Alto, back during the long afternoons we used to have in that relaxed year of freedom. I found the logic of his argument persuasive, then as I do now. Spirituality is a vague, amorphous category, and people mean as many things by it as they do by the word 'work'. The word 'work' clearly refers to some kind of activity, and one can say a great about that kind of activity and its importance in human life. But one would be hard pressed to say that the word 'work' picks out a discrete form of scholarly competence, or a mastery of a distinctive skill. Work encompasses many various skills. That is why Howard says that his most recent scholarship, on "good work," has little to do with multiple intelligences.

And yet back in that idyllic year I was uneasy with Howard's conclusion. It seemed to me that there was a skill-like quality in spirituality which was recognizable and demonstrable in many of the pursuits of spiritual experience throughout the world, and that their practice would meet most of the criteria which he laid out. At the time, I had not done the research which would allow me to make my case with confidence. There still is much to do. But now, a decade later, I feel ready to broach a hypothesis: that there is a psychological proclivity towards 'absorption' which may have a developmental path, which seems to be differentially distributed across individuals, which can be trained, and whose skilled use sits at the heart of most serious attempts to develop spiritual experience. I explore the evidence for this hypothesis here. Yet while I believe that I may have identified a skill at the heart of much spiritual practice, I have also come to believe that the skill is not unique to spirituality. In fact, it may be one of those evolutionary accidents, a skill that emerged to meet one kind of need—to manage terror, pain and shock—and was co-opted by another.

On the Track of Spiritual Experience

I first began to think about spiritual experience when I was a graduate student in anthropology. I had arrived in my program fascinated by the problem of mind: how humans thought, what constrained our thought, and in particular, the problem of irrational thought. At the time, most anthropologists attributed a belief in magic either to life in a prescientific society (as Frazer and Horton had done) or they explained it away as not really being belief, but the symbolic management of anxiety and distress (as Malinowksi and Leach had done). Evans-Pritchard's brilliant monograph, *Witchcraft, Oracles, and Magic among the Azande (1937),* chronicled the everyday life of preliterate Sudanese living along the Nile who believed that strange forces worked in their lives much as we understand chance to work in ours. The Azande did not doubt that when the granary fell on a man (to use a famous example) the man was killed by the weight of the building—but why was this man, and not another, sitting beneath the granary when it fell? That was what witchcraft explained. Evans-Pritchard laid out what I came to think of as a cognitive model of witchcraft, and described the way that the Azande learned to use it to interpret events in their lives. The Azande, he argued, were logical, but not scientific. They thought coherently and consistently about particular events, but they never abstracted across contexts to examine the overall logic of their argument.

By this point I had discovered that there were middle-class white Britons, well educated and living in London, who called themselves witches and magicians (Luhrmann 1989). They seemed to believe in magic in the good, old Frazerian sense. They talked about strange forces, manipulated by the mind, which could change the outcome of illness, job interviews and government discussion. Their models of witchcraft and magic were similar in many ways to those of the Azande. Yet by any measure, they lived in a scientific society, and they spoke and acted as if they believed that their magic was real. I set out to understand their interpretive structure. In those days cognitive science was relatively new. It was, in any event, new in anthropology and unknown to me. Later, when I came across *The Mind's New Science*, I devoured it, and I set out to reconstruct the biases, schemas and heuristics in the models my magicians used and in the way they used them. When I first went to the field (in darkest London) I looked for cognitive structure the old-fashioned way, in the narratives, metaphors and representations on which people relied in order to interpret their magical ideas as valid.

But the cognitive story—the account of the kinds of knowledge people acquired, how those ideas were structured and the way they were learned—turned out to be only one part of the story, and not the most important part. People were trained in particular techniques which they thought enabled them to recognize, to generate and to manipulate magical forces. The exact purpose of the training varied from group to group (people who called themselves witches talked more about generating power, while those who thought of themselves as practicing 'high magic' talked about recognizing existing power) but the actual training structure was common. Moreover, all groups recognized the need for training, and all groups identified some people as skilled, and a smaller group of people as experts. Some groups even had formal, take home courses. Before I could be initiated into the most elaborately hierarchical and secretive of magical groups, I was required to take a nine-month home-study course complete with supervisor and monthly essays. It was one of two home-study courses I took. These courses were not dissimilar from other published courses offered to new students in magic. Lessons typically demanded that the student learn to cognitive knowledge associated with that brand of magic (who divinity was, how magical power was understood, which symbols represented it) and, typically, they asked students to personalize that knowledge, to see it as relevant to and embedded within their lives. But they also demanded the acquisition of two attentional skills: meditation and visualization. Each course demanded that the student learn to quieten the mind, and to focus on some internal experience (an image, a word, or on the apparently empty mind itself). Each course also demanded that the student learn to visualize. Here, the student relaxed into a meditative study and tried to see with the mind's eye some unfolding narrative sequence. This is an example from one of my early lessons:

> *Work through these exercises, practicing one of them for a few minutes each day, either before or after your meditation session.*
>
> 1. *Stand up and examine the room in which you are working. Turn a full circle, scanning the room. Now sit down, close the eyes and build the room in imagination. Note where the memory or visualizing power fails. At the end of the exercise briefly re-examine the room and check your accuracy. Note the results in your diary.*
>
> 2. *Carefully visualize yourself leaving the room in which you are working, going for a short walk you know well, and returning to your room. Note clarity, breaks in concentration, etc, as before.*
>
> 3. *Go for an imaginary walk; an imaginary companion, human or animal, can accompany you. Always start and finish the walk in the room you use for the exercises. Note the results, etc, as before.*
>
> 4. *Build up in imagination a journey from your physical plane home to your ideal room. Start the journey in real surrounds then gradually make the transition to the imaginary journey by any means you wish. Make the journey to and from the room until it is entirely familiar.*

The point of the exercises was to develop the capacity to use magical images in a state of physical relaxation and mental concentration, in which the student was trying to see those mental images clearly, with borders, duration, and stability.

What startled me, as a young ethnographer, was that this training worked. That is, after about a year of this kind of training (not only in one of the home study courses, but in a weekly Monday night "exercise class," and through trying the suggestions offered in the many popular training books on developing magical skills) my mental imagery *did* seem to become clearer. I thought that my images had sharper borders, greater solidity and more endurance. I began to feel that my concentration states were deeper and more sharply different from the everyday. And I began to have more of what a psychologist would call 'anomalous experience'. I had a hypnopompic vision: I had been reading a novel written by this kind of magical practitioner, really trying to imagine what the characters were experiencing, and one morning I awoke to see some of the characters standing by my window. I shot up in bed when I saw them, and they vanished. But for a moment, I really saw them. And I felt different in rituals, when we shut our eyes, sank into meditative states, and visualized what the group leader told us to. At those times, when I was trying so hard to see with my mind's eye and to be completely relaxed but mentally alert, it seemed as if there was something altered about the way I experienced the world—in my sense of self, sense of time, sense of focus. This was not true for all ritual gatherings, but in those rituals in which I felt fully absorbed, the difference from the everyday was striking. Moreover, I did not feel as if I was simply acquiring a new language to interpret everyday experience, but that I was acquiring a new experiential skill, and that the skill could be taught and mastered.

Spiritual Skills

And indeed there is a great deal of historical and ethnographic evidence that the attentional skills of meditation and visualization have been taught throughout history and across cultures, that they are learnable skills, and that mastery of those skills is associated with intense spiritual experience. Systematic visualization practice is found in Asian monastic tradition (Beyer 1978) and in medieval Christianity (Carruthers 1998), and it remains the cornerstone of arguably the most successful spiritual conversion practice in Catholicism, the Ignatian Spiritual Exercises. The practice of visualization is also widely distributed in shamanic or shamanic-style religions (such as Crocker 1985), although the training may appear less systematic to an observer, in part because it is apprentice-based and taught in a preliterate context. Most ethnographies of shamanism are clear that the shaman must be apprenticed and trained. Those ethnographies that describe the training in detail suggests that such training consists in expert coaching to enable the apprentice to enter an altered state and to see certain kinds of images clearly and reliably.

The practice of meditation is equally widely distributed, and famously present in many Eastern spiritual systems, where it is presumed to be a skill that can be learned and which, when learned, will deliver to the practitioner a series of intense spiritual experiences. Meditation has garnered the lion's share of the scientific study of spiritual practice, and because of this we know that consistent practice may produce physiological changes (Austin 1999). It is less appreciated that Christian prayer is a meditational system, although usually used in a less focused manner. The worshipper withdraws himself from the everyday, focuses inwardly, and attempts to bend his mind to hear the small, still voice of God.

Trance States

The common description we give of such practices is that they create a form of trance, a simple behavioral pattern in which a subject displays intense absorption in internal sensory stimuli with diminished peripheral awareness. An interest in trance states is even more widely distributed that the specific attentional practices of mediation and visualization. Trance states play a role in nearly every know culture, although their role in those cultures seems to wax and wane. In a still authoritative survey of religious practice, based on the Human Relations Area Files (HRAF), Erika Bourguignon (1970) discovered that 89 percent of the 488 cultures studied used some ritualized forms of dissociation states. (She suggests that if the HRAF were more complete, the numbers would be higher; most negative examples may reflect the absence of good records rather than the absence of the practice.)

While the specific attentional techniques of meditation and visualization may not be used, typically the trance is entered through the use of some kind of sensory manipulation: chanting, altering the light, fantasy, pain, rapid whirling—techniques which decrease peripheral awareness and enhance absorption in internal sensory stimuli. Meditation probably inhibits sensory responsiveness to external sensory stimulation, while visualization may work by intensifying internal stimuli and in effect drowning out external sensory stimulation.

The psychological puzzle, of course, is what is actually being learnt. There are no (or at least, no as-yet-identified) physiological markers of a trance state (Spiegel and Spiegel 2004). As individuals enter more deeply into these highly absorbed states, they tend to experience reduced responsiveness to external stimuli (it may be more difficult to attract their attention), an altered sense of time (which usually passes more slowly), an altered sense of self (they feel differently about their "selves") and an altered sense of control (they often experience phenomena as happening to them, rather than in being control of their experience as agents). It seems clear even from the historical and ethnographic literature that there are individual variations in a person's capacity to enter such states, and possibly in the depth of trance a person is able to enter. It is also clear that while most unusual spiritual experiences (visions and more dramatic trance phenomena like mystical and near death experiences) are reported as occurring spontaneously, individuals with expertise can learn to enter trance experience predictably. After all, in many religious settings (for example, shamanism and possession practices) the expert's expertise relies upon his or her ability to enter such states on demand. And while it may be possible to 'fake' an altered state, the vast literature does not suggest that such expert command practices are normatively faked.

There are two clear candidates for the psychological mechanism of trance, both of them abundantly studied, both obviously associated with trance, and neither of them satisfactory as accounts of the skill associated with learning to go into trance. ('Flow', as defined by Csikszentmihalyi 1990, might be thought to be another, but the construct of flow focuses on task performance, rather than psychological mechanism. The phenomena, however, seem to be related.) The first is hypnosis, which is often presented concretely as a trance experience. Spiegel and Spiegel describe the clinical use of hypnosis straightforwardly as the experience of trance. "The trance experience is often best explained to new patients who have questions about it as being very much like being absorbed in a good novel; one loses awareness of noises and distractions in the immediate environment and, when a novel is finished, a moment of reorientation to the surrounding world is required" (2004,p. 21). They argue that "the crux of the trance state is the dialectic between focal and peripheral awareness" and they define hypnotic trance as "characterized by an ability to sustain a state of attentive, receptive, intense focused concentration with peripheral awareness in response to a signal" (2004, p. 19).

The problem with hypnosis as a mechanism is the tool that has been used to infer its presence. What scientists have actually studied is the practice of one person (the hypnotist) putting another person (the to-be-hypnotized subject) into a hypnotic state. Yet the willingness to go into trance might plausibly be thought to reflect the subject's willingness to respond to authority, and so the test for hypnotic ability might reveal as much about the personality traits of high responders than about their ability to go into trance. In fact in the 1980s, the field of hypnosis research was consumed by what was called the 'state-trait' debate. Some (like Hilgard and the Spiegels) argued that the hypnotic state arose through the manipulation of attention, and reflected something about consciousness. The other side (Spanos and Barber, for example) argued that hypnosis was a cognitive condition of suspended judgment and suggestibility (see the able discussion in Kihlstrom 1997). In any event, the actual practice of what is called 'hetero-hypnosis' does not resemble the spiritual practice we are trying to model here.

The other candidate is dissociation, a psychological construct which was described by Janet and then disappeared in the scientific literature (and seemingly, in the culture) as Freud's concept of repression came to dominate models of the mind, reappearing in the 1970s when new patients began to flood into the psychiatric consulting room (see Luhrmann 2004). Dissociation is described in the official psychiatric nosology (the DSM) as "a disruption in the usually integrated functions of consciousness, memory, identity or perception of the environment" (APA 1994, p. 447). While dissociation is a complex empirical construct, poorly understood and used in a variety of different ways, trance is central to the phenomenon. Patients are often described as going into trance or being in a state of intense internal absorption with limited responsiveness to an observer. The prototypical trance state (for example, the practitioner of a spirit possession religion like Santeria in the state that observers recognize as their possessed state) would certainly count as falling with the DSM definition. The 'switching' behavior of dissociative identity disorder, while not identified explicitly as trance behavior in the diagnostic handbook, often looks to an observer as if the subject were going into trance.

Again, the problem with dissociation as a construct, at least for the purpose of discussing a putative spiritual intelligence, arises with the tools used to detect it. The term is used primarily as a psychiatric description of symptoms and experiences associated with trauma and intense distress. The model is that the dissociating individual responds to a situation in which he is terrified and helpless by entering an altered state. The little girl panics when her stepfather enters her bedroom at night—and so she just goes somewhere else in her head. Over time, the model suggests, this 'dissociation' becomes her preferred (and ultimately, maladaptive) unconscious defense against emotional distress. It is true that the clinical writing on dissociation often refers loosely to trance-inducing religious practices as involving "normal" or "non-pathological" dissociation. The psychiatrist Stanley Krippner, for example, begins a collection entitled *Broken Images, Broken Selves* (Krippner and Powers 1997) with a ritual from the Afro-Caribbean spirit possession religion of Santeria, which he uses to caution readers about too quickly accepting what he calls the western paradigm of dissociation as always trauma-related. Nevertheless, the scientific literature on dissociation models the trance phenomena as a response to intense emotional distress, often accompanied by a feeling of helplessness. Moreover, as in the literature on hypnosis, the construct of dissociation is doing more than describing trance: it describes a variety of disruptions in awareness and identity, whose psychological relationships are not clear.

In fact, the different reach of the constructs of dissociation and hypnosis have lead to an active debate within these scientific literatures about the relationship between the two. Hilgard (1977), one of the early researchers on hypnosis, treated the concepts of hypnosis and dissociation as effectively interchangeable. And at least some researchers have demonstrated that people with the most dramatic and trance-like form of dissociative disorder, dissociative identity disorder (once called multiple personality disorder) were likely to be judged "high hypnotizable" (Bliss 1984; Fritchholz *et.al.* 1992). However, scores on two widely used tests of dissociation and hypnosis are not in fact associated in nonclinical populations, nor in several studies of clinical populations (Whalen and Nash 1996). The psychiatrist Lisa Butler (1996) argues that this finding makes sense because the test of hypnotic susceptibility judges the potential to enter hypnotic states, while the test of dissociation judges a subject's active use of such states to protect themselves. She argues that someone is not likely to use dissociative states unless they have been traumatized, and unless, having been traumatized, they use their capacity for self-hypnosis as a defense. She describes this as a hypnotic diathesis theory of dissociation. Yet it is also true that the dissociation model of altered states presumes that such states arise in response to emotional distress, and that they are not controllable: that's why the client comes to the psychiatrist's consulting office. There is presumed to be a skill component to her altered states, in that the young child is thought to go into trance spontaneously and then repeatedly as a learned defense against emotional distress. And still the child's control over the practice is understood to be as limited as conscious control over any unconscious defense mechanism. The meditator or religious practitioner, by contrast, deliberately sets out to practice the entry into altered states. While unusual phenomena may arise unbidden in his life, the daily practice of trance states is deliberate and chosen.

Absorption as a Measure of Spiritual Experience

My candidate for a psychological construct which best captures the skills associated with spiritual experience is absorption, as measured by a scale introduced by Tellegen and Atkinson in 1974. The researchers had set out to find personality correlates of hypnotic experience. They factor analyzed a large set of questions and identified a cluster that they called a measure of absorption, which correlated modestly with hypnotic susceptibility. From the results, Tellegen developed what came to be known as the Tellegen absorption scale, a thirty-four question true-false scale. Widely available on the Internet, the questions tap subjects' willingness to be caught up in their experience—particularly their imaginative experience, and in nature and music. Tellegen and Atkinson argued that the attentional style captured by the questions created "a heightened sense of the reality of the attentional object, imperviousness to distracting events, and an altered sense of reality in general, including an empathically altered sense of self" (Tellegen and Atkinson 1974, p. 268).

Later, Tellegen argued that there were clusters of experiential response within the scale. He identified eight such clusters: 1. *Imaginative involvement* in items like these: "If I wish I can imagine (or daydream) some things so vividly that they hold my attention as a good movie or story does" and "When I listen to music I can get so caught up in it that I don't notice anything else." 2. *Emotional responsiveness* in items like these: "I can be deeply moved by a sunset" and "I like to watch cloud shapes change in the sky." 3. *Responsiveness to highly inductive (for example hypnosis-inducing) stimuli* in items like these: "When listening to organ music or other powerful music I sometimes feel as if I am being lifted into the air" and "The sound of a voice can be so fascinating to me that I can just go on listening to it." 4. *Vivid re-experiencing of the past* in items like these: "Sometimes I feel and experience things as I did as a child" and "I can sometimes recollect certain past experiences in my life with such clarity and vividness that it is like living them again or almost so." 5. *Expansion of awareness* in items like these: "I sometimes "step outside" my usual self and experience an entirely different state of being" and "At time I somehow feel the presence of someone who is not physically there." 6. *Powerful imaging* in items like these: "If I wish I can imagine that my body is so heavy that I could not move it if I wanted to" and "Sometimes I can change noise into music by the way I listen to it." 7. *Imaginal thinking* in items like these: "My thoughts often don't occur as words but as visual images" and "Sometimes thoughts and images come to me without the slightest effort on my part." 8. *Cross-modal experiencing* in items like these: "Different colors have distinctive and special meanings for me" and "I find that different odors have different colors" (Tellegen 1981, pp. 220–21).

What the instrument seems to capture is someone's willingness to allow him- or herself to be absorbed in internal or external sensory experience for its own sake, to enjoy the involvement in itself rather than experiencing it primarily as a means to some other goal. And that of course is precisely the domain that magical training (and, as I shall argue, prayer training) encourages. That kind of spiritual training specifically asks the exercitant to focus inwardly the absorbed attention on internal sensory experience. Tellegen even argues, in an aside, that the attention to one's internal thoughts "hangs together" with vivid imagery and altered states, suggesting that the construct of absorption captures that combination of imagery, internal focus and altered state that seemed central to magical practice as I described it ethnographically.

Moreover, absorption as measured by this scale seems closely connected both to hypnotic and dissociative experience. A subject's response to the absorption scale is correlated both with dissociation measures and with hypnotic susceptibility. The Dissociative Experiences scale, probably the most widely used measure of dissociation, bases a third of its items on absorption. (Another third measures amnesia, and the final third, depersonalization). Spiegel and Spiegel (2004) suggest that hypnosis can be thought of as one third absorption, one third suggestion and one third dissociation Many studies have found a moderate correlation between response to the Tellegen and hypnotizbility (Nadon *et. al.* 1991). And while there are still debates on the relationship between dissociation and hypnotizability, there is no doubt that absorption is clearly moderately to strongly correlated with both (Whalen and Nash 1996).

There is surprisingly little empirical work on absorption, and what work has been done has tended to focus on "openness to self-altering experiences," "imaginative involvement," or fantasy (McCrae and Costa 1983; Glisky *et. al.* 1991; Wild, Kuiken, and Schopflocher 1995). One well-known paper discusses absorption in the context of a "fantasy prone" personality style (Wilson and Barber 1983). Other papers demonstrate that high absorption, as measured by the Tellegen scale, correlates with enjoying reading novels and listening to music (Nell 1988; Snodgrass and Lynn 1989) and with the ability not only to have altered states, but while in such states to experience greater alterations in imagery and awareness (Pekala, Wenger, and Levine 1985). A summary paper, written fifteen years ago, pointed out that the constructs of imaginative involvement, absorption and openness to experience overlap considerably, and that we needed more 'work of a primary kind" on absorption (Roche and McConkey 1990, p. 99). That paper also pointed out that some work focused on absorption as a state, as a certain kind of experience, and that other work focused on absorption as a set of personality traits.

What I find useful about Tellegen's construct of absorption, however, is that it is the only psychological measure I have encountered which seems to distinguish between people who report intense spiritual experience, and those who do not.

New Paradigm Churches

Since 1977 I have spent hundreds of hours in the growing points of American religion, in churches, temples and other religious groups which have seen significant growth since 1965. In particular, I have spent a great deal of time in new paradigm Christian churches, which are among the fastest growing expressions of evangelical Christianity. The term 'new paradigm' was initially coined to describe churches coming out of California and their combination of casual social style and conservative theology. Churches associated with Calvary Chapel, Vineyard Christian Fellowship, Hope Chapel, and their many descendants were likely to meet in gyms, not in formal church buildings; to use rock bands, rather than a choir; to play contemporary music, lyrics projected with powerpoint, rather than ordinary hymns. They were Bible-based, in that their teaching and practice focused directly on the scriptures, and for them, the point of worship was to develop a personal relationship with Jesus.

My ethnographic focus for the last fifteen months has been a Vineyard Christian Fellowship in Chicago. I have attended services weekly; participated in a "housegroup" of five to ten people which meets weekly to read the Bible; taken weekend courses with titles like "the Art of Hearing God" and "Healing and Deliverance;" sat through the ten week "Alpha" course for newcomers to Christianity (this is one of the most widely taught courses on Christianity today—its website says that more than two million have taken it worldwide); formally interviewed over twenty people, with well over forty hours of transcribed conversation; listened to some of the popular Vineyard music and read many of the books which Vineyard congregants read.

This is a culture in which people actively seek out spiritual experience. I had been coming to housegroup for over a year by the time Zeke made the decision that he was not going to go to graduate school in sociology, but that instead he would pursue a seminary degree, and he wanted more than anything to feel a close, intimate relationship with God. One evening we were going around the group, asking what people wanted us to pray for on their behalf. Zeke mournfully explained that he really wanted God to speak to him in a booming voice which he could hear outside his head, and that God had not done so yet. He wanted us to pray for him that God would be unmistakably present in his life. He assumed, as most Vineyard congregants assume, that it is very important to have an intimate personal relationship with God, and that one of the signs of this intimacy is that congregant will have concrete, sensory experiences of God's presence.

Vineyard services are overtly conventional (at least the ones I have attended are) but they do tolerate speaking in tongues and other charismatic phenomena, normally in small groups outside the larger services. That, in fact, was why the church originally split from Calvary Chapel. John Wimber, the man who founded the Vineyard, believed that God could speak to humans as he had done in the Hebrew Bible, and that Jesus could still heal as He had done in Palestine. It is said that the early Vineyard churches were more overtly charismatic than their services are now, but there is no question that charismatic phenomena are a source of pride and authority in the church. People speak openly and happily about hearing God speak to them in prayer, and even about hearing God speak audibly. They talk about their visions and the images they have "received" in prayer. At the end of the Sunday service, the "prayer team" will line up against the wall in the back. "Do not leave until you have had prayer, if you want prayer" the leader will say, and indeed, people will be clustered around the prayer team, waiting for someone to pray for them individually. The people who are on the prayer team, and who are known to pray "well" for others, are called "prayer warriors." This is a term of admiration and respect, and people expect prayer warriors to have more intimate relationships with God, and to have more concrete spiritual experiences.

Conversing with the Deity

Many, many books and courses offer to teach the congregant how to develop that more intimate relationship and to experience it concretely. One well-known evangelical text is *Hearing God: Developing a Conversational Relationship with God*. The author Dallas Willard begins by saying that God's face-to-face conversations with Moses are examples of the "normal human life God intended for us" (Willard 1999, p. 18). He recalls Augustine's famous conversion experience in which he heard, from outside of him, a disembodied voice saying "take up and read," and says, "I cite these cases here not because they are exceptional, but precisely because they are so common" (p. 21). The book was published as a manual to teach the reader to do likewise. That was also the point of the "Art of Hearing God," a three-day how-to conference held at one of the Vineyard churches. It was also the point, more obliquely, of the Alpha course, which builds into its schedule a weekend retreat that is usually called 'the Holy Spirit day'. On that day, the hope of the organizers is that the participants will come to develop an experiential relationship with God. In our case, we heard lectures and spent some quiet time in contemplation, and the other group leaders prayed over each one of us individually. "Did you feel hot?" someone eagerly asked me afterwards. "That's often the sign of the Holy Spirit."

Clearly congregants are being taught in part to interpret everyday experience as bearing the signs of God's presence. This interpretation is explicitly part of the learning process described in *Dialogue with God*, a book recommended by the leader of "the Art of Hearing God" conference. The author begins by saying that he used to live in a rationalist box. He yearned to hear God speak to him the way God spoke to others in the Hebrew Bible—and he believed that God still spoke to others the way he did in ancient Canaan. Alas, he was unable to hear God speak to him until he realized that God's voice often sounds like his own stream of consciousness, and that the Christian just needs to know how to pay attention to his own awareness in order to hear God speaking directly and clearly. "God's voice normally sounds like a flow of spontaneous thoughts, rather than an audible voice. I have since discovered certain characteristics of God's interjected thoughts which help me to recognize them" (1986, p. 29). That is the point of the book: to help you to identify what, in your experience of your own mind, are God's thoughts. "You need to learn to distinguish God's interjected thoughts from the cognitive thoughts that are coming from your own mind" (1986, p. 31). God's voice, the book explains, has an unusual content. You will recognize it as different from your ordinary thoughts. You feel different when you hear God. "There is often a sense of excitement, conviction, faith, vibrant life, awe or peace that accompanies receiving God's word" (1986, p. 30).

At the same time, it is also clear that congregants are being taught the classic attentional techniques that have been used to general religious experience across the ages. *Dialogue with God*'s central example of a man who knew how hear God's voice begins by saying that he "knew how to go to a quiet place and quiet his own thoughts and emotions so that he could sense the spontaneous flow of God within" (1986, p. 6). The author provides explicit exercises to help his readers do likewise. He sells a 'centering cassette' for that purpose on their website. In fact, he recommends a 'prayer closet', a place where you can go, unplug the phone, and be fully quiet in prayer. He recommends journaling to write down and discard distracting thoughts; he recommends simple song to focus the mind in worship; he recommends breathing techniques to breathe out your sin and breathe in the healing Holy Spirit; he recommends the complete focus of the mind and heart on Jesus. He acknowledges that many of these techniques seem very eastern, but distinguishes them from Zen and other forms of meditation on the grounds that eastern meditation contacts "the evil one," while he uses the techniques to contact God.

Many of the best selling Christian books are books on technique. One such example is Richard Foster's *Celebration of Disciplines*. Published by HarperCollins in 1978, by 2003 it had sold more than a million and a quarter copies. The book is a straightforward and accessible summary of the classic spiritual disciplines, and it leads with chapters on each of what he calls 'the inward disciplines:" meditation, prayer, fasting and solitude. He describes prayer as a learning process, and describes meditation—his first discipline—as most effectively achieved through the imagination. "Perhaps some rare individuals experience God through abstract contemplation alone, but most of us need to be more deeply rooted in the senses" (2003, p. 25). He says that meditation cannot be learned from a book, but only from its practice, and advises the reader to find a comfortable position that won't be distracting, relax, and focus on the written word of God. "Seek to live the experience, remembering the encouragement of Ignatius of Loyola to apply all our senses to the task. Smell the sea. Hear the lap of water along the shore. See the crowd. Feel the sun on your head and the hunger in your stomach. Taste the salt in the air. Touch the hem of his garment . . ." (pp.

29–30). The actual technique is taught exactly as it was in the course I took on magic.

Prayer of course is an attentional technique. The subject focuses attention inwardly, on thoughts and feelings and inner sensations, and tries to shut out the obtruding world. Many of the books read by members of this Vineyard would speak about a "prayer closet," a place where you could really concentrate on prayer. At least two Christian I know had a literal closet they used for prayer when they were younger. And they consistently spoke of prayer as a discipline which you had to master, and as a skill which you could improve with practice. One man explained: "When I first became a Christian my prayer life was very, um, more rigid—I needed to set aside half an hour before I go to bed to pray and be very diligent about that. . . . You only go to boot camp once, but then after that, you rely on the training." He was someone who really did use a closet in those early days, when he became a Christian at the end of high school. "I would read [through the Gospel of John] and I would take some notes, and then I'd actually get in my closet—I had a decent-sized closet in my parent's house—because it would be quiet there and I could read with the light, and then I would just pray on my knees."

Measuring Spiritual Differences

And yet despite the emphasis on prayer and despite all the prestige of intense spiritual experience, not everyone had those experiences, and fewer still actually heard God speak audibly. Why?

By the time I began the fieldwork with the Chicago Vineyard church, I decided to supplement my ethnographic participant observation and my open ended interviews with more focused interviews which asked people specifically about their spiritual experience, and about what a psychologist would call anomalous experience. Because I was also interested in the psychological routes to these experiences, I had people fill out all kinds of different questionnaires. I gave them the Tellegen absorption scale. I also gave them the DES (dissociative experiences scale); a version of the DES intended for a non-clinical population; when those failed, I tried the Kennedy dissociation scale and another dissociation scale; I gave them various psychosis proneness scales, like the Launay-Slade Hallucination Proneness scale. The only scale that was at all useful was the Tellegen absorption scale. By that I mean that different people responded differently. Some people loved it. One woman told me that the man who had designed it "lived inside my head." Others didn't find many items that they could affirm. This was different from the dissociation and psychosis scales, most of which people rejected entirely.

The Tellegen picked out the people who had unusual, intense spiritual experiences. The woman who explained that Tellegen had lived inside her head affirmed 33 of the 34 questions. She was the most highly regarded of the prayer warriors. When she prayed, she had vivid mental imagery. She often felt sensory sensations, often during prayer, which she attributed to the presence of the Holy Spirit. She talked about "seeing" images, and while she could say that for the most part they were not as real as ordinary sight, there were times when the images seemed more real than others. She had heard God speak audibly to her on three occasions. By contrast, a man who confessed that he'd struggled to pray and didn't do it very well, said yes to only four out of the thirty-four items. He did say that he often felt more peaceful after prayer, and he did recount one moment when he was worshipping in church in St Louis, at a time when he and his wife were thinking about whether they should move to Chicago and if so, where, and "I really just felt really clearly that God put [this] Vineyard into my head." Yet that was the only spiritual experience he was able to recall for me—despite having really wanted to have more such experiences earlier in his life. When he was in high school, for example, he recalled that "I remember desperately wanting to draw closer to God, and [to have] one of these inspired Holy Spirit moments . . . I wanted those [experiences] and I sought them out, but I never found myself encountering them."

By this point, I have given the Tellegen to twenty people, for whom I have some other evidence of spiritual experience. For eighteen of those people I have formally taped interviews that have lasted well over an hour, and all but one of them I have come to know in the context of my participant observation. Four of them said yes to fewer than a third of the items; eleven of them said yes to half or more of the items, and eight of them said yes to two thirds (twenty-two) or more (one of those responses, however, I will leave aside here because my uncertainty of the level of her understanding). That group which said yes to fewer of a third of them items, with the exception of one person, uniformly reported little unusual experience; the group which said yes to at least two thirds of the items reported the most sensory experience of God, and in general, contained the people regarded as the "prayer warriors" and the people regarded as having the richest interior prayer lives. They were also more likely to have had a frank hallucination. Of the four people who clearly affirmed having heard an audible voice when alone, two were Tellegen high-scorers (the other two I will shortly discuss).

Exceptions

In general, then, the Tellegen picks out something about disposition or proclivity among these individuals. It does not seem to pull out the difference in training, at least among these individuals. At a church like this one, everybody prays. People are constantly reminded that they should be in prayer constantly—"that's what the Bible says"—and if you begin a conversation with them about prayer, they will usually make some remark to that effect. Christian radio, Christian writing, and the culture of the church all underscore the centrality of prayer, that prayer is the only way to begin and to maintain a relationship with Jesus. People in the church know that they should set aside a significant amount of time each day to spend in "quiet time" with Jesus (the normative amount of time seems to be thirty minutes). Many congregants keep "Dear God" journals, which they use to record their prayers and which they also use, sometimes at a different point than at their quiet time, to record what they regard as God's 'answers', which come to them as God guides them in which words to use.

Rather, the Tellegen seems to pick out the ability to respond to prayer practice—or to absorption training. Zeke, for example, was another man who affirmed only four of the questions. In our interview, as I was probing for hallucinations, out of body experiences, mystical experiences, and other phenomena, he said (a bit glumly), "I don't have these superpowerful experiences that make me fall to my knees." And in response to several of the Tellegen questions (for example, "if I wish I can imagine (or daydream) some things so vividly that they hold my attention as a good movie or story does") he scribbled, "there are such people?" At the same time, inclination or interest play some kind of role. For example, a woman who said yes to just over a third of the items (thirteen out of thirty-four) said in talking about prayer, "I'm not like, like some people are prayer warriors, I'm not, it's hard for me to pray sometimes." Later she said, "I don't understand the gift of prophecy completely. I probably never will and I don't have it and I don't want it because it would scare me."

By contrast, consider the experience of another woman, the second highest scorer (twenty-seven out of thirty-four). Jane is also known as a prayer warrior. She has never heard God audibly, and she says that she has never had a vision, although she seems to have had an out-of-body experience when she was baptized as a young teen (she saw herself as if she was outside of her body). But she often loses track of time and even her surroundings when she prays, she often has powerful vivid images and sensory impressions, and she treats her prayer experience as in some ways more real than the world around her. For example, she said that in prayer, "sometimes I want to be in a different place, and so in my mind, I'll go to that place." Jane finds that for her, prayer becomes a way to make God real. "I feel like the more I treat God as if he were sitting where you are, the more real He is to me."

Two people really stand out from this general account. The first is a woman who was among the lowest scorers, and yet who clearly wanted to have dramatic charismatic experiences and probably did so. I watched her change over time. When I first met her, back when I first began to attend the church in April 2004, she seemed remarkably uninterested in psychological and imaginative experience, and much more focused on leading a good and moral life. She said in our first interview, that April, that "prayer is a hard thing for me" and that "for me, my prayer life is radically different from Nora's"—the highest of the Tellegen scorers. She did talk about God speaking to her, and gave an example of the way that he did, but she explicitly denied having heard an audible voice (although one story was ambiguous in the interview, and a year later, she re-told that story explicitly as about an audible voice). When I gave her the Tellegen scale, I had the impression that she regarded the questions as frivolous, and disapproved of them. She was also at this point uncertain of her career, and was contemplating law school.

Then she went to a conference in which people with charismatic experience were clearly and specifically presented as having more authority within the church than those without that experience. (The conference took place at a church—the Toronto Christian Airport church—which the national Vineyard organization had regarded as overly charismatic, and from which it had separated.) At that meeting, Elaine felt a blast—"like a big strong wind"—as the Holy Spirit blew down along the audience of some 1800 people, and it knocked her over. "It felt like a power coming on me." She was deeply impressed by this, and very excited. After she came back, she started going to as many charismatic Christian conferences as she could, of the sort sponsored by the different Vineyard churches, and she threw herself into experiencing God intensely and concretely. She would pray prostrate, nose into the ground, even at church. She took in as a roommate a homeless woman whom the church was trying to help (they paid her share of the rent). At one point she stopped a drunkard, reeking of whisky, late at night on an urban street, and prayed for him. She reported that he cried. By the following spring, she had decided to become a missionary and to devote her life to the church.

And yet even with her yearning for experience and her intense, committed prayer, she seemed more interested in prophecy than in sensory experience during prayer. Elaine was in my housegroup—in fact, she had organized it—and so I saw her weekly. By that spring, she had become very interested in dreams and in the way they could be used to discern the plan God had for you, and she had read many evangelical texts on spirituality. She really liked the books which spoke about the concrete reality of spiritual phenomena (for example, those written by John Paul Jackson) and she became excited by ideas about spiritual reality which few congregants at the church took seriously. (For example, she explained to our housegroup that if you recorded a cricket's chirps, and slowed the recording down to the rate it would take if a cricket's life were as long as a human's, you would discover that the cricket was really singing the hallelujah chorus from Handel's Messiah.) But she did not describe her prayer life the way Jane described hers, with all its visual, sensory lushness. Elaine talked about talking with God and hearing from God—all auditory, linguistic descriptions—and she was very focused on the ability to prophesy, rather than on the sensory quality of spiritual experiences.

In the world of magical practitioners, people often drew distinctions between practitioners who easily had rich, powerful anomalous experiences—people with vivid imagery, who seemed easily to enter altered states—and people who were "psychic," who were thought able to discern truths about other people and to predict their futures. (You could be gifted in one or the other or both.) That kind of naturalistic distinction may pick out a psychological distinction between word-oriented and image-oriented individuals. At least one person spontaneously offered a version to me in this Christian setting. I sat down with Augusta one evening and asked her to help me to understand what was different between one group of people (who happened to be the high Tellegen scorers) and another group, in which I placed people clearly quite eager for religious experience but who did not score highly (a group in which I placed both Elaine and herself). She said that the two groups prayed differently. The first group was more flexible, she said. They were more "touchy-feely," more compassionate, and they liked metaphor. They liked to use metaphors when they prayed. She didn't. She and those in that second group "spoke truth." She said that they saw things in black and white. They were, in effect, more interested in words of prophecy, and less interested in the story.

Augusta had affirmed only eighteen items, just over half of the Tellegen. And yet she was well-identified as a prayer warrior, did receive images during prayer, and she heard the audible voice of God so often that I thought of her as someone whom Gordon Claridge (1997) would call a 'healthy schizotype.' Claridge is among the growing number of

Europeans who do not treat hallucinations as pathognomic symptoms of psychiatric illness, but instead point to their distribution in the normal population—a phenomenon that has been known for a long time, but is poorly studied—and who have concluded that psychiatric illnesses may not be as discrete as American psychiatric formulations assume.

Most people in the church—or for that matter, among the magicians or in any other religious setting in which I have worked—report hallucinations as rare, unusual events. They occur, to those who experience them, one, twice, perhaps thrice. The individual reporting them often remembers exactly when they occurred, and they are momentous events precisely because they are so unusual. (It is relatively easy to identify a true auditory hallucination; people are generally able to answer clearly whether they heard a voice "outside their head" or "inside their head." Visual hallucinations are somewhat more ambiguous, but again, people are usually able to distinguish inside the head from outside). This was not true for Augusta, who seemed to experience hallucinatory phenomena with something like the frequency that people with psychotic disorders experience distressing voices. In her case, however, there was no emotional impairment, no difficulty in life tasks, and no discomfort. Moreover, the voices were not distressing, and they were appropriate to the cultural setting in which she found herself. Augusta, in her middle twenties, was a leader in the church, highly successful in her competitive job, and surrounded by friends.

Augusta says that the first time she heard a voice outside of her head, she was eleven. It was really hot, and she was listening to the television, and she heard things and they bothered her so she shut off the television. She still heard "a little voice" so she shut the window. So she went to lie in bed with her mom. Then "I think there was a season in my life, like a really long season, where I didn't hear anything." She heard something again at the end of high school. She was out driving after dark, which she wasn't supposed to do, and felt such a distinct presence in the car that she stopped and pulled over. Then a voice said, "God is here, and God is everywhere, and God will always be with you." It was a monotone male voice. She drove on to her friend's house, and while she knew that the voice was God and that this was a good thing, she didn't tell her friend and her friend asked her whether she was all right. She joined a Pentecostal church some years later.

These days, Augusta says that she hears God's voice outside of her head "all the time," and "every day." Often, it is like a voice whispering just outside her ears, as if "when your nose and your ears are stopped up and you know you're speaking but you can't really hear that you're speaking but you can hear your voice sort of reverberating within you." She had pointed to the air just behind her ears to describe where the voice was located. This is a particularly striking gesture, because ambiguous, soft whisperings just outside the ears are not uncommon in psychotic patients. For instance, Pat Deegan's tapes for her "Hearing Voices" curriculum, created to enable non-voice hearers to develop empathy for those who hear distressing voices, begin with those sounds. A woman (not in the church, but in a housing program for people with substance abuse and serious mental illness) described her first, terrifying psychotic episode to me as the experience of listening to a field of rats, scratching and squeaking, rushing towards her.

And yet August did tell stories about images and their power during prayer that were much like those told by the other prayer warriors. She led a course on prayer that I took (it was meant to equip you to pray for people as a member of the prayer team in church). She cautioned us never to give concrete advice after prayer, and never to prophesy about birth, death, or marriage, a move that a skeptic might see as a hedge, but which is understood within the church as a caution from the human fallibility of prayer. Then she went on to tell a story about violating the rules. She was then, she said, quite inexperienced, and she was pretty uncertain about what she was doing. She didn't have enough experience to trust her intuition. She was praying after church for a woman, someone she didn't know, and as she prayed she began to get images of a child. Do you have children?, she asked the woman, and the woman said no. Nor had she nieces or nephews. Augusta continued to pray, but her images of children were so powerful and persistent that finally she blurted out (as she told the story) that "a child will come into your life." She felt awful afterwards, she said. She'd just broken one of the cardinal rules. She felt like fool, too, that she'd misused the woman's trust and failed the most basic task that God had directed her towards. But a month later, the woman came back to church and came up to her and thanked her, because she'd been pregnant when Augusta had prayed for her and she hadn't known it. The point, of course, is that those unexpected images you get in prayer may well be God speaking to you directly.

Spirituality and Gardner's Eight Criteria

Despite these exceptions, there is enough evidence here to take seriously the hypothesis that the Tellegen absorption scale taps some capacity to have visual images, to concentrate on inner stimuli, and to enter altered states—and some comfort, on the part of the individual, with these capacities. Because a positive response to the scale requires both some of these capacities (to answer honestly) and some degree of comfort with them (to admit the honest answer) one can call the scale a measurement of the proclivity to absorption. In the absence of experimental work on training absorption, I infer from the large body of ethnographic and historical work that this proclivity can be trained, and that the attempt to train absorption is central to most serious attempts to generate spiritual experience. But does trained absorption meet Howard's eight criteria for an intelligence? For the most part, yes, at least if you include the evidence about hypnosis and dissociation.

Is There Potential Isolation by Brain Damage?

Some studies suggest that religiosity in general and trance states in particular are associated with activity in the temporal lobe, and there is a strong associated between epilepsy and religiosity (Waxman and Geschwind 1975; Bear and Fedio 1977; Mandel 1980; Geschwind 1983; Persinger 2001). Dissociative disorders in which flashbacks and altered states play a prior role, such as PTSD, are arguably other examples of an assault to the body which leads to the increased use of absorption, and an emerging body of research argues that emotional trauma may generate pseudoseizures (non epileptic seizures) with dissociative disorder symptom profiles (Harden 1997; Bowman and Markand 1996).

Are There Idiots Savants, Prodigies, and Other Exceptional Individuals?

There clearly have been individuals throughout the ages famous for their ability to withdraw into distinct and seemingly observable altered states and, while in them, to have powerful experiences they have called spiritual. These are, of course, the mystics. The sixteenth-century St. Theresa of Avila is a prominent example of someone known not only for the fact of her prayer, but for her capacity to entered deeply into an absorbed state. Of the "fourth degree of prayer" she says, "[the soul] dissolves utterly . . . to rest more and more in God" (in Happold 1963, p. 353).

Is There an Identifiable Core Operation or Set of Operations?

Yes, absorption is the capacity to focus inwardly and to ignore external sensory stimuli. The 'gold standard' test for hypnotizability, the Stanford

C, is in fact a progressive test of the ability to ignore external distractions and to attend to an internal imagined stimulus.

Is There a Distinctive Developmental History?

There is a developmental history to hypnosis, although the data do not make that much sense to me. It has been know for some time that all children are highly hypnotizable (Spiegel and Spiegel 2004). This begins to change at puberty, and people develop different degrees of hypnotizability which are thought from that point on to be extremely stable. One well known study followed once-Stanford undergraduates for ten, fifteen and then twenty five years and found that their scores on the Stanford C were extremely stable, more so that the scores of IQ tests (Piccione *et al.* 1989). One of the awkward gaps in the research literature, however, is that there are few studies that attempt to train people in absorption tasks, and test them before and afterwards for hypnotizability; there are even very few such studies looking at training effects in visualization. (Fromm and Katz 1990, who did a training study on students who were highly hypnotizable, did find training effects in the experienced depth of trance and on the vividness of visual imagery.) And clearly there are identifiable 'end-state' experts, although exactly what that expert looks like will vary with the cultural setting: an adept for a magician, a priest or priestess for a possession cult member, a prayer warrior for a Vineyard church member.

Is There Support from Experimental Psychological Tasks?

Yes, hypnotic induction is such a task, as are experiments in self hypnosis (Fromm and Katz 1990), meditation (Austin 1999) and so forth.

Is There Support from Psychometric Findings?

Yes, that is the Tellegen absorption scale.

Is There Susceptibility to an Encoding in a Symbolic System?

Well, that is a little harder, unless one includes the detailed accounting in various religious texts of the progressive depth of absorption. The Visuddhimagga is an example of such a progressive encoding of increasingly absorbed meditation states (Goleman 1974).

And yet there is a significant caveat: the psychological capacity that I see as central to so much spiritual experience is not, after all, unique to that experience. The trance state which I believe is produced by trained absorption is also produced by significant emotional trauma. People who have frightening car accidents can find themselves looking down on their bodies as if from above, as can terrified and inadequately anesthetized patients in operating rooms and soldiers during combat. Perhaps spiritual experience is one of those evolutionary spandrels, an ability accidentally produced by or co-opted from an ability which evolved to serve some other need. It would have been helpful, in our ancestral past, to be able to walk home on a broken ankle, or to fight without emotion, despite our terror. Perhaps that ability to separate ordinary self and emotion from awareness by focused absorption then became the means by which a sense of extraordinary otherness emerged. Spiritual experience may be an accident of the complexity of human consciousness—though if it is, that accident says nothing about the ontological reality of the divine. One thinks of Rousseau, whose great spiritual experience came when he was knocked down by a rampaging dog, and who woke into a temporarily disconnected state of absorption.

> Night was coming on. I saw the sky, some stars, and a few leaves. The first sensation was a moment of delight. I was conscious of nothing else. In this instant I was being born again, and it seemed as if all I perceived was filled with my frail existence. Entirely taken up by the present, I could remember nothing; I had no distinct notion of myself as a person, nor had I the least idea of what had just happened to me. I did not know who I was, nor where I was; I felt neither pain, fear, nor anxiety. I watched my blood flowing as I might have watched a stream, without even thinking that the blood had anything to do with me. I felt throughout my whole being such a wonderful calm, that whenever I recall this feeling I can find nothing to compare with it in all the pleasures that stir our lives. (1979, p. 39)

Whatever Howard concludes about absorption and the argument I present here for its role in spiritual experience, I have gained enormously from our conversations over the years, and the discussions we had back at Stanford have shaped my thinking in powerful ways. It has been an honor to be his friend.

REFERENCES

Austin, J.H. 1999. Zen and the Brain. Cambridge, Massachusetts: MIT Press.

Bear, D., and P. Fedio. 1977. Quantitative Analysis of Interictal Behavior in Temporal Lobe Epilepsy." *Archives of Neurology* 34, pp. 454–467.

Beyer, S. 1978. The Cult of Tara. Berkeley: University of California Press.

Bliss, E. 1984. Multiple Personality: A Report of Fourteen Cases with Implications for Schizophrenia and Hysteria. *Archives of General Psychiatry* 174, pp. 727–734.

Bourguignon, E. 1979. Hallucination and Trance: An Anthropologist's Perspective. In W. Keup, *Origins and Mechanisms of Hallucinations* (New York: Plenum), pp. 183–190.

Bowman, E. S., and O.N. Markand. 1996. Psychodynamics and Psychiatric Diagnoses of Pseudoseizure subjects. *American Journal of Psychiatry* 153: 1, pp. 57–63.

Butler, L., E. Duran, P. Jasiukaitus, C. Koopman, and D. Spiegel. 1996. Hypnotizability and Traumatic Experience. *American Journal of Psychiatry* 153:1, pp. 42–63.

Carruthers, M. 1998. The Craft of Thought: Meditation, Rhetoric, and the Making of Images. Cambridge: Cambridge University Press.

Claridge, G., ed. 1997. *Schizotypy*. Oxford: Oxford University Press.

Crocker, C. 1985. Vital Souls. Tucson: University of Arizona Press.

Csikszentmihalyi, M. 1990. Flow: The Psychology of Optimal Experience. New York: Harper and Row.

Evans-Pritchard, E.E. 1937. Witchcraft, Oracles, and Magic among the Azande. Oxford: Oxford University Press.

Frischholz, E., L. Lipman, B. Braun, and R. Sachs. 1992. Psychopathology, Hypnotizability and Dissociation. *American Journal of Psychiatry* 149, pp. 1521–25.

Fromm, E., and S. Katz. 1990. Self-Hypnosis. New York: Guilford Press.

Geschwind, N. 1983. Interictal Behavior Changes in Epilepsy. *Epilepsia* 24 (Supplement 1), pp. S23–S30.

Glisky, M., D. Tataryn, K. McConkey, B. Tobias, and J. Kihlstrom. 1991. Absorption, Openness to Experience, and Hypnotizability. *Journal of Personality and Social Psychology* 60, pp. 263–272.

Goleman, D. 1974. *The Varieties of the Meditative Experience*. New York: Dutton.

Happold, F.C., ed. 1963. *Mysticism*. Harmondsworth: Penguin.

Harden, C.L. 1977. Pseudoseizures and Dissociative Disorders: A Common Mechanism Involving Traumatic Experiences. *Seizure* 6: 2, pp. 151–55.

Hilgard, E, 1977. Divided Consciousness: Multiple Controls in Human Thought and Action. New York: Wiley.

Kihlstrom, J. 1996. Convergence in Understanding Hypnosis? *International Journal of Clinical and Experimental Hypnosis* 45: 3, pp. 324–331.

Krippner, S., and S. Powers, eds. 1997. Broken Images, Broken Selves. Washington, D.C.: Brunner-Mazel.

Luhrmann, T.M. 1989. Persuasions of the Witch's Craft. Cambridge, Massachusetts: Harvard University Press.

———. 2004. Yearning for God: Trance as a Culturally Specific Practice and Its Implications for Understanding Dissociative Disorders. *Journal of Trauma and Dissociation* 5, pp. 101–129.

Mandel, A. 1980. Toward a Psychobiology of Transcendence: God in the Brain. In J. Davidson and R. Davidson, eds., The Psychobiology of Consciousness (New York: Plenum), pp. 379–464.

McCrae, R., and P. Costa. 1983. Joint Factors in Self-reports and Ratings: Neuroticism, Extraversion, and Openness to Experience. *Personality and Individual Differences* 4, pp. 245–255.

Nadon, R., I. Hoyt, P. Register, and J. Kihlstrom. 1991. Absorption and Hypnotizability. *Journal of Personality and Social Psychology* 60, pp. 144–153.

Nell, V. 1988. The Psychology of Reading for Pleasure. *Reading Research Quarterly* 23, pp. 6–50.

Pekala, R.C., C.F. Wenger, and R. Levine. 1985. Individual Differences in Phenomenological Experience: States of Consciousness as a Function of Absorption. *Journal of Personality and Social Psychology* 48, pp. 125–132.

Persinger, M. 2001. The Neuropsychiatry of Paranormal Experiences. *Journal of Neuropsychiatry* 13, pp. 515–524.

Piccione, C., E.R. Hilgard, *et.al.* 1989. On the Degree of Stability of Measured Hypnotizability over a 25 Year Period. *Journal of Personality and Social Psychology* 56, pp. 289–295.

Roche, S., and K. McConkey. 1990. Absorption: Nature, Assessment, Correlates. *Journal of Personality and Social Psychology* 59, pp. 91–101.

Rousseau, J.-J. 1979. *Reveries of the Solitary Walker*. Harmonsdworth: Penguin.

Snodgrass, M., and S. Lynn. 1989. Music Absorption and Hypnotizability. *International Journal of Clinical and Experimental Hypnosis* 37, pp. 41–54.

Tellegen, A. 1981. Practicing the Two Disciplines for Relaxation and Enlightenment: Comment on Qualls and Sheehan. *Journal of Eperimental Psychology: General* 110, pp. 217≠226.,

Tellegen, A., and G. Atkinson. 1974. Openness to Absorption and Self altering Experiences ('Absorption'): A Trait Related to Hypnotic Susceptibility. *Journal of Abnormal Psychology* 83, pp. 268–277.

Virkler, M., and P. Virkler. 1986. *Dialogue with God*. Gainesville: BridgeLogos.

Waxman, S.G., and N. Geschwind. 1975. The Interictal Syndrome of Temporal Lobe Epilepsy. *Archives of General Psychiatry* 32: 12, pp. 1580–86.

Whalen, J., and M. Nash. 1996. Hypnosis and Dissociation: Theoretical, Empirical, and Clinical Perspectives. In L. Michelson and W. Ray, eds., Handbook of Dissociation (New York: Plenum), pp. 191–206.

Wild, T.C., D. Kuiken, and D. Schopflocher. 1995. The Role of Absorption in Experiential Involvement. *Journal of Personality and Social Psychology* 69, pp. 569–579.

Willard, D. 1999. *Hearing God*. Downer's Grove: Intervarsity Press.

Wilson, S., and T. Barber. 1983. The fantasy-prone Personality. In A. Sheikh, ed., *Imagery: Current Theory, Research, and Application*. New York: Wiley.

7

Creativity in *Creating Minds*

DEAN KEITH SIMONTON

Although Howard Gardner would not consider creativity his core area of research, he nonetheless has been a prolific and influential contributor to that topic. The PsycINFO electronic database maintained by the American Psychological Association lists about two dozen contributions, and this likely represents a serious underestimate given the multidisciplinary nature of his scholarly output. These publications include chapters in some important edited volumes on creativity, such as Sternberg's (1988) *The Nature of Creativity* (Gardner 1988), Brockman's 1993 *Creativity: The Reality Club IV* (Gardner 1993b), Boden's (1994) *Dimensions of Creativity* (Gardner 1994), and Sternberg's 1999 *Handbook of Creativity* (Policastro and Gardner 1999). Moreover, Gardner's interest in creativity as a phenomenon is evident in his other professional activities. For example, he has served for many years on the editorial boards of the two leading journals in the field— the *Journal of Creative Behavior* and the *Creativity Research Journal*— and on the executive advisory board for the *Encyclopedia of Creativity*, the definitive reference work on the topic (Runco and Pritzker 1999). Hence, Gardner can certainly be said to have earned the credentials of a highly visible "creativity researcher."

But what exactly is the nature of his contributions? What is the impact of his ideas on creativity research? Which of his discoveries are most likely to survive the test of time? To help address such questions I wish to focus my attention on a solitary publication: *Creating Minds: An*

Anatomy of Creativity Seen through the Lives of Freud, Einstein, Picasso, Stravinsky, Eliot, Graham, and Gandhi (Gardner 1993a). I have selected this book for two major reasons. First, unlike many psychologists who take the journal article as the primary means of scientific communication, Gardner clearly finds books a more convivial publication vehicle (Gardner 2002). Second, there can be no doubt that this book can be considered his most influential single writing on creativity. This conclusion is evident in the attention it has received in the professional literature—well over a hundred citations since its publication.

Given that focus, I wish to write what might be considered a retrospective book review. I start by providing an overview of the book's contents and key ideas. I then provide a critique of those ideas.

Overview

The book can be considered like a sandwich. More specifically, it consists of three parts, the second part rather thicker than either the first or the last, and containing the hugest portion of the intellectual meat. In terms of page counts, Part I consists of forty-five pages, Part II of 309, and Part III of forty-nine pages—a genuine Dagwood sandwich in which the center is three times the size of the end pieces combined. Let me provide the details about this creative concoction.

Part I: Introduction

Gardner opens the book with two chapters that provide the foundation for the rest of the book. The first entitled "Chance Encounters in Wartime Zurich" provides basis for selecting the seven creative minds that provide the raw data for the psychological analysis: Sigmund Freud, Albert Einstein, Pablo Picasso, Igor Stravinsky, T.S. Eliot, Martha Graham, and Mahatma Gandhi. Given this research sample, Gardner then presents his goals in writing the book. These are three. First, he wants to tease out the patterns that underlie the breakthroughs that each of these creators were able to achieve. Second, he wishes to use these seven exemplars to discern the more general characteristics of exceptional creativity. Third, and perhaps a bit discrepant from the first two, Gardner seeks to draw conclusions about the nature of the "modern era," with these creators located at a pivotal point in that era—the point, indeed, at which it became truly modern. Then the author presents the main organizing themes that will permeate his analysis of the seven figures, and discusses some of the problems in trying to capture the essence of a historical period.

Unlike what holds for the first chapter, the second chapter has a title that makes it quite explicit what it is all about: "Approaches to Creativity." After observing that "the study of creativity shadows the study of intelligence" (p. 19), Gardner describes the main research strategies, namely, the cognitive, personality-motivational (encompassing the psychoanalytic, behaviorist, and intrinsic motivational), and the historiometric. This establishes the background for discussing his approach to the study of creativity. This consists of four distinct components that can be characterized as organizing themes, an organizing framework, some issues for empirical investigation, and two emerging themes. The last, especially the "Faustian bargain," embody ideas that surfaced during the course of Gardner's immersion in the primary biographical data.

Part II: The Creators of the Modern Era

The sample, goals, and methods of the inquiry thus defined, Gardner proceeds to the most substantial ingredient of this offering: seven chapters on the seven creators of the modern era. Actually, the chapters are arranged into three clusters, each cluster followed by an "interlude" that analyzes what has just transpired. The first cluster treats "Sigmund Freud: Alone with the World" and "Albert Einstein: The Perennial Child," the second cluster "Pablo Picasso: Prodigiousness and Beyond," "Igor Stravinsky: The Poetics and Politics of Music," and "T.S. Eliot: The Marginal Master," and the final cluster "Martha Graham: Discovering the Dance of America" and "Mahatma Gandhi: A Hold upon Others." Notice that the subtitles for each chapter provide a sort of thumbnail summary of each creator's key characteristic or core contribution. Nevertheless, each of the seven chapters is rich in biographical details and psychological observations. Indeed, each chapter is almost as long as the entire length of either Part I or Part II. It's like a Dagwood sandwich in which each slice of meat, cheese, lettuce, and tomato is about as thick as each slice of bread.

Part III: Conclusion

Most sandwiches have the same type of bread on top and bottom. Gardner's product does not. The first slice is white bread, the last slice whole wheat. I say this even though it consists of only one *bona fide* chapter on "Creativity across the Domains" plus an epilogue on "The Modern Era and Beyond." The latter treats issues that are more peripheral to evaluating Gardner's contributions to our understanding of creativity, and thus can be ignored. The former, in contrast, counts as the single most significant chapter in the entire book. Here the author returns to the organizing framework outlined in Chapter 2, provides a prototypical profile of the exceptional creator, deals with several critical issues, discusses the two emerging themes, and raises some additional issues. Most of the critique that follows will concentrate on the observations and speculations contained in this concluding chapter.

Critique

Before I launch into the evaluation, I must confess my limitations as an evaluator. Those limitations stem from the fact that Gardner's *Creating Minds* is actually two books, not one. On the one hand, it can be considered a work of history and biography—an attempt to describe the nature of the modern era and seven creators who helped defined the nature of that era. Indeed, Part II of the book, the section that dominates the page counts, can be viewed largely as a collection of seven biographies. If one edited out anything that refers to creativity as a general phenomenon, I doubt that the length of these chapters would be reduced very substantially. Even so, my competence to evaluate these biographical essays is minimal. In fact, for most of the seven figures my main knowledge comes from reading this book rather than any outside reading (Freud, Einstein, and Stravinsky constituting the sole exceptions). On the other hand, Gardner's contribution can be viewed as a scientific investigation into creativity. That is, it purports to be a work of social science in general and psychological science in particular. As a psychologist who has studied creativity for over thirty years, and who has published over two hundred articles and books on the subject, I feel much more capable of judging the merits of Gardner's ideas from a scientific perspective. It is for that reason that my critique focuses on the two slices of bread rather than the cold cuts, cheese, lettuce, and tomato.

That constraint in mind, I will concentrate on the following features of Gardner's book: its methodological approach and its substantive findings.

Methodological Approach

Gardner chose to study creativity by adopting a rather distinct method. To appreciate the nature of the departure, it is necessary to realize that most psychological research—including most research on creativity—is conducted on college students who volunteer to participate in laboratory experiments or correlational studies. Those who serve as participants in experiments are usually given problems to solve, the experimenter manipulating the nature of the problems or the conditions in which those problems must be solved (see for example Smith, Ward, and Finke 1995; Sternberg and Davidson 1995). Those who participate in correlational studies will be given a battery of cognitive tests, personality inventories, and other psychometric instruments (see for instance Cattell and Drevdahl 1955; Feist 1993, 1997). No matter what the specific details, one thing is certain: Such research is dedicated to investigating everyday forms of creativity, not the kinds of creativity that make people famous for their creative achievements. Creativity researchers often express this contrast as that between "little-c" creativity and "Big-C" Creativity. Given the seven creators that provide the basis for Gardner's inquiry, it is manifest that he is studying Big-C Creativity. These seven can be considered unchallengeable exemplars of the phenomenon.

Although Gardner's concentration on Big-C creators is distinctive, it is not unique. Psychologists have devised a number of approaches to studying eminent individuals, including big-name exemplars of creativity (Simonton 1999b). Of these approaches, the following four stand out:

1. *Historiometric method*—The oldest approach is historiometry, a technique in which biographical and historical data about a large sample of eminent individuals are subjected to quantitative measurement and statistical analysis (Simonton 1990). The first historiometric investigation was conducted by Quételet in 1835, albeit the first classic historiometric study was published by Galton in 1869. As Gardner (1993a) points out in Chapter 2, this is the methodology that I have used in the vast majority of my own studies of creative genius (see Simonton 1984b).

2. *Psychometric method*—Here eminent individuals are subjected to psychological assessment using a variety of questionnaires, interviews, tests, and inventories. The first example was Galton's (1874) study of a sample of famous British scientists, but the technique did not really become common until the latter half of the twentieth century. Representative investigations include Roe's 1953 study of sixty-four

eminent scientists and the inquiries into distinguished writers, architects, and mathematicians conducted at the Institute for Personality Assessment and Research at the University of California at Berkeley (for example Barron 1969; MacKinnon 1978).

3. *Psychobiographical method*—Freud's 1910 psychoanalysis of Leonardo da Vinci constitutes the classic instance of this approach. Although psychobiography has tended to concentrate on political leaders (Tetlock, Crosby, and Crosby 1981), a fair number have looked at eminent creators, such as Beethoven, Darwin, Dickinson, Dostoyevsky, Goethe, Poe, Newton, Nietzsche, Shakespeare, Socrates, and Van Gogh.

4. *Comparative method*—This is essentially the method used by Gardner (1993a). A collection of distinguished figures is subjected to various comparisons and contrasts. Usually the number of luminaries is kept small to render the analysis more manageable. In an inclusive sense, this approach can be said to date back to Plutarch's classic *Parallel Lives* of eminent Greeks and Romans, albeit comparative studies by psychologists are more recent. For instance, Hershman and Lieb's (1988) studied the relation between manic-depression and creativity by conducting connected case studies of Newton, Beethoven, Dickens, and Van Gogh (see also McCurdy 1960; Rothenberg 1987).

These methods have different advantages and disadvantages, as well as distinct goals and functions (Simonton 1999b). To understand better the nature of the contrasts, let us examine the following issues: sampling, measurement, and inference.

Sampling. Any psychological study of creativity must begin with an appropriate sample. In the case of the four approaches described above, two issues have to be addressed. First, how is the sample of eminent creators to be selected? Second, how large should the sample be? For historiometric and psychometric research the answer to the first question is to sample systematically from a given population. Most commonly, the subjects for study are selected according to some eminence criterion. Thus, historiometric subjects are often chosen according to the amount of space assigned various creators in standard reference works (for instance Cox 1926; Galton, 1869; Murray 2003) while psychometric subjects are often selected because they have won major honors or because they were identified as top creators by experts in the field (for example Helson 1980; Roe 1953; Zuckerman 1977). Historiometric and psychometric methods also have similar answers to the second question: Obtain as big of a sample as possible. Hence, historiometric samples typically encompass a hundred or more creators (for example Cox 1926;

Raskin 1936; Simonton 1980), while psychometric samples usually involve dozens of creators (for instance Cattell and Drevdahl 1955; Feist 1997; Roe 1953). Historiometric samples tend to be much larger than psychometric samples because historiometric studies can include deceased celebrities and because psychometric studies must face severe logistic problems in the assessment of contemporary celebrities.

Psychobiographical and comparative investigations answer the two core sampling questions in a very different way. First, the sampling is less systematic, the creators being chosen largely because they are intrinsically fascinating. This is especially true in the case of psychobiography in which a creator may be studied largely because he or she has some personality quirk. For instance, Van Gogh has inspired lots of psychobiographers to tackle the problem of why he cut off a portion of his ear (Runyan 1981). Second, the samples in psychobiography and comparative studies are less ample than found in historiometric studies—just a single case in psychobiography and a dozen or less in comparative studies. In the specific case of Gardner's *Creating Minds*, the creators were not selected by some objective scheme—such as eminence scores or expert ratings—but rather according to a subjective judgment of (a) who best represented each type of intelligence in his theory of multiple intelligences (Gardner 1983) and (b) who best characterized certain core features of the modern era (Gardner 1993a). Moreover, there are just seven creators, rather than a dozen or even hundreds.

The sampling contrasts are important because the conclusions drawn in any empirical inquiry presume that the sample is representative of the phenomenon under investigation. There are two ways to ensure this goal in studies of Big-C creators. First, study a large sample of such creators. Second, make sure that those sampled include the most distinguished exemplars. Because Gardner's (1993a) inquiry includes only seven creative minds, it becomes especially urgent that they be representative. In fairness, Gardner himself is aware of this fact and makes some effort to deal with the issue (see p. 388). Nevertheless, it is conceivable that some of his conclusions might have changed had he obtained a sample of creators that was more representative of the larger population of outstanding creators. Let me give one example.

Gardner (1993a) has inferred that the productive output of each of his seven creators displays a similar life pattern, what he has called the "Ten-Year Rule" (see especially 371). Specifically, each seemed to conceive a major creative product—whether radical breakthrough or comprehensive work—every ten years. The first landmark work would come ten years into the career, the second after twenty years, and the third after thirty years. In the case of Picasso, for example, the three creative achievements are marked by *Les demoiselles d'Avignon* and Cubism (radical breakthroughs) in the first decade, the Neoclassical style in the second decade, and *Guernica* (a comprehensive work) in the third decade of his career. Similar spacing of notable creations is shown for Freud, Einstein, Stravinsky, Eliot, Graham, and Gandhi. So the inference appears plausible. However, can this Ten-Year Rule be generalized to other exemplary creators besides these seven?

Extensive historiometric research suggests otherwise. The economist David Galenson (2005) has conducted a series of investigations into large samples of painters from the Renaissance to the modern era. He discovered that painters display two distinct styles of creativity: the conceptual and experimental. The former carefully plan their work in advance, compose paintings that embody artistic breakthroughs, make contributions relatively early in their careers, and tend to be known for a small number of distinct works. The latter tinker around as they paint, slowly developing their ideas in a series of paintings, attain their career peaks relatively late, and may not have any single work stand out above the rest but instead are known for a complete body of work. Significantly, Picasso was identified as the typical conceptual painter in a manner compatible with Gardner's analysis. Yet Paul Cezanne exemplified the typical experimental artist.

In additional analyses Galenson (2005) showed that this conceptual-experimental distinction applies to other forms of artistic creativity, including sculpture, poetry, novels, and film. In fact, T.S. Eliot was specifically shown to be a conceptual poet. Although Galenson did not deal with musical or choreographic creativity, it seems probably that the same distinction applies in those domains as well. Indeed, the contrast between conceptual and experimental creativity may extend into the sciences. For instance, where Einstein might be considered a conceptual scientist, Enrico Fermi could be viewed as an experimental scientist—a physicist whose ideas slowly evolved rather than appearing in major paradigm shifts. If this contrast applies to all forms of creativity, then it is possible that the Ten-Year Rule is only relevant to conceptual creators. The experimental creators, by comparison, would not have their careers so easily demarcated by discrete and qualitatively distinct achievements.

If Gardner (1993a) had collected a larger sample of creators, he probably would have realized that the Ten-Year Rule might not be applicable to all creative minds. Even if he had only sampled two painters from the modern era, he would have been obliged to include Cezanne, and thereby encounter an experimental artist whose career output violates the rule. At least that would be the case if the painters were sampled according to their eminence, for Cezanne rates as the second most famous painter of the twentieth century (Murray 2003, p. 137). This illustrates one of the advantages of historiometric and psychometric approaches to the study of exemplary creativity. Given that they typically operate with samples several times larger than comparative investigation, the investigator can have more confidence that any conclusions are truly representative of Big-C creators in general. Indeed, historiometric investigations will sometimes sample *all* creators who have attained any distinction in a given domain, thus ensuring the generalizability of any inferences. Examples include studies of 2,012 philosophers (Simonton 1976), 2,026 scientists (Simonton 1991a), 696 classical composers (Simonton 1977b), and 772 painters and sculptors (Simonton 1984a). Results derived from these large-sample investigations cannot possibly be idiosyncratic to a handful of creative individuals.

Measurement. Galenson's 2005 study differs from Gardner's 1993a in another crucial manner: the conclusions in the former were based on objective measurement rather than subjective judgment. For instance, Galenson determined the life cycle of creative output in experimental and conceptual artists by introducing quantitative measures of a painting's aesthetic impact. The latter variable was quantified according to a diversity of operational definitions, such as how much the work was sold for in open auctions and the number of times the work appears in reference works (see also Simonton 1980; 1998a). As already mentioned, objective quantification is characteristic of both historiometric and psychometric research—as the roots "metric" in both words implies. Comparative and psychobiographical investigations, by comparison, tend to favor qualitative analyses (Simonton 1999b).

Quantitative measurement has several advantages over qualitative evaluation (Simonton 2003). In the first place, quantification obliges the researcher to define concepts and variables in a more rigorous and precise manner. Something cannot be measured without first providing an operational definition of what needs to be measured. Measurement consists of counts, and nothing can be counted until the researcher defines what counts and what does not count. Furthermore, quantified measures permit the use of statistical analyses that enable an investigator to determine objectively the direction and magnitude of relationship between two variables. These analyses even allow the relationship between two variables to be assessed after introducing controls for the possible contaminating effects of other variables (Simonton 1990). Finally, the superior objectivity and power of quantitative analyses can lead to inferences that qualitative analyses, with their more intuitive approach, either get wrong or overlook entirely.

To offer an illustration, many psychobiographers have offered explanations for why King George III of Great Britain suffered from recurrent bouts of mental illness (Runyan 1988). Yet these accounts are predicated on the assumption that the emotional breakdowns did not result from stressful events in the monarch's personal and political life, a premise insecurely founded on the mere qualitative scan of the historical record (Simonton 1989a). When the same record is subjected to quantitative measurement and statistical analysis, this assumption turns out to be unwarranted (Simonton 1998b). Not only did the appearance of these pathological episodes follow the intrusion of extremely stressful life events, but also the magnitude of the relationship between the two variables is about the same size as found in empirical research on everyday populations.

It is not unlikely that comparative studies, such as Gardner's 1993a, might also benefit by replacing qualitative with quantitative analysis. May one example suffice to show how. Gardner (1993a) argued that the seven creators in his study could have benefited from a "fruitful asynchrony." This signifies a lack of fit between the individual creator, the creator's domain or discipline of achievement, and the field, that is, the colleagues active in the same domain who must ultimately evaluate the creator's contributions. "Pure synchrony," in contrast, means that the individual, the domain, and the field exhibit intermesh very smoothly and completely.

Although Gardner (1993a) did an impressive job documenting the asynchronies in his sampled creators, it is not apparent how much faith can be placed in this factor. How important is its contribution? What is the relative impact of different types of asynchronies, such as that between the individual and the field versus the individual and the domain?

Unlike the case of King George's maladies, I know of no quantitative investigations that explicitly scrutinize the place of asynchrony in exceptional creativity. Nonetheless, a few historiometric studies have tested hypotheses that bear a clear connection with Gardner's (1993a) conjecture. For instance, an inquiry into the differential eminence of 2,012 Western philosophers showed that the more illustrious thinkers were more likely to advocate positions that were inconsistent with the views maintained by most of their contemporaries (Simonton 1976). Another study of 479 classical composers indicated that their most successful works—at least in the long term—tended to depart from the stylistic conventions that defined the era in which they worked (Simonton 1980). Finally, an investigation of fifty-four eminent psychologists demonstrated that whose who had the most long-term impact had a higher likelihood of advocating extremist positions on the big questions that dominate psychological research (Simonton 2000b). Hence, there appears to be some historiometric support for the conclusions drawn from Gardner's comparative study.

These historiometric inquiries, besides finding some evidence for the positive impact of asynchrony, also feature assets unique to quantitative methods. For example, the relationships between asynchrony and eminence are estimated while introducing statistical controls for possible contaminating or confounding factors. Just as significant, the statistical analyses also provide explicit and precise information about the substantive importance of the relationship. For instance, the study of Western philosophers showed that the asynchrony between the thinker's beliefs and those of his or her contemporaries accounted for a little bit more than one percent of the variation in a philosopher's ultimate eminence (Simonton 1976). Hence, asynchrony has some role to play, but the role is not all that substantial. For example, the number of philosophical issues addressed by a given thinker has over five times the impact as the degree of asynchrony. Needless to say, this latter comparison could only be made using a quantitative approach, such as that favored by historiometric and psychometric research.

Inference. In one respect, the foregoing discussion was a little misleading. Quantitative studies of exemplary creators cannot draw any useful conclusions without there being appreciable variation in the degree of creativity exhibited in the sampled individuals. In psychometric research, this necessity is often attained by assessing two groups, one consisting of exceptional creators and another made up of a control group who are comparable in terms of gender, age, and geographic origins but who are otherwise undistinguished (for instance Barron 1969). In historiometric research, this same requirement is met by gathering a sample of creators who vary immensely in the level of achieved eminence. For instance, the eminence of the 2,012 philosophers ranged from Xenocrates to Aristotle and from Henri du Roy to Descartes (Simonton 1976). Similarly, the study of 772 artists had representatives ranging from Hendrick Bloemaert to Michelangelo (Simonton 1984a). If all of the sampled persons in psychometric and historiometric studies had the same degree of distinction, no conclusions could be drawn about the factors that contribute to creative achievement. Although the eminent who defined the sample might have certain traits or experiences in common, these attributes might be shared with all individuals making contributions to the same domain (Simonton 1986b).

The need for variance raises an inferential problem for both psychobiographical and comparative methods, approaches with rather diminutive samples sizes. In the psychobiography there is no variation at all, whereas in the comparative approach the variation is minimal. This certainly holds for Gardner's (1993a) seven creative intellects. Each of the seven is responsible for supreme achievements in his or her respective field. None can be considered an also-ran, and certainly none is a virtual nonentity. Accordingly, given this homogeneous sample it is not logically possible to infer the factors that differentiate these seven luminaries from far lesser lights. In concrete terms, consider the following contrasting pairs of contemporaries who created in the same domain and yet who have dramatically contrasting reputations: Albert Einstein versus Friedrich Hasenöhrl, Sigmund Freud versus Emile Coué, Eliot versus Robinson Jeffers, Igor Stravinsky versus Karol Szymanowski, and Pablo Picasso versus Carlo Carra. The comparative method, lacking a control or comparison group of lesser figures, cannot discern why the first member of each pair was evidently much more creative than the second member. As a result, the method is insufficient to support some of the substantive conclusions Gardner ventured in *Creating Minds*.

As a case in point, consider Gardner's (1993a) inference regarding what he calls the "Faustian Bargain." That is,

> in one way or another, each of the creators became embedded in some kind of a bargain, deal, or Faustian arrangement, executed as a means of ensuring the preservation of his or her unusual gifts. In general, the creators were so caught up in the pursuit of their work mission that they sacrificed all, especially the possibility of a rounded personal existence. (p. 44)

For the moment let us ignore the conceptual ambiguities inherent in this inductive conclusion. What concerns us here is what this actually tells us about creativity. Granted that the seven all engaged in the Faustian Bargain, does that engagement set these creators apart from Hasenöhrl, Coué, Jeffers, Szymanowski, and Carra? Does the degree of commitment to that bargain separate the latter from other figures in the same field who never came close to attaining even minimal acclaim? There is absolutely no way of answering these questions because his sample consists solely of the cream of the crop, completely ignoring those in the dregs.

Substantive Findings

Gardner's 1993a book is rich in claims about the nature of the creative person. In fact, I know of no investigation using the comparative approach that surpasses this work in the depth and range of insights. At the same time, it should now be evident that the comparative approach suffers from certain methodological limitations that might render some of these conclusions less convincing that might hold otherwise. Even so, some of these statements have received confirmation from investigations using alternative approaches to the scientific study of exemplary creators. Other statements have not been confirmed, and even disconfirmed. Consequently, in this final stage in my evaluation of Gardner's 1993a work I would like to indicate which of his conclusions have received confirmation and which still await empirical verification. To accomplish this task, I will focus on the propositions that delineate "A Portrait of the Exemplary Creator" in the last chapter (pp. 360–363). Gardner was "struck by the extent to which common themes ... emerge in the lives of these creators" and therefore he felt "comfortable in putting forth a portrait of the Exemplary Creator, whom I shall nickname E.C. and speak of as female" (p. 360). The specific features of this portrait can be grouped into three categories: confirmed, unconfirmed, and disconfirmed.

Confirmed

Several of Gardner's generalizations have received partial or complete endorsement in other empirical studies using either historiometric or psychometric methods. In particular, I would like to document the following dozen confirmations:

1. "E.C. comes from a locale somewhat removed from the actual centers of power and influence of her society, but not so far away that she and her family are entirely ignorant of what is going on elsewhere" (Gardner 1993a, p. 360). Galton (1874) was the first to study this question, using a sample of eminent British scientists. Although he concluded that these creators were more likely to be born in urban rather than rural settings (see also Eiduson 1962), Galton did not correct for population size. In other words, do metropolitan areas produce more outstanding creators on a per capita basis? Most studies show that small towns may be more productive of great scientists than big cities (Cattell 1910; Poffenberger 1930; but see Berry 1981). At the same time there is reason to believe that one can be born too far away from the intellectu-

al, cultural, aesthetic centers. At least the adverse effect of such provincial origins has been found in classical composers (Simonton 1977b, 1986a). Although more research needs to be done on this issue, tentative support exists for this feature of the E.C. profile.

2. "The family is neither wealthy nor in dire financial straits, and life for the young creator is reasonably comfortable, in a material sense" (Gardner 1993a, pp. 360–361). Galton (1874) was again the first researcher to address this question, finding that nearly three quarters of his eminent scientists had fathers who engaged in either business or professional occupations. Similar results have obtained for other studies of distinguished contributors to the sciences (Eiduson 1962; Roe 1953), including Nobel laureates (Berry 1981; Zuckerman 1977). However, when the samples of creators are extended to achievement domains beyond science, professional and business backgrounds become a bit less predominant (Cox 1926; Ellis 1926; Goertzel, Goertzel, and Goertzel 1978). The reason for this difference is that artistic creators, in comparison to scientific creators, tend to have somewhat less advantaged socioeconomic origins (Raskin 1936). The fact remains, however, that the vast majority of outstanding creators in all domains grew up in homes that were neither luxurious nor impoverished.

3. "E.C.'s areas of strength emerged at a relatively young age, and her family encouraged these interests, thought they are ambivalent about a career that falls outside of the established professions" (Gardner 1993a, p. 361). There is ample evidence that creative geniuses tend to display precocious development in their chosen domain of achievement (for example Simonton 1977b; 1991b; 1992a). Empirical research also supports the importance of parental support for early creative development (Bloom 1985). Only the last statement about family ambivalence has not received scrutiny in historiometric and psychometric inquiries.

4. "There comes a time when the growing child, now an adolescent, seems to have outgrown her home environment. E.C. has already invested a decade of work in the mastery of a domain and is near the forefront; she has little in addition to learn from her family and from local experts, and she feels a quickened impulse to test herself against the other leading young people in the domain" (Gardner 1993a, p. 361). Empirical investigations have shown that it requires about 10 years of extensive study and practice before a young talent attains the expertise necessary for world-class creativity (Ericsson 1996; Hayes 1989). The only essential qualification is that the most creative individuals require less time in expertise acquisition than do their less creative colleagues (Simonton

1991b; 2000a). The two assertions that flank this core claim still await empirical verification.

5. "And so, as an adolescent or young adult, E.C. ventures toward the city that is seen as a center of vital activities for her domain. With surprising speed, E.C. discovers in the metropolis a set of peers who share the same interests; together, they explore the terrain of the domain, often organizing institutions, issuing manifestos, and stimulating one another to new heights" (Gardner 1993a, p. 361). Empirical investigations have shown that eminent creators are far from "lone geniuses." On the contrary, they tend to be intermeshed in a network of colleagues, associates, correspondents, and competitors (Simonton 1984a, 1992a, 1992b). Indeed, the higher the degree of eminence attained, the richer this domain-specific network tends to be. This is true in both the arts and sciences.

7. "Sometimes E.C. proceeds directly to work in a chosen domain although she might just as well have flirted with a number of different career lines until a crystallizing moment occurred" (Gardner 1993a, p. 361; see also Walters and Gardner 1986). Although Gardner is not claiming that a crystallizing experience is an essential part of the profile, some research suggests that it may play a role in the sciences. Specifically, Roe (1953) found that many of her sixty-four eminent scientists did not decide upon their career until they had the opportunity to engage in original research as a college undergraduate. The unexpected joy of discovery propelled them into a life of scientific inquiry.

8. "So special does E.C. feel [after recognition for the breakthrough] that she appears willing to enter into special arrangements—a Faustian bargain—to maintain the flow that comes from effective, innovative work. For E.C., this bargain involves masochism and unbecoming behavior toward others, and, on occasion, the feeling of a direct pact with God" (Gardner 1993a, p. 362). Although the Faustian bargain has not been the subject of empirical scrutiny, I can cite some indirect support for at least a portion of this statement. Eysenck (1995) has shown that creativity is positively associated with elevated scores on the Psychoticism scale of the Eysenck Personality Questionnaire. High scores are associated with the following personal characteristics: aggressive, cold, egocentric, impersonal, impulsive, antisocial, unempathetic, and tough-minded. Such individuals would certainly be more inclined to engage in the hypothesized bargain than persons scoring low on this scale.

9. "E.C. works nearly all the time, making tremendous demands on herself and on others, constantly raising the ante. In William Butler

Yeats's formation, she chooses perfection of the work over perfection of the life (Gardner 1993a, p. 362). The empirical support for this generalization is overwhelming: Eminent creators in all fields are workaholics who devote most of their waking hours to their work and do so day after day, including most weekends (Roe 1953; Simon 1974). It is rare in the extreme to identify any outstanding creator who put in just forty hours per week.

10. "She is self-confident, able to deal with false starts, proud and stubborn, and reluctant to admit mistakes" (Gardner 1993a, p. 362). Both historiometric and psychometric inquiries into the personality of exceptional creators have found that they have considerable ego-strength, self-sufficiency, determination, and persistence in the face of obstacles and failures (Barron 1969; Cattell and Drevdahl 1955; Cox 1926). As far as I know, nothing has been done on any putative reluctance to admit mistakes.

11. "When E.C. produces an outpouring of works, a few of them stand out as *defining*, both for E.C. herself and for members of the surrounding field" (Gardner 1993a, p. 362). If I am free to provide a quantitative operational definition for "defining," then this assertion is abundantly true. The output of any notable creator varies immensely in impact, the vast majority of works being largely ignored and only a very small percentage having impressive influence (Simonton 1997b). For instance, most scientific journal articles receive no citations, and only a tiny proportion attains the status of a "citation classic" (Price 1963; Redner 1998). Similarly, only a fraction of the total output of even the greatest composers has found a lasting place in the concert repertoire (Simonton 1977a, 1998a). Hence, if "defining" is taken to mean "high-impact" by an appropriate domain-specific criterion, then Gardner's generalization is confirmed. Nonetheless, there is one small qualification: Great creators may not necessarily agree with their colleagues about which of their works can be considered defining (Simonton 1999a).

12. "Some creators die young, of course, but in the case of our E.C., she lives on until old age, gains many followers, and continues to make significant contribution [sic] until her death" (Gardner 1993a, p. 362). An appreciable literature has grown around the subject of the life span of illustrious creators, and in most domains their life expectancy surpasses that of the general population (for example Cassandro 1998; Cox 1926; Simonton 1997a). It is also true that the differential eminence of creators is positively correlated with the number of followers (Simonton 1984a; 1992a). These followers may be either direct, such as students

and disciples, or indirect, such as admirers and imitators. Finally, the higher the magnitude of eminence a creator attains, the higher the probability that he or she will produce major works late in life (Lindauer 1993b; Simonton 1988; 1991a; 1997b). Of special interest in this regard is the production of "swan-song" compositions in music (Simonton 1989b) and "old-age style" compositions in the visual arts (Lindauer 1993a).

Unconfirmed

In this category I have placed all of Gardner's (1993a) conclusions about the Exemplary Creator that have not yet been explicitly addressed in psychometric and historiometric research. These are eight in number.

1. "The atmosphere at home is more correct than it is warm, and the young creator often feels a bit estranged from her biological family; even though E.C. has close ties to one of her parents, she feels ambivalence, too. Intimate ties are more likely to exist between E.C. and a nanny, a nursemaid, or a more distant member of her family" (Gardner 1993a, p. 361). Notwithstanding the fact that some investigators have addressed issues relating to the claims made in this quote (for example Goertzel and Goertzel 1962; Goertzel, Goertzel, and Goertzel 1978; McCurdy 1960; Simonton 1986b; Walberg, Rasher, and Parkerson 1980), nothing sufficiently specific is available that would permit an assessment of its empirical validity.

2. "There is a moral, if not a religious, atmosphere around the home, and E.C. develops a strict conscience, which can be turned against herself but also against others who do not adhere to behavioral patterns she expects" (Gardner 1993a, p. 361). A great many investigations have looked at the religious backgrounds of eminent creators (Galton 1874; Roe 1953; Simonton 1986b), but I know of none that deals with the development of a "strict conscience."

3. "The creator often passes through a period of religiosity that is rejected and that may, but need not, be revisited in later life" (Gardner 1993a, p. 361). This idea that distinguished creators go through one or two phases of faith merits further inquiry. The research literature has found that highly eminent creators are usually not religious, at least not during the periods that they have come under study, which is often mid-career (for instance Lehman and Witty 1931; Roe 1953). Interestingly, it is possible that a late-life resurgence of religiosity might be part of the swan-song phenomenon (Simonton 2002).

4. "Still, with greater or lesser speed, E.C. discovers a problem area or realm of special interest, one that promises to take the domain into uncharted waters. This is a highly charged moment. At this point E.C. becomes isolated from her peers and must work mostly on her own. She sense that she is on the verge of a breakthrough that is as yet little understood, even by her. Surprisingly, at this crucial moment, E.C. craves both cognitive and affective support, so that she can retrain her bearings. Without such support she might well experience some kind of breakdown" (Gardner 1993a, p. 361). I am unaware of any research of any kind that documents the critical period that Gardner describes here. It is certainly worth further inquiry.

5. "Of course, in the happy circumstances that we have examined, E.C. succeeds in effecting at least one major breakthrough. And, the field rather rapidly acknowledges the power of the breakthrough" (Gardner 1993a, p. 362). The truth of this assertion I suppose hinges on what is meant by "rather rapidly." Certainly in some cases the delay in recognition can be substantial. We lack empirical research on this question. It would be of special interest to know whether the time lapse is positively associated with the magnitude of the breakthrough.

6. "E.C. attempts to retain her creativity; she will seek marginal status or heighten the ante of asynchrony to maintain freshness and to secure the flow that accompanies great challenges and exciting discoveries" (Gardner 1993a, p. 362). Research on creative scientists show that they tend to be upwardly mobile, highly prolific investigators moving into the most prestigious institutions (for example Allison and Long 1987). This seems to run counter to Gardner's suggestion. On the other hand, one content analysis of 15,618 themes by 479 classical composers did reveal a tendency for these creators, as they aged, to write music that departed increasingly from the stylistic conventions of their day (Simonton 1980). This might be taken as evidence for enhanced asynchrony. Yet no empirical study published date addresses these questions directly.

7. "Inevitably with aging, limits on E.C.'s creative powers emerge. She sometimes exploits young persons as a means of rejuvenation" (Gardner 1993a, 362). It would be good to discover whether the relation between outstanding creators and the next generation of talent is truly exploitive. The research has instead concentrated on the beneficial effects that mentors or masters have on their students or apprentices (Simonton 1984a; 1992a; 1992b; Zuckerman 1977; Walberg, Rasher, and Parkerson 1980).

8. "Finding it increasingly difficult to achieve original new works, E.C. becomes a valued critic or commentator" (Gardner 1993a, p. 362).

I know of no systematic inquiries into this specific career shift. However, some research has documented how the productivity of scientists must often increasingly compete with increased administrative responsibilities, albeit it is difficult to determine the directly of the causal connection (Horner, Murray, and Rushton 1994; Roe 1965). Do scientists go into administration because their research program has become less effective do expanded administrative detract from the research effort? Of course, the same causal ambiguity might attend the relationship suggested in Gardner's proposition.

Disconfirmed

In the final category are three assertions that appear to be inconsistent with the literature on exceptionally creative individuals.

1. "E.C.'s family is not highly educated, but they value learning and achievement, about which they hold high expectations. In a word, they are prototypically bourgeois, holding dear the ambitions, respectability, and valuing of hard work that have come to be associated with that class, particularly in the late nineteenth century" (Gardner 1993a, p. 361). In contrast to this statement, a disproportionate number of eminent creators come from families where one or both parents pursue learned professions, such as medicine, law, education, and the clergy (Cox 1926; Ellis 1926; Raskin 1936). The family background can thus be considered highly educated with respect to the general population. This familial circumstance holds especially for outstanding scientists (Raskin 1936).

2. "Given E.C.'s enormous energy and commitment, she has an opportunity for a second breakthrough, which occurs about a decade after the first one. The succeeding breakthrough is less radical, but it is more comprehensive and more intimately integrated with E.C.'s previous work in the domain" (Gardner 1993a, p. 362). I already mentioned Galenson's (2005) distinction between conceptual and experimental artists, the latter not having breakthroughs of the kind required by this claim. But there are other unhappy niceties besides. Take, for example, the research on career landmarks (Raskin 1936; Simonton 1991a, 1991b; Zusne 1976). These investigations attempt to determine the ages at which creators produce their first major work, their single best work, and their last major work. Typically, this research shows that the first landmark appears sometime in the late twenties, the second in the late thirties to early forties, and the last in the mid-to-late fifties. If these landmarks can be equated with breakthrough works, then the separations are about twelve years between the first two and about fifteen years

between the last two. One might say "close enough" and conclude that the Ten-Year Rule is confirmed. However, the more eminent the creator, the earlier the first landmark appears and the later the last landmark appears (the placement of the middle landmark remaining unchanged). This means that the most distinguished creators will have the three landmarks separated by even more intervening years. At the same time, the lesser creators will have their landmarks separated by much fewer years, even much less than a decade. Finally, it should be emphasized that regardless of creative impact, it is the middle career landmark that defines the best work, not the first. Of course, it could be argued that the best work is "less radical" and "more comprehensive." Yet at least in the sciences the evidence shows that breakthrough contributions are most likely to emerge in mid-career rather than early career (Wray 2003; 2004).

3. "The nature of E.C.'s domain determines whether an opportunity for further breakthroughs arises. (Remaining highly creative is easier in the arts than in the sciences.)" (Gardner 1993a, p. 362). The first assertion is true if a qualifier is inserted between "domain" and "determines," such as "partially." Other factors besides the domain of creative achievement determine the likelihood that an individual will continue to produce breakthroughs. As noted in the preceding paragraph, for example, highly prolific creators are more prone to make an important contribution late in life (Simonton 1988; 1997b). On the other hand, the parenthetical statement may not be consistent with multi-case quantitative research. For example, Dennis (1966) found that the age decrement in creative output was far more pronounced in the arts than in the sciences. Actually, it may be difficult to make such a broad generalization because career trajectories vary tremendously within various artistic and scientific disciplines (Dennis 1966; Lehman 1953; Simonton 1991a). For example, poets tend to have shorter careers than novelists and the careers of mathematicians tend to be more abbreviated than the careers of geologists (for an explanation, see Simonton 1997b).

This is not a bad success rate. A dozen propositions about E.C. have been confirmed, eight remain unconfirmed, and just three have been disconfirmed.

Conclusion

I began this critique of Gardner's views on creativity by identifying *Creating Minds* as the target for commentary. This choice was based on the acknowledgment that this book represents his greatest single contribution to the study of creativity. After providing an overview of the book's contents, I then evaluate its contributions to a scientific understanding of creativity. This evaluation was both methodological and substantive. On the methodological side, I discussed the four major approaches to the psychological study of eminent creators, and then discussed how Gardner's approach compared with the others in terms of sampling, measurement, and inference. This comparison revealed some major limitations in his method. On the substantive side, I evaluated his profile of the Exemplary Creator in light of empirical findings in the psychometric and historiometric literature. Although most of Gardner's generalizations receive endorsement, a large proportion remains untested by any method, and a few have been disconfirmed outright. The fact that not every conclusion has been confirmed suggests that some of the untested inferences might also not survive empirical scrutiny. Hence, it is hoped that *Creating Minds* will inspire research that directly tests some of his most intriguing conjectures. However, those future investigations will have to adopt approaches that apply quantitative methods to large samples of distinguished creators. In other words, the verification should depend on psychometric and historiometric approaches.

REFERENCES

Allison, Paul D., and J. Scott Long. 1987. Interuniversity Mobility of Academic Scientists. *American Sociological Review* 52, pp. 643–652.

Barron, Frank X. 1969. *Creative Person and Creative Process*. New York: Holt, Rinehart.

Berry, Colin.1981. The Nobel Scientists and the Origins of Scientific Achievement. *British Journal of Sociology* 32, pp. 381–391.

Bloom, Benjamin S., ed. 1985. *Developing Talent in Young People*. New York: Ballantine.

Brockman, John, ed. 1993. *Creativity: The Reality Club IV*. New York: Simon and Schuster.

Cassandro, Vincent J. 1998. Explaining Premature Mortality across Fields of Creative Endeavor. *Journal of Personality* 66, pp. 805–833.

Cattell, James M. 1910. A Further Statistical Study of American Men of Science. *Science* (4th November).

Cattell, R.B., and John E. Drevdahl. 1955. A Comparison of the Personality Profile (16 P.F.) of Eminent Researchers with That of Eminent Teachers and Administrators, and of the General Population. *British Journal of Psychology* 46, pp. 248–261.

Cox, Catharine. 1926. *The Early Mental Traits of Three Hundred Geniuses.* Stanford: Stanford University Press.

Dennis, Wayne. 1966. Creative Productivity between the Ages of 20 and 80 Years. *Journal of Gerontology* 21, pp. 1–8.

Eiduson, Bernice T. 1962. *Scientists: Their Psychological World.* New York: Basic Books.

Ellis, Havelock 1926. *A Study of British Genius.* Revised edition. Boston: Houghton Mifflin.

Ericsson, K. Anders. 1996. The Acquisition of Expert Performance: An Introduction to Some of the Issues. In K. Anders Ericsson, ed., *The Road to Expert Performance: Empirical Evidence from the Arts and Sciences, Sports, and Games* (Mahwah: Erlbaum), pp. 1–50.

Eysenck, Hans J. 1995. *Genius: The Natural History of Creativity.* Cambridge: Cambridge University Press.

Feist, Gregory J. 1993. A Structural Model of Scientific Eminence. *Psychological Science* 4, pp. 366–371.

Feist, Gregory J. 1997. Quantity, Quality, and Depth of Research as Influences on Scientific Eminence: Is Quantity Most Important? *Creativity Research Journal* 10, pp. 325–335.

Freud, Sigmund. 1964 [1910]. *Leonardo da Vinci and a Memory of His Childhood.* New York: Norton.

Galton, Francis. 1869. *Hereditary Genius: An Inquiry into its Laws and Consequences.* London: Macmillan.

Galton, Francis. 1874. *English Men of Science: Their Nature and Nurture.* London: Macmillan.

Galenson, David. 2005. *The Art of Innovation: The Life Cycles of Creative Artists.* Princeton: Princeton University Press.

Gardner, Howard. 1983. *Frames of Mind: A Theory of Multiple Intelligences.* New York: Basic Books.

———. 1988. Creative Lives and Creative Works: A Synthetic Scientific Approach. In Robert J. Sternberg, ed., *The Nature of Creativity: Contemporary Psychological Perspectives* (New York: Cambridge University Press), pp. 298–321.

———. 1993a. *Creating Minds: An Anatomy of Creativity Seen through the Lives of Freud, Einstein, Picasso, Stravinsky, Eliot, Graham, and Gandhi.* New York: Basic Books.

———. 1993b. Seven Creators of the Modern Era. In John Brockman, ed., *Creativity: The Reality Club IV* (New York: Simon and Schuster), pp. 28–47.

———. 1994. The Creators' Patterns. In Margaret A. Boden, ed., *Dimensions of Creativity* (Cambridge, Massachusetts: MIT Press), pp. 143–158.

———. 2002. My Way. In Robert J. Sternberg, ed., *Psychologists Defying the Crowd: Stories of Those Who Battled the Establishment and Won* (Washington, DC: American Psychological Association), pp. 79–88.

Goertzel, Mildred G., Victor Goertzel, and Ted G. Goertzel. 1978. *300 Eminent Personalities: A Psychosocial Analysis of the Famous*. San Francisco: Jossey-Bass.

Goertzel, Victor, and Mildred G. Goertzel. 1962. *Cradles of Eminence*. Boston: Little, Brown.

Hayes, John R. 1989. *The Complete Problem Solver*. Second edition. Hillsdale: Erlbaum.

Helson, Ravenna. 1980. The Creative Woman Mathematician. In Lynn H. Fox, Linda Brody, and Dianne Tobin, eds., *Women and the Mathematical Mystique* (Baltimore: Johns Hopkins University Press), pp. 23–54.

Hershman, D., Jablow, and Julian Lieb. 1988. *The Key to Genius: Manic-Depression and the Creative Life*. Loughton: Prometheus UK.

Horner, Karen L., Harry G. Murray, and J. Philippe Rushton. 1994. Aging and Administration in Academic Psychologists. *Social Behavior and Personality* 22, pp. 343–46.

Lehman, Harvey C. 1953. *Age and Achievement*. Princeton: Princeton University Press.

Lehman, Harvey C., and Paul A. Witty. 1931. Scientific Eminence and Church Membership. *Scientific Monthly* 33, pp. 544–49.

Lindauer, Martin S. 1993a. The Old-Age Style and Its Artists. *Empirical Studies and the Arts* 11, pp. 135–146.

———. 1993b. The Span of Creativity among Long-lived Historical Artists. *Creativity Research Journal* 6, pp. 231–39.

MacKinnon, Donald W. 1978. *In Search of Human Effectiveness*. Buffalo: Creative Education Foundation.

McCurdy, Harold G. 1960. The Childhood Pattern of Genius. *Horizon* 2, pp. 33–38.

Murray, Charles. 2003. *Human Accomplishment: The Pursuit of Excellence in the Arts and Sciences, 800 B.C. to 1950*. New York: HarperCollins.

Policastro, Emma, and Howard Gardner. 1999. From Case Studies to Robust Generalizations: An Approach to the Study of Creativity. In Robert J. Sternberg, ed., *Handbook of Creativity* (New York: Cambridge University Press), pp. 213–225.

Poffenberger, A.T. 1930. The Development of Men of Science. *Journal of Social Psychology* 1, pp. 31–47.

Price, Derek da Solla. 1963. *Little Science, Big Science*. New York: Columbia University Press.

Quételet, Adolphe. 1968 [1835]. *A Treatise on Man and the Development of His Faculties*. New York: Franklin. Reprint of 1842 Edinburgh translation of 1835 French original.

Raskin, Evelyn. 1936. Comparison of Scientific and Literary Ability: A Biographical Study of Eminent Scientists and Men of Letters of the Nineteenth Century. *Journal of Abnormal and Social Psychology* 31, pp. 20–35.

Redner, S. 1998. How Popular Is Your Paper? An Empirical Study of the Citation Distribution. *European Physical Journal* B4, pp. 131–34.

Roe, Anne. 1953. *The Making of a Scientist*. New York: Dodd, Mead.

———. 1965. Changes in Scientific Activities with Age. *Science* 150 (15th October), pp. 113–18.

Rothenberg, Albert. 1987. Einstein, Bohr, and Creative Thinking in Science. *History of Science* 25, pp. 147–166.

Runco, Mark A., and Steven R. Pritzker, eds. 1999. *Encyclopedia of Creativity*. San Diego: Academic Press.

Runyan, William M. 1981. Why Did Van Gogh Cut Off His Ear? The Problem of Alternative Explanations in Psychobiography. *Journal of Personality and Social Psychology* 40, pp. 1070–77.

———. Runyan, William M. 1988. Progress in Psychobiography. *Journal of Personality* 56, pp. 295–326.

Simon, R.J. 1974. The Work Habits of Eminent Scientists. *Sociology of Work and Occupations* 1, pp. 327–335.

Simonton, Dean Keith.1976. Philosophical Eminence, Beliefs, and Zeitgeist: An Individual-generational Analysis. *Journal of Personality and Social Psychology* 34, pp. 630–640.

———. 1977a. Creative Productivity, Age, and Stress: A Biographical Time-series Analysis of 10 Classical Composers. *Journal of Personality and Social Psychology* 35, pp. 791–804.

———. 1977b. Eminence, Creativity, and Geographic Marginality: A Recursive Structural Equation Model. *Journal of Personality and Social Psychology* 35, pp. 805–816.

———. 1980. Thematic Fame, Melodic Originality, and Musical Zeitgeist: A Biographical and Transhistorical Content Analysis. *Journal of Personality and Social Psychology* 38, pp. 972–983.

———. 1984a. Artistic Creativity and Interpersonal Relationships Across and Within Generations. *Journal of Personality and Social Psychology* 46, pp. 1273–286.

———. 1984b. *Genius, Creativity, and Leadership: Historiometric inquiries*. Cambridge, Massachusetts: Harvard University Press.

———. 1986a. Aesthetic Success in Classical Music: A Computer Analysis of 1935 Compositions. *Empirical Studies of the Arts* 4, pp. 1–17.

———. 1986b. Biographical Typicality, Eminence, and Achievement Style. *Journal of Creative Behavior* 20, pp. 14–22.

———. 1988. Age and Outstanding Achievement: What Do We Know After a Century of Research? *Psychological Bulletin* 104, pp. 251–267.

———. 1989a. Shakespeare's Sonnets: A Case of and for Single-case Historiometry. *Journal of Personality* 57, pp. 695–721.

———. 1989b. The Swan-Song Phenomenon: Last-Works Effects for 172 Classical Composers. *Psychology and Aging* 4, pp. 42–47.

————. 1990. *Psychology, Science, and History: An Introduction to Historiometry*. New Haven: Yale University Press.

————. 1991a. Career Landmarks in Science: Individual Differences and Interdisciplinary Contrasts. *Developmental Psychology* 27, pp. 119–130.

————. 1991b. Emergence and Realization of Genius: The Lives and Works of 120 Classical Composers. *Journal of Personality and Social Psychology* 61, pp. 829–840.

————. 1992a. Leaders of American Psychology, 1879–1967: Career Development, Creative Output, and Professional Achievement. *Journal of Personality and Social Psychology* 62, pp. 5–17.

————. 1992b. The Social Context of Career Success and Course for 2,026 Scientists and Inventors. *Personality and Social Psychology Bulletin* 18, pp. 452–463.

————. 1997a. Achievement Domain and Life Expectancies in Japanese Civilization. *International Journal of Aging and Human Development* 44, pp. 103–114.

————. 1997b. Creative Productivity: A Predictive and Explanatory Model of Career Trajectories and Landmarks. *Psychological Review* 104, pp. 66–89.

————. 1998a. Fickle Fashion versus Immortal Fame: Transhistorical Assessments of Creative Products in the Opera House. *Journal of Personality and Social Psychology* 75, pp. 198–210.

————. 1998b. Mad King George: The Impact of Personal and Political Stress on Mental and Physical Health. *Journal of Personality* 66, pp. 443–466.

————. 1999a. *Origins of Genius: Darwinian Perspectives on Creativity*. New York: Oxford University Press.

————. 1999b. Significant Samples: The Psychological Study of Eminent Individuals. *Psychological Methods* 4, pp. 425–451.

————. 2000a. Creative Development as Acquired Expertise: Theoretical Issues and an Empirical Test. *Developmental Review* 20, pp. 283–318.

————. 2000b. Methodological and Theoretical Orientation and the Long-term Disciplinary Impact of 54 Eminent Psychologists. *Review of General Psychology* 4, pp. 1–13.

————. 2002. *Great Psychologists and Their Times: Scientific Insights into Psychology's History*. Washington, DC: APA Books.

————. 2003. Qualitative and Quantitative Analyses of Historical Data. *Annual Review of Psychology* 54, pp. 617–640.

Smith, Steve M., Tom B. Ward, and Ronald A. Finke, eds. 1995. *The Creative Cognition Approach*. Cambridge, Massachusetts: MIT Press.

Sternberg, Robert J., ed. 1988. *The Nature of Creativity: Contemporary Psychological Perspectives*. New York: Cambridge University Press.

————. 1999. *Handbook of Creativity*. Cambridge: Cambridge University Press.

Sternberg, Robert J., and Janet E. Davidson, eds. 1995. *The Nature of Insight.* Cambridge, Massachusetts: MIT Press.

Tetlock, Philip E., Fay Crosby, and Travis L. Crosby. 1981. Political Psychobiography. *Micropolitics* 1, pp. 191–213.

Walberg, Herbert J., Sue P. Rasher, and Joann Parkerson. 1980. Childhood and Eminence. *Journal of Creative Behavior* 13, pp. 225–231.

Walters, Joseph, and Howard Gardner. 1986. The Crystallizing Experience: Discovering an Intellectual Gift. In Robert J. Sternberg and Janet E. Davidson, eds., *Conceptions of Giftedness* (New York: Cambridge University Press), pp. 306–331.

Wray, K. Brad. 2003. Is Science Really a Young Man's Game? *Social Studies of Science* 33, pp. 137–149.

———. 2004. An Examination of the Contributions of Young Scientists in New Fields. *Scientometrics* 61, pp. 117–128.

Zuckerman, Harriet. 1977. *Scientific Elite.* New York: Free Press.

Zusne, Leonard. 1976. Age and Achievement in Psychology: The Harmonic Mean as a Model. *American Psychologist* 31, pp. 805–07.

8

Creativity Is Always
Personal and Only Sometimes
Social

MARK A. RUNCO

This chapter is a kind of microcosm. Like all microcosms, it is easiest
to understand when the macrocosm is defined. The macrocosm in this
instance might be called "all possible perspectives on the creative
process." There is a huge number of possible perspectives (for instance
Runco 2003; Runco and Pritzker, 1999). This chapter could also be
called *self-referential* (Hofstadter 1985), or I might simply say that I am
trying herein to practice what I preach. The last of these descriptions is
trite, however, and the self-referential alternative may be a bit preten-
tious. The reader can him- or herself decide which descriptor (microcosm, self-referential, or preaching) best fits.

The principle being described (and I hope demonstrated and practiced)
involves interpretive processes. These are vital for creativity. They are also
compatible with Howard Gardner's (1988; 1993; Gardner and
Nemirovksy 1991) theory of creativity. The fit is most obvious when we
use the right language. Indeed, this is the interpretive process being
demonstrated: In this chapter I do not simply quote Gardner when describing how our theories mesh. Instead, I interpret his theory using the concept of interpretation and the terminology of *personal creativity* (Runco
1996; 2000). (That is why I described this as a microcosm.) The compat-
ibility of theories is my own interpretation—which is the self-referential
aspect of this chapter I mentioned above. I will, however, be much more
precise in connecting interpretative tendencies to the creative process and
in identifying how this meshes with Gardner's (1993) work. I will also
raise some concerns about the social and historical stance taken by

Gardner. In that sense this is a critique; I believe more emphasis should be given to the individual and to the role of interpretive processes.

I am well aware of Gardner's (1993) reasons for relegating the individual, and "critique" is probably too strong a word for this chapter. Gardner's (1993) perspective is enormously useful and informative. It is, however, one perspective on the creative process. As he describes it (at least in *Creating Minds: An Anatomy of Creativity Seen through the Lives of Freud, Einstein, Picasso, Stravinsky, Eliot, Graham, and Gandhi*, and especially in the section titled, "My Approach to Creativity"), his perspective is historical and biographical. He has developed a theory of creativity in large part based on biographies of famous creators. Or it might be more accurate to say that his theory of creativity was motivated in part by his interest in history and biography and co-evolved as he studied them. Gardner has also conducted and cited developmental research, but his intention in *Creating Minds* seems to have been to understand unambiguous cases of creativity.

This approach is fascinating, but it can blind us to the potentials of children and non-eminent individuals and to the creative process as it is used before and independently of creative achievement and accomplishment. It was this concern about studies of eminent creators that lead to the theory of *personal creativity* (Runco 1995; 1996; 2003). Personal creativity begins with "original interpretations of experience." There is more to it (see below) but interpretation is critical for the present purposes because it fills a gap in Gardner's (1993) theory (I should say "may be interpreted as a gap"). That gap is best identified and defined when we look more closely at the historical and biographical perspective.

Historical and Biographical Approach

Gardner's (1993) theory is a very useful one and consistent with data. The data, however, were biographical and historical. In *Creating Minds*, Gardner examined seven individuals. These individuals may be representative of eminent individuals, but they are not representative of everyone. One problem, then, is that of generalizability. Gardner found eminent creators to employ both adult and child-like tendencies. Are these same tendencies vital for the creativity of other creators, in other eras, and at other levels of ability? Gardner is well aware of these questions and carefully defends the choice of historical eras and choice of creators. Similarly, he acknowledges that his relied on one sample, and that other individuals or other domains could have been studied. Gardner is careful and thoughtful in his work.

In some ways he is more careful than I. The focus on unambiguous cases of creativity allows him to be entirely certain about what he is studying. No one would question the creativity of Freud, Einstein, Picasso, Stravinsky, Eliot, Graham, and Gandhi. But again, can we apply what we find in their cases (such as child-like tendencies) to more ambiguously creative persons? Perhaps not. Of course, those other persons may not be creative! Unlike Gardner, I am willing to take that risk. I am willing to assume that *every* person has creative potential, even if I am wrong some of the time. I am similarly willing to invest resources in studying ambiguously creative persons. This is because the potential pay-off is so large. If I am correct, and every individual has creative potential, and if we study creative potentials and find a way to help each individual, even just a little bit, the cumulative result (across huge numbers, basically the entire human population) will be enormous.

Gardner prefers unambiguous cases, and I am glad he is studying them. But they provide us with only one source of data. Errors are inherent in these data: biographies and autobiographies can, for example, be biased, or at least incomplete. It helps that Gardner bridges his findings with the work of Gruber (for example Davis, Gruber, and Keegan, in press) and Simonton (1999), but they too emphasize unambiguously creative persons. At one point Gardner describes his case study approach as one end of a continuum, and Simonton's (1999) historiometric approach at another end, and he acknowledges how useful it would be to "span the gap between these two approaches" (p. 27). The problem here is that both of these approaches represent only historical examples of creative performances. Only actual achievement is recorded in history; potential and everyday creativity are not recorded. Clearly a meta-theory of creativity must acknowledge Gardner's (1993, 1994) findings, as well as Simonton's (1999). But it should also considers findings from other kinds of research, including that which does not fall between the historiometric and the case study perspectives but instead captures creativity that is either not of a nature that is was recorded in history[1] or is

---

[1] There is also concern about mistaken judgments and changes in opinion. Runco (1995) described *reputational paths*, with fame and influence increasing and decreasing as time passes. Influence is subjective, and a historical reading of it is only as accurate as the recorded information. For some famous creators, we have plenty of information, but for others, we have very little—and all of it is open to bias. Think of revisionist history and the idea that our historical records may reflect mostly the winners of the past, not the losers (whose records may have been destroyed or distorted). Our history also reflects the impressions of literate people and those who saw the value in recording their experiences.

so immediate and contemporary that it cannot be considered historical. This takes us to the theory of personal creativity.

Personal Creativity

The theory of personal creativity was developed as a reaction to existing theories. I was particularly dissatisfied with research on creative products (for instance citations, publication counts, artworks, inventions) and research spotlighting the social aspects of creative performance and eminent persons (for example Kasof 1995). Products are often studied, but they tell us little about the creative process, and even less about individuals with creative potential but who are not yet productive. Research on creative products is yet another interesting source of information—but it does not give us anything near a complete picture. Studies of eminent persons are also highly objective; as noted above, there is no doubt about the creativity of Einstein or someone of similar stature. But eminence is often a matter of persuasion (Simonton 1989), and attributions play a large role (Kasof 1995; Runco 1995). Yet attributions influence the *impact* of the creative work; they do not directly influence the creative process. Admittedly some creators change their efforts or products in response to public reaction. Any creator who is trying to sell his or her work may do that, but only the extrinsically motivated would, and extrinsic motivation makes originality difficult. Also, sometimes eminence is attained for reasons unrelated to creativity.

The theory of personal creativity is an attempt to separate (a) an individual's creative potential and (b) the personal aspects of the creative process from (c) the social processes involved in creative achievement. Personal creativity is fundamental in the sense that very likely the personal processes must operate before the social processes. The theory of personal creativity does not, then, dismiss social processes (attributions and the like) but instead suggests that they occur later and are sometimes irrelevant. They are irrelevant when the individual is still developing his or her creative potential and not yet performing in an unambiguously and social fashion. They are also irrelevant in most instances of everyday creativity (Runco and Richards 1998) and for children's creativity.

Personal creativity involves interpretation, discretion, and intentions. The first of these is very much like the assimilatory process, described by Piaget (1970; 1976). Information is brought into the individual's cognitive system, but since there are no cognitive structures to support it (in other words understanding is incomplete), the information must be altered in order to be considered. The best example of assimilation may be imaginative play. Gardner (1993) quoted Freud's description of what would seem to be a similar, if not identical, process:

> Might we not say that every child at play behaves like a creative writer, in that he creates a world of his own, or, rather, rearranges the things of his world in new ways which pleases him? . . . The creative writer does the same as the child at play. He creates a world of phantasy which he takes very seriously—that is, which he invests with large amounts of emotion—while separating it from reality. (p. 24)

Freud's description of what I refer to as assimilation during imaginative play is speculative at best, given that it was based on questionable data (Gardner 1993, p. 25). Though also inferential, Piaget's (1970; 1976) description of assimilation is, on the other hand, consistent with a large number of observations. For Piaget, children lost in their imaginary worlds often ignore many pieces of information imposed by the objective experience. They often distort objective experience such that their doll can dance or their pet can talk. Surely, it is not useful to construct this kind of original interpretation all of the time, and for that reason *discretion* is a part of creative process. By that I mean that it is best to be original some of the time, to conform some of the time, and to know when to do one or the other! Making this kind of decision may be effortful, however. Indeed, after childhood, the creative process does require some effort. (Think here of Gardner's [1993] observations about "marginality of choice" [p. 30] and his finding that "creative individuals want to be creative, and they organize their lives to heighten the likelihood that they will achieve a series of creative breakthroughs" [p. 35].) Adults may need to be tactical about it (Runco 1999b). For these reasons the creative process reflects intentions, intrinsic motivation, and values. If an individual values creative things and perhaps admires creative people, he or she will probably look for opportunities and be willing to invest the effort into constructing original interpretations and be careful to do so at the right time.

Developmental Continuities and an Alternative View of Child-Like Tendencies

One advantage of this perspective, with interpretation playing a key role in creative thinking, is that it recognizes developmental continuities. Each of us constructs interpretations of experience, and we do so throughout our lives. It may become more difficult as we get older. At least there are indications of rigidity in late adulthood (Chown 1961). Rubenson and Runco (1995) suggested that the tendency to become less flexible and more rigid reflects the investments made—and the corresponding risk avoidance. The more we have invested in something, the more we have to lose and the less likely we are to change. This is one reason there is a cost to expertise: Experts have invested huge amounts of time into their fields, and they thus have much to lose if that field (or their own niche within it) loses respect. It is analogous to financial investment risk-aversion, which increases as an investment increases.

This implies that experts and older adults could remain flexible. In fact, this is one explanation for creative achievement late in life: The creator employs a *late life style* (Lindauer 1991a; 1991b) which keeps him or her flexible and allows exploration and discovery of original insights or ideas. This is also another reason for including *intentions* in the theory of creativity: If the individual so chooses, he or she can maintain the effort to be creative. But late-life changes and other tactics will not be used unless the individual decides to do so and invests effort accordingly. Apparently the childlike behaviors Gardner (1992) observed in Freud, Picasso, Einstein, and the others were intentional. Removing oneself from outside pressure and convention may also be intentional, for as Gardner (1993, p. 11) described it, "creative individuals may strive to make themselves more marginal." Those individuals may have been trying to maintain their originality and recognized that there was a benefit to the child-like perspectives. In that light intentions play a role in personal creativity and in the work of Freud, Picasso, Einstein, and the others.

The same can be said for assimilation and the capacity for original interpretations. I would go as far as to suggest that it is a key cognitive mechanism used in adult accomplishment, and it is certainly used during childhood. Perhaps the eminent creator learns to appreciate the construction of original interpretations and continues to employ them, while the rest of us fall into routine and make more and more assumptions as we get older. Note that this possibility–eminent creators finding their original ideas with the same mechanism they used as children–is congruent with Gardner's (1993) ideas. He described Freud and the other luminaries as childlike and identified "important dimensions of adult creativity [that] have their roots in the childhood of the creator" (p. 30). I am suggesting that creators sometimes use the assimilatory capacities they had as children. Gardner (1993, p. 31) seems very close to this when he reported that "the very process of discovering themselves become models for later exploratory behaviors, including efforts to probe phenomena never before conceptualized." On a behavioral level, the use of assimilatory capacities might very well make the adult appear to be childlike.

Gruber (1996) once described how during his childhood Jean Piaget was already actively involved in collecting and in the scientific method. (Gruber himself claimed that during his own childhood he was learning to jump rope backwards.) I do not know for certain, but if Piaget was investing in his studies of biology instead of learning to jump rope, we might assume that imaginative play was not important to him, and therefore perhaps not a marker of later creative success. Yet assimilation takes many forms. It might be that a child is very imaginative and constructs imaginary worlds or friends (Hoff, in press), and that this is predictive of later adult creativity, but then again another child may have equal assimilatory capacities but direct them to something other than imaginative play. It would be interesting to identify other manifestations of assimilatory capacity and then use them to predict later creative performance. Keep in mind, however, that assimilatory capacity just supplies cognitive potential. A child may have all kind of potential but not fulfill it. He or she may be outstanding in assimilatory capacity but not acquire the expertise that is necessary for actual accomplishment. I am sure the social processes Gardner (1993) described, and those identified by Albert (1980a; 1980b) and Helson (1990), are important for transforming potential into the complex of skills and motivations which are required for high-level creative accomplishment.

There is some indication of what I have said in that famous creators do show talent early in life. Gardner (1993) gave a number of examples of Picasso, whose early work was remarkable. Picasso's early assimilatory capacity may not have been obvious in his imaginative play, but it was obvious in his early (and then later) art work. He certainly offered his own original interpretations in his artwork. Gardner (1993, p. 10) also described Einstein, who developed his theory by "returning to the conceptual world of childhood: the search for basic understandings unhampered by conventional tendencies of a question." Gardner further suggested that "all creativity grows, first, out of the relationship between an individual and the objective world" (p. 9). He may not have been thinking about assimilation here, but then again, he did refer to his early interest in Piaget's theory of cognitive development. These observations seem to be compatible with what I am suggesting about the role of interpretation and assimilation in the creative process.

Effective Creativity

Indeed, I am by no means suggesting that Gardner (1993) is incorrect in his description of the development of creative talent. I merely think his description, with the inclusion of social processes, applies with certainty only to eminent creators and individuals who eventually change the domains in which they work. (He defines creativity so that the work is at some point "accepted in a particular cultural setting" [p. 35].) Some of the things he finds in his case studies may not be necessary for a child to paint an original picture or for an average professor to teach in a creative fashion. Yet the eminent creator, the child, and the professor each do need to construct original interpretations of experience.[2] If these are in fact effective or adaptive, as well as original, they are creative.

Creative things must be effective or adaptive. Otherwise their originality is unrealistic and the behavior may be irrelevant or psychotic. For this reason something like "effectiveness" or "fit" or "adaptive value" is always included, along with originality, in definitions of creativity. Bruner (1972) described creativity as "effective surprise." The best term may indeed be effectiveness; adaptiveness implies a kind of reaction. Usually, adaptations are elicited by a problem or demand, but creativity can be *proactive* rather than reactive (Heinzen 1999). This is a minor point in some ways, but it is a critical one, especially for moral and ethical creativity (cf. Gruber 1993). The distinction between reactive and proactive creativity can be difficult, especially when the situation is simplified such that the former are viewed as reactions to problems. Problems can be quite hazy and personal. Creative persons sometimes get lost in a problem, and the problem actually disappears! The individual does not think he or she is working on a problem. The individual is, instead, so involved, so motivated, so immersed, that he or she is simply doing what they want to do. Others may fail to see the task at hand as a problem as well. The "problem" is in the eyes of the creator: It is a personal one, a matter of interpretation.

Ideas and Other Indicators of Potential

Gardner (1993; and see Feldman, Csikszentmihalyi, and Gardner 1994) does not see much (if any) value in psychometric tests of talent, nor in

---

[2] Experience may not be entirely objective. Piaget (1976), for example, referred to reflective abstraction, the basic idea being that we sometime think about our thoughts,

the capacity for divergent thinking. If we accept the idea of potential, these may in fact have some use in a overarching meta-theory of creativity. Divergent thinking tests do, for example, have reasonable predictive and discriminant validities, especially compared to the IQ and other oft-used indicators of giftedness (Plucker 2000; Runco 1986: 1991: 1999; Runco, Plucker, and Lim 2000–2001). I refer to the divergent thinking indices as *estimates of the potential for creative problem solving*. The emphasis is on *estimates* (which may be imperfect) and *potential* (rather than actual performance).

As a matter of fact, Gardner (1993) refers to problem identification as beyond the reach of psychometric techniques, but inroads have been made in this regard. Csikzentmihalyi and Getzels (1976) got things moving in regards to the skills which fall under the umbrella of *problem discovery* and *problem-finding*, and several psychometric techniques now allow the examinee to first define a task and then solve it (for example Runco 1994; Wakefield 1985). Admittedly, the examinee is still placed in the testing setting, which means that intrinsic motivation is minimal (and generalizability likewise), but these tests do offer information about the potential for problem discovery and definition. They can be used in combination with assessments of intrinsic motivation and perhaps with some indicator of the intention to do creative work. In one recent study Runco *et al.* (in press) used data from divergent thinking along with data representing *discretionary time on task* (the latter being used as an estimate of motivation) to improve predictions actual creative accomplishment. Perhaps psychometric measures can supply useful information. Such measures do have serious limitations, but nonetheless useful information can be obtained and used along with that provided by other kinds of studies of creativity. In this fashion we may develop the fullest possible picture of creativity.

Conclusions

B.F. Skinner (1975) argued that science should rely on objective experimentation and data that were valid in the sense that they could be used to "predict and control" behavior. It is not enough to describe, for that does not explain, and Skinner wanted to fully explain behavior. Pribram (1999, p. 213) argued much the same and stated that "the job of science is to show 'how' a process works." Jay and Perkins (1998) put it this way:

---

and we can have reactions (and interpretations) to them. We are not directly responding to objective experience.

In efforts to understand cognitive processes, progress requires going beyond definitions to gain insight into mechanism. Broadly speaking, the quest for mechanism involves developing causal models for the phenomenon in question. Searching for mechanism typically includes trying to understand *why* and *how* people exhibit particular patterns of behavior or thought. (p. 260)

I favor the interpretive view of creativity because it applies across the lifespan and to both everyday and eminent creativity. I also favor it because it is a theory of mechanism. Assimilation is not easy to experimentally manipulate, but there are sound experimental demonstrations of how interpretations are formed and how they relate to creative insights (for example Rothenberg 1999; Smith and Carlsson 1990; Smith 1999). It is best viewed as a theory (not a fact), but it is a theory describing the mechanism or process which is involved in various expressions of creative talent.

The key difference between the interpretive view of personal creativity and Gardner's (1993) theory may be that he explains unambiguous creative *achievement* while I have attempted to explain creative *potential*. For reasons like this I once suggested that the word *creativity* not be used (Runco 1991). There are too many disagreements when we use the noun. My recommendation was to always be specific and instead of referring to creativity as a thing by itself we use it only in the form of an adjective. In this manner we would have creative *products*, creative *achievements*, creative *potential*, and so on. As the present chapter demonstrates, these various emphases might lead to certain discrepancies (a few of which exist between Gardner's view and my own), but there also might be commonalities (for example the child-like or assimilatory capacity of creative people, both eminent and the non-eminent). Avoiding the noun "creativity" might help, but of course, the reader is welcome to construct his or her own interpretation.

This chapter is titled "Creativity is Always Personal and Only Sometimes Social" because I wanted to highlight the point that even the eminent levels of creative achievement may depend on the interpretive processes described in the theory of personal creativity. Eminent creative achievement, and for that matter all social expressions of creativity, depend on many other things, in addition to interpretation. Gardner (1993; 1994) does an excellent job of identifying and explaining those others things. Curiosity and a tendency towards self-promotion, for example, often play a role in high-level achievement. It does, however, seem the most parsimonious to separate the social from the personal. I say that in part because eminent creators are famous, as well as creative, but fame can be obtained in many different ways. It is therefore extricable from the creative process. I am also concerned with a reliance on reputation as a part of creativity, given how frequently reputations change (Runco 1999). Even the reputations of Freud and Einstein could diminish given a long enough perspective. It makes no sense to me to focus on qualities that come and go. That would be analogous to describing a person by their attitudes, which by definition are temporary and malleable, instead of their personality traits, which are relatively stable. Alternatively, since reputation depends on influence and social attributions (Kasof 1995; Runco 1995), judging a creator on their reputation would be a bit like judging a person based on his or her family and friends instead of personal qualities of the individual him- or herself. Gardner is quite insistent that "creativity is inherently a communal or cultural judgment" (p. 36). He admits that his approach to creativity "reflects the 'great man/great woman' view of creativity" (p. 37). Gardner and Nemirovksy (1991) put it this way:

> It is a mistake to view creative process as simply an activity which occurs within the mind of a single individual (or small set of individuals). Rather, understanding of the creative process requires a consideration of a dynamic system involving at least three vantage points: the cognitive process and talents exhibited by specific individuals; the structure of knowledge as it exists—and can be transformed—within a particular cultural domain or discipline; and the set of *individuals or institutions empowered to make judgments about the quality of work carried on within specific domains*. (p. 3, emphasis added)

I am a psychologist, not a historian, and for this reason I see greatness, fame, and reputation as social judgments, but creativity as something that is at least initially personal. I see it as interpretive, discretionary, and intentional, and as something that might either be used to change a domain, or used to adapt to experience and solve day-to-day problems in an original and effective manner. In this light it may be that the distinction between potential and high-level performance is not sufficient. Perhaps the compromise necessary for a meta-theory is to view what I am describing as everyday creativity and what Gardner (1993) describes as eminent creativity. Recall here the idea I offered earlier in this chapter about continua and quadrants representing different kinds and levels of creativity. One continuum might represent everyday creativity at some moderate level and eminent creativity at the high extreme. Other continua would be necessary to allow studies of creative potential (not yet expressed) to contribute to the meta-theory.

Creativity is a good thing, a very good thing, and society needs to invest in it (Florida 2005; Rubenson and Runco 1991; 1995). If we focus on an individual's potentials, much can be done; we can invest in many different ways. We can make a difference. This is especially true because we might find individuals who have enormous potential but are not yet using it. The gains there would be huge. What kinds of gains are possible when we focus on eminent creators? Only marginal ones. We may dramatically improve our understanding of history and eminent creativity, but I for one would like to know what to do in the schools to help children solve their problems in a creative fashion.

Before concluding I suggest that we adopt a tactic uncovered by Gardner (1993), namely, simplify the situation, just as the seven creators in his *Creative Minds* simplified their thinking. Recall here how Einstein returned to "the conceptual world of his childhood" (Gardner 1993, p. 10). Gardner even explored the possibility that this tendency to simplify was used in different domains, which is significant given how much emphasis he places on domain differences (Gardner 1983). Again in his words, "I find a noteworthy similarity . . . in the search for the most elementary, the most elemental forms within a domain" (1993, p. 18). This tactic may in turn reflect an interpretive tendency of unambiguously creative individuals. Indeed, Gardner (1993, p. 26) noted how, in the arts, "the seasoned master may develop *highly personal interpretations* of familiar pieces, or, alternatively, *return to those deceptively simple pieces* that may actually prove difficult to execute convincingly and powerfully. Such an analysis helps to explain why creative individual continue to engage in the area of their expertise despite its frustrations, and why so many of them continue to raise the ante, posing evergreater challenges for themselves, even at the risk of sacrificing the customary rewards" (emphases added).

Using this simplification tactic, it would seem that the differences between his ideas and those of the theory of personal creativity come down to the definition of "creativity." Gardner focuses on creative achievement, and for that reason can be quite certain he is in fact discussing creativity. The problem is that generalizations to other persons (and perhaps eras) are questionable. I prefer to look to creative potentials. The problem there is that the people I study may never change a domain or attain any significant reputation. These people may only be creative in adapting to day-to-day problems and hassles or in the self-expression of choosing clothes for the day. Yet that to me seems to be worthwhile, especially if we occasionally stand back and compare the theories that describe eminent and everyday creativity, as we have done here.

REFERENCES

Chown, S.M. 1961. Age and the Rigidities. *Journal of Gerontology* 16, pp. 353–362.

Gardner, H. 1988. Creativity: An Interdisciplinary Perspective. *Creativity Research Journal* 1, pp. 8–26.

———. 1993. *Creating Minds: An Anatomy of Creativity Seen through the Lives of Freud, Einstein, Picasso, Stravinsky, Eliot, Graham, and Gandhi.* New York: Basic Books.

Gardner, H., and R. Nemirovksy. 1991. From Private Institutions to Public Symbol Systems: An Examination of Creative Process in Georg Cantor and Sigmund Freud. *Creativity Research Journal* 4, pp. 1–22.

Gardner, H., and C. Wolf. 1988. The Fruits of Asynchrony: A Psychological Examination of Creativity. *Adolescent Psychiatry* 15, pp. 96–120.

Gruber, H.E. 1996. The Life Space of a Scientist: The Visionary Function and Other Aspects of Jean Piaget's Thinking. *Creativity Research Journal*, pp. 251–265.

Lindauer, M.S. 1992. Creativity in Aging Artists: Contributions from the Humanities to the Psychology of Aging. *Creativity Research Journal* 5, pp. 211–232.

———. 1993. The Span of Creativity among Long-lived Historical Artists. *Creativity Research Journal* 6, pp. 221–239.

Okuda, S.M., M.A. Runco, and D.E. Berger. 1991. Creativity and the Finding and Solving of Real-World Problems. *Journal of Psychoeducational Assessment* 9, pp. 45–53.

Piaget, J. 1976. *To Understand Is to Invent.* New York: Penguin.

———. 1981. Foreword. In H.E. Gruber, *Darwin on Man: A Psychological Study of Scientific Creativity.* Chicago: University of Chicago Press.

Pribram, K.H. 1999. Brain and Creative Activity. In M.A. Runco and S. Pritzker, eds., *Encylcopedia of Creativity* (San Diego: Academic Press), pp. 213–17.

Richards, R. 1990. Everyday Creativity, Eminent Creativity, and Health: Afterview of CRJ Special Issues on Creativity and Health. *Creativity Research Journal* 3, pp. 300–326.

Rubenson, D.L., and M.A. Runco. 1992. The Psychoeconomic Approach to Creativity. *New Ideas in Psychology* 10, pp. 131–147.

Runco, M.A. 1993. On Reputational Paths and Case Studies. *Creativity Research Journal* 6, pp. 487–88.

————. 1995. Insight for Creativity, Expression for Impact. *Creativity Research Journal* 8, pp. 377–390.

————. 1996. Personal Creativity: Definition and Developmental Issues. *New Directions for Child Development* 72 (Summer), pp. 3–30.

Runco, M.A., and I. Chand. 1994. Problem Finding, Evaluative Thinking, and Creativity. In M. A. Runco, ed., *Problem Finding, Problem Solving, and Creativity* (Norwood: Ablex).

Runco, M.A., and R. Richards. 1998. *Eminent Creativity, Everyday Creativity, and Health.* Norwood: Ablex.

9

Gardner on Leadership

ROBERT SPILLANE

There is no psychology; there is only biography and autobiography.

—THOMAS SZASZ

The term 'leadership' is an incantation for the bewitchment of the led.

—CHRISTOPHER HODGKINSON

Leading Minds

Teachers and students of management know Howard Gardner as the author of *Leading Minds: An Anatomy of Leadership* (1997). This celebrated book, written with the collaboration of Emma Laskin, offers a cognitive approach to leadership (Gardner is interested in the 'minds' of leaders and followers), discusses leadership in relation to stages of human development, and provides readers with a fascinating series of case studies of eleven 'leaders': Margaret Mead, J. Robert Oppenheimer, Robert Maynard Hutchins, Alfred P. Sloan, George C. Marshall, Pope John XXIII, Eleanor Roosevelt, Martin Luther King, Margaret Thatcher, Jean Monnet, and Mahatma Gandhi. These eleven 'leaders' are compared with a 'control group' of ten political and military leaders of the twentieth century. They are leaders because Gardner describes a leader as "an individual (or, rarely, a set of individuals), who significantly affects the thoughts, feelings and/or behaviors, of a significant number of individuals" (1997, p. xiii). Some leaders affect others directly through story-telling (Thatcher) and others indirectly through their creations (Mead). Gardner's leaders are of different personalities and they appear before us as, alas, human-all-too-human.

Gardner's eleven vignettes represent a rich source of biographical data and he does not spare us details of the strengths and weaknesses of his leaders. Their human frailties and Gardner's biographical honesty are such that we pause to wonder how these people became leaders, which is, of course, the point of the book. Too often readers encounter, in the leadership literature, sanitised descriptions of the lives of the authors' heroes. Gardner goes to the heart of the achievements and failures of his leaders so that we are left to reflect on the necessary or sufficient conditions for the emergence of leaders. To assist us in our reflections he acknowledges that he is interested in the minds (thoughts, feelings, images) of leaders (and followers); he is not interested in their personalities or motivational states.

Readers should be grateful to Gardner for sparing them another study of the personalities of so-called leaders since the dispositionalist approach to leadership has singularly failed to produce any meaningful generalisations, although tautologies abound. When authors emphasise the personalities or motivational needs of leaders they invariably depend on tautologies for their plausibility. One reads, for example, in the leadership literature, that 'charismatic leaders have special personal qualities'. Gardner flirts with tautologies (for example his central thesis is that leaders influence their fellow human beings), but he does not claim that there is a 'leader personality'. Indeed, his eleven biographies quickly disabuse readers of the very idea of a consistent leader personality. The personality trait approach to the study of leadership—based on inferences from leader behavior—faces the challenge of explaining the behavior of followers, and it runs into insuperable problems (Spillane and Martin 2005).

Yet there is in Gardner's cognitive approach to leadership a lingering sense that there are consistent qualities of people which qualify them for the status of leader. In the section headed *The Antecedents of Leading* Gardner offers several generalizations about the personal qualities of future leaders and their relations with others (loss of parent, contrasting set of relations with parents, unhappy childhood, striking appearance, predisposition to risk-taking, sense of personal toughness, need of power, linguistic intelligence) (pp. 32–34). To be fair, he does not claim that these qualities and relations are necessary conditions. He does, however, write of the "early markers of leadership" which apply to "some" proto-leaders. These are, at best, generalisations with little or no predictive power.

It can confidently be said that the search for stable and enduring personal qualities of leaders has failed, and must fail, because leaders cannot adequately be understood apart from the dialectical relationship in which they are involved with their followers. Both must be considered partners in the game of leadership and attempts to analyse one party at the expense of the other are invalid. Leadership is a relationship between leader and followers.

Gardner acknowledges the truism that leaders cannot exist without followers (p. 36) and uses story-telling as the basis for the dialectical relationship between (direct) leaders and their followers, but confuses the issue by recommending his 'cognitive approach' with its emphasis on the 'minds' of leaders and followers. He never explains the relationship between the behavior of story-telling and 'minds', leaving it to the reader to wonder whether the term 'mind' is merely a metaphor. In fact, the word 'mind' does not even appear in his subject index.

The back cover of the paperback edition tells readers that, although there have been many previous studies of leadership, Gardner's book is the first to concentrate on "the crucial component of leadership—the human mind"—by exploring the dynamic relationship between the minds of leaders and those of their followers. Gardner's cognitive approach views leadership as a process which occurs within the minds of individuals who live in a culture. He is interested in

> *the mind* of the leader and *the minds* of the followers (whom I sometimes refer to as audience members or collaborators). Accordingly, this book is a sustained examination, first, of the ways in which leaders of different types achieve varying degrees of success in characterizing and resolving important life issues *in their own minds* and, second, of how in parallel or in turn, they attempt *to alter the minds* of their various audiences to effect desired changes. (p. 15, emphasis added)

This is what Gardner means by a cognitive approach to leadership: he studies ideas, thoughts or images rather than observed behavior, personality, or motivational factors.

> Confronted with the phenomenon of leadership, a cognitively oriented scientist is likely to ask such questions as, What are the ideas (or stories) of the leader? How have they developed? How are they communicated, understood and misunderstood? How do they interact with other stories, especially competing counterstories, that have already drenched the conscious-

ness of audience members? How do key ideas (or stories) affect the thoughts, feelings and behaviors of other individuals? (p. 16)

Just how his cognitive approach can provide an answer to the last (and, given his definition of leadership, the crucial) question is by no means clear on Gardner's account. Questions about the thoughts and feelings of individuals cannot be answered from the eleven biographical sketches. In fact, they cannot be answered at all because it is impossible to study the 'minds' (thoughts, feelings, images, and so forth) of leaders or followers. One can study what they do and what they say; one cannot study thoughts and feelings except as inductive inferences from observed behavior (public data) or from communications about private data. As a cognitivist Gardner would argue that inductive inferences from observed behavior and communications are reasonable and helpful; nominalists, behaviorists, and existentialists would argue they are unreasonable and unhelpful. Critics would want to ask Gardner to explain how thoughts and feelings differ from behavior and how they can be variously assessed. What do we add to our understanding of leader/follower behavior by invoking such concepts as thoughts and feelings, which are at best inferences from behavior, and at worst abstract nouns which we reify at our (linguistic) peril?

Gardner is not just interested in leadership, which would be pointless given the scope of his description of leaders as individuals who significantly influence others, he is interested in effective leadership. In one sense 'effective leadership' is a pleonasm since the fact of leadership attests to its effectiveness, so that leadership cannot be ineffective. In another sense, 'effective leadership' means that the relationship is to be judged pragmatically by its consequences, and this is the sense in which Gardner uses the term. But pragmatic interpretations invariably suffer from problems of circularity, i.e. leaders are successful when they succeed. It is a truism that leaders achieve a degree of success and an historical fact that their effectiveness is finite and, in many cases, short-lived. Is it accurate to say that, for example, Churchill was an effective leader in 1940 and an ineffective leader in 1945? Or was it the case that he was a leader in 1940 and he was not a leader in 1945? The scope of Gardner's definition of a leader is, however, so wide that he is able to say that Churchill was a leader in 1940 and remained so until his death (since he significantly influenced a significant number of people every year of his life after 1940). The advantage of Gardner's pragmatism is that it enables him to use the criterion of effectiveness after the event without modifying the status of a leader. So he can say that Churchill was effective in 1940 as a leader because of the effectiveness of his communications, and he was ineffective in 1945 *as a leader* because of the ineffectiveness of his communications. Circular reasoning of this type has haunted pragmatic thinkers since the days of William James.

Gardner's central thesis is: leaders fashion stories, especially and importantly stories of identity. Not only should leaders be good storytellers, they should embody the stories in their lives. "The ultimate impact of the leader depends most significantly on the particular story that he or she relates or embodies, and the reception to that story on the part of the audiences (or collaborators or followers)" (p. 14). The pragmatism is obvious in the assertion that "(w)hat links the eleven individuals with whom I lead off, and the score of others from this century whose names could readily have been substituted for them, is the fact that they arrived at a story that worked for them and, ultimately, for others as well" (p. 14).

It is well known that, philosophically, pragmatism is concerned with consequences rather than causes and Gardner's pragmatism is no exception. Gardner says that leaders tell stories "about themselves and their groups, about where they were coming from and where they were headed, about what was to be feared, struggled against, and dreamed about" (p. 14). But most people tell such stories (to priests, psychotherapists, friends, lovers, students, business subordinates, football teams, and so on), so what is special or different about leaders' stories? Presumably individuals become leaders when their stories 'significantly affect' a 'significant number of people'. In short, particular stories do not guarantee leadership; an individual becomes a leader by virtue of the consequences of his story-telling for a significant number of people.

Pragmatic philosophers say that truth is what works. Gardner says that leaders' stories are those that work. If the stories don't work, the story-tellers are not leaders and Gardner is forced back to his general description of leaders as individuals who *influence* others. Clearly, some types of stories do not produce followers, and so they don't 'work'. We are led, therefore, to the pragmatic (and circular) conclusion that we only know that leaders' stories work, when they work. But a theory which explains everything (after the event), can predict nothing (before the event). So leaders fashion stories which work for them and for others. A particular story is only known to be successful after it succeeds. We are caught again in circular reasoning—leaders relate influential stories, they are influential because leaders relate them. And moreover, "ordinary leaders relate ordinary stories, innovative leaders relate innovative stories, visionary leaders relate visionary stories" (pp. 10–11). Well, yes.

To escape the charge of circularity Gardner has to offer an account of the special nature of leaders' stories. He attempts this difficult task in the chapter headed *The Leaders' Stories*. He begins by admitting that he uses the term 'story' in a broad sense, in that he includes narratives (in the linguistic sense), but also "invented accounts in any symbol system, ranging from a new form of explanation in the physical sciences to a novel mode of expression in dance or poetry" (p. 42). Very broad indeed.

In short, Gardner offers readers the tautology that leaders communicate with followers and the truism that stories reflect different levels of sophistication. More specifically, and of empirical interest to researchers, is the proposition that leaders attempt to convince others of a clear vision of life based on personal and group identity. "I maintain that the most fundamental stories fashioned by leaders concern issues of personal and group identity; those leaders who presume to bring about major alterations across a significant population must in some way help their audience members think through who they are" (p. 62). Now this proposition applies to many categories of people who would not normally be called 'leaders', for example factory supervisors, football coaches, business executives, professors. If Gardner wants to say that leadership is, or can be, a feature of these job categories, then he has an interesting view, to say the least, of followership.

'Leader' derives from 'laedare' which means to lead people on a journey. The concept carries the assumption that followers choose to accompany the leader on his travels and this assumes that there is no conflict of interest between the parties. Obviously, these assumptions cannot be said necessarily to apply to all super- and subordinate relationships. Factory supervisors and business executives have coercive power over their subordinate colleagues and it is naive to believe that the latter freely choose to 'follow' the former. Gardner's dependence on the general relationship of 'influence' means that he fails adequately to consider the power relationships involved in hierarchical relationships and the diverse ways in which people 'follow' others, most of which are not examples of leadership.

Leading Minds concludes with 'six constant features of leaders' and six features which characterise modern leadership. According to Gardner the ideal-typical qualities of an exemplary leader include: youthful interest in people and excellent speaking skills; willingness to confront individuals in authority; willingness to take risks; concern with moral issues; widely travelled; wide range of contacts; capacity for sustained reflection. The six constants of leadership are: the story (leader must have a central message); the audience (must be receptive to the message); the organisation (as a basis for leadership); the embodiment (leaders must embody their stories); direct and indirect leadership (creative leaders influence others through their creations, political leaders influence audiences directly); the issue of expertise (as a basis for technical authority). Finally, Gardner offers guidelines for effective leadership built around the need to: appreciate enduring features of leadership; anticipate and deal with new trends; encourage recognition of the problems, paradoxes and possibilities of leadership.

These conclusions are derived from Gardner's sample of 'leaders' and so the validity of his conclusions depends on the validity of his sample. Neither is convincing. For example, Gardner makes such astonishing assertions as "(t)here is little question, however, that from an early age, certain individuals stand out among others for their personal attractiveness, as is true of E.L. (the exemplary leader). Most often, the traits are physical—leaders are often tall, good-looking, and graceful" (p. 288). The first sentence is a tautology and so trivially true. The second sentence is empirical and false. Not only is the second sentence not true of leaders generally (Alexander, Julius Caesar, Napoleon, Hitler, Stalin, Mussolini, Churchill, for starters), it is not even true of Gardner's sample. He qualifies his assertion with the following tautology: "If they lack these physical characteristics, they may at least have strong defining facial characteristics or piercing eyes" (p. 288). Well, they may and then again they may not. Furthermore, these sentences would seem to cover all cases because it is difficult to imagine who would be exempted from these descriptions. Who lacks strong defining facial characteristics?

The main problem is that, in trying to work with the relational concept of 'influence', Gardner casts his net too wide. When we start calling academics, business executives and administrators 'leaders' there is no line of demarcation between those who influence others because of the position they occupy and those who influence others because of their exemplary personal qualities. We can be influenced by others in various ways (positively or negatively, voluntarily or involuntarily), and we follow others for diverse reasons (traditional, legal, rational). By relying on 'influence' as the fundamental relationship between leader and followers, Gardner fails to acknowledge cases where a conflict of interest exists between the parties and where it does not. This would seem to be an important issue where people are 'influenced' coercively by people in positions of power compared with those whose influence is personal and benign. And Gardner's distinction between direct and indirect leadership allows, say, builders and architects to be called leaders simply because a significant number of people have to live in their 'creations'. Since, indirect leadership, through artistic creations, does not require story-telling the status of leader is based on the very general concept 'influence'.

Obviously proud of his theory of direct and indirect leadership, Gardner writes: "The distinction between indirect leadership, through the creation of symbolic products, and direct leadership, through story-telling and embodying, is also novel: I have sought to build bridges between the influence exerted by a creative individual and the influence wielded by a traditional organizational or national leader" (p. 296). Without the qualifying requirement of story-telling, Gardner's approach to leadership reverts to the study of those individuals who significantly influence a significant number of people, directly or indirectly. The potential number of leaders is therefore indeterminate and the analysis of leadership pointless. With the inclusion of story-telling (narratives, messages) as a necessary condition of (direct) leadership (that is, leaders communicate with their followers), the theory is tautological since the negation of Gardner's proposition is self-contradictory. The pragmatic claim that his study has focused on "individuals generally seen as leaders by their contemporaries" (p. 296) begs the question. That, say, Hutchins and Sloan were capable administrators is clear; that they were leaders is not.

As if to anticipate objections to his description of leaders, Gardner writes: "It remains an open question whether leaders defined in a radically different way can still satisfy my criterion of 'affecting thoughts, feelings, and behaviors of a significant number of individuals'" (p. 296). That his criterion is so elastic as to be pointless to try to satisfy seems to have escaped him. And should we be able, in a 'scientific' study, to define 'leaders' in radically different ways?

Gardner acknowledges that his study raises several obvious questions. He admits to a traditionalist approach in that his "focus is on the single leader—generally recognised as such—and on the considerable agency that the person may gain because of his authoritative position and/or powers of persuasion" (p. 295). He accepts that he has not emphasised or questioned the validity of other approaches to leadership, based on power, politics, the public or the personality of leaders. Nor has he concerned himself with "contemporary revisionist critiques of leadership—leadership as collective; leadership as instigated by the audience, rather than by the nominal leader; leadership on the part of those who have been relatively 'without voice' or 'without a place at the table', or a deconstructionist or postmodernist critique that would question the entire legitimacy of talk about leadership" (for which many thanks) (p.

295). He admits that he has focused on individuals "generally seen as leaders" by their contemporaries and, in so doing, begs the question about the crucial relationship that obtains between them. For Gardner that relationship is 'influence'. I shall argue that it is 'authority'.

Leadership as Relationship

When Gardner writes about the several choices confronting a student of leadership—a choice between the study of leaders or the study of followers—he gives the impression that these are, methodologically, viable alternatives. They are not. The leader-follower dichotomy is false and it is not a viable method for the study of leadership. The only viable prospect for studying leadership is the relational approach favored by social psychologists. Here one chooses to regard the relationships between leader and followers as the objective element in the picture. At first blush this seems unpromising as a scientific strategy because the very words used to name these relationships are unavoidably abstract and lack the kind of physical referent commonly associated with science. Nevertheless, science often works with abstract constructs. Several important thinkers in the social sciences have taken the stand that the key to the puzzle of how to be scientific about personality and society, leaders and followers, managers and subordinates, psychiatrists and 'patients', and so forth, lies in regarding these relationships as the primary reality. George Herbert Mead in sociology and Thomas Szasz in psychiatry are well-known contributors to the discipline of social psychology in which this orientation persists most strongly.

According to the social psychological perspective, a relationship once named refers to an irreducible element in the researcher's conceptual scheme. There is no way in which the relationship between leaders and their followers can be analysed in terms of component relationships. Leadership stands for a relationship; it is not the sum of leaders' personalities or minds. We may, of course, make inferences about the personalities or motivational states of individual leaders and their followers from the way the relationship manifests itself, and these inferences can be used as explanations for particular cases of leadership. It is also true that leadership overlaps with other relationships between the parties, such as conformity, obedience, influence, power and authority. But all of these may be present and leadership absent. So a relationship correctly identified can be regarded as irreducible, and this gives it valid status as a scientific starting-point (Spillane and Martin 2005, pp. 16–17).

Gardner, as we have seen, emphasises 'influence' as the key relationship underpinning leadership. So inclusive is this concept that he is faced with the difficult, if not impossible, task of deciding who are leaders and who are not. Because he fails to undertake an adequate conceptual analysis of the relationships between influence, power, and authority, his selection of leaders is unconvincing. And because his generalisations and conclusions are based on his sample, they too are unconvincing.

Influence and Power

Gardner's eleven 'leaders' represent an odd collection of prominent men and women, or what Americans call 'celebrities'. Of their fame and influence there can be no doubt. But it is not at all clear why celebrities should be called leaders—not clear until one realises that the scope of Gardner's description of a leader is so broad that celebrities would qualify. A leader is, for Gardner, an individual who significantly affects (that is to say, influences) the thoughts, feelings, or behaviors of a significant number of individuals. This description is qualified by the admission that a significant number of individuals has to recognise (authorise) the individual as a leader. The notions of influence and authority are thus confounded.

That 'affect's is synonymous with 'influences' is apparent when Gardner writes: "I see both Churchill and Einstein as leaders—as individuals who significantly influence the thoughts, behaviours and/or feelings of others . . . Einstein and Churchill mark two ends of a continuum that denotes the capacity of a person (or group of persons) to *influence* other people" (p. 6, italics in the original). "(Indeed, I could have termed this study *An Examination of Influence*, but that lexical move would have undermined the reorientation in thinking about both creativity and leadership that is my goal)" (p. 6). It is unfortunate that Gardner did not elaborate because this sentence in parentheses is of primary importance.

It is clear throughout his book that Gardner is indeed concerned with the process of 'influence'. He asserts that "these eleven individuals all became leaders in the sense that I am using the term: persons who by word and/or personal example, markedly influence the behavior, thoughts, and/or feelings of a significant number of their fellow human beings (here termed followers or audience members)" (pp. 8–9). These descriptions of leaders, built on the notion of 'influence', inform Gardner's theory, methodology, and conclusions and raise, as we shall see, a number of conceptual and logical problems which Gardner does not adequately deal with. For example, he does not analyse the relation-

ships between influence, power, and authority which is especially indicated given the difficulties facing researchers who try to separate a
leader's personal influence from his positional power. This separation is
important for Gardner's study because he is interested in 'leading
minds', in other words, influential *individuals* (Thatcher) rather than
influential *positions* (Prime Minister).

What does it mean to talk of a leader 'affecting' the behavior of followers? It is not clear whether Gardner, who claims scientific legitimacy for his study, assumes a causal relationship when he uses the word
'affects'. If so, a power relationship must apply—so that any case in
which the behaviour of person A is affected by person B is an instance
of the power of B over A. But Gardner's analysis suggests that for this
power to exist it has to be accepted (or authorised) by followers (otherwise they would not qualify as collaborators or followers). The quandary
which then arises can be expressed thus: (a) leader power is equivalent
to cause; (b) its operation requires the consent of the persons operated
upon (followers); hence, by deduction, (c) followers must consent before
a leader may cause anything to happen to them. The absurdity of this
conclusion attests to the falsity of the premises. It is of the essence of
power, as it operates upon people, that their consent is irrelevant. Where
a person's consent is relevant, the situation has moved beyond power to
authority. By relying on the general term 'influence' Gardner obscures
the important differences between power and authority.

Gardner's failure to set up conceptual distinctions between influence
and power means that the issue of conflict of interest is by-passed. This
is important when we compare such 'leaders' as Pope John XXIII and
Gandhi with, say, Hutchins and Sloan, where conflict of interest is more
likely to be an issue in the two latter cases. Where no conflict of interest
between the parties exists influence is not regarded as power, for such
activities as inducement, encouragement and education are then simply
what the terms suggest. But where a conflict of interest does exist, even
if latent, such activities are defined as manipulation and regarded as
cases in which the terms 'influence' and 'power' are synonymous.
Where a conflict of interest exists and either force or coercion comes
into play, power of a kind not classified as influence is present.

In the study of leadership it is important to identify power independently from influence. Followers may be influenced by anything and
everything about a leader, including his habits, manners, actions and
rhetoric, whether or not these are directed at influencing them. That
seems to be incontrovertible. But it is not the same as saying that a
leader is exercising power over followers, or that what is influencing

followers is the leader's power. Followers may be quite correct in believing that a leader has certain powers and may be suitably impressed; but they may be equally impressed when their beliefs about the leader's power are in fact false. On the other hand, a leader may make every effort to influence followers psychologically and fail completely, even if his powers extend to beating them to death. Even at this extreme it can be said that followers are influenced by the leader since they do something (die) that they would not otherwise do. Obviously, the extent of confusion that can be engendered by conflating two such terms is infinite.

Gardner acknowledges the importance of power in the study of leadership but offers a remarkable opinion about its effects—or non-effects. "I do not for a moment underestimate the importance of power as a motivation or a force in its own right, but I insist that, of itself, power—as opposed to terror—cannot bring about significant changes. The vantage point of power, however achieved, needs to be yoked to specific messages—to stories—that can direct and guide an inner circle and a wider polity" (p. 16). This assertion is patently false. Power can, and does, bring about significant change. An individual's personal power may be used in unauthorised ways. This may occur within a formal organisation but is more usually found outside it (for example, crime). A state of affairs in which personal powers were not bounded by authority would, accordingly, be a state of barbarism. The movement towards a civil state, or organisation, is characterised by success in the struggle to bring power and its exercise under the moderating control of authority. This involves profound social and psychological developments: social because consensus has to be achieved as to which actions are morally acceptable; psychological because individuals have to control themselves according to these rules. Gardner is surely right to suggest that power is conditional upon the concession of authority. Whether that is achieved through leaders' stories and their acceptance (or authorisation) by followers is another matter.

Power and Authority

Power and authority must also be distinguished. The power exercised by leaders is dependent on their abilities to mobilise the activities of their followers and this is, in turn, dependent on the extent to which followers concede authority to leaders. The power attributed to leaders is, therefore, conditional on the concession of authority and is defined and circumscribed by these concessions. It is not enough merely to state the tautology that leaders influence people. Nor is it enough to say that leaders have the power to influence people because of the stories they relate. Their stories are successful insofar as they are judged to be authoritative.

The assent of the person to whom a story is addressed is a necessary condition for the establishment of it as authoritative, and if this is to occur certain conditions must be met. It must be such that a follower understands it, believes it to be consistent with the purposes of his group (if any), and believes it to be compatible with his personal interests. Authority is, therefore, a quality of a communication (or story) by virtue of which it is accepted. Carl Friedrich (1963) would add that, in the case of political, bureaucratic and managerial authority, it is a quality of a communication that is capable of *reasoned elaboration*. And reasoning means the ability to argue about relevant issues. Arguing is not, however, a necessary condition of leadership and is often not a feature of it at all.

Authority, then, refers to a relationship between persons or between person surrogates (such as institutional positions) and it is dissolved by dissent. Since authority implies more than a net advantage to individuals, it contains a moral element relating to the common good. Accordingly, it is sensitive to psychological factors. Power, on the other hand, does not require assent and its effects are not cancelled by dissent. Power is morally neutral and insensitive to psychological evaluation. Particular uses of power, by leaders for example, are morally evaluated and classed as being in accord with or counter to authority. The use by a leader of power that runs counter to authority may induce assent but not authority (Spillane and Martin 2005, p. 91).

Rulership and Leadership

To describe a leader as "an individual who significantly affects the thoughts, feelings and/or behaviours of a significant number of individuals" raises two questions. First, are there individuals who meet this descriptive requirement and yet are patently not leaders? Is, for example, a policeman on point-duty a leader? And Donald Duck would, on Gardner's account, qualify as a leader. He might answer in the negative to both questions since he has selected for study individuals "seen as leaders by their contemporaries." But this qualification entails more than a relation of influence; it entails one of authority because it assumes a relation involving some form of concession or authorisation.

Second, is the leader's influence positive or negative in its effects? Are notorious serial killers who significantly affect our behavior leaders? Again, Gardner's answer is, presumably, that since serial killers are not 'seen as leaders by their contemporaries' (or at least not by a significant number of people), they do not qualify as leaders. But should they become freedom fighters, and their killings re-defined as heroic actions, they may become leaders. Again this involves a series of judgements by potential followers about the right or legitimacy of the potential leader's actions and their effects on followers and the wider community. And this places us in the domain of authority.

Third, what is the relationship between rulership and leadership? Gardner does not address this issue even though it is clear that most of his 'leaders' were rulers in the literal sense of the term—there was a strong probability that their commands would be obeyed, voluntarily or involuntarily. Is this equally true of leaders? Clearly not if we mean Gardner's indirect leaders. But what of his direct leaders? Do they get their following in the same way rulers get theirs? Both rulership and leadership entail obedience. In the case of rulership it may be voluntary or involuntary, coercive or consensual. If this is true of leadership then there is no difference between the two concepts. If, however, we allow a difference between rulership and leadership, it would seem that leadership entails voluntary, but not involuntary, obedience.

Max Weber can help us here with his analysis of rulership (*Herrshaft*) in modern capitalist societies. His essay *The Protestant Ethic and the Spirit of Capitalism* (1904–05) maintains that Calvinism and other Puritan sects set up those psychological conditions which account for the appearance in the West of a form of capitalism not seen anywhere else in the world at any other time in history; and also, indirectly, the conditions for the accumulation of a uniquely successful body of scientific knowledge. Both capitalism and science have existed elsewhere and at other times, but never with the emphasis on the rational which is the legacy of the New Capitalism. Given Gardner's choice of leaders (especially Oppenheimer, Sloan, Hutchins, Marshall) it is worth rehearsing some of Weber's main points so that a more effective distinction can be made between rulers and leaders.

Bureaucratic Rulership

Essentially Weber sees capitalism as a form of social organisation based on the allocation of fixed duties to hierarchically arranged positions. The duties are fixed through the introduction of general rules, often written regulations. Since this applies not only to the separate institutions of the state but to the state itself (in which the general rules take the form of laws), a high degree of concord can be developed between the state and its constituent institutions, although the extent to which every institution is forced to conform in function to the requirements of the centralised authority may vary. So far as the person is concerned, his job within the total pattern of co-operation is specified in terms of routines designed to deal with the general case. In fact these routines and their concordant regulations may create the general case, since they define all other cases as aberrations or emergencies. The organisation is one which can best produce a standard article or service, so this defining manoeuvre is essential.

The formal power to give the orders required for the carrying out of these duties is distributed in a stable way and includes rules delimiting the coercive means at the disposal of officials. Only persons who have the 'generally regulated qualifications' to serve are employed. The hierarchy and the graded levels of authority generate a firmly ordered system of super- and subordination in which there is always a supervisor to every office (except the highest). Ideally the governed have the right of appealing against the decision of any office-holder to a higher authority, in a definitely regulated manner.

Associated with finite roles are regulations specifying what must be done and/or what must not. The role specifications and the regulations then constitute the basis for the institution's claim that it has rationalised action, since by following them the person should be able to serve the aims of the institution and by implication the good of society at large. Theoretically, he has no need to understand the purposes served by the organisation nor to be able to judge whether any member's actions support it. He has merely to accept a very narrow responsibility - that of carrying out his own 'part' with precision and reliability. On this basis, social structure can be rationalised to stricter and stricter degrees, and so it may be brought to resemble the conceptual model of a social machine.

Weber is explicit that bureaucracy is a machine and that it is an instrument in which people are merely functionaries. This impersonal character means that the mechanism—in contrast to structures based on personal loyalty—will readily work for anyone who knows how to gain control over it. The system specifies powers to be exercised by the person occupying each position in the organisation; formal power is made to cover the functions required in each office as exhaustively as possible. This power is attached to the *position* itself rather than to persons and is defined as explicitly as possible.

`It is evident that the form of rulership which operates in this system differs from the earlier types. It is attached to a position, not a person, so it is the position which claims the greater stability and importance. It gains this character because its functions are considered essential to the production of some material or service. The rationale for conceding rulership to such a position therefore rests ultimately on the desirability of the item being produced. There could, of course, be much argument about the desirability of producing this or that item, but the Protestant Ethic cut short any debate on the matter simply by asserting that the ultimate value of anything was not to be ascertained by men. With this as a major premise, no argument about the desirability of anything, whether it be bombs or mustard gas, can be conclusive. All participants in these organisations from top to bottom, must take it on faith that production is desirable on its own account, and therefore everyone is relieved of any obligation to show that the organisation serves such abstract purposes as contributing to human welfare or happiness. When the process did actually lead to desirable goods becoming available in quantities, the concession of rulership to the organisational hierarchy came to appear to be simply rational. If there is something a little odd in a conscience which acknowledges the positional rather than the personal, the rational rather than the moral as its source, it is nevertheless effective.

Weber's analysis leads, therefore, to the question of the difference between rulership and leadership, and on this issue there has been considerable debate. He reduced rulership to three 'ideal-types', the 'charismatic', the 'traditional' and the 'legal-rational'. Briefly, charismatic rulership is based on a person, usually one who offers a solution to some very deep-seated and recalcitrant problem, and the solution offered is usually of a kind which both defines the problem more clearly than has been done before and gives the impression that the person offering it holds the key to understanding the central problems of existence. Charismatics are, therefore, leaders in the thousand-year tradition of the Anglo-Saxon word 'laedare'—to lead people on a journey. Weber would class Gandhi and Martin Luther King as charismatic. Charismatics, it should be noted, are almost always assassinated. In Machiavelli's terms, they are unarmed prophets who always come to grief.

Traditional rulership is well represented in the feudal system where person and position were usually connected by birth ('ascribed status') and there was a certain element of paternalism expected, so that the welfare of the inferior depended to some extent on the personal favor of the superior. Here, the inferior's estimate of the superior as a person could intrude on what was due to his position.

Legal-rational rulership, in contrast, eliminates the personal and much of the uncertainty that goes with it and concentrates directly on whether a certain task gets fulfilled. Unlike the traditional and charismatic claims to rulership, legal-rational rulership is embedded in the social order. It extends to individuals only in so far as they occupy an organisational office and even then their powers are limited to a 'sphere of competence' as defined within that social order. Obedience is due to individuals because they occupy a particular office and perform in their role with the appropriate technical competence. There is no other reason to obey their commands.

The great social change set in motion by the Reformation was, in these terms, a rise to predominance of legal-rational rulership over the traditional type which characterised the feudal system. But the Reformation also saw the transfer of spiritual rulership to the secular rulers, for monarchs and other heads of state became 'spiritual leaders' of their nations, and some took on mystical attributes in the eyes of their members. In these cases, the direction of transformation was from charismatic 'leadership' to legal-rational 'rulership'. An obvious case is Hitler who institutionalised his charisma by creating the office of the Führer of the Third Reich, recognised by the personal salute 'Heil Hitler'.

Gardner's Leaders

It is the merit of Weber's analysis that we can appreciate the difficulty in classifying as leaders (rather than rulers), business executives (Sloan), military officers (Marshall), scientists (Oppenheimer), administrators (Hutchins), academics (Mead). Charismatics, like Gandhi, Hitler, and Mao Zedong are clearly leaders. Where the basis of rulership is legal-rational (without prior charismatic status) it is difficult to understand why such people, however effective they are, should be called leaders. And this is where Gardner's dependence on 'influence' weakens his case. He repeats the truism that leaders need followers but most of the people we follow are not leaders. We follow the policeman who directs us to the side of the road, but we do not call him a leader no matter how efficient he is. We follow the advice of the car mechanic to sell our car but we do not call him a leader no matter how competent he is. And so it goes for politicians, managers, military officers and bureaucrats. If we follow them, and it is frequently a rational decision not to do so, it is for legal reasons or because we judge them to be technical experts. Who they are as *persons* is not important.

Charismatics are in a different category altogether, as Weber realised when he referred to them as 'leaders'. Charismatics acquire their following because of an "uncommon and extraordinary devotion of a group of followers to the sacredness or the heroic force or the exemplariness of an individual and the order revealed or created by him" (Weber 1947, pp. 358–59). In following a charismatic, individuals have to be prepared to suspend their critical judgements and invest considerable emotion, and thus faith, in the person and his proposed journey. Gardner is right to emphasise the importance of story-telling in this endeavor but he is wrong to attribute the success of other celebrities and rulers to this ability.

Contra Gardner, it can be argued that in matters of everyday life we don't need leaders. If we follow individuals it is because of the role they occupy or the technical skills they possess. In short, we follow competent individuals because it is rational to do so. But when we are faced with emergencies, with attendant extraordinary needs, leadership is called forth. History teaches us that 'natural' leaders in moments of distress were neither appointed office-holders nor 'professionals' but the bearers of specific gifts that were considered extraordinary.

Charisma is radically opposed to bureaucratic organisation because it is self-determined and sets its own limits. It is opposed to the economic infrastructure of bureaucracies and to their rules, roles and rewards. Charismatic leadership is naturally unstable because the mere fact of recognising the personal mission and extraordinary powers of charismatics establishes their status. They must perform heroic, miraculous deeds and should they cease to do so, their status and power evaporate.

If we choose to confine the study of leadership to charismatics, the range of candidates is narrow. If we embrace Gardner's approach, the range is very wide indeed. Moreover, there is no reason to accept Weber's trichotomy—other approaches to rulership and leadership are possible.

Weber, for example, makes rationality a basis for legal-rational rulership and considers all personal rulership to be based on non-rational criteria. The competent individual, on this account, derives his power from exceptional personal characteristics of a non-rational nature. Yet it is apparent that some people may secure a sizeable following, not because of their charismatic qualities, but because they propose to solve problems with which others are grappling. One thinks here of survivors of a plane crash who turn to a competent stranger to lead them out of the jungle. In short, there is nothing so rational as following a person because he is likely to solve important problems, even though he may fall well short of charismatic status. We need a separate category that would account for the fact that certain people have special knowledge and abilities, even though they do not hold a formal office. This is to say that particular, non-charismatic individuals may have their personal power sanctioned rationally because of their ability to help a group achieve its goals. Such people may become leaders.

Why Leadership?

Rulers throughout history have wanted to believe that others obeyed them, not because they had the power to enforce obedience, but because they were 'born leaders'. This myth was invented by Plato and has been so successful that it is still debated seriously in business schools and management conferences. Plato, in *The Republic*, called the story of the 'born leader' the great lordly lie. "Could we perhaps fabricate one of those very handy lies? With the help of one single lordly lie we may, if we are lucky, persuade even the rulers themselves" (414). In this way rulers can become leaders and (attempt to) bewitch their followers.

'Leadership' is today a popular notion and especially appeals to politicians, journalists, managers and bureaucrats. Among managers this concern with leadership has been, for more than half a century, a fetish. In 1951 two American sociologists argued that managers' fixation with leadership derived from the fact that they wanted to believe that their power over their subordinates resulted from the latter's recognition of their superior ability. Power was, of course, left out of the story (Miller and Form 1951, p. 195). The way in which the notion of leadership has been used by 'servants of power' in industry and government has been well documented by Baritz (1960) but his book has had little impact on modern management. Today there is no more popular topic in management and government administration than leadership.

Wittgenstein (1997) argued that the meaning of a word depends on its role in the language game of which it is a member. The words 'ruler' and 'leader' operate in quite different language games—as rulers know only too well. That they (and others) want us to believe they are leaders by invoking a language game which includes the ideas of gifted and superior individuals leading others on a journey to paradise, would appeal to Plato (and to Machiavelli). But history tells us that leaders are just as (if not more) likely to lead us to hell. Gardner tells us that he has selected his 'leaders' carefully, a result of which is the convenient allocation to the status of a 'control group' such leaders as Hitler, Lenin, Stalin and Mao Zedong. Had he included them in his sample, his conclusions would have been quite different.

Gardner's book is a bold attempt to analyse leadership. But most of his 'leaders' are rulers—Gandhi and King are the exceptions in that they achieved their following largely without the assistance of formal power.

There is, however, the possibility in Gardner's study of separating the rulers from the leaders and conducting a comparative analysis of their backgrounds, skills and rhetorical abilities. There can be little doubt that leaders (but not necessarily rulers) throughout the ages have been masters of rhetoric. So Gardner is surely right to emphasise the importance of story-telling in leadership. But his attempt to explain the success of such rulers as Mead, Oppenheimer, Hutchins, Sloan, Marshall, and Roosevelt by an appeal to their rhetorical powers is unconvincing. By failing to distinguish between rulership and leadership he has promoted celebrities and bureaucratic functionaries to a dubious status.

REFERENCES

Baritz, Loren. 1960. *The Servants of Power: A History of the Use of Social Science in American Industry*. New York: Wiley.

Friedrich, Carl. 1963. *Man and His Government*. New York: McGraw-Hill.

Gardner, Howard. 1997. *Leading Minds: An Anatomy of Leadership*. London: Harper Collins.

Hodgkinson, Christopher. 1983. *The Philosophy of Leadership*. Oxford: Blackwell.

Miller, Delbert, and William Form. 1951. *Industrial Sociology: The Sociology of Work Organisations*. New York: Harper and Row.

Plato. 1968. *The Republic of Plato*. New York: Basic Books.

Spillane, Robert, and John Martin. 2005. *Personality and Performance: Foundations for Managerial Psychology*. Sydney: University of New South Wales Press.

Szasz, Thomas. 1976. *Heresies*. Garden City: Doubleday.

Weber, Max. 1947. *The Theory of Social and Economic Organisation*. Oxford: Oxford University Press.

———. 1985. *The Protestant Ethic and the Spirit of Capitalism*. London: Counterpoint.

Wittgenstein, Ludwig. 1997. *Philosophical Investigations*. Oxford: Blackwell.

10

The Second Gardner's Late Shift: From Psychology to Outer Space?

CARLOS E. VASCO

Introduction

As with many famous authors, there are now not one but two Howard Gardners. There is the first Gardner (1980–2000), the brilliant author of *Artful Scribbles; Art, Mind, and Brain; Frames of Mind; The Mind's New Science; The Unschooled Mind; The Disciplined Mind; Creating Minds; Leading Minds,* and *Intelligence Revisited.* There is now the second Gardner (2001 to our day), the thoughtful co-author of *Good Work* (2001) and *Making Good* (2003), the first fruits of the *GoodWork* Project.

The first Gardner of the old millennium is well known throughout the world: his Theory of Multiple Intelligences is now twenty-one years old and thriving. Canada, Sweden, Spain, Italy, Argentina, Colombia, Mexico: you name it, and he can quote to you quite a few successful MI-experiences there. No doubt, he is one of the top-ranking psychologists of America, the Americas, the world.

The second Gardner of the new millennium is hardly known yet. The second-Gardner's manifesto was *Good Work* (2001), a joint effort with two other top-ranking psychologists in America, M. Csicszentmihalyi and W. Damon. It was followed two years later by a paperback edition with a new "Afterword: Good Work in 2002", and one year later by a second book, written with his research assistants, W. Fischman, B. Solomon, and D. Greenspan, *Making Good* (2004), no longer with Basic Books but back home at the Harvard University Press. (These three writings of the second Gardner will be quoted in this chapter as GW, AW, MG).

The boundaries between psychology and social psychology (Harré 1993), cultural psychology (Shweder 1990), and sociology are foggy and slippery; but the question arises: why did three of the top-ranking psychologists in America, instead of persisting on doing first-rate psychology, agree on dabbling in second-rate sociology and folk moral philosophy? Is the second Gardner still a psychologist? Or has he wandered away from psychology to sociology, or cultural anthropology, or moral philosophy, or beyond, perhaps to outer space? Let us call this late change of focus from the first to the second Howard Gardner, for short, "Gardner's shift".

The Crisis of Psychology

Gardner's shift might be due to the drying up of psychology between neurology on the hard side and socio-cultural discourse analysis on the soft side. The advent of high-resolution scanners, real-time brain imaging, neural networks and massive parallel-processing computing have thinned out the ranks of psychologists towards neurology and soft AI modeling in cognitive science, activities still nostalgically referred to by some fugitives as 'neuropsychology'.

The linguistic turn initiated by Peter Winch's and Richard Rorty's reading of the second Wittgenstein, J.L. Austin's analytic philosophy, and the mounting post-modern pressure on reducing everything to discourse, from Michel Foucault in France, through Basil Bernstein in England, to the Georgetown group in the U.S., (see Deborah Schiffrin's Handbook, Schiffrin *et al.* 2001) is thinning out the ranks of true believers in psychology as an independent, well defined academic discipline worth pursuing on its own.

Gardner's dilemma must have been either to deepen the neurological view through the dark glasses of MRI, PET and other scanners, or to widen the socio-cultural view through the metaphors of domains and fields, forces and resistances, alignments and misalignments. Good-bye, psychology. Good morning, sociology. The "*GoodWork* Project" started.

The Moral Calling

A second hypothesis is that Gardner's shift might be due to the slow maturing of a moral calling, prepared by his own work in *Creating*

Minds (1993) and *Leading Minds* (1995). Interviewing live celebrities or perusing biographies of dead ones, Gardner began to ponder why some highly talented people used their talents to further their own careers, fortunes or at least to increase their public acclaim, while others turned their focus on altruistic causes. The nagging question 'Why?' started to challenge the first Gardner to move away from himself. That was, indeed a hard—and worthy—challenge, not only for himself, but for psychology in general, and, in particular, for the theory of multiple intelligences.

In fact, according to the second hypothesis, it must have turned out to be too much of a challenge for psychology. When no significant differences could be found in child-rearing practices, childhood memories, close friends, distressing episodes in adolescence, youth or maturity, or in other direct influences on the personal psychology of the person, where could one go? Again, the hard way would be to look into neural density, synaptic networks or neurotransmitters. The Scylla of neurology. The soft way would be to look more and more outside of the personal psyche towards the socio-cultural micro-, meso- and macro-environments. The Charybdis of sociology. Those two legendary perils were not enough to stop Howard Gardner. He decided to sail beyond, risking shipwreck.

Thus, the moral question opened up a moral dilemma: stay within psychology and reject the moral question, or roam at large into the social sciences, and even beyond their self-imposed frontiers, in a quest for answers to the nagging question.

In the Preface of *Making Good* (MG, p. vii), the authors start with the sentence: "It is often said that the quality of social scientists' research is proportional to the distance they maintain from the objects of their investigation. Yet it is also clear that many social scientists study issues that are of deep personal concern." The shift away from psychology into other social sciences might be coded in the last sentence. The moral imperative must have compelled Gardner to look towards the work on morality by William Damon, and to the study of the social conditions enabling states of flow by Mihail Csicszentmihalyi; the trio started on the way out of psychology.

God bless them! The world needs moral guidance, and who could provide better advice than three of the leading psychologists of America? Very few people, indeed, but our authors could perform that service only at the cost of leaving their secure bases in the rocky mountains of psychology. Good-bye psychology. The "*GoodWork* Project" started.

The Quicksand of Ethics

Let us identify, for the moment, ethics with moral philosophy, not with morals or morale. Morality is what people think they ought to do or not to do, and what they say is moral or immoral, whether they act in contrary ways to what they think and say. Ethics or moral philosophy is the art of analyzing the criteria that people use to classify deeds and practices into good and bad, moral or immoral, as distinct from legal or illegal, useful or counterproductive, pleasing or taxing, and of pondering the grounds for such criteria.

The trouble is that you cannot do moral philosophy out of the psychological, sociological or anthropological facts. The gap between "is" and "ought" is wide and dangerous. The naturalistic fallacy is a sword of Damocles hanging on top of every committed social scientist worth its mettle. Though not explicitly named, the anti-naturalistic fallacy also hangs up there. The first warns against the slide from "is" to "ought", from "everybody does it" to "it is right", a slip dear to optimists and philanthropists; the second warns against the pessimists' and misanthropists' preferred slip: from "is" to "ought-not", from "everybody does it" to "it is wrong".

Those philosophers' warnings still loom in the air, but what can you do? If your research results are to become direct contributions to the betterment of the human condition, "Wertfreiheit" is an unsurmountable barrier. One must praise or blame, promote or restrain, preach to young people trying to make it good and denounce those who cut corners. On what grounds?

Beyond the Social Sciences

Perhaps the established factual base of psychology, social psychology, cultural psychology and sociology could provide such grounds; but looking back at research results in the social sciences, they turn out to be—in the best of worlds—as close to established facts as a researcher could wish (discounting the natural scientist's belief that they are not even "facts", let alone "scientific"). That means those results are on the "is"-side. How could one go to the "ought"-side of the tracks? One must tread the quicksand of ethics.

The social sciences, whatever you think "social" or "science" means, still provide a century-old tradition of scholarship where you can choose schools, methods, models, theories, corpuses and databases. You strive to go beyond the information given, to outdo the best social scientists, to stretch the boundaries of the current social sciences. The trouble is the quicksand of ethics beyond those old or new boundaries. There you find no longer science but philosophy, and when you do philosophy, people no longer believe you, unless they were already in agreement with you on the same opinions you hold dear. Out there you find no longer "episteme" but "doxa". Have the second Gardner and his brave friends gone beyond thick psychology to thin sociology, and beyond the already thin atmosphere of the social sciences to the empty outer space of opinion?

The Threats of Outer Space

At least, the second Gardner and his co-authors have been hardy and honest enough to follow their good intentions and launch their space ships out of psychology to sociology and beyond. Now, there are the costs of bravery. You expose yourself to criticism coming from all directions: from social scientists shooting from behind, from moral philosophers ahead of you, and from assorted laypeople hitting from right and left, above and below.

That is why, as an outside critic, I dare disparage the authors' sociology as second-rate, their moral philosophy as folksy, and their two books—Afterword and all—as disappointing. Critics have an unfair advantage over authors. The music critic need not play the piano well to lambaste the virtuoso performer. All those critics must know is a small sample of what transpires in the air of music audiences and music critics. In this case, we critics need not fear the naturalistic or the anti-naturalistic fallacy. We may go from facts to value judgments without restraint, as long as we manage to persuade the readers. All we critics must know is a small sample of the general feeling of social scientists, philosophers, readers and book critics. Irresponsibly enough, we critics may preach without applying to ourselves what we preach. Too bad, but that is the role of critics, be they psychologists, sociologists, philosophers, or laypeople.

Sociological Qualms

One misgiving that lingers as an aftertaste when you finish reading and re-reading the *GoodWork* books is the set of categories used as a framework for data analysis. There is a suggestive mapping of professional realms into four regions: individual practitioners, domain, field, and stakeholders (GW, pp. 21–26; Gardner *et al.* 1997), but the distinction between individual practitioners and the field is hard to envision. In the use of the word in the books, it looks as if the field is composed of individuals, but it is explicitly said that it is composed of roles (GW, pp. 26). This way, the field becomes a more sociological category, but one that is not clearly used in the analysis as distinct from the individuals roaming in that field. That might be why individuals and stakeholders disappear in *Making Good*: besides domains and fields, instead of individuals, only the person—or self—appears now, perhaps as a return path to psychology (MG, pp. 19–21). A careful reading of the list of causes of misalignment in the following paragraph will also reveal the elusiveness of individuals.

There is a problem with the other main category of analysis: alignment/misalignment, to be predicated of professional realms (GW, pp. 27–36; compare AW, pp. 251–53; MG, pp. 14–17). Several strains of misalignment are identified: "Thus, alignment can fail because of tension between domains . . . between fields . . . within domains . . . within fields . . . between a domain and the wider culture . . . between a field and the wider society . . . [or] domains and fields can clash with the demands of stakeholders" (GW, p. 33). So far, so good, but how to judge misalignments? From the voiced misgivings of misaligned individuals? Could not these voiced feelings also be interpreted as alignment of the field with the culture and wider society (if fields are to be interpreted as composed of roles, not of individuals)?

When people talk about what they do, the chances are they could be—consciously or not—polishing up their story. Sociology of science, journalism or theater knows better than giving credence to self-reports. There are ethnographic techniques borrowed from anthropology, and polished up by sociologists, to follow up a group of professionals in their day-to-day routines. In the *GoodWork* studies, too little or no crosschecking of real-world behavior was conducted in the style of Steve Fuller in England, Bruno Latour in France, or Peter Galison in the U.S. As sociologists say, there was no triangulation of interview results.

There is also a problem that qualitative analysis has brought to the fore: the value of deviant cases, outliers, and exceptions that challenge the majority opinion. The *GoodWork* Project is especially sensitive in this respect, because there are bright people from Harvard doing the interviewing, there is a tape recorder on the table, and every subject knew that the Harvard people were going to write a book or two about whatever they would say. The text analysis of interviews still stays at the level of content analysis (see, for instance, the content tables in GW, pp. 193–96). There is no trace of a deeper discourse analysis, where the positioning game between the interviewed and interviewing subjects would be attended to, as they co-construct each other at every turn. The lack of this level of analysis will cause trouble when we deal with outliers and exceptions, as we shall see below in the case of Matt Drudge.

Then, there are the conclusions. Let us start with those of *Good Work*. The options to restore good work are called "five levers for good work" (GW, p. 212), and they are the following:

- Creating new institutions (GW, pp. 212–14)
- Expanding the functions of existing institutions (GW, pp. 214–15)
- Reconfiguring the membership of existing institutions (GW, pp. 215–16)
- Reaffirming the values of existing institutions (GW, pp. 216–17).
- Taking personal stands (GW, pp. 217–18).

The authors also suggest three things that a good worker can do: expanding the domain (by "clarifying the values on which it is based, bringing new knowledge to bear on the tasks, or instituting better procedures to serve the profession's purposes"), reconfiguring the field ("to work directly with individuals and institutions already in place to confirm the domain's crucial norms and values"), and taking personal stands (GW, pp. 232–36).

They advocate developing coherent new visions (GW, pp. 236–39): "To develop a joint vision is the task of national leaders. But if our leaders lack the courage such a task requires, the burden to articulate tomorrow's vision falls on our shoulders" (GW, p. 236).

Then, the authors insert a dialogue between two fictional characters: Rick Sutton, a thirty-nine-year-old cardiologist who works for a large HMO in Boston, and Cynthia French, an acquaintance and a retired physician who was visiting her grandchildren (GW, pp. 239–242). Rick is fed up with the HMO he works with and wants to quit the profession; now he would go so far as to advise his child not to be a doctor; the older physician, Cynthia, challenges his views, reminds him of his ideals, recalls other paradigms of good work in medicine, and tries to show the better side of things in a very stereotyped school-counselor role. What is a dialogue about a medical doctor's "burn-out" doing in a book on genetics and journalism? It looks as if it had strayed away from a data set taken from another project, if it were data and not fiction, that is.

After the dialogue, the authors give some ideas on the foundations of a new vision; they mention "four key elements that could lay the foundation for good work in our time. (If mnemonics are of any help, we can speak of the 'three DEs–development, decency, and democracy–and the one ED, education)'" (GW, p. 242).

We can compare the conclusions of *Good Work* with those of *Making Good*: now we have six factors influencing the route to good work: long-standing belief and value systems, role models and mentors, peers, pivotal experiences, institutional milieu, and periodic inoculations (MG, pp. 168–174), and the five levers for good work are now only four, easily recalled as "the four M's": Mission, Models, Mirror tests, and Messages (MG, pp. 174–183).

Judicious, insightful, elevating conclusions, but they have little connection to the data and the analysis. They do reveal the valuable insights and the accumulated wisdom of the authors, but practically all of them could have been written before the research was done. Thus, sociologists may have some cause to think this is not first-rate sociology.

Philosophical Misgivings

There is a troubling "excommunication" perpetrated by the authors on one of their subjects: the notorious, infamous, counter-example of Matt Drudge: "A different innovation, which we examined in Chapter 7, has been introduced by the Internet 'journalist' [scare quotes by the authors of GW] Matt Drudge. In our view, the *Drudge Report* has exceeded the boundary of what should qualify as journalism, since its inclusion of gossip represents the kind of expansion that strikes at the domain's soul and threatens to destroy it" (GW, p. 213). But what paper does not include gossip? What news hour? If you go past the supermarket cash registers, you see twenty newspapers there: the *Boston Globe*, the *New York Times*, and eighteen tabloids of celebrity gossip. What is journalism? This is journalism: ninety percent gossip and ten percent serious reporting at its best, not counting the gossip mingled with the serious reporting. Why pretend the contrary?

On what grounds is the accused to be declared guilty? It seems that the "domain's soul" is just a Weberian ideal type, belied by the harsh reality of earthly journalism. If the overwhelming majority of people pay for gossip on the web and on tabloids, watch trash on TV and follow *realities* for months, pay dearly for hardcore cable channels or Internet porn sites, is that alignment or misalignment? Sociology is at a loss. Only the *GoodWork* team seems to know how to use the category.

In a sense, Matt Drudge was the most honest to the interviewers (in spite of not being so honest to the public and the victims of possibly false gossip). He does think he serves the public better by publishing what is suppressed in the proper journals by their very proper editors. Matt Drudge tore the veil of propriety cast by his colleagues.

In a similar fashion, the "casualty of the system" (GW, pp. 105–07), a geneticist speaking anonymously, told the truth about the respected professors at NIH, and David Ledbetter blew the whistle on the respected professors at "Harvard, MIT, Stanford, UCSE, where there's not a single faculty member who doesn't own a company or have multiple patents and gets more money from . . . the commercial profits than from their salary" (GW, p. 112).

On what grounds can the authors condemn Matt Drudge? Or those professors who own private labs on the other side of College Avenue? Not on social science research results. Not on philosophical principles, either. Moral philosophers have despaired on finding firm grounds for the moral imperative. Nietzsche, Marx, and Freud, the masters of suspicion, eroded all foundations. The only grounds left for excommunication are the beliefs of honest-to-goodness middle class American citizens, too close for comfort to the "Moral Majority".

The lack of careful moral philosophy in the books forces the authors to take the current politically correct stances in order to judge—both 'etically' and 'ethically'—the realms, domains and fields they survey, and to rely on bland principles agreed upon by the so-called public opinion, which is just as manipulated and suspect as private opinion.

Perhaps because of the avoidance of moral-philosophical reflection in these two books, too much attention is paid to the opinions of the majority of practitioners of each profession, who can be reliably predicted to agree on most shared moral truisms whenever interviewed for the record. Their subjects seem to agree sincerely on those opinions, judging from what comes up in the interviews and the methodological caveats taken by the researchers, but that is not the point: most people sincerely do agree on those truisms; the point is that most of us do not act consistently with what we profess, and the same happens to them. Thus, just as sociologists might have felt because of the lack of triangulation, moral philosophers might also feel that these books built their cases on the shaky grounds of folk morality.

A Layman's Complaint

In a *GoodWork* Project meeting in October, 2001, Isaac Mwase, not really a layman but a Baptist minister from Malawi, now living in the U.S., pointed out a shortcoming of *Good Work*: the bias of defining good work by looking only inside the U.S. society, and forgetting the marginal, the poor, the suffering of the rest of the world. According to Mwase, those suffering the most by biased reporting or by geneticists' and biochemists' patents are the peoples of the Third World, not the people in the U.S. His idea can be made precise by looking at the way stakeholders are defined in the *GoodWork* Project, as part of the professional realm (GW, p. 21).

Let us call this bias 'Americocentrism', to mimic the word 'Eurocentrism', which we are so fond of using to criticize Europeans. Rev. Mwase asked where in the book are the poor, the suffering of the Third World. Nowhere to be seen.

My version of Mwase's complaint is that the *GoodWork* Project defined stakeholders too narrowly. Let us look at their definition: "1. Corporate shareholders and executives. 2. General public–consumers and citizens" (GW, p.26).

There seems to be enough breadth in the above definition, but there is an empirical test for the factual narrowness of the way this definition of stakeholders is actually used in the book. To perform that test, I would suggest an experiment: change a few expressions throughout the book, like "the stakeholders", "the public", "the general public", "the citizens", and similar ones, to "the American stakeholders", "the American public", "the American citizens", and "American" similar ones, and see if any reader would notice the change. It is so self-evident that America is what is talked about, that the effects of decisions made in the United States are easily reduced to waves and ripples inside the country, but they might create *tsunamis* abroad.

It is seldom noticed in the U.S. that, for Latin Americans like me, America goes all the way from Canada to Tierra del Fuego; but even the confines of the American continent would be too restrictive if stakeholders were to be limited to people inside it. At least all North-, Central-, and South-Americans are also involved in whatever happens in the U.S., but one must consider the trend towards globalization, the open-market global economy, and the U.S. hegemonic status as the only World Power. These new geopolitical realities force us to conclude that stakeholders in the professional realms of genetics and journalism are now everywhere in the world. Who is not a stakeholder of CNN reporting—not to mention Fox News—or of the U.S. Patent Office when patenting and licensing genetic materials, AIDS medicines or genetically engineered foods and organisms?

Let us not try to define stakeholders: let us try to find some inhabitant of the world who is not a stakeholder of U.S. journalism, U.S. genetics or what have you. Hard to find.

Conclusion

The last two books, *Good Work* Afterword and all—and *Making Good*, are quite disappointing for those who have read *Frames of Mind, Creative Minds, Leading Minds, Flow* or *The Moral Child*. Perhaps too many expectations make you too harsh on judging a new product, no matter how good it might be. The big names on the cover make those expectations soar, but the print inside the covers is there to be critically read and pondered. This critic found no trace of the hypothetical influencing factors that might come out of the first Gardner's earlier books, like a period of distress and suffering in the early years, or the presence of a knowledgeable friend and confidant in the crucial periods of decision-making, or the attitude towards religious belief.

In fact, there were no causal chains or psychological hypotheses, no plausible conclusions on the internal motions of the subjects' reflective or intra-personal intelligences to be found. There were no new conceptual tools for analysis: the division of the professional realm into individual practitioners, domain, field, and stakeholders is still fuzzy in its boundaries and shaky in its use, and 'alignment' turns out to be a thin notion without much clout, as soon as we realize that the realities of practice are as hopelessly different from the verbal agreements on ethical standards in genetics as they are in journalism, the theater or other professional realms.

Is journalism better aligned now, after September 11th (AW, pp. 252–53)? Or is it only better aligned with a terrorized American public inside the nation's borders? For outsiders like me, journalism in the U.S. is in a worse condition now than before the fall of the Twin Towers. The silence of American media on Attorney General Ashcroft's slow and deep erosion of one hundred years of progress in civil liberties in the U.S. in just four years; on the Guantanamo shame; on the appointment of the new Attorney General Gonzales, whose memo allowed for torture to Iraqi prisoners; on the Likud government's apartheid practices and selective assassinations that foster Arab hatred and terror plots, to mention a few, leave much to ponder. Through a flick of the remote control on cable TV, the quality of CNN reporting, and even worse, of Fox News, about the invasions of Afghanistan and Iraq could be judged by direct comparison to BBC or Deutsche Welle reports. Have U.S. journalists translated and commented on copy from Arab news agencies? Never, except for buying sensationalist video-clips from the al-Jazeera network. Is that alignment or "entente"? The impossibility of answering these questions is enough to show the limitations of the alignment-misalignment metaphor.

It is time to stop. Venturing on moral philosophy is dangerous for the *GoodWork* team and for their critics. I, as a critic, might have wandered too far beyond the limits of technical, sociological and philosophical criticism about the professional work of a group of committed social scientists reporting on journalists, geneticists, and theatrical artists, but I must clearly state here that I have no moral complaints about their work. I admire the authors' rewarding of honesty and integrity and their speaking out against malpractice in the professions they selected for scrutiny. I agree with many of their moral judgments, sharing most of their culture and being a loyal admirer of American scholarship and academic life. My graduate studies were carried out in the U.S., and I am a frequent visitor at several American universities, often a welcome guest at Harvard's Project Zero. How could I, or the average American, disagree with their conclusions and their advice? Nevertheless, my impression about Gardner's shift is still dim; but when he was writing his first two books twenty-five years ago, the first Gardner did not shine so brightly, either. Now look how far he has gone.

At the present time, the second Gardner and his good co-workers must be learning hard and fast social psychology, cultural psychology, critical discourse analysis, sociology, anthropology, and moral philosophy. We must allow them more time. The *GoodWork* Project is a very difficult, complex, interdisciplinary endeavor of wide scope and great social value; the first two books give us grounded hope that its grand design will materialize soon in a series of books and papers that will live up to their authors' and my very high expectations; but they have not arrived there yet. Let us wait till next year.

REFERENCES

Fischman, W., B. Solomon, D. Greeenspan, and H. Gardner. 2004. *Making Good: How Young People Cope with Moral Dilemmas at Work.* Cambridge, Massachusetts: Harvard University Press.

Gardner, H. 1993. *Creating Minds.* New York: Basic Books.

Gardner, H. 1995. *Leading Minds.* New York: Basic Books.

Gardner, H., M. Csicszentmihalyi, and W. Damon. 2001. *The Empirical Basis of GoodWork: When Excellence and Ethics Meet.* New York: Basic Books. [Paperback edition: 2003, with a seven-page *Afterword* on pp. 251–56: "Afterword: Good Work in 2002."]

Gardner, H., A. Gregory, M. Csicszentmihalyi, W. Damon, and M. Michaelson. 1997. Good Work: Methodological Considerations. Research paper No. 3. www.goodworkproject.org/publications/papersbynumbers.htm.

Harré, R. 1993. *Social Being: A Theory for a Social Psychology II.* Oxford: Blackwell.

Schiffrin, D., D. Tannen, and H.E. Hamilton, eds. 2001. *Handbook of Discourse Analysis.* Oxford: Blackwell, 2001 (Paperback ed. 2003).

Shweder, R.A. 1990. Cultural Psychology: What Is It? In J.W. Stigler, R.A. Shweder, and G. Herdt, eds., *Cultural Psychology* (New York: Cambridge University Press), pp. 1–46.

11

Changing Minds about GoodWork?

ANNA CRAFT

The Original Mind-Set: The GoodWork Project

Howard Gardner and his colleagues explore the notion of excellence and ethics, particularly in the workplace, in their large scale GoodWork Project. Gardner argues that "a society needs GoodWorkers, and especially so at a time when things are changing rapidly, our sense of time and space is being radically altered by technology, and market forces are tremendously influential, with few counter-forces of equal power" (Gardner 2004a, p.207). It could be argued that at the heart of this is the study of human generativity—or creativity, exploring issues which arise when workers in a range of professional contexts, strive for excellence in an ethical framework. For, as Gardner puts it, we can choose whether we use our creativity "in ways that are selfish and destructive or in ways that are generous and life-enhancing" (Gardner 2004a, p. 212).

A collaboration between Csiksentmihalyi, Damon, and Gardner, the GoodWork project grew, in part, out of a set of concerns which brought into question the pervasive nature of the market model, such that "any human sphere threatens to be overwhelmed by the search for profit—when the bottom line becomes the only line that matters" (Gardner *et al.* 2001, p. 14). Thus, this long-term study of the professions emerged, looking first at veterans or senior figures in their professions (Gardner *et al.* 2001) and then at the dilemmas faced by younger people (Fischman *et al.*, 2004). It has so far focused on professionals in a range of fields including genetics research, higher education, journalism, different art forms, law, business and philanthropy and has used in depth interviewing with supplementary techniques, to elicit perspectives of both veterans and novices.

The first book from the project (Gardner *et al.* 2001) was published just after the 11th September World Trade Centre terrorist attack which shook many parts of the world, and the authors note an immediate and initial shift in the career-choices of many young Americans, away from making money and toward those which we might see as socially oriented, for example, teaching, intelligence, counter-intelligence, public services, the armed forces.

The study is so far mainly confined to the United States, however it does help us to understand the pervasive forces of the market and its influence on how successful veterans and those eager to become so, go about leading their professions. It demonstrates many ways in which ethics and excellence struggle to co-exist in an increasingly contorted tension. And the study also reminds us that that, in part due to the marketization of society, none of us is free from moral and ethical dilemmas.

The findings and dimensions of the project are wide and varied, encompassing explorations of what it means to work in an inter-disciplinary way in making new knowledge at the forefront of a profession, together with the nature of professionality and the sorts of ethical and other dilemmas which face those with little experience but high aspirations (novices) on the one hand, and those who have enormous experience and expertise together with a track record of excellence (veterans), on the other. The study has revealed that in most of the professions studied, there is an identifiable, shared sense of what it means to be a professional in that domain. It has also explored the conditions in which GoodWork is more likely to be developed and has proposed the notion of 'alignment'. That is, where the values of doing excellent work in the profession align closely with a belief in what is worthwhile to society and align also with the values of the individual; a profession which is 'aligned' is one where "all of the different interest groups basically all call for the same kinds of performances" (GoodWork Project 2004, p. 23)

It would be impossible to discuss all elements of this enormous project. Instead, in this chapter I have chosen to focus in particular on some aspects of what could be described as the original mind-set, raising some questions about its focus and rationale, and raising the possibility that some fundamental issues may be absent from the project team's foci. I look at the work on young people in particular, posing three challenges arising from issues around that work (although these may not be limited to that work in particular)—and make the case for a change of mind with respect to all three.

Young People's Aspirations: What Is Not Asked?

One of the findings of the GoodWork project's work with younger people was that "too many of the young workers . . . espous[ed] a dubious brand of moral freedom—asserting that they were the ultimate judges of the ethics of their work" (Fischman *et al.*, p. 182). This may reflect a 'consumer as always right' mirror to the 'Market as God' model of living in so many parts of the world (as documented in the case of the United States so well by Kincheloe, 2002); and yet we socialise young people into believing that they alone are the judge of the appropriateness of their or anyone else's actions and ideas, to our peril. As Fischman *et al.* put it, "the entire world could use many more individuals who unite their considerable personal capacities with a commitment to act responsibly, ethically, morally" (2004, p. 182). The project also explores the role of spirituality, and Solomon and Hunter (2002) suggest that bringing one's spirituality which they see as "a sense of profound connection to things beyond and/or within one's self" (Solomon and Hunter 2002, p. 39) into one's working or public identity, might be one step; this too could have implications for teachers and teaching.

In making the critique which follows, I am mindful that the GoodWork project, its data collection, analysis and synthesis, is still work in progress. There may be work underway, not yet in the public domain, which would address some or all of the points which follow; nevertheless at this point in time they are offered as points for debate.

Three Challenges

However, it could be argued that a number of fundamental questions are buried within the GoodWork project. Without engaging with these the study, although extensive, may be missing some significant elements: consideration of which way GoodWork may face, the consideration of models of ethical engagement—both of which may include exploration of gender issues, and finally, engagement with the cultural situatedness of GoodWork.

Challenge 1: Which Way Does GoodWork Face?

Promoting the generativity of young people in the context of wider ethical dimensions of our existence is not an optional extra (Craft 2005a). As Fischman *et al.* put it: "At a time when the world is inexorably interconnected and the potential for destruction has never been greater, a perennial concern with the implications and applications of work seems an imperative, not an option" (Fischman *et al.* 2004, p. 182). An immense challenge facing those concerned with nurturing and teaching young people and their aspirations, is to work out how we do this, and how to do it in such a way that takes account of GoodWork that not only faces out, to the world of work, but 'faces in', as it were to home and personal lives, too. This seems to be a question which the GoodWork project does not currently address.

An integral element to this is of course gender. The expansion of equality of opportunity in the world beyond the home for both women and men leads to a further set of dilemmas as work effort is poured into contexts that could be described as 'facing out' rather than 'facing in'.

It would seem that women's and men's choices about where they put their work efforts, have shifted considerably from the position documented by Colette Dowling (1982) where women were seen to be very likely to sabotage their own career success in favor of a domestic role, seen in terms of 'being taken care of' by a partner with economic and perhaps other security. At the time of writing, in England for example, more than half of women with a child under five are in paid employment. This figure rises to seventy percent of all women of working age when age of child is not taken into account (Fawcett Campaigns 2005); figures published by the Department of Trade and Industry (DTI) in England in 2004 note that seven out of ten mothers working full time say they would work even if they did not have to, that fifty percent of mothers with children under five work—and that forty-four percent of lone parents go out to work (DTI 2004). The extent of women's responsibilities and the impact of this in society at large are recognized by government. The Department of Trade and Industry commissioned a poll from MORI in 2005. In it, 78 percent of employees are reported as expecting to be able to balance work lives with their home lives in a way that they choose to, with 85 percent believing that allowances should be made for working parents with young or disabled dependents (DTI 2005). The focus of policy emerging from this and other findings highlights the notion of "work-life balance" (*ibid.*). And from the perspective of the care and education of young children, there is increasing recognition of the need to provide high quality and affordable care and education for children. *Every Child Matters: Change for Children,* is a new Government initiative in England, aiming to support the well-being of children and young children, from birth to nineteen, which brings together organizations which provide services for children so as to share information and work together in order protect children and young people from harm and help them achieve their aspirations. In addition, March 2005 saw for the first time, the appointment of a Children's Commissioner for England, whose role was to give children and young people a voice in government and in public life (DFES 2005). Such government support for women and families has been described as travelling in another direction in the United States, where most of the GoodWork project has been undertaken—with little support being given by the state to encourage and support children and young families particularly where both parents are working (National Organization for Women 2004).

What sorts of decisions are made by both men and women as the home context for doing GoodWork expands beyond a dyad and into a family? How is the balance of GoodWork achieved? Some attention is being paid to these questions in the project, but perhaps an even bigger issue than the one of how excellence and ethics are maintained in the professions, is the extent to which excellence and ethics are also maintained in the home, by professionals trying to do GoodWork in both directions. For although we are beginning to have a good sense of what might be involved in doing excellent creative work that 'faces out'—and in particular some of the moral and ethical dimensions to this (Gardner *et al.* 2001), we have yet to document and understand the issues involved in striking that balance.

A further issue not addressed within the project, is what the consequences may be for families where both parents are 'facing out'. Kubo (2004) explores the fostering of creativity in Japan and Singapore, arguing that a major threat to creativity is in the sub-contracting of parenting of small children. It is an issue, he notes, that young adults do not consider home making as a viable option. Kubo documents the transference of focus for creative engagement to the external context, for both genders the world beyond the family itself is seen as a primary context for creativity. Kubo's thesis is that the transference of focus to outside of the home and family, has a deleterious effect on creative engagement in the home.

There is some evidence that for those who aspire to high creativity and excellence at work rely on strong support from those close to the creator, including those in the home (Gardner 1993)—even, for some, collaboration with partners and family (John-Steiner 2000). But how this shifting balance of roles in the twenty-first century home, plays out for all involved, could be explored, particularly in the context of striving for excellence and making the efforts needed to balance aspirations and responsibilities with some wisdom.

In terms of GoodWork that faces out, the stories of women such as Judith Richards Hope, the first female associate director of the White House Domestic Council and in the first class of women admitted to study Law at Harvard and others like her (Richards Hope 2003) are testimony to the creative challenges and opportunities that the dual roles bring. How might the project explore this issue in relation to other extraordinary achievers like Richards Hope? How do GoodWorkers, and particularly women, broker the challenges of dual roles? To what extent may this involve a version of the Faustian Bargain described by Gardner (1993) in his analysis of great creators, where in order to pursue creativity at a level of excellence, very often the home life and relationships are neglected.

And what of those whose creativity faces in, and whose lives may be more ordinary but just as demanding—and just as aspirational in terms of raising a family? What role does generative creativity, excellence and ethics, play in the home for both children and also their parents (Schwager 2005)—and how would we characterize alignment in this context?

All of these questions serve to illustrate a need to unravel rather more, the context of young people's aspirations, and the conceptual frame for GoodWork in terms of what counts.

Challenge 2: Whose Models of Ethical Engagement?

What kinds of underpinning moral or ethical models are implicit in the interpretation of actual or predicted choices made by subjects in the GoodWork study? It is intriguing that the project does not yet probe the underpinning moral or ethical model that may lie behind the interpretation of choices of young adults, insofar as there are conflicting developmental interpretations of moral and ethical development within cognitive psychology which could help to frame interpretations, or which could give rise to new ways of thinking about development.

One of these is the widely-accepted Kohlbergian model of six identifiable stages of moral development, which traverse a journey from preconventional reasoning to conventional through to post-conventional (Kohlberg 1981; 1984), is one of these. The theory is dependent on the thinking of the Swiss psychologist Jean Piaget and the American philosopher John Dewey.

However the Kohlbergian model of stages of moral development has been challenged as gendered by Gilligan (1982; 1993) positing another, perhaps equally gendered, model, offering a feminine account. Clearly, the model that we use for how moral or ethical behavior is conceived of and develops, will affect the way that we interpret how young adults make choices about their futures, and deal with ethical dilemmas facing them in their chosen paths. To what degree is such a model in development?

To the extent that the GoodWork project is looking at the development of ethically responsible attitudes of pre-collegiate young people, the ethical model is not explicit or interrogated; an omission, it seems?

Challenge 3: How Culturally Saturated Is GoodWork?

How far is the fact that the study has been almost totally located in North America, significant—in other words how important is the particular cultural context for the findings? We might expect, perhaps, in some of the professions, similarities in perspective from culture to culture, in terms of the core values of the profession. But what of possible cultural differences in the individual's relationship and loyalty to these?

It is possibly uncontested that the role of the social is now recognised widely in studies of human behaviour. As Feldman (2000) notes, the era of the cognitive psychology interpreting generativity as a purely individually-located process had its heyday in the mid to late twentieth century, and has now been replaced by perspectives based on Vygotskian constructivism which offer a powerful role to social engagement (as exemplified, for example, by the work of John-Steiner, 2000). However, how that social engagement is situated may be powerfully culturally-specific, reflecting wider social values.

Within studies of creativity, it is argued by some that Confucian societies of the East put a greater emphasis on the social group *vis-à-vis* the individual; society is often tightly organised, there are many social rules and regulations to govern the behaviour of the person who is socialized from when young to conform with the in-group (Ng 2003). This perspective contrasts with the one more dominant in the West, which places greater emphasis on the individual as by far more important than the social group (Bellah, Madsen, Sullivan, Swidler, and Tipton, 1985). Such macro-differences in value are bound also to lead to differences in the ways that those living and working in different cultures construe themselves. This is borne out by the work of Markus and Kitayama (1991; 1994) which suggests that in a collectivistic society, the individual's need for validation is toward conformity with the social group whereas in an individualistic society the social pressures are toward differentiation, difference, and behaviour which is individuated to a much greater degree.

Unpicking what this could mean in the context of doing GoodWork, feeling responsible to a profession, and to a public or client group, and to wider society, whilst being socialised in a Western Individualist model, seems important; and an element of this is the identification of which is the dominant social pull. In Eastern cultures, the immediate and extended family may form an equally strong pull in terms of feelings of responsibility in doing GoodWork, and may in fact be the stronger determinant of how ethical and moral dilemmas are resolved, in such cultures.

Added to this cultural frame, some studies document pressure for acculturation to occur in the direction of cultural individualism rather than in the direction of cultural collectivism (Ng 2001; Smith and Bond 1993). This would also seem to be borne out by the fact that the first book from the GoodWork Project (Gardner *et al.* 2001) was selected in 2003 as one of the most important books published in Hong Kong.

The case for consideration of cultural situatedness would be supported by the work of Nisbett (2003) who offers a socio-historical and economic account of East-West differences as emerging from foundations laid in contrasting forms of social and economic organisation in ancient China and Greece.

Both Nisbettt and Ng acknowledge the finer differentiations which may be invisible in a simple categorisation which describes Asian-Western, or liberal—but it is both the broad brush and the fine grained analysis—or at the very least, acknowledgement, which is currently invisible in the GoodWork project.

The only dimension that I have raised here is the individual-collectivist one. But there could be all kinds of others, not necessarily based on geography but rather on socio-economic status, ethnic identity, spiritual perspective and so on. However the East-West dimension has been emphasised here because of the role that Western Individualism can be seen to be having within the globalized marketplace, on Eastern values and ways of operating (in that the pressure toward a Western Individualised model, based on a capitalist market economy, is immense).

There are at least three reasons why we should be taking heed of these potentially complex cultural differences.

Firstly, there is a particular moral or ethical stance which we might describe as GoodWork, implicit in the project contributing to a reframing of what it means to be a professional, which takes account of cultural context and which therefore situates aspirations within this wider contextual frame. The workers in the GoodWork project perhaps have a role to play in exploring and exposing aspects of "cultural imperialism" (Craft 2005), in explaining professional conduct. The project has a role to play in documenting some of these apparent pressures from the West, on Eastern models of professional engagement.

The second reason for taking account of cultural context stems from the difficulty of offering models which interpret and explain behaviour in ways which appear to have universal application; another dimension of cultural imperialism (Craft, *ibid.*), particularly where such work is developed in first-class Universities in the United States, with a potential to influence behaviours in other cultures.

Thirdly, there may be many influences on young people's choices; some of these may arise from values held in the family and its sub-cultural networks. How can the project engage with these, particularly from the perspective of individual and collectivist approaches?

Levers for Shifting the GoodWork Focus?

In his recent book, *Changing Minds* (Gardner 2004b), Gardner proposes seven 'levers' to changing minds. These he characterises as Reason, Research, Resonance, Redescriptions, Resources and Rewards, Real World Events and Resistances.

How might these be applied to the arguments advanced in this chapter?

Lever 1: Reason

As its title suggests this lever for changing minds appeals to rational argument. I would hope that the chapter so far has laid out rational arguments for the inclusion in the GoodWork project, of the perspectives of which way GoodWork faces, models of ethical engagement, and the role of culture in the situating of GoodWork.

Lever 2: Research

During the first part of this chapter empirical and conceptual research has been drawn upon and cited, to support the arguments being made for considering each of the three challenges as worth addressing within the

GoodWork project. Research and policy literatures which document and study gender and family issues with respect to the economy, moral and ethical development, and aspects of creativity, are all drawn upon to make the case for considering seriously the three challenges of which way GoodWork faces (or what 'counts' as GoodWork), the question of which moral/ethical frame is being used to interpret the data, and the extent to which the account of GoodWork offered in the project may be culturally saturated. The case can, then, be supported by research.

Lever 3: Resonance

Gardner acknowledges the role of the affective in persuasion. He suggests that what he calls several other "'re" terms' (*ibid.*, p.16) play a role here and may arise when "one feels a 'relation' to a mind-change" (*ibid.*, p. 16), believing that the person in question is worthy of respect, or is reliable. It is not for me to judge this. However, having had the privilege of working with Howard Gardner now as a scholar of his work over nearly ten years one way or another, my hope would be that there may be sufficient resonance for these arguments to be taken seriously at least in his response to them in this text. Gardner recognises the role also of rhetoric in changing minds, drawing on logic, relevant research and also resonance—all intentions of this chapter.

Lever 4: Representational Redescriptions

Each of the cases made above could be represented in multiple ways, although I have not chosen to do this here. The case of which way GoodWork faces, for example, could be represented for example by the image of a see-saw, or by a doorway to an open vista, with symbolic representations of domain (professional) aspirations in the outdoors, and representations of home aspirations in the indoors. Statistics quoted could be represented through graphs. The case regarding models of ethical engagement could be represented by the well-known stage model frequently laid out in tabular form to represent Kohlberg's perspective, compared with Gilligan's challenge which might be represented through sociograms. The East-West models of cultural engagement could be shown through diagrams of sparring engagement with oppositional forces represented, compared with diagrams demonstrating the search for consensus with shared engagement represented.

Lever 5: Resources and Rewards

Clearly, the addressing of such issues as raised earlier in the chapter might demand greater resources to facilitate such enquiry. Whilst these may be hard to come by with respect to cultural situatedness and modes of ethical engagement, the fact that life-work balance remains in focus for employers (eg deloitte) and for governmental policy makers together with not-for-profit organisations, suggests that the exploration of the direction in which GoodWork faces may be a candidate for resource.

Lever 6: Real World Events

As indicated in the previous discussions, number of different real-world events should serve to shift the foci to encompass the points about direction, ethical models and culture. First, on which way GoodWork faces, there is ample evidence from the real world that the issue of dual responsibilities is an increasing one. Therefore, it seems likely that for those aspiring to do not simply work, but GoodWork, there are tensions and dilemmas which the project would do well to address. Second, on ethical models, we know from Gilligan's empirical documentation discussed earlier, that this is a contested area and that multiple models may therefore exist. And finally on the question of culture—evidence of differences in approach to creativity was cited in the earlier discussion; whether this counts as 'real world events' may be a moot point, but it seems undisputable that culture should be explored in terms of how GoodWork plays out.

Lever 7: Resistances

The establishment of this long-term project, by senior researchers in three of the most highly respected Universities in the world, has been a landmark achievement, particularly at this point in history in the United States, where market-driven change infiltrates all aspects of professional life including the lives of researchers, and the identities of University departments. In many respects the project can be seen as forward looking, even visionary. The part of the project based at Harvard, has developed, perhaps in part as a consequence of its unusualness in the landscape of research projects at this time, a strong coherence around themes that it has been researching. As well as collective identities (for the GoodWork project even on this one of the three sites, is in reality a complex web of several interconnected projects, each one substantial in its own right) there are the historically laid down reputations and interests of those leading the overall project and its parts. These factors together may mean that the ideas proposed in this chapter may fall on stony ground.

Reaching the Tipping Point?

It is proposed that the GoodWork project team, under the leadership of Gardner and colleagues, consider issues raised here under the headings of which way GoodWork faces, which models of ethical engagement are implicit in their interpretations of GoodWork data, and finally the extent to which the project could be exploring the role of cultural context.

Whether the arguments advanced here are sufficient to reach what Gardner (2004b) calls the "tipping point" of mind-change remains to be seen.

REFERENCES

Craft, A. 2005a. *Creativity in Schools: Tensions and Dilemmas.* London: RoutledgeFalmer.
————. 2005b. Creativity in Schools: Tensions and Dilemmas. Keynote lecture at ESRC Seminar, Creativity and Wisdom, University of Cambridge, April 2005.
Department for Education and Skills. 2005. Every Child Matters. Website: http://www.everychildmatters.gov.uk/aims/?asset=documentandid=15516. Last accessed 12th June, 2005.
Department for Trade and Industry. 2004. Key Facts on Women in the Labour Market.   Website: http://www.womenandequalityunit.gov.uk/women_work_commission/. Last accessed 16th June, 2005.
Department of Trade and Industry. 2005. Work-Life Balance: The Employee's Perspective, March 2005. Website: http://www.dti.gov.uk/bestpractice/assets/er-research.pdf. Last accessed 12th June, 2005.
Dowling, C. 1982. *The Cinderella Complex.* New York: Pocket Books.
Fawcett Campaigns. 2005. Website: http://www.fawcettsociety.org.uk/Campaign_Employ.htm). Last accessed 12th June, 2005.
Feldman, D.H. 2000. Foreword to John-Steiner 2000.
Fischmann, W., B. Solomon, D. Greenspan, and H. Gardner. 2004. *Making Good: How YA Cope with Moral Dilemmas at Work.* Cambridge, Massachusetts: Harvard University Press.

Gardner, H. 1993. *Creating Minds: An Anatomy of Creativity Seen Through the Lives of Freud, Einstein, Picasso, Stravinsky, Eliot, Graham and Gandhi.* New York: Basic Books.

———. 2004a. *Can There Be Societal Trustees in America Today?* Working paper: Harvard Graduate School of Education (November).

———. 2004. *Changing Minds: The Art and Science of Changing Our Own and Other People's Minds.* Boston: Harvard Business School Press.

Gardner, H., M. Csikszentmihalyi, and W. Damon. 2001. *Good Work: When Excellence and Ethics Meet.* New York: Basic Books.

Gilligan, C. 1982.*In a Different Voice.* Cambridge, Massachusetts: Harvard University Press.

———. 1993. *In a Different Voice,* Cambridge, Massachusetts: Harvard University Press.

GoodWork Project Team. 2004. *The GoodWork Project: An Overview.* Published on GoodWork Website: http://www.goodworkproject.org/ GoodWork%20Project%20Overview.pdf. Last accessed 16th June, 2005.

John-Steiner, V. 2000. *Creative Collaboration.* New York: Oxford University Press.

Kincheloe, J.L. 2002. *The Sign of the Burger: McDonalds and the Culture of Power.* Philadelphia: Temple University Press.

Kohlberg, L. 1981a. *Philosophy of Moral Development: Moral Stages and the Idea of Justice.* San Franscisco: Harper and Row.

———. 1981b. *Essays on Moral Development.* First edition. San Fransisco: Harper and Row.

———. 1984. *Essays on Moral Development, Volume II.* San Francisco: Harper and Row.

Kubo, Y. 2004. Challenges for Creativity in Singapore and Japan: Confucious's Influence and Professionalism. In M. Fryer, ed., *Creativity and Cultural Diversity* (Leeds: The Creativity Centre Educational Trust).

National Organization for Women. 2004. Web page on recent legislation: http://www.now.org/nnt/fall-2004/legupdate.html. Last accessed 12th June, 2005.

Richards Hope, J. 2003. *Pinstripes and Pearls: The Women of the Harvard Law Class of '64 Who Forged an Old-Girl Network and Paved the Way for Future Generations.* New York: Scribner.

Schwager, I. 2005 [2000]. Parenting Challenges for the New Millenium. First published in 2000, now available at http://www.creativeparents .com/ar020200.html. Last accessed 25th January, 2005.

Solomon, J., and J. Hunter. 2002. A Psychological View of Spirituality and Leadership. *School Administrator* (September), pp. 38–41.

12

Artful Practice: A Reflexive Analysis

GRAEME SULLIVAN

Reflexive Perspectives

Since his period of prodigious output in arts education from the 1970s to the 1990s the work of Howard Gardner continues to inspire widespread confidence and some ambivalence among many arts educators. Throughout these decades of influence the capacity of Gardner to take on the enormous challenge of looking directly into the basic workings of the developing mind and to put in place a regime of research that sought to explain the variability of human knowing has been unsurpassed in scope and ambition. How best to respond to the educational demands that arose from these insights was the primary agenda pursued through the later years of inquiry undertaken by Gardner and his associates at Harvard Project Zero (HPZ).[1] In recent times this impact has been felt more directly as a source of support in shaping educational theory and practice that share Gardner's belief in the multiplicity of

---

[1] Harvard Project Zero was originally established by Nelson Goodman in 1967; the wry title implied that 'zero' was known about the arts and human development. Goodman's original research associates, Howard Gardner and David Perkins, subsequently took over responsibility for the theoretical direction and operation of HPZ with Gardner being the Director of the Development Group (1972–2000), and Perkins the Director of the Cognitive Skills Group (1972–2000). The image used to describe this apparent zero understanding was both a quantitative measure and a philosophical inference, which captured the two central concerns of the HPZ researchers.

human capacity and proclivity, and his conviction about the cognitive basis of arts learning.

It is with a sense of perspective and a measure of critical distance that sets the scene for this critical review of Gardner's artful and mindful approach to theorizing about the contribution of the arts to the learning life of individuals. Consequently it is the twin areas of practice that ground his studies of the arts, human development, and education, which are covered, namely: *arts education practice* and *research practice*. The term 'practice' is purposefully used to refer to a melding of concerns about research and development that characterize the evolution from an initial focus on basic studies of perception, conceptualization and symbolization, to a later emphasis on applied approaches to curriculum and assessment that responded more directly to changing educational and community demands. The vast publication output that repackaged core HPZ studies to constituencies across many disciplines was in part an advocacy effort to help those interested but not expert in the arts to reconsider their preferences and possible misconceptions about the importance of the arts in human development. The breadth of the audiences embraced and the tendency in the early years to partially bypass discipline-specific interests in the arts and aesthetic education produced areas of criticism. However, throughout the emergence of HPZ as a significant research group the desire of Gardner has been to offer suggestive pathways for others to consider, although he has never been timid in his response to his critics. On balance, therefore, there is a spirit of debate amid the defense and it is with this in mind that I have undertaken what I define as a 'reflexive analysis' of his artful practice. So as to clearly position the structures, strategies and subjectivities that frame this essay there is a need to define what I mean by a reflexive analysis.

A reflexive response implies an action that 'works against' a stimulus in a way that acknowledges the impact of the source, yet is open to interpretation. A reflexive encounter yields outcomes that may not be referenced to strict standards or normalized within any discipline structure, rather a breadth of approaches is used that open up the debate around circumstances and outcomes as they emerge. This kind of situated reaction is especially relevant in the review of issues grounded in the arts because it is directed by personal and public interests as well as being a quest for imaginative insight that is informed by discipline expertise. In other words, a critical review that is open to a reflexive impulse has a creative element to it that encourages us to look anew at a set of practices, while at the same time allows us to reconsider existing domains of knowledge. This requires a transparent understanding whereby we can 'see through' the data, texts, and contexts at hand—in this case, information about Gardner's conceptions of the arts, his research, and educational practices—so as to be aware of the possibility of imaginative options and alternative ideas. Further, to fully respond to the plausibility and the possibility of the outcomes opened up by Gardner as a consequence of the inquiries undertaken at HPZ over the years there is a need to re-visit some of the original conceptions and operations that shaped how arts education was seen at the outset. Although a revisionist tendency is apparent in taking any historical snapshot, there is merit in being reminded of formative decisions for they set in place distinctive patterns of practice and help identify possible sustaining factors. Consequently the metaphor guiding this review is that of a retrospective exhibition–in this case the exhibits are several texts published by Gardner that chronicle his theories and practices that have had a significant impact on arts education.[2] These texts are seen as a representative sample that contain evidence that can be interpreted; a series of cultural artifacts that are specific to the time in which they were produced and the discourse that surrounded them; and components in a process-folio that maps ongoing decision-making and contexts as ideas and theories are conceptualized and given form.

There are three stances adopted in undertaking a reflexive analysis that include *dialogue, questioning*, and *reflection*. Dialogue addresses the issue of the plausibility of the information under review as a debate is opened up between the researcher—in this case, Gardner—and relevant communities of inquiry. Here, a dialogue surrounding Gardner's notion of arts practice is reviewed by bringing to attention issues raised by some of his critics from areas of the arts and aesthetics. Gardner's educational practice plays a central role in his conception of the arts and human development and here the ideas and issues he advances are subject to questioning. Raising questions does not merely draw attention to the adequacy of policies or programs, but looks to the implications of the actions and outcomes that result. Reflection, on the other hand, involves an assessment of research outcomes and empirical understandings so as to

---

[2] The primary texts referenced are: *The Arts and Human Development* (1973); *Artful Scribbles* (1980); *Art Education and Human Development* (1990); *Art, Mind, and Brain* (1982a); *Art, Mind and Education* (Gardner and Perkins, eds., 1989); *The Unschooled Mind* (1991). Although Gardner's conceptions of creativity and his multiple intelligences theory have had an impact on arts education their influence is best seen within broader educational and social contexts and others cover these issues in this volume.

review the conceptual and operational structures used in theorizing. Reflection is thus a meta-analytic process that reviews decision-making and is used here to critique the structure of Gardner's research practice.

Arts Education Practices

The founding of Harvard Project Zero within a climate of bustling confidence surrounding the Harvard Graduate School of Education in the late 1960s put in place the opportunity for sustained research and development in the arts. As a research enterprise HPZ continues to exist and the purpose has broadened since its inception where today the "mission is to understand and enhance learning, thinking, and creativity in the arts, as well as humanistic and scientific disciplines, at the individual and institutional levels."[3] As a research entity that has maintained remarkable focus and institutional identity HPZ has always been self-supporting and in the early years survived mostly on research grants from the federal government, whereas in recent decades support has come mostly from private foundations. During its genesis what has changed most has been the structure of the HPZ enterprise. Today, a more formalized administrative model is in place that supports ongoing research projects that address a variety of educational and community needs and interests and oversees the development and production of research resources.

The definition of the arts that Gardner proposed in the earlier years has changed little and bears a stamp of conceptual consistency. In his 1973 book, *The Arts and Human Development*, Gardner presented his version of a psychology of the arts within which the arts were described as a basic and distinctively human process that involved the "communication of subjective knowledge" by means of a symbolic object that someone had created and someone had to "understand, react to, or appreciate" (1973, p. 30). In rejecting the tendency in psychology to partition knowing in dichotomous terms around cognitive and affective polarities, Gardner saw in the arts a form of human functioning where thoughts and feelings were inextricably connected and subsequently presented as "art." In reviewing psychological attempts to reconcile cognitive and affective approaches he explained that

> such attempts suggest that the integration of affect and cognition is most likely to be realized if one focuses on pursuits where feeling and knowing

---

[3] For full details of a history of Harvard Project Zero, past and current research projects, personnel, products, and services, see http://www.pz.harvard.edu

are recognized as being intertwined, such as the arts. In my view, any psychological analysis of the arts and the artist presupposes an integrated view of human development. I suggest that, collectively, the artist, audience member, performer, and critic provide a viable and holistic end state for human development. (1973, p. 7)

To ground his psychology of the artistic process Gardner identified three systems—making, feeling and perceiving—and the process of symbolic functioning as the means by which to experience and come to know things through these doing and thinking processes. Much of the thesis in the 1973 text revolved around a review of the variable evidence assembled around arguments of how individuals and species can be seen to develop in these psychological systems, which ultimately give rise to the various ways that we participate in artistic processes. And it is in the gradual integration of these making, feeling and perceiving structures through symbolic functioning that the full range of human cognition becomes evident in actions, affects, and discriminations. In presenting his symbolic-developmental perspective of the arts in *Art Education and Human Development* (1990) Gardner described a similar process:

> Human artistry is viewed first and foremost as an activity of the mind, an activity that involves the use of and transformation of various kinds of symbols and systems of symbols. Individuals who wish to participate meaningfully in artistic perception must learn to decode, the "read," the various symbolic vehicles in their culture; individuals who wish to participate in artistic creation must learn how to manipulate, how to "write with" the various symbolic forms present in their culture; and, finally, individuals who wish to engage fully in the artistic realm must also gain mastery of certain central artistic concepts. (1990, p. 9)

To understand the genesis of Gardner's definition of the arts and the educational consequences that he later advocated, it is necessary to track the structuralist genealogy on which it was based and to consider the kind of dialogue opened up around these views. A brief historical snapshot is in order.

Notational Structures and Notional Starts

In the early days of HPZ conceptions of the arts drew inspiration from the ideas of Nelson Goodman, from which Gardner and his associates adapted both conceptual and operational definitions in the empirical studies undertaken, especially in the 1970s. In describing the philosophical climate around the publication in 1968 of Goodman's *Languages of Art*, Gardner (1982a) echoed his mentor's assertion that the philosophy of art had become caught in a definitional slipknot as a result of furtive attempts to define notions such as value, beauty and emotions. Goodman's response was to focus on symptoms of the artistic process that were accessible and conducive to analytical study, namely, symbols. Goodman's theory built on the belief that there were different kinds of symbols and they functioned in different ways. This was explained in his theory of notation and described within a notational and non-notational continuum. Within this range, symbols were positioned according to the degree of notation exhibited, whereby a notational scheme was a highly conventional symbol system and during translation there was little loss of meaning (for example, interpreting a musical score). A non-notational symbol system on the other hand could elicit multiple meanings (for example, interpreting visual arts). In considering the relative position of symbol systems within this range Goodman introduced two criteria he defined as semantic and syntactical differences, the former having to do with meaning gleaned from a symbol, and the latter referred to the structural conventions of a symbol system.

Goodman's perspective was grounded in philosophical science because he felt distinctions between the sciences and aesthetics were rooted in assumed differences between knowing and feeling, between the cognitive and the emotive. Goodman's excursion into the arts was taken up by Gardner and fueled by the belief that "the entrenched dichotomy is in itself dubious on many grounds, and its application here becomes especially puzzling when aesthetic and scientific experience alike are seen to be fundamentally cognitive in character" (Goodman 1968, p. 245). Goodman explained the way symbols function as art forms in terms of the concepts of denotation, representation and exemplification. The denotative character of a symbol was descriptive, while a symbol could also represent properties or qualities, and exemplify either literal qualities or metaphorical features. For Goodman, the term metaphorical exemplification and expression were synonymous and this conflation did little to impress some aestheticians at the time.[4] Goodman's notion that expression was embedded within particular symbols rather than being carried by what was being represented also irked

---

[4] See *The Monist* 58: 2, (1974), for a series of critical essays on aspects of Goodman's aesthetic position generated in response to the publication of *Languages of Art*. See also articles by Pole (1974) and Savile (1971) in *The British Journal of Aesthetics*.

others. Goodman's response would reiterate the core of his thesis and that symbols function in different ways depending on what properties were attended to. This qualifying statement described Goodman's strategy for detecting the difference between art and non-art. The notion that circumstance determined if a symbol functioned as art was what Goodman meant when he asked, not "*what* is art?" but "*when* is art?" The point that symbolic forms were neither inherently artistic or not,[5] was at the core of Gardner's emerging theory of artistic development and he acknowledged this debt to Goodman.

> Through a quirk of language, art objects are spoken of as *symbols*, even as their constituent elements are also called symbols. What is meant here is that paintings, poems, novels, dances, and so forth, whatever their intrinsic interest and appeal, possess the potential of reference to the external world, to the world of subjective experience, and even to themselves. As Nelson Goodman has pointed out, a painting can, when functioning as a symbol, denote a man, express sadness, and exemplify grayness. The capacity to create and to appreciate symbols in a *medium* (such as sound or gesture) or in an *art form* (such as dance or music) is regarded here as the major prerequisite for artistic development, one which may be restricted to human beings. (1973, p. 43. Emphasis in the original)

Debate and Dialogue around Artistry

Although the presence of Goodman as a catalyst and a confidant helped energize the climate of inquiry in the early days of HPZ, the response to the publication of *The Arts and Human Development* (1973) indicated that Gardner was clearly setting in place a conceptual and empirical framework for sustained study of the artistic process. John M. Kennedy (1974) expressed measured confidence in the potential of the socio-cognitive approach to development being sketched by Gardner and the rendering of individual development and participation in artistic processes in all its complexity. Despite positioning the arts within a workable psychological framework, Kennedy detected a softness in the definitions and descriptions that, he felt, would need to be further focused for clinical investigation. Kennedy also noted areas where Gardner would also be subject to "empirical pursuit" by psychologists

---

[5] The view that circumstance and purpose were the determinants used to identify characteristics of human knowing was later applied by Gardner (1983) to his conception of multiple intelligences, where no intelligence was seen as inherently artistic or not, as all forms of intelligence could be used for artistic ends.

in need of more concrete evidence. For some reviewers, however, Gardner was too conservative in his speculations about the developing perceiving and feeling modes. Dale Harris's review (1976) highlighted some consistent behavioral styles or dispositions evident in studies of early development that he felt could strengthen Gardner's arguments about affective states. The developmental studies in early symbolization undertaken at HPZ during the mid and late 1970s that explored cognitive styles across different media picked up on this area of development although the outcomes were inconclusive and did not stand up to confirmatory analysis.[6] For Efland (1976), Gardner's text was an amalgam of features drawn from competing psychological perspectives where a shortcoming was a general lack of critical engagement with relevant literature in art and aesthetics. Efland did, however, applaud the effort to bridge cognitive and affective traditions and the originality of characterizing the audience member as a participant in the artistic process. Efland's suggestion that Gardner's conceptual overview could be used as a basis for a program of research to test the claims made proved to be prescient.

The critical elements identified by some commentators in the 1970s took on a sharper focus as the empirical studies, technical reports and publications from HPZ gained wider exposure throughout the arts education community. The cognitive orientation that saw arts learning as a composite of making, perceiving and feeling processes was gaining widespread acceptance as the psychological emphasis shifted away from a focus on behavior to the construction of knowledge as the primary quest for learning. The symbol processing approach being proposed by Gardner consequently offered opportunities for arts educators to align with a view that, on balance, spoke clearly to the notions of art knowing that had an intuitive and intellectual resonance. Creating visual symbols and interpreting them through the processes of making, perceiving, and appreciating was a description of art practice that mapped relatively easily onto curriculum structures that sought to ground art learning in content domains as well as developmental perspectives. What sometimes irked art educators was that characterizing the art learner as an expressive and responsive individual, and the trajectory of content-based cur-

---

[6] See, for example, Gardner, Wolf, and Smith 1975; Ives, Silverman, Kelly, and Gardner 1979; Wolf and Gardner 1979. In a structural equation modeling study of over two hundred second graders, the author was unable to provide statistical support for the 'patterner-dramatist' cognitive style construct and the relationships across drawing, storytelling and clay modeling as proposed by earlier HPZ studies (Sullivan 1986).

riculum development, was well chronicled in art education, but didn't seem to feature much in the model Gardner was crafting. In some cases the complaints raised legitimate issues such as concerns over the lack of focus on the mediating influence of socio-cultural contexts; technical questions about squeezing art experiences through psychological instruments that satisfied controls but maybe compromised validity; and incorrect readings that attributed to Gardner stances that were the very opposite of what he was advocating.[7]

Later versions of Gardner's conception of the arts reflected a more modulated view that was educationally oriented as he responded to the broader challenges of what his views on human development and artistic knowing might look like within schooling. Still evident in his writing was his enthusiasm for the uncertainties of child art and his unwavering conviction about the significance of artistic growth within a developmental frame that was captured in the portfolio of incidents, encounters and anecdotes in *Artful Scribbles* (1980). Although Gardner maintained firm views about his conception of developmental aesthetics in this text, some notions were more nuanced. It was generally not the case that Gardner was responding to criticism, but rather his assessment of the impact of empirical findings that offered plausible alternatives. For instance, the cross-cultural research of Alexander Alland (1983) questioned the assumed universalism of certain graphic conventions and highlighted the importance of cultural influences on the child art–something that had not featured strongly in Gardner's research.

In his essay on *Art Education and Human Development* (1990), Gardner ponders the observation that cultural variability is much more pronounced in the arts than in more 'notational' disciplines such as mathematics or language instruction. Yet he remains wedded to the view that it is through a scientific approach to the study of human development that suitable parameters for art educational progress might be revealed. Working within constraints is a strategy that has long been a feature of imaginative undertakings in the arts so there is merit in continuing the quest Gardner proposes. On the other hand, having to continually re-craft art practices to conform to the conditions of scientific

---

[7] For a response to the HPZ studies of perception, conceptions of the arts, and symbolization studies undertaken in the 1970s see Lovano-Kerr and Rush 1982; Rosario 1977. For a review of the literature on children's aesthetic development see Taunton 1982; and for a critique of the u-shaped curve of development see Wilson 1981; Duncum 1986; and *Studies in Art Education* 38:3. David Pariser continues this debate in this volume.

inquiry can be legitimately questioned as the scientific findings revealed to date are less than robust in their explanatory power.

The ambivalence in accounting for cultural variables as agents in artistic development reflects a broader difficulty in reconciling the way information processing using symbols gives rise to meaning making that can be generalized across contexts. In its most basic sense, a symbol systems approach to arts learning of the kind proposed by Gardner places the cognitive architecture in the mind, which is best located in the head, and that symbolic functioning takes place by manipulating forms and media that can carry meaning. In his critique of the symbol processing model of cognition endorsed by Gardner, Efland (2002) raises several concerns. He questions the use of the computer analogy, as others have, noting that the reduction of information to modular bits and to operations carried out on symbols means that the necessary mix between the hardware of the mind and the software of the content is hard to reconcile. Efland also feels that the metaphoric meaning characteristic of the arts is less readily accounted for within a computational model of cognition. Another quibble Efland raises gets at concerns about the apparent context neutral aspect of symbolic processing. He describes an artificial separation of the individual and the environment whereby actions in the real world need to be translated into symbolic representations that disembody them from the individual and the context. In Gardner's case, he is a firm advocate of Mihaly Csikszentmihalyi's situated view of creativity (Gardner 1982; Feldman, Csikszentmihalyi and Gardner 1994), and David Perkins's 1992 version of distributed intelligence, therefore he is well aware of the need to give form to symbolic understanding in social contexts. Nor can another of Efland's criticisms of symbolic processing, the tendency to separate feeling from knowing, be aligned with Gardner, who has, from the outset, sought to reconcile cognition and affect. A final concern of Elfand's is a more generic issue that permeates the cognitive sciences in general and this is the inclination to see individuals as passive participants who have little agency over the construction of knowledge. This problem seems more directed towards hard nosed cognitivists who ascribe to a computer model of the mind rather than interdisciplinary oriented theorists such as Gardner.

Despite debates and dissention about symbolic functioning and information processing that is well documented by Gardner (1987) in the cognitive science literature, he has been able to fashion considerable theoretical capital from his research. One of the key findings to emerge from his studies of symbolization and his views on children's artistic production and conceptions of the arts was the variability found in the way individuals made meaning through the use of symbols across media. In examining this variability Gardner was able to look at a similar 'data set' that others such as Piaget had dismissed as arcane and was able to explain it as a consequence of the varied way that individuals used different symbolic forms to construct understanding. By linking different information processing biologies with various symbolic media Gardner (1983) was able to draft the core of his theory of multiple intelligences. Although his conclusions drew on a diverse array of data that had its genesis in many of the HPZ studies, in essence his theoretical claims were based on a qualitative analysis that may not have had the certitude of probability measures that Gardner would have preferred. Still, his version of a 'subjective factor analysis' was consistent with the evidence he assembled and the plausibility of his account of intelligences has since been both supported and savaged by many.[8]

Multiple Views of Arts Education Practice

In looking again at Gardner's original description of the way individuals participate in the artistic process–as artists, audience members, critics, and performers–these appear surprising resilient. Although conceived over thirty years ago and having gone through iterations that consolidate around conceptual, perceptual and productive knowledge, what was consistently presented as a unique form of artistic knowing achieved through symbolization may now be considered in a new light. However, one has to consider alternatives to the reliance on the structural limitations of symbolic functioning and to relinquish the mantle of essentialism and align more closely with the realities of contemporary arts practice. It is within the contexts of the arts disciplines themselves that offers the most promising descriptions of how individuals, communities and institutions participate in arts practices. There are some consistencies in the intentions, roles and functions with the descriptions Gardner adopted in his original premise, however there are also important differences in these practices these days.

It is easy to appreciate the lure of essentialism for the rationalist assumption that things have essences or inherent characteristics means that it is possible to identify features that represent these qualities. It is

---

[8] There is a tantalizing doctoral dissertation waiting to be undertaken by an enterprising and theoretically savvy student who can apply a similar strategy of analyzing the same data set Gardner used to construct his theory of multiple intelligences, but who might come up with a completely different but equally plausible theoretical conception.

easier to investigate aspects of reality if they can be seen to have a fixed nature. This kind of thinking is at the heart of a rationalist view of the world for if it is agreed that thoughts, actions and things have an essential nature then it is reasonable to assume that these attributes are distributed across systems, genres or settings. This helps explain observable differences and assists in scientific analysis. Although essentialist conceptions have been successfully used in the study of the physical world, when used to freeze-frame the ever-changing dynamics of human nature the outcomes are problematic.

Essentialism is an enduring perspective in the arts where many enthusiasts argue that the arts represent a unique way of knowing and this has been a central tenet in causes such as aesthetic education, sensory-based learning, visual literacy, and so on (Eisner 2002). In advancing claims about the unique nature of visual symbolization Gardner is consistent in assigning an essentialist stamp to the forms of perceptual, conceptual and productive knowledge he sees as central to artistic knowing. Even with minor concessions made in acknowledging the interplay of situated factors and socio-cultural influences that shape what and how we learn, Gardner remains a rationalist at heart.

Yet, as people participate in arts experiences today they can be seen to take on the roles of artists, audience members, critics and performers, or in the case of many multi-media contemporary artists, *all* of these roles at the same time. Being described as an artistic participant who merely encodes or decodes symbolic forms is an inadequate account of the complex way we create, conceptualize and confront the arts today. The limitations of symbolic processing as a model of arts knowing in this day and age is sharpened by the emergence of other models of the mind that have the potential to explain in a more plausible way the variance *seen*, the regularity *known*, and the distinctiveness *felt* in and across the arts. At the end of his engaging essays on the emergence of the cognitive sciences Gardner draws attention to the "computational paradox" facing those who want to understand the complexity of human thought and action (Gardner 1985). For those of us who subscribe to the view that the arts are a cognitive coalition located in the mind, body, settings, and circumstances that we inhabit, we cannot ignore this kind of challenge.

The computational paradox arises, as Gardner sees it, through the historical preference to view thinking as an ordered, rational process that can be represented as a function not unlike a mathematical algorithm. Unfortunately the human mind in all its logical and imaginative diversity cannot be so neatly captured. Gardner acknowledges this "messy" quality.

Human thought emerges as messy, intuitive, subject to subjective representations—not as pure and immaculate calculation. These processes may ultimately be modeled by a computer, but the end result will bear little resemblance to that view of cognition canonically lurking in computationally inspired accounts. (1985, p. 386)

The computational bind arose in part because of the convenience of computers as modeling instruments and the study of thinking became an exercise in explaining human behavior in terms of the workings of the computer, rather than the other way round. Just as the behaviorists found it easy if foolhardy to ignore language in their clinical snapshots, it seems the cognitivists will face the same redundancy if they fail to consider the real if messy role of context and culture. Although the research agenda Gardner proposes in concluding his review of cognitive science shares the ambition of the early days at HPZ, it understandably remains locked into a conception of thinking that is primarily scientific. Yet even in the sciences, there are intriguing developments that are aligned more closely with the interests and practices of both the sciences and the arts. I am thinking here of areas such as complexity and emergence theory, complex adaptive systems, and other 'chaotic' studies into our micro and macro worlds.[9] These kinds of investigations may not be located within the traditional disciplines of the sciences and might be dismissed as boutique inquiries. They do, however, mostly represent interdisciplinary studies that are less governed by codified practices and more open to newer perspectives.

Those interested in human encounters in a changing social, cultural and global world now sharpened by the critical jabs of postmodernism and the pervasive influence of digital technologies should be enthused by the possibility of new attitudes and alliances. Within this uncertain yet imaginative prospect there are dilemmas as past convictions are questioned. For instance, the reductive archetype that served the arts and the sciences so well for so long no longer reveals the elusive truths believed to reside within matter and motion. Scientists and artists interested in dealing with the untidy complexity of the real world are often working in the spaces between disciplines while being conscious of but not bound by the safety net of canonical practices. An intriguing example for me are those teams of scientists and artists working on ideas such as complex, scale-free networks[10] that explore ways of thinking about

---

[9] See for example Coveney and Highfield 1995; Gell-Mann 1995, 2003.
[10] See for example Eve, Horsfall, and Lee 1997; Wilson 2002.

how phenomena are related, which adds to our understanding of ways we partition knowledge into structural forms such as taxonomies, hierarchies, matrices, frequency distributions and so on. As conceptual organizers these devices serve as editing strategies that allow us to represent information for ready interpretation. Representing large-scale phenomena is mostly arranged under hierarchical structures where the parts are indexed to the whole in successive levels. Yet not all things readily conform to such a structure therefore it is instructive to ponder other possibilities. What is especially attractive to researchers who put a premium on visual configurations and dynamic structures is the way that complex phenomena such as scale-free networks, no matter how large or how small, have elements that have both unique and universal features. This is quite different from normal distributions that reflect random occurrences and probability characteristics that are so central to concepts in scientific research. Scale-free environments are not exotic phenomena but can easily be seen, for example, in the workings of the Internet where 'real' life events are played out, some of which are content neutral such as computer viruses, while others are purpose-driven such as ideologically based web sites. As a real-world environment, the Internet can't be fully studied by relying on traditional methods and practices, yet imaginative scientists and thoughtful artists who are open to other possibilities do indeed offer the possibility of seeing and studying things in new ways.

In this reflexive encounter with Howard Gardner's arts practice I have identified the genesis of basic conceptions and how these informed the research program he directed and shaped the applications later developed in arts educational theory. Clear sightlines can be seen that locate these ideas within the collective mindset of those who helped give HPZ it's vision and voice at the outset. What is disappointing for me is that the momentum of serious and imaginative questioning waned after the intensity of the early years of HPZ that Nelson Goodman described this way:

> It [HPZ] had no fixed program and no firm doctrines but only a profound conviction of the importance of the arts, and a loose collection of attitudes, hunches, problems, objectives, and ideas for exploration. (1989, p. 1)

Obviously HPZ would have ended up an energetic if well meaning academic exercise without the extraordinary intensity on the part of the Gardner and his associates to take the cause out into the field. The outcome in advocacy and audience building has been impressive by any standards; yet there is little doubt that the full potential of the theories, constructs and ideas about art that gave spark to the original HPZ remain unfulfilled.

Research Practices

The second area covered in this review deals with Howard Gardner's research practices. The approaches that frame the art-based inquiries undertaken at HPZ in the 1970s through the 1990s cover a spectrum that includes experimental studies, descriptive accounts, and applied projects in educational settings. Grounded in the scientific traditions of psychology and later adapted to wider contexts using more qualitative approaches, the research program pursued always sought to maintain rigorous and systematic procedures. Gardner has never shied away from his preference for clinical methods that offer the potential for explanatory insight. However, as the scope of HPZ expanded in the mid 1980s in response to a change in the political and community perceptions about the needs of education as the research funding priorities changed, the fieldwork projects undertaken required the use of a range of methodological practices. In order to capture the mood of the times it seems appropriate to introduce this section with a personal anecdote that reflects the intensity of the research environment at HPZ and some dilemmas faced in taking a lead from avenues opened up by Gardner and his research colleagues.

As an art education graduate student at the Ohio State University in the 1980s I became fascinated by the studies of children's symbolic development and cognition generated by the researchers at HPZ. My doctoral research evolved in response to the symbolization studies undertaken at HPZ in the late 1970s and sought to test the empirical basis of the theory of cognitive style being promoted at HPZ at the time. The idea of cognitively grounded forms of symbolization that centered on the making, perceiving and feeling world of children held great promise for art educators like myself. A generous response from Howard Gardner meant that I was given direct access to the early symbolization research files, reports, and publications at HPZ. This helped me design a multivariate analysis of a model of symbolic functioning that sought to confirm the perceived relationships among cognitive style framed around the visual and verbal distinctions ('patterners' and 'dramatists') proposed by Gardner and his associates at the time, and areas of storytelling, drawing and clay modeling This was in part a replicative study as I modified instruments developed at HPZ in their symbolization studies, which I applied as measures in a structural equation analyses of responses to tasks around cognitive style and in various media from over two hundred seven-year-olds (Sullivan 1986). While examining the original data and designs of one of the symbolization studies I became puzzled by a particular instrument. Of the inventive tasks included I was intrigued to find that the material used for clay modeling was not clay, but play-doh. In the 1970s play-doh was relatively new as a play material used with young children. As a modeling compound it was certainly malleable and allowed for the imaginative construction of all manner of forms. But the natural body heat of young hands soon made play-doh crumble and rather hard to work into detailed forms and shapes. Therefore, to have youngsters create objects using play-doh, and then measure them on scales such as amount of complexity of detail in a three dimensional version of the 'draw/make-a-person' task, would raise validity problems. An alternative would be to use white earthenware (which is what I used in my study) for this form of clay certainly retained its full modeling properties for the time needed, and when it dried on small hands it looked like white talcum power so the youngsters never felt they were getting dirty. I remember being non-plussed at the time in thinking that an arts researcher with a basic knowledge of the visual arts would have been aware of the inherent problems posed by using inappropriate materials and processes.

Despite my need to modify some operational components in the testing of a theory proposed by Gardner and his associates at HPZ, this scenario reflects how I was informed and puzzled by their work at the time. On a broader level, the comprehensive way the researchers at HPZ approached the study of the cognitive complexity of human development generated excitement among many arts educators, as well as skepticism among others. In a reference to the innovative program of arts research opened up by Gardner and others at HPZ in the 1970s and 80s I wrote:

> The scope of Project Zero is indeed vast. In the unfolding of new areas of research, attention needs to be given to providing directions for others to follow. Even paths bulldozed with statistical efficiency remain insignificant if they are too numerous and obscure. The use of complex machinery should not be intimidating, as this does not change the potency or paucity of the ideas that power it. (Sullivan 1986, p. 29)

How might my assessment of the research practice of those at HPZ stand up today?

Systems and Structures of Arts Inquiry

The approach to research pursued by Gardner from the early days of HPZ was shaped by a firm belief in the capacity of scientific inquiry to yield the knowledge needed to better understand the role of the arts in human development. The guiding structure owed allegiance to astute observers such as Piaget and the strategy of detecting breakdowns in the thinking and reasoning capacities of individuals as they confronted cognitive problems and puzzles. Gardner's overall goal was to construct a profile of learning that accounted for comprehensive ways of knowing that was well grounded in the performance and practices of the arts. Taking on the arts agenda meant that Gardner had to define a broad theoretical framework that was psychologically sound and offered a coherent structure for operationalizing concepts for subsequent scientific study. This is what he called seeking a "first order approximation to the natural developmental history of key artistic capacities." He added:

> Against this background, it should then be possible to ascertain the flexibility of this portrait, the differences which background and training can make, the effects of intervention or of a highly unusual home or school setting, the role of individual differences, and the like. In other words, first, the approximation: then refinements, alterations or possibly even the scuttling of the initial model. (1982b, p. 83)

By describing a defensible account of artistic development that was well grounded within developmental and cognitive psychology it was assumed that focused inquiries into specific arts performances and responses could be carried out to help identify more complex explanatory models of artistic behavior.

In line with conventional rationalist practices that distinguish between basic and applied research the early years of HPZ were devoted to answering core theoretical questions, which were later applied in various community and educational contexts. Constructing a sound theory of development in the arts that could be logically and seamlessly extended into a theory of instruction became more evident as the trajectory of research carried out at HPZ during the first couple of decades evolved. Quibbles over methodological problems expressed by others in early critiques of HPZ research generally focused on concerns about the validity of instrumentation—and here the often cited problem of well meaning psychologists squeezing art constructs into unsympathetic measurement protocols was a common complaint—and broader issues such as the lack of cultural diversity in the samples used in HPZ studies. In some cases these concerns were well founded as the increasing importance of contextual variables became more obvious as the research program moved beyond clinical studies. In other cases it was argued by those at HPZ that some procedural problems would even themselves out due to the number of studies undertaken so that the replicative feature of scientific inquiry served as an in-house defense mechanism.

Where research practices changed most was as a consequence of the evolution of HPZ into an applied program of field based projects during the 1980s. The changing research market place and cultural climate that saw a new emphasis on educational accountability increased the opportunities for site based inquiries and innovative programs and proposals. This was opportune for HPZ as the theories being developed were ready for exploration in educational settings. The cross-disciplinary interest and the mix of eclecticism and pragmatism evident in the late 1970s and early 1980s was used to good effect in designing a new generation of research projects. Mostly funded by private foundations, these often had practical and procedural requirements yet also allowed the investigators at HPZ the opportunity to design multi-year projects, often in collaboration with other institutions and cultural agencies. In implementing these projects use was also made of those researchers at HPZ who brought educational expertise as well as experience in field studies so that the range of methodologies noticeably expanded. Yet, the insistent voice of Gardner was evident as he saw the need to nest experimental elements and control group mechanisms into the design of large-scale projects. The more extensive use of descriptive and interventionist quantitative methods also meant that comprehensive demographic data was always close at hand so as to enhance the interpretive yield of findings and outcomes.[11]

During the 1980s when the research program at HPZ expanded to address educational demands it was also a time of considerable debate about educational research methodologies. Amid this dialogue the large-scale, collaborative research projects in the arts that HPZ pioneered served as an institutional model that few others could hope to emulate in scope. Yet the discipline-specific impact on basic research in the arts has been sporadic after the initial flurry in the late 1980s to the mid 1990s[12]

---

[11] See, for example, the HPZ Project Co-Arts (Davis 1993), a typical research design that incorporated various descriptive techniques such as surveys and questionnaires from which more comprehensive case studies were carried out at selected sites. Other long-term arts HPZ research projects that featured a combination of qualitative and quantitative approaches included Arts Propel and the Lincoln Center Institute Study.

[12] Extensive arts research projects undertaken during this time included Arts PRO-PEL (Gardner 1989); Project Co-Arts (Davis 1993; Davis, Soep, Maira, Remba, and Putnoi 1993; Davis, Solomon, Eppel, and Dameshek 1996); and The Lincoln Center Institute Project: Curricular Frameworks in Aesthetic Education.

as the focus turned to interdisciplinary areas and broader educational interests in pedagogical practice and policy. More recent efforts in arts research by Gardner's associates continue to explore applied projects within school settings.[13] Studies at HPZ that specifically address basic research questions in the arts have been limited. An exception, however, was the meta-analytic critique of the published evidence for the transfer of arts learning to other areas of educational performances that made good use of the well-honed methodological expertise among HPZ researchers.[14] As well as taking on a reactive research role within the arts education community, it is intriguing to consider the elements of research practice that might endure, and those that might change, if Gardner and his colleagues were to re-invest in asking basic questions about the arts.

A Methodological Reprise

If Howard Gardner decided to look again at the questions first posed in the heady days of HPZ what conceptual structure might be used to investigate areas of artistic perception, conception, and production? If interventionist studies were seen to be necessary to address hypotheses about artistic preferences, ways of thinking, creative problem solving and the like, then it might be expected that mixed methodology approaches (Tashakkori and Teddlie 2003) would be used so as to position controlled investigations within broader contextual frameworks. Essential to such inquiries would be a critical review of the relevant research literature in arts education disciplines, critical and cultural studies, art history, and contemporary arts practice to ensure the construct validity of conceptual and operational measures. Although some past notions would be abandoned,[15] a view firmly maintained would be that arts forms carry meaning and can be used as data from which information can be gathered and interpreted. In other words, arts images and forms are replete with potential evidence of knowledge and images function as texts, artifacts, and events that embody individual and cultural meaning. Further, there would be a need to account not only for

---

[13] See the three-phase Studio Thinking Project, 2001–2006.

[14] See the special edition of *The Journal of Aesthetic Education* edited by Ellen Winner and Lois Hetland, 34: 3–4 (Fall–Winter, 2000).

[15] Constructs such as 'art style,' and criteria such as 'flavorfulness' would readily be seen to reflect reductive formalist conceptions and have little explanatory power as variables.

independent elements that might be constituent variables, but also to accommodate interdependencies among components and processes that might have a transformative or interactive role as thinking and making systems are enacted.

Allied to this attention given to various particularities and contexts might be the realization that the symbol processing approach to cognition favored by Gardner may not have the explanatory power needed to account for the variability of artistic knowing. Presently there are plausible alternatives that offer intriguing possibilities. For instance, the computational paradox that Gardner highlighted in his 1987 publication can be reconfigured in light of alternative metaphors of the mind. For instance, those advocating a connectionist model (Rumelhart 1998) assert that there is no index of ready-made symbolic meanings in the brain which are filed away that we access as we re-construct new understandings. Rather, it is argued the architecture of the mind consists of a vast array of parallel neural networks and learning is a process of making rapid connections as meanings are made in the action and associations forged. As a potential model for thinking about the 'arts' mind I describe connectionism this way:

> As a parallel rather than a serial process, connectionism is not governed by any executive function or central processor. Rather, cognitive processing activates links strengthened by previous learning, but is also open to intuitive and opportunistic connections. Many visual artists would have little difficulty endorsing a view that favors this kind of intuitive integration of prior knowledge and the possibility of new associations. (Sullivan 2005, pp. 120–121)

Even more intriguing might be "dynamicist" models (Thelan and Smith 1994) of cognitive functioning that describe a systems-like process whereby meanings continually change as a consequence of the interactions between the individual and the context. This conception builds on the 'self-organizing' capacity of dynamic systems which means that thoughts are able to connect or relate to each other in multiple, non-linear ways. For those invested in the arts, visualizing the interplay of thoughts and actions in a dynamic mix of mindful activity that is mediated by contextual constraints has a lot of appeal.

Whether complex conceptions of the mind lend themselves to sustained study in arts research is unknown. It is certainly feasible, given the opportunities for interdisciplinary inquiries, especially if artists and arts researchers have direct input alongside their colleagues from the sciences. We were given a chance to see collaborations of this kind with the workings of HPZ, and these programs have the potential to yield results that can capture the elegance and complexity of arts knowing. Within renewed regimes of research needed today it is equally intriguing to consider the direction such studies might take had Gardner maintained his enthusiasm for asking these difficult questions.

Final Reflection

The purpose of this review was to present a critique of some core ideas about the arts education and research practices of Howard Gardner. The stance adopted was selective in that the sample of texts that display Gardner's emergence as an arts researcher was mined for the source and salience of the ideas they exhibit. As products of their time, the interpretation of these texts came in part from their documentation of the practices and programs of inquiry, and in part from the debate and discourse they set in play. Seen in retrospect, the generative power of Gardner's conceptions and their influence on how they changed the way we think about arts education was shown to be uneven. The tendency to change the point of impact as new interests arose meant that creative energies often dissipated. As texts that might be expected to sustain meaningful encounters the sources re-visited in this essay appear more like works-in-progress rather than visions of conviction. As a witness to this evolving paradigm I have been informed and remain indebted to the work of Howard Gardner, and I continue to be enlivened for I am able to get a hoist up on his shoulders as it helps me see more clearly in other directions.

REFERENCES

Alland, A. 1983. *Playing with Form: Children Draw in Six Cultures.* New York: Columbia University Press.

Coveney, P., and R. Highfield. 1995. *Frontiers of Complexity: The Search for Order in a Chaotic World.* New York: Fawcett Columbine.

Davis, J. 1993. *The Co-Arts Assessment Handbook.* Cambridge, Massachusetts: Harvard Project Zero.

Davis, J., E. Soep, S. Maira, N. Remba, and D. Putnoi. 1993. *Safe Havens: Portraits of Educational Effectiveness in Community Art Centers that Focus on Education.* Cambridge, Massachusetts: Project Zero.

Davis, J., B. Solomon, M. Eppel, and W. Dameshek. 1996. *The Wheel in Motion: The Co-Arts Assessment Plan from Theory to Practice.* Cambridge, Massachusetts: Harvard Project Zero.

Duncum, P. 1986. Breaking Down the U-curve of Artistic Development. *Visual Arts Research* 12: 1, pp. 43–54.

Efland, A.D. 1976. Book Review: *The Arts and Human Development*, by Howard Gardner. *Studies in Art Education* 17: 2, pp. 67–69.

———. 2002. *Art and Cognition: Integrating the Visual Arts in the Curriculum.* New York: Teachers College Press.

Eisner, E.W. 2002. *The Arts and the Creation of Minds.* New Haven: Yale University Press.

Eve, R.A., S. Horsfall, and M. E. Lee, eds. 1997. *Chaos, Complexity, and Sociology: Myths, Models, and Theories.* Thousand Oaks: Sage.

Feldman, D.H., M. Csikszentmihalyi, and H. Gardner. 1994. *Changing the World: A Framework for the Study of Creativity.* Westport: Praeger.

Gardner, H. 1973. *The Arts and Human Development: A Psychological Study of the Artistic Process.* New York: Wiley.

———. 1980. *Artful Scribbles: The Significance of Children's Drawings.* New York: Basic Books.

———. 1982a. *Art, Mind, and Brain. A Cognitive Approach to Creativity.* New York: Basic Books.

———. 1982b. Response to Comment on Project Zero by Jessie Lovano-Kerr and Jean Rush. *Review of Visual Arts Research Education* 15, pp. 83–84.

———. 1983. *Frames of Mind: The Theory of Multiple Intelligences.* New York: Basic Books.

———. 1985. *The Mind's New Science: A History of the Cognitive Revolution.* New York: Basic Books.

———. 1989. Zero-Based Arts Education: An Introduction to Arts PROPEL. *Studies in Art Education: A Journal of Issues and Research* 30: 2, pp. 71–83.

———. 1990. *Art Education and Human Development.* Los Angeles: Getty Center for Education in the Arts.

———. 1991. *The Unschooled Mind: How Children Think and How Schools Should Teach.* New York: Basic Books.

Gardner, H., and D. Perkins, eds. 1989. *Art, Mind, and Education: Research from Project Zero.* Urbana: University of Illinois Press.

Gardner, H., D. Wolf, and A. Smith. 1975. Artistic Symbols in Early Childhood. *New York University Education Quarterly* (Summer 1975), pp. 13–21.

Gell-Mann, M. 1995. Plectics. In J. Brockman, ed., *The Third Culture: Beyond the Scientific Revolution* (New York: Touchstone), pp. 316–332.

———. 2003. Regularities and Randomness: Evolving Schemata in Science and the Arts. In J. Casti and A. Karlqvist, eds., *Art and Complexity* (Amsterdam: Elsevier), pp. 47–58.

Goodman, N. 1968. *Languages of Art: An Approach to a Theory of Symbols.* Indianapolis: Bobbs-Merrill.

————. 1989. Introduction: Aims and Claims. In H. Gardner and D. Perkins, eds., *Art, Mind, and Education: Research from Project Zero* (Urbana: University of Illinois Press), pp. 1–2.

Harris, D.B. 1976. Book Review: *The Arts and Human Development*, by Howard Gardner. *Journal of Aesthetic Education* 10: 3–4, pp. 243–45.

Ives, W., J. Silverman, H. Kelly, and H. Gardner. 1979. Artistic Development in the Early School Years: A Cross-Media Study of Storytelling, Drawing and Clay Modeling. Technical Report #8. National Institute of Education (DHEW). Washington D.C.: Spencer Foundation.

Kennedy, J.M. 1974. Book Review: *The Arts and Human Development: A Psychological Study of the Artistic Process. Journal of Aesthetics and Art Criticism* 33: 2, pp. 228–231.

Lovano-Kerr, J. and J. Rush. 1982. Project Zero: The Evolution of Visual Arts Research in the Seventies. *Review of Research in Visual Arts Education* 15, pp. 61–81.

Perkins, D.N. 1992. *Smart Schools: From Training Memories to Educating Minds.* New York: Free Press.

Pole, D. 1974. Goodman and the 'Naive' View of Representation. *British Journal of Aesthetics* 14: 1, pp. 68–80.

Rosario, J. 1977. Children's Conception of the Arts: A Critical Response to Howard Gardner. *Journal of Aesthetic Education* 11: 1, pp. 91–100.

Rumelhart, D.E. 1998. The Architecture of Mind: A Connectionist Approach. In P. Thagard, ed., *Mind Readings* (Cambridge, Massachusetts: MIT Press), pp. 207–238.

Savile, A. 1971. Nelson Goodman's 'Language of Art': A Study. *British Journal of Aesthetics* 11: 1, pp. 3–27.

Sparshott, F.E. 1974. Goodman on Expression. *The Monist* 58: 2, pp. 187–202.

Sullivan, G. 1986. A Covariance Structure Model of Symbolic Functioning: A Study of Children's Cognitive Style, Drawing, Clay Modeling, and Storytelling. *Visual Arts Research* 12: 1, pp. 11–32.

Sullivan, G. 2005. *Art Practice as Research: Inquiry in the Visual Arts.* Thousand Oaks: Sage.

Tashakkori, A. and C. Teddlie. 2003. *Handbook of Mixed Methods in Social and Behavioral Research.* Thousand Oaks: Sage.

Taunton, M. 1982. Aesthetic Response of Young Children to the Visual Arts: A Review of the Literature. *The Journal of Aesthetic Education* 16: 3, pp. 93–109.

Thelan, E. and L.B. Smith. 1994. *A Dynamic Systems Approach to the Development of Cognition and Action.* Cambridge, Massachusetts: MIT Press.

Wilson, B. 1981. Response to Winner and Gardner. *Review of Research in Visual Arts Education* 14, pp. 32–33.

Wilson, S. 2002. *Information Arts: Intersections of Art, Science, and Technology*. Cambridge, Massachusetts: MIT Press.

Wolf, D. and H. Gardner. 1979. Style and Sequence in Early Symbolic Play. In N.R. Smith and M.B. Franklin, eds., *Symbolic Functioning in Childhood* (Hillsdale: Erlbaum).

13

Considering the U-Curve

DAVID PARISER

Introduction

In this essay I will be questioning the origins and viability of Gardner's u-curved aesthetic development hypothesis. I will advance two sorts of critical material—contextual-historical and empirical. But before I question the premises and predictive power of one of Gardner's very numerous and robust intellectual offspring, I first must acknowledge his support over the years. He has been a generous mentor and he has functioned as a prolific and inspiring researcher. His work in the fields of multiple intelligences, creativity, giftedness and the arts have all been important landmarks in my professional landscape.

It is true of original and synoptic thinkers like Gardner, that their predictions and observations are hugely generative. Thus for example, MI theory has been a fruitful source for practical change and theoretical research in education. Educators do need to have a clearer idea of what constitutes intelligence and MI theory has certainly prodded them into thinking afresh on this topic. The same can be said of the u-curve theory—its claims, provable or not, have brought about an important debate in art education and psychology.

The Claim

But, to start at the beginning. It has long been an article of faith among the culturati that the genius of childhood is much the same gem as that which adorns the highest achievements of mature artists (Malvern 1988). Baudelaire was among those who first explored the commonalities that exist between the genius of the adult artist and the child's gift. The Romantic tradition provided the basis for asserting a link—if not an identity—between the genius of childhood and adult genius. Some Western visual artists—especially the Modernists—have embraced this vision of the child as the prototypical artist. Robert Motherwell (1970) spoke about the ways in which the child's grasp of visual language is testimony to the universal reach of the same visual language employed by Modernist artists:

> Part of the enterprise of modern art is to strip away from painting the costumes, the masquerades, the status symbols of church and state and politics—hence its so-called abstraction, which is actually a . . . universalism. This universalism is not unparallel to that of small children, as when the French Fauves and German Expressionists began to paint more and more directly,colorfully, immediately and expressively . . . (pp. 26–27)

Equally telling, Motherwell grieves over what he perceives as the way in which most young children lose the marks of visual genius as they enter adolescence and early adulthood. Henkes (1990) makes the same point about graphic development from a cognitive-developmental perspective. It is therefore unexceptional that Rosensteil and Gardner (1977) stated:

> In most areas of human development, ranging from scientific understanding . . . to moral judgment, a smooth regular improvement in task performance can be observed from early childhood to adolescence. The child's artistic and creative capacities have always posed somewhat of a puzzle in this respect; the clear decline in artistic activity . . . and the apparent decline in certain artistic skills . . . seems to contradict a general developmental principle . . . (p. 36)

Gardner and Winner (1982) give final form to this speculation about development and the demise of creative power in the visual arts with the label "u-shaped development." They use this term to characterise the highly aesthetic performance of young children, followed by a period of falling-off and, for some, a return to aesthetic excellence. Gardner and Winner introduce the term in a book edited by Strauss (1982) devoted to u-shaped development in cognition. In 1991 Gardner again articulated the model:

> In the arts, for example, young children prove to be better metaphor makers and to produce drawings with more originality and flavor than older

children mired in the so-called "literal stage" of aesthetic development. Some children remain at the trough in the u, some cease drawing or metaphorizing altogether, and selected others eventually produce fine drawings or innovative metaphoric figures. (p. 107)

The operative terms in this discussion are the the qualifiers, "originality," "flavor," and "fine." As long as these qualifiers are somewhat aligned with the Modernist aesthetic espoused by Motherwell and others, the observation remains uncontroversial.

One of the basic criticisms levelled at the notion of u-shaped aesthetic growth arises from an understanding of the pervasive legacy of Modernist artists. In a remarkable work, Fineberg (1997) uncovers the fact that many well-known Modernist artists (Dubuffet, Kandinsky, Klee, Larionov, Miro, Munter, Picasso) were all keen students of young children's drawings and paintings. They owned extensive collections of children's drawings and paintings-and they were not above appropriating images and styles from the children's work. This has been a well-kept secret according to Fineberg: "The influence of child art on Modern artists has barely been mentioned as a possiblity in the scholarship on Modern art and not even the artists have been eager to discuss it . . ." (p. 14).

It is thus no surprise that people steeped in the Modernist aesthetic, with a knowledge of the great Moderns will quite naturally see many shared formal characteristics in child art and that of mature artists. After all, many of the Modern masters deliberately incorporated the child's visual syntax, approach to form and spontaneous use of color into their own work. The comparison works in both directions. Modernist art looks like children's art and *vice versa*. Perhaps this bias went unnoticed when Gardner and Winner made their observation about the u-shaped trajectory of children's aesthetic growth.

We (Kindler *et al.* 2002) were not the first to have difficulty with what appeared to be a Modernist-inspired formulation for aesthetic development. Several art educators—Wilson and Wilson(1981), Duncum (1986), Korzenik (1995), and Wilson (1997)—suggest that the much-noted decline in aesthetic quality may well be an artifact of the pre-eminence of Modernist tastes among the researchers who look at the visual work of young children. Duncum (1986) presented a thorough review of the criticism that had been levelled at the u-curve hypothesis. He identified three flaws: 1) There was a significant lack of agreement among the u-curve proponents concerning the exact moment in the child's life when the slump in aesthetic performance occurred. The trough of the U was notoriously hard to pin down. 2) There was little agreement among the proponents as to precisely what features of the children's artwork declined- descriptive terms like "flavorful" seemed vague and *ad hoc*. 3)The u-curve seems to be a normative description that depends on a Modernist-Abstract Expressionist vision of the ultimate goal. Duncum adds, "I have argued that the 'u' curve is based on confusion and stylistic prejudice. I have been particularly mindful that not all artistic endpoints conform to the stylistic biases of self-expression theorists and aesthetic formalists" (p. 54).

Others in psychology have pointed out the limitations of the theory. Golomb (1992) cites the work of Halkiadiakis (1983) for empirical evidence from children's drawings that does not support the Gardner and Winner model. Rostan (1997) states that the u-curve is only observed in populations where the youngest childen do not receive art instruction. Where children do receive art instruction, Rostan claims that the graph of aesthetic growth is an upwardly sloping line indicating a linear relationship between aesthetic excellence and age.

There is another aspect to this choice of the young child as a model for artistic greatness, and that is the concomitant disdain for artistic skill, technical achievement, and the ability to make recognizable, naturalistic images. Paul Klee (1924) one of the pre-eminent Modernists wrote as follows about realism:

> The artist . . . does not attach such intense importance to natural forms as do so many realist critics, because for him, these original forms are not the real stuff of the process of natural creation. For he places more value on the powers which do the forming than on the final forms themselves. (p. 87)

Thus for the Modernist there are two cardinal values. First, respect and love for the child's spontaneous imagery—so different from the platitudes sanctioned by the discredited and defunct academy and second, a certain disdain for technical ability. These two principles establish Modernism's special relationship to children and child-art. It is in fact with the rise of Modernism that the puzzling honorific "child artist" becomes possible. Before Modernism the child may have been an inspiration but would hardly have been confused with the artist. The u-curve model is a contemporary way of securing the child's place in the pantheon of artists.

My claim thus far is that the u-curve hypothesis is largely the result of an implicit aesthetic bias in favor of Modernist art. Moreover, due to the fact that many of the Moderns emulated the work of young children, the waters of aesthetic objectivity are hopelessly muddied. Young children's visual work looks like the work of unsullied genius, in part because world-class Modern artists have studiously copied and emulated the imagery, colors, and graphics of the very young child.

Thus, it seems to me that Gardner did not consider the possibility that what seemed like an "objective" observatioin was in fact the reflection of a deeply ingrained aesthetic credo.

We now turn to another aspect of this model for aesthetic development. Can the relationship between children's graphics and artists' graphics be demonstrated? Does the model predict what we find when we examine samples of child, adolescent and adult art?

On the face of it, the model suggests that, if one takes a longitudinal sample of an artistic individual's visual work covering the time span from early childhood to adulthood one ought to find proof for what Davis (1997) describes as follows:

> This course of development from display of early facility, to disenfranchisement in middle childhood, to mature realization only by an artistic minority, has been described as u-shaped. . . . In this configuration, the highly expressive drawings of the youngest children and the adult artists are envisioned at the two high peaks of the u, with the conventionalized drawings of children in middle childhood bottoming out on the floor of the u. (pp. 132–33).

So the question is, if one does in fact look at work from individuals spaced along the lifespan from childhood to artistic adulthood, does one in fact note the effloresence, decline, and return of aesthetic quality? This question has been asked and tested operationally at least three times.

Looking for Proof: Empirical Attempts to Find the U-curve

The Davis Study

Pre-eminent among those who sought to empirically demonstrate the u-curve, is Davis (1991). For her doctoral dissertation, Davis constructed a two-part study. First, she obtained drawings from seven different age and training groups (five-, eight-, eleven-, and fourteen-year-old children with art training, fourteen-year-olds without art training, adult artists, and adult non-artists). These experimental subjects were asked to make four drawings: a control drawing and then three other drawings each depicting one of three emotions, happy, sad, and angry. Davis intentionally left the drawing request vague, for example "Draw happy," so that there would be a chance for those who were so inclined to make "abstract" drawings—that is, images with no clear referent. For the second half of her study, Davis trained two judges, both with a background in the arts, to apply a sophisticated scoring protocol to the drawings. In the end, all drawings were awarded a numerical score-and could be plotted against each other as to their relative aesthetic merit. The Davis scoring protocol was consciously constructed around aesthetic formulations taken from the work of Goodman (1976) and Arnheim (1969, 1971). Both of these scholars provided the Formalist-Modernist aesthetic concepts (balance, organization, repleteness, and so forth) that Davis operationalized in her scoring protocol.

The results of Davis's study were impressive. She did indeed arrive at a canonical u-curve in which the drawings of the five-year-olds (as a group) and those of the adult artists (as a group) scored demonstrably higher on measures of aesthetic value than the scores of all the five other intervening groups of draughtsmen. Her two judges did in fact see a u-shaped curve in the aesthetic merit of drawings by individuals from childhood through adulthood. For adherents, Davis's work remains an important demonstration. So, Eisner, in a recent publication (2002) cites Davis's work as strong evidence for the existence of the u-curve.

Further Empirical Explorations: Inserting a Cross-cultural Element

For lots of reasons, Davis's findings proved to be a catalyst for our own speculations and resulted in two studies that tested the robustness of her claims-and by implication, the reach and applicability of the u-curve hypothesis itself. In the first study Davis, Pariser, and van den Berg collaborated to replicate Davis's original research (Pariser, Van den Berg 1997a), with two significant differences: instead of using only Western judges with art backgrounds, we also used art-trained judges from China, and we obtained the drawings from an age sample identical to Davis's original, but this time from members of the Chinese community in Montreal. We thus sought to look for the u-curve among members of a culture that has a rich and distinct aesthetic heritage, though not untainted by Western Modernism (See Andrews 1998, Gao 1996). One hundred sixty-five test drawings were solicited from fifty-five individuals in the Montreal Chinese community. These drawings were asssessed by two pairs of judges: two male Chinese art-trained judges from Montreal, and two female art-trained judges from the Boston area.

Figure 1 Emotion Drawing: Sad—Brazilian adult artist

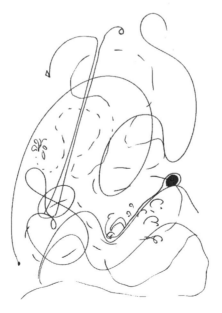

Figure 2 Emotion Drawing: Happy—Taiwanese adult artist

We made one more significant change to Davis's original study design. In addition to using the Davis scoring protocol for assessing the drawings, we also asked the judges to make a much simpler and less nuanced assessment of the drawings. This was a three-way sort. Both pairs of judges were asked to sort the 165 drawings into three piles: Good, Poor, and Indifferent. Judges were free to use their own criteria for making these sortings-and in interviews following the sorting process , the judges were asked to give an explanation for why they sorted the drawing as they did. The only constraint was that there had to be at least one drawing in each pile-that is, the judges could not simply put all drawings in the "good" or "poor" pile.

Our results did not provide much empirical comfort for the notion that the u-curve effect is a widespread and cross-cultural phenomenon. They suggested that the judges were as critical a variable as the drawings themselves. We found that while the two Western-trained judges produced canonical u-curves, regardless of the assessment instrument, the Chinese judges produced an uneven but upwardly sloping linear pattern (a dragon, as we dubbed it.) regardless of which assessment procedure they used. This upward sloping line reflected their assumptions (articulated in the interviews) that as the age of the artists increased, so too did the aesthetic merits of their work.

Particularly telling was the difference in the treatment of the five-year-olds' drawings. Where the North American judges ranked the five-year-olds' drawings as better than or only slightly inferior to those by adolescents and adult artists, the Montreal Chinese judges invariably ranked these same drawings as inferior to those by all other groups in the sample. In other words, for the Chinese judges, there was nothing that special aesthetically about the five-year-old children's drawings. And, as we have seen, privileging the young child's work is the bedrock on which the u-curve rests.

As far as van den Berg and I (1997a) were concerned, the results of this replication of Davis's original study failed to confirm that the u-curve was a widespread developmental trend. Evidence for this was the fact that art-trained judges from two different artistic traditions did not agree on the relative merits of the same set of drawings. This suggested to us that judgments of aesthetic merit were at least as much a function of the judges' dispositions and training, as a reflection of the "objective properties" of the drawings themselves. Davis (1997) was not in agreement with us, and we engaged in an extensive debate on this topic in the pages of the Spring Issue of Studies In Art Education (Davis 1997b; Pariser, van den Berg 1997b).

In addition to questioning the generalizability of the u-curve claim, one other important methodological element emerged from this small study. We (Pariser, van den Berg) observed that in the case of both pairs of judges, the results of their assessments were strikingly similar, regardless of the instrument used. That is, the judges' characteristic sorting patterns were the same , whether or not they used the Davis protocol or the three-way sort. This observation proved useful when it came time to frame a larger follow-up study on the same question, because we opted to use the simple three-way sort rather than the more intricate and time-consuming Davis scoring protocol.

At this point we (Kindler *et al.* 2000) were intrigued by two issues: One was, how to get a better sense for the impact of the judges' age,education, and cultural backgrounds as they affected their aesthetic choices. And the the other was to try to look at a wider spectrum of repertoires in drawing. In the Montreal replication of the Davis study , the drawing task (draw an emotion) reflected what was essentially a single terminus model of artistic growth, the ideal endpoint being expressive and authentic imagery that used formal means to convey feeling-an essentially Modernist vision of authentic art. Kindler and Darras (1997) among others (See Wolf and Perry 1988) had developed a model of graphic-artistic development as a network of possible pathways leading to a number of artistic goals. Graphic imagery could and did serve a number of different functions, expression was certainly one of these,but there were others as well.

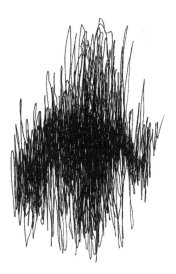

Figure 3 Emotion Drawing: Angry—Taiwanese adult artist

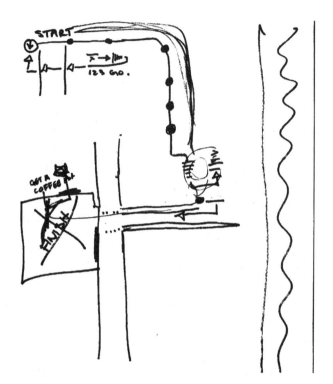

Figure 4 Map Drawing—Canadian adult artist

That is, graphic representations have many uses beyond expression; communication, instruction, enumeration, mapping, modelling, caricature . . . Each of these aims may quite plausibly have a different developmental trajectory and most certainly embody different criteria for aesthetic success. In the next phase of our investigation we looked more closely at these multiple graphic repertoires.

The Three-Country Study: Summary and Results

In our second and larger study we decided to incorporate the notion of multiple pathways (or graphic repertoires) into our research design. For our follow-up study (Kindler, Pariser, van den Berg 2000)we collected drawings from 360 subjects, 120 individuals from each of three countries (Brazil, Canada, and Taiwan). Drawings were made by six groups of people: five-, eight-, eleven-, and fourteen-year-olds, adult non artists, and adult artists. Our subject-groups were similar to those chosen by Davis in her study, but we omitted artistically trained fourteen year olds.

Each participant in the study was asked to make four drawings. All of the participants were asked to make a "control" drawing of anything they wanted. There were then two different experimental tasks. Half of the participants were asked to make three images representing "happy, sad and angry." (Figures 1, 2, and 3 illustrate drawing responses to this request). The request for "emotion" drawings was a replication of Davis's original task. The other half of the participants were asked to make three drawings reflecting some of the multiple repertoires Kindler and Darras had identified: one drawing was to represent the route they take from home to school or work. We assumed that this request would generate "map-like" drawings which emphasize landmarks and which are constructed for easy reading, rather than realism. Many of these drawings did indeed incorporate map-like features (see Figure 4). A second drawing request was to draw a favorite cartoon figure. With this request we tapped into imagery based on icons readily available in the popular media (see Figures 5, 6). The fourth drawing request was to show several people doing something together. We intended this task to focus the participants on a very common theme in drawing development, one that incorporates interest in the human figure and narrative (see Figure 7).

As in the Davis study, the second phase of our study involved judging the drawings. We asked four judge-groups to look at 720 drawings out of the 1,440 that we collected. The judge-groups were made up of eight-year-old children, fourteen-year-olds, adult non-artists, and adult artists. There was a total of 192 judges, 64 from each country, and 16 in each judge-group. Each judge made a three-way sort of the drawings, assigning them to one of three piles. Judges were also interviewed after making their assessments. Our purpose in having such a wide variety of judges from three different countries, was to examine even more closely the role that the judges' age and background played in aesthetic assessment.

As is evident, this study enabled us to ask a lot of questions beyond examining the simple robustness of the u-curve. We were able to look at: the impact of different cultural backgrounds on aesthetic assessment and the differential responses to drawings that come from different graphic repertoires—for example, the difference in response to cartoons versus "expressive" images like the happy, angry, sad drawings.

As far as the u-curve assessment pattern is concerned, the results were clear (see Figure 8). We found that there were four distinct assessment patterns: a u-curve, a flat line, an inverted u, and a rightward sloping line that suggested a linear relationship between age and aesthetic merit.

Figure 5 Cartoon Drawing—Taiwanese adult artist

Figure 6 Cartoon Drawing—Brazilian adult artist

Figure 7 People Drawing—Brazilian adult artist

The u-curve pattern reveals that the judge finds equally high merit in the drawings of the five-year olds and those of adult artists. The inverted u-curve is constructed by those judges who find the work of those individuals in the middle range (fourteen-year-olds and adult non-artists) better than that of the adult artists or the youngest children. There are several possible reasons for this pattern- one might be an "anti-Modernist" bias (that is, a preference for the literal drawing style of late adolescence) and the other has to do with the judge's own learning needs. (This is especially the case for the eight-year-old judges.)

The linear-upward sloping line reflects the judges' positive regard for the gradual increase in mastery that comes with age. The operative motto here is "practice makes perfect." The flat line is perhaps a variant of the u-curve, for with this configuration, the judge makes it clear that he or she values the work of all the drawing subjects equally. Only five percent of all the judges in the study produced this configuration.

When we look at the frequency of these patterns of assessment, some interesting facts emerge (see Table 1). The first and most important finding in terms of the issue under discussion here is that the u-curve pattern is created only by the art-trained judges and practically no one else. More than this, it is only one third of all artist-judges from each of the three countries who create this pattern. We can see that the u-curve pattern is found cross-culturally among art-trained judges. But even among those who have been trained in the arts, only one third showed that they believe that the work of young children and adult artists has equivalent aesthetic merit.

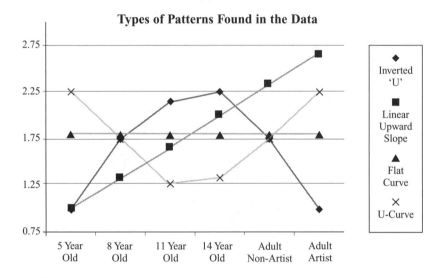

Figure 8 Typical sorting patterns for all judges in three countries study.

It is clear that the most "popular" and widespread conception of aesthetic development is in fact the notion that practice makes perfect— reflected in the upward linear pattern. Over sixty percent of all the 192 judges in our study constructed this sort of pattern.

We can make several observations based on our second study:

1. The u-curve sorting pattern reflects a specialized and somewhat rarified view of aesthetic development, one associated exclusively with training in the arts and rarely found among non-art trained judges (see Table 1). It is found amongst the art-trained judges from Brazil, Canada, and Taiwan. It is not found in any of the other judge-groups.

2. The most widespread vision of aesthetic development is the idea that the aesthetic quality of work improves with age. About two thirds of our judges regardless of age and country shared this view (see Table 1).

3. As a group, the artist judges, regardless of the country they came from, responded as a homogeneous group—especially when it

JUDGE CATEGORIES

SORTING PATTERNS	Adult Artists (N = 48)	Adult Non-Artists (N = 48)	14 Year Olds (N = 48)	8 Year Olds (N = 48)	Average % (N = 192)
MODERNIST (U-curve)	29.2%	2.1%	0%	0%	7.8%
NO AESTHETIC PREFERENCE (Flat line)	8.3%	4.2%	2.1%	6.3%	5.2%
TRADITIONALIST (Linear, Right-sloping)	54.2%	70.8%	68.8%	47.9%	60.4%
ANTI-MODERNIST (Inverted U)	8.3%	22.9%	29.1%	45.8%	26.6%
Total %	100	100	100	100	100

Table 1 Percentage of types of judge from all three countries who made different sorting patterns.

ALL JUDGES ON THEIR OWN COUNTRIES' DRAWINGS

Eight year old judges		Fourteen year old judges		Adult non-artist judges		Adult artist judges	
Cartoon	1.940056	People	1.659251	People	1.75	People	1.884181
Map	1.883681	Emotion	1.648843	Emotion	1.702546	Emotion	1.818519
People	1.883274	Cartoon	1.599299	Cartoon	1.651733	Map	1.701042
Emotion	1.827623	Map	1.566852	Map	1.604167	Cartoon	1.629483

Table 2 Table showing thematic preferences for each judge-group. (Three countries combined.)

came to their preferences for different parts of the graphic repertoire (see Tables 2, 3, 4, and 5). The thematic rankings of the artist-judges are identical across all three countries-and their pattern of choice is statistically significant. (The common ranking pattern, from high to low is: People, Emotions, Cartoons, and Maps.)

4. As a group, the eight-year-old judges were also a cross-culturally homogenoeous group: Their patterns of thematic preference were quite consistent accross the three countries, and were distinctively different from the preferences of the older judges (see Table 2). Especially noteworthy is the way in which the youngest

Eight year old judges	Fourteen year old judges	Adult non-artist judges	Adult artist judges**
Map 2.097917	Emotion 1.616667	Cartoon 1.616667	People 1.70339
Cartoon 2.086458	People 1.585805	Emotion 1.572917	Emotion 1.60625
Emotion 2.047917	Cartoon 1.555208	People 1.535417	Map 1.484375
People 2.012712	Map 1.535417	Map 1.571875	Cartoon 1.404167

** Ranking is significant at the .000 level.

Table 3 Showing Brazilian Judge-groups' rankings for four types of thematic drawing.
(Average score is given in right half of each column.)

Eight year old judges	Fourteen year old judges	Adult non-artist judges*	Adult artist judges**
Cartoon 1.81568	Emotion 1.71042	People 1.82733	People 2.04449
People 1.80236	People 1.70657	Emotion 1.73542	Emotion 1.95417
Emotion 1.77037	Map 1.63125	Map 1.6625	Map 1.92292
Map 1.66667	Cartoon 1.62076	Cartoon 1.63771	Cartoon 1.80191

* Ranking is significant at the .011 level.
** Ranking is significant at the .000 level.

Table 4 Showing Canadian Judge-groups' rankings for four types of thematic drawing.
(Average score is given in right half of each column.)

Eight year old judges**	Fourteen year old judges*	Adult non-artist judges**	Adult artist judges**
Cartoon 1.918033	People 1.685381	Emotion 1.799306	People 1.904661
Map 1.886458	Cartoon 1.621926	People 1.784958	Emotion 1.895139
People 1.834746	Emotion 1.619444	Cartoon 1.70082	Map 1.695833
Emotion 1.664583	Map 1.533889	Map 1.578125	Cartoon 1.682377

* Ranking is significant at the .042 level.
** Ranking is significant at the .000 level.

Table 5 Showing Taiwanese Judge-groups' rankings for four types of thematic drawing.
(Average score is given in right half of each column.)

judges consistently chose cartoons as their favorite type of drawing within the drawing repertoire.

It is interesting that the eight-year-old's sorting patterns were split
between the "traditional" upward sloping line at 48 percent, and the
inverted-u curve at 45 percent. The inverted-u privileges those
draughtsmen in the center of the sample—the eleven- and fourteen-
year-olds and the adult non-artists. So the criteria that some of the
eight-year-olds used for assessing drawings may have been to choose
drawings from people who have mastered representational drawing
skills that they value—literal, and conventional, rather than the less stylistic accomplishments of the adult artists. In other words, the eight-
year-olds chose as their most popular drawings those which they felt
they could learn from—rather than those that were "the most beautiful"
or aesthetically accomplished.

It is evident that the notion of "a good drawing" meant different
things to members of our judge-groups. The clearest evidence of this is
the fact that judge-groups from the three different countries ranked the
types of drawings (Emotion, Map, Cartoon, and People) very differently. For example, the Taiwanese eight-year-old judges were highly enthu-
siastic about the cartoon drawings, ranking them first of four, while the
Taiwanese adult artists held cartoons in low esteem, ranking them fourth
on the list. Similarly, "People" drawings were differently appreciated by
the four judge-groups. As the purposes of cartoon drawing, map drawing, and telling stories about people interacting are very different, it only
follows that the criteria for evaluating these drawings will be different as
well.

Our three-country study made one thing perfectly clear: people
posess divergent notions of how children's artworks relate to the work of
mature adults. For some judges, the relationship is infact a u-curved pattern, for other judges there is a straightforward relationship between aesthetic quality and the age of the draughtsman (as in the Traditionalist
sorting pattern; see Table 1). But this is not the only dimension on which
there are clear differences. As Tables 3, 4, and 5 illustrate, judges of different ages and from different countries have different preferences for
parts of the graphic repertoire. Interestingly enough, the adult artists are
the most uniform in their repertoire ranking: in all three cases they rank
their thematic preferences from high to low as follows: People, Emotion,
Map, and Cartoon. One might expect artists to be a little more spontaneous and hard to predict but on the contrary, the artists are the most
uniform in terms of their thematic choices.

What our second study has demonstrated is that there are a number of different ways in which people organize drawings by children, adults, and artists, and that these kinds of organization seem to be the products of educational formation as well as cultural background. What we have also shown is that even though adherents of the u-curve do exist in three different cultural settings, this sort of aesthetic judgement is not the province of children or untrained adults. In fact, a far more universal view of graphic development is the simple upward-sloping linear relation between aesthetic merit and age. So, there does seem to be something to be said for the observation that much aesthetic assessment is in the eye of the beholder. Marx Wartofsky (1994)-speaking of developmental theories of art history makes this same point well: "Not only is a developmental history of art possible, but any number of such histories is possible. The domain of art history is strewn with the bleached bones and fossil remains of different species of developmental histories of art" (p. 228). What he says of art history is very aptly applied to personal art history—a description of the development of individual artistry—as well.

We are stuck with a difficult problem here: all of these sorting patterns, springing as they do from the judges' a prioris, bring us no closer to an "objective" view of the relationship of graphic development to aesthetic qualities. And for art teachers like myself, this is not an idle question—it is one that has direct bearing on classroom practice. For, depending on one's criteria and needs "good drawings" will be differently defined. And these definitions will determine which sorts of drawings will dominate the rankings-and serve as models for pedagogy. If some people define "good" drawings as those that exhibit skill and mastery of conventional forms—with little or no concern for expression or authenticity, then those people are going to expect art instruction that emphasizes those values and qualities. They will not be concerned with the qualities associated with Modernism: expression, the use of formal properties to convey meaning, and disdain for "mere" technique and skill.

Thus Gardner's u-curve hypothesis may well lead art teachers astray if they assume that it is an objective description of the actual process of graphic development. If, on the other hand, they understand the Gardner hypothesis as a demonstration of the way in which aesthetic a-prioris can alter one's perception of graphic development, then one may well stumble upon a number of new and interesting facts about graphic development-which is the case here with our own research.

As this essay has dealt with Gardner's speculative foray into the realm of artistic development, I will close with my own speculation within the same universe. This one bridges Gardner's MI theory with Kindler and Darras's notion of multiple graphic pathways. Although Gardner (1999) argues for the existence of many different sorts of intelligences (ten at last count), he has gone on record as discounting the existence of "artistic" intelligence *per se*." Strictly speaking, no artistic intelligence exists. Rather, intelligences function artistically—or nonartistcally—to the extent that they exploit certain properties of a symbol system . . . spatial intelligence can be exploited by a sculptor or painter, and non aesthetically by a geometer or surgeon" (p. 108). He has explained that the visual artist may well use a number of intelligences for artistic purposes, and nowadays, given the openness of the artistic domain, it is not hard to find artists who employ many of Gardner's intelligences in the pursuit of their art. Christo's interpersonal IQ makes it possible for him to exercise his visual-spatial skills when he wraps buildings and makes installations in public spaces.

MI theory suggests that artists' works will reflect artists' special IQ's. Thus, the introspective genius of Rembrandt or Lucien Freud can be found in visual images that display a mastery of classical painting, while exploring the artists' inner worlds. Mathematically or logically inclined artists like Escher, Magritte, or Mark Tansey manipulate visual symbols in an exploration of space (Visual Spatial IQ), or the paradoxes of language and philosophy (Logical-mathematical IQ).

These sorts of explorations map nicely onto a conception of development in the visual arts as a passage through a network of pathways rather than movement along a single road with a single, known terminus. Kindler and Darras (1997) draw our attention to the multiple uses of imagery; they suggest that any model of graphic development needs to take these multiple purposes into account. Thus, a far better way of looking at aesthetic development might be through the multiple lenses of MI theory rather than the telescope of the u-curve hypothesis.

REFERENCES

Andrews, Julia. 1998. Introduction to Julia Andrews and Kuiyi Shen, eds., *A Century in Crisis: Modernity and Tradition in the Art of 20th Century China*. New York: Abrams.

Arnheim, Rudolf. 1969. *Visual Thinking*. Berkeley: University of California Press.

———. 1971. *Art and Visual Perception*. Berkeley: University of California Press.

Davis, Jessica. 1991. *Artistry Lost: U-Shaped Development in Graphic Symbolization*, Ph.D. Thesis, Graduate School of Education, Harvard University.

———. 1997a. Drawing's Demise: U-Shaped Development in Graphic Symbolization. *Studies in Art Education* 38: 3, pp. 132–157.

———. 1997b, Does the U in the U-Curve Also Stand for Universal? Reflections on Provisional Doubts. *Studies in Art Education* 38: 3, pp. 179–185.

Duncum, Paul, 1986. Breaking Down the U-Curve of Artistic Development. *Visual Arts Research* 12: 1, pp. 43–54.

Eisner, Elliot, 2002. *The Arts and the Creation of Mind*. New Haven, Yale University Press.

Fineberg, Jonathan, 1997. *The Innocent Eye: Children's Art and the Modern Artist*. Princeton: Princeton University Press.

Gardner, Howard, 1999. *Intelligence Reframed. Multiple Intelligences for the 21st Century.* New York: Basic Books.

Gardner, Howard, and Winner, Ellen. 1982. First Intimations of Artistry. In S. Strauss, ed., *U-Shaped Development*. New York: Academic Press, pp. 147–168.

Gao, Jianping. 1996. *The Expressive Act in Chinese Art: From Calligraphy to Painting*. Uppsala: Acta Universitatis Upsaliensis.

Golomb, Claire. 1992. *The Child's Creation of a Pictorial World*. Berkeley: University of California Press.

Goodman, Nelson. 1976. *The Languages of Art.* Indianapolis: Bobbs-Merrill.

Halkidiakis, S. 1983. The Effects of Repeated Experience with a Single Drawing Scheme. Boston: University of Massachusetts, unpublished paper.

Henkes, Robert. 1990. The Child and Abstract Expressionism. *Early Child Development and Care* 57, pp. 51–74.

Kindler, Anna, David Pariser, Axel van den Berg, Liu Wancen, and Belidson Dias. 2002. Aesthetic Modernism, the First Among Equals? A Look at Aesthetic Value Systems in Cross-Cultural, Age and Visual Arts Educated and Non-Visual Arts Educated Judging Cohorts. *The International Journal of Cultural Policy* 8: 2, pp. 135–152.

Kindler, Anna and Bernard Darras. 1997. Development of Pictorial Representation: A Teleology-based Model. *Journal of Art and Design Education* 16: 3, pp. 217–222.

Kindler, Anna, Axel van den Berg, and David Pariser. 2000. Making Drawings, Judging Drawings: A Cross-Cultural Study of Graphic Development and Aesthetic Development. Proposal funded by the Social Sciences and Humanities Research Council of Canada, #410-2000-0453.

Klee, Paul, 1964 [1924]. On Modern Art. In Robert L. Herbert, ed., *Modern Artists on Art: Ten Unabridged Essays* (Englewood Cliffs: Prentice Hall, 1964), pp. 74–92.

Korzenik, Diana, 1995. The Changing Concept of Artistic Giftedness. In Claire Golomb, ed., *The Development of Artisitically Gifted Children* (Mahwah: Erlbaum), pp. 1–30.

Malvern, Sue. 1988. Modernism, Primitivism, and the Child: Universal Aesthetics and the Teaching of Franz Cizek and Marion Richardson. Presented at the International Seminar on the History of Art and Design Education, 26th November.

Motherwell, Robert. 1970. The Universal Language of Children's Art and Modernism. An address opening the plenary session of the International Exchange in the Arts (29th April). In T*he Scholar* (nd), pp. 24–27.

Pariser, David and Axel van den Berg. 1997a. The Mind of the Beholder: Some Provisional Doubts About the U-Curved Aesthetic Development Thesis. *Studies in Art Education* 38: 3, pp. 158–178.

———. 1997b. Beholder Beware: A Reply to Jessica Davis. *Studies in Art Education* 8: 3, pp. 186–192.

———. 2001. Teaching Art vs. Teaching Taste: What Art Teachers Can Learn from Looking at a Cross-Cultural Evaluation of Cross-Cultural Evaluation of Children's Art. *Poetics* 29, pp. 331–350.

Rosenstiel, Anne, and Howard Gardner. 1977. The Effects of Critical Comparisons upon Children's Drawings. *Studies in Art Education* 9:1, pp. 36–43.

Rostan, Susan. 1997. A Study of Young Artists. The Development of Talent and Creativity. *Creativity Research Journal* 10, pp. 175–192.

Strauss, Sidney. 1982. *U-Shaped Development.* New York: Academic Press.

Wartofsky, Marx, 1994. Is a Developmental History of Art Possible? In Margery Franklin and Bernard Kaplan, eds., *Development and the Arts: Critical Perspectives* (Mahwah: Erlbaum), pp. 227–243.

Wilson, Brent. 1997. Child Art, Multiple Interpretations, and Conflicts of Interest. In Anna Kindler, ed., *Child Development in Art* (Reston: National Art Education Association), pp. 81–94.

Wilson, Brent, and Margery Wilson. 1981. Review of *Artful Scribbles: The Significance of Children's Drawings*, by Howard Gardner. *Studies in Visual Communication* 7: 1, pp. 86–99.

Wolf, Denny and Susan Perry. 1988. From Endpoints to Repertoires: New Conclusions about Drawing Development. *Journal of Aesthetic Education* 22: 1, pp. 17–35.

Replies to My Critics

HOWARD GARDNER

Though the image of "under fire" is a bit inflammatory, it is an honor to have a volume dedicated to one's work. I am grateful to Jeffrey Schaler for envisioning the volume, assembling the critics, and presiding over the editorial process. Each of the critics took the mission seriously and I am grateful for their individual efforts. Some of the contributors are close colleagues, others I have never met. Some are in substantial agreement with my enterprise, while others see little value in it. In my responses I have sought to be impersonal and to respond to each contribution on its merits. I will be pleased if readers will not be able to infer, from my responses, the nature of my relation to the critic.

Before offering individual responses, it is necessary for me—and I have every confidence that it will be helpful to both readers and critics—to make some preliminary remarks. Thereafter, I have grouped the essays into five categories that are both convenient and appropriate. In each case, I offer introductory remarks that contextualize the essays in that category and then move on to specific, targeted responses.

My Scholarship and Writing

By formal training I am a psychologist. But I am properly construed as an individual who embodies five different roles. In descending order of importance, they are:

1. A psychological conceptualizer—one who probes various psychological concepts and their relation to one another (for example, the relationship between intelligence and creativity);

2. An empirical psychologist—one who conducts observations and/or formal experiments, analyzes the data, surveys the findings of others, and continually ponders how to operationalize a contentious issue;

3. A social scientist—I was originally trained in the hybrid social scientific field of Social Relations, not psychology proper. I think readily in terms of other social sciences, including sociology, anthropology, and, more recently, economics as well;

4. A public intellectual—From early in my career, I have sought to write for a broad audience, through the authoring of trade books and occasional articles in wide circulation magazine. I appear with some regularity on National Public Radio and, on occasion, on television. It is important for me to share my ideas with the educated public, both in the United States and abroad;

5. A politically engaged scholar, author, and speaker. Until the age of fifty, I was not involved in controversial political issues—not through any deliberate decision but rather because the several aforementioned roles did not call for such involvement. Both because of my own recent work in professional ethics, and because of circumstances in the world that concern me, I have become increasingly involved in the discussion of political matters—in the jargon, in punditry.

In this volume, it is primarily my work as a psychologist that is under examination. So it should be. But it is important to lay out these varying roles, because they help to explain the nature of evidence on which I draw, the style in which I present my ideas, and, most importantly, certain simplifications that I explicitly employ in order to make my work accessible to a wider audience. The other subjects of past and projected volumes in this *Under Fire* series are also scholars whose works have been widely discussed outside their chosen professional specialties.

Motivation of my Work

At various times in my scholarly career, my work has reflected three quite different motivations:

1. I have been intrigued by an empirical phenomenon. My initial decision to study brain-damaged adults was stimulated by my realization that their symptom profiles are deeply counterintuitive—for example, a stroke victim might lose her linguistic skills but remain competent in the musical arena, or *vice versa*. Or, to take an example from this volume, I was struck by the several ways in which the art works of young children resembled those of modern masters—and so I began to investigate the possibilities of 'u-shaped curves' in development.

   Only rarely is my work stimulated by a desire to address some current controversy in the professional literature, be it theoretical or empirical. I think of myself as a 'phenomenon person' and I am attracted to work that identifies and illuminates an enigmatic phenomenon.

2. I have heard about a body of knowledge that sounds intriguing but I can't find out what I want to know. No compelling synthesis exists. This was the state of knowledge when, in the late 1960s, I decided to write a book about the French intellectual movement called structuralism. The result was my first trade book: *The Quest for Mind: Piaget, Lévi-Strauss, and the Structuralist Movement* (1973). In the early 1980s, growing discussions of cognitive science led me to conduct numerous interviews and to author *The Mind's New Science: A History of the Cognitive Revolution* (1985). My decision to write a book about leadership reflected my judgment that leadership deserved to be considered from a cognitive angle: *Leading Minds: An Anatomy of Leadership* (1995).

3. More recently, my work has been motivated by problems that have been festering in society. I begin by seeking to understand the problem better, using whatever analytic and empirical tools are available. Thereafter I strive to address that problem in a practical manner. Some of my educational efforts in the 1980s and 1990s were engendered by a concern with the quality of pre-collegiate education in American and my belief that current efforts at amelioration were, at least in certain respects, ill-advised. The GoodWork Project®, a collaborative undertaking, is addressed to the question of how professions can survive during a time when markets are enormously powerful and there are few significant forces that can counter these market pressures. Newly launched work on the nature of trust, and its importance in every society, is

similarly motivated by my conclusion that the perhaps warranted lack of trust poses an enormous threat in the United States and perhaps other societies as well (Gardner, Benjamin, and Pettingill 2006).

How I Approach My Work

I am very interested in theory but I do not see myself as a theorist. Nor do I consider myself a controversialist. When critiqued, I rise to the occasion and defend myself vigorously, but I do not particularly enjoy the thrust and parry of scholarly controversy. While I have documented the numerous ways in which common sense can be misleading, I still take common sense and folk wisdom seriously. And I am suspicious of conclusions that stray too far from beliefs that have endured over the centuries. Jarring conclusions often make more polemical sense than they make genuine sense.

My procedure in scholarship is avowedly multidisciplinary. In this tack I was inspired above all by the Russian psychologist Alexander Luria (1902–1979). Following his own teacher, Lev Vygotsky, Luria believed that psychological phenomena are most likely to be elucidated if they can be approached from a variety of disciplinary and subdisciplinary angles. And so, for example, in trying to comprehend the nature of the human linguistic faculty, I (following Luria's example) found it congenial to examine language from the perspective of genetics, brain anatomy and physiology, psychology, sociology, cultural studies, and, of course, linguistics. I learned a tremendous amount about scholarship through my decades-long immersion in the study of aphasia—a phenomenon that can only be elucidated by intensive and extensive cross-disciplinary investigations.

Within the broad field of psychology, I customarily employ four principal lenses. When examining a phenomenon like language, I consider *development*: what is the 'end state' of linguistic competence, what is the initial state, and through what states or stages does the language faculty pass? I consider *cognition*: in which ways is language represented mentally, which operations are involved in linguistic production and expression? I consider *brain*: how are linguistic capacities represented in the human nervous system, how flexible is this representation, what happens should various brain loci and pathways be impaired at different points in development? Finally, I consider *cultural expression*: how is language used in various cultures (for example literate versus non-literate cultures), and in different settings within a single culture?

I am well aware that each of these lenses has its limitations—and should I momentarily forget their limitations, my critics are only too happy to remind me of them! This multi-disciplinary focus keeps me honest: whenever I risk becoming too immersed in a single perspective, I bring myself up short by peering through a different lens. I hope that the regular employment of multiple perspectives increases the likelihood that I will come to understand a phenomenon in its deserved fullness.

As a social scientist, I am sensitive to various confusions to which my approach is susceptible. These include the danger of confusing description with prescription; of confounding the 'emic' (internal) perspective with the 'etic' (external) perspective on a phenomenon; of intermingling objective with subjective analyses. Over the years, I have become more comfortable in addressing the issue of values: I no longer shudder at the prospect of offering prescriptions, value judgments, an 'etic' perspective, a subjective comment. But I seek to remain fully aware of which analytic hat I am wearing at a particular moment.

A few other points about my approach to scholarship. I see myself as a synthesizer and a systematizer. I like to offer ideal types, taxonomies, classifications which others are free to accept, build upon, or reject. I am especially interested in the modern era and in modernism, and many of my examples come from the arts and sciences of the past century. At the same time, however, I am deeply immersed in more traditional scholarship and in examples drawn from history; and I remain suspicious of many of the products and most of the concepts of post-modernism. I am leery of hedgehogs—scholars who believe in a single monopolistic concept that can organize all knowledge—be it leadership as power, or intelligence as 'g'. At the same time, however, I also resist conclusions that stress the uniqueness of each and every thing. Humanistic studies properly revel in the particular; social scientific studies should search for patterns, for ways of simplifying the indisputable complexity of human activity. In many cases, I see myself searching for a productive 'middle ground'.

Personally I have never felt particularly adventurous or courageous. The life of the scholar, even the popularizer, is primarily sedentary and seemingly risk free. Yet, as I reflect on my career thus far, I see how it can be seen as being adventurous. I have taken on the subjects that others of a scholarly disposition might have shied away from, and I have put forth analyses that can be seen as daring or even foolhardy. I have preferred to stray far from the beaten path, rather than treading the paths that my colleagues have already followed. I never expect to have the last word about a topic; I am much too intellectually restless for that. I hope that at times I have been able to put forth one of the first words.

Attitude toward Critiques

While I do not relish argument or controversy, I am quite comfortable with the notion of critiques. I welcome detailed analyses and critiques of what I have said. I like to engage with individuals who conceptualize a topic of mutual interest in a distinctly different manner. I especially welcome empirical data that bear on my principal assertions as well as indications of areas that I have neglected or misconstrued. At the same time, I must confess that I have less patience for endless terminological dickering, definitional infighting, and nitpicking about small points. I do not like individuals who cannot see the forest for the trees. And I do not enjoy critiques that are so insistent on putting forth the author's own perspective that they fail to engage the efforts that I have made. A good critic should have—or at least be able to adopt *pro tem*—a sympathetic sense of what the to-be-critiqued authority is trying to achieve.

My very first scholarly article was a comparison of the structuralist approaches of Jean Piaget and Claude Lévi-Strauss. As a graduate student who wrote in English, I was tremendously moved to receive personal letters from both Piaget and Lévi-Strauss. Piaget's was in French, Lévi-Strauss's in almost perfect English. I want to quote from Lévi-Strauss' response, because in a way that I could not have appreciated at the time, he reflects some of my own views about criticism. Lévi-Strauss first thanks me for the comparison with Piaget, and says that he is largely in agreement with what I have to say. Turning then to a more specific critique that I offered about his analyses of myth:

> Concerning your other paper, to be quite frank, the kind of criticism you level at me makes me shrug. I look at myself as a rustic explorer equipped with a woodman's axe to open a path in an unknown land and you reproach me for not having drawn a complete map, calculated accurately my bearings and for not having yet landscaped the country! Forgive me for saying so but it looks as if Lewis and Clark were taken to task for not having designed the plans of General Motors while on their way to Oregon. Science is not the work of one man. I may have broken new ground but it will take a great many years and the labour of many individuals to till it and make the harvest. (Personal communication, 10th April, 1970)

I have no illusions that my contributions approach those of Lévi-Strauss: I say, again, the comparison is only with reference to our attitudes toward critiques. In what follows, you will see that my patience for those whose grain size resembles my own is far greater than my patience for those who seem fundamentally to have misconceived what I am trying to achieve.

Organizing the Current Critiques

I have grouped the current set of critiques into five separate categories, which, roughly speaking, follow my own intellectual development. For the most part, the separate critiques fall chiefly into one category, though a few overlap more than one category. Critiques also differ in whether they are general or more specific: I have indicated my characterization of each, as well as my own assessment of their degree of generality or specificity.

Development and Education

It is fitting that Deanna Kuhn and David Olson are the initial critics in this volume. Roughly speaking, we are members of the same scholarly generation and the same disciplinary cohort. All three of us have primary affiliations with the fields of psychology, human development, and education. In the 1960s we were among the first generation of young American scholars who read texts by the founding cognitive developmentalist Jean Piaget; and we brought to this reading some of the pragmatist concerns of the American psychologist and educator Jerome Bruner. Over the years we have each become increasingly involved in educational issues, such that our most recent books have as much to do with schools and teaching as with the developmental trajectory of the individual child or of children in general. And, indeed, for many years, though we may think of ourselves as psychologists, our teaching and research have take place in faculties of education. Viewed from afar, we are similarly contoured peas in the same psychological pod.

Yet, even a cursory reading of our works indicates that we approach our central concerns in distinctly different ways. Within our ranks, Kuhn remains much the closest to the central tradition in developmental psychology: her focus is on the mind of the individual developing child. Moreover, she is sympathetic to the idea that a general developmental trajectory colors the cognition of the child, independent of the subject matter that he is tackling. And in Piagetian terms, she identifies the most crucial capacities for education: the capacities to inquire and to argue in a sophisticated manner. Olson's attention falls squarely on the community into which the student is being socialized: what are the relevant skills that he needs to develop, what norms obtain within that community, how does the young person go about acquiring and abiding by these norms. He goes so far as to question whether, as psychologists, we should devote time to the investigation of an individual child's specific intellectual capacities, or dispositions, as he terms them.

Before turning attention to these specific contributions, I feel the need to lay out my own views about the relationship among these three scholarly avenues. Beginning with psychology, I see that motley discipline as having two distinct bases. On the one hand, psychology necessarily reflects the biological—the neurological and genetic—bases of our species. We cannot carry out psychological analyses in the absence of the most current information about our genetic heritage and the ways in which our brain develops and is organized. Powerful constraints are imposed on the species as a whole—and on each of us individually—by these biological forces; we ignore them at our analytic peril.

At the same time, however, human psychology does not exist in a vacuum. From birth, perhaps before, we are strongly affected by other persons, and, more broadly, by the ambient culture. We observe and attempt to follow the models and practices of significant others in our lives. We are socialized into roles and into institutions. Much of our development, in fact, depends on our capacities to utilize our biologically-given proclivities as we attempt to master practices of our culture as a whole, as well as the far more specific details of our own family values and our own future lives in their fullness.

Awareness of these twinned sets of inputs has informed my psychological investigations from the first. It was for this reason that I long ago elected to focus on human symbol-using capacities—those in the arts, to be sure, but the full range of symbolic systems that affect human life as well. Indeed, susceptibility to encoding in a symbol systems has always been a chief desideratum for a candidate intelligence. The focus on symbols allows me to take advantage of the Janus-faced aspects of psychology. The discipline simultaneously builds on our brain capacities to symbolize—to appreciate that one element can stand for, or represent or be embedded within another—and to build upon these representational capacities as we acquire and create knowledge scientifically, artistically, pragmatically. At the same time, and evidently, the particular symbols and symbol systems that we acquire are clearly human inventions: developed over the millennia in various cultures. We can only acquire them by being immersed in our society, receiving training, having the opportunity to practice symbol-using skills, and ultimately contributing to the transmission of semiotic capacities and skills to successive generations.

Developmental psychologists believe that much can be learned by focussing on origins, genesis, moment-to-moment (microgenetic) changes, and more molar (stage-like) changes. This position is not without critics: Kant doubted that anything useful could be learned by studying processes of cognitive maturation; Nelson Goodman, my own skeptical teacher, said that development could be subsumed by the unrevealingly simple rule "As they get older, kids get smarter." Developmental psychology, as practiced by cognitivists like Piaget, personality theories like Erik Erikson, moral experts like Lawrence Kohlberg, is a sustained wager that such critics are mistaken. Developmentalists focus on the determination of end states of development; the knowledge base and competence present at birth or in early life; the various stages through which the person passes; and, as Kuhn stresses, the factors that motivate or thwart progress from one state to the next.

Forty years ago, we developmentalists largely sang from the same hymnal—one whose melodies were composed in large measure by Jean Piaget, with alternative harmonic patterns by Jerome Bruner, Alexander Luria, Lev Vygotsky, Heinz Werner, and a few other significant figures. But as the field has expanded, and as knowledge has deepened, deep divisions have emerged within developmental psychology about how best to proceed. For present purposes, it is important to point out that developmentalists disagree about the extent to which development occurs in one piece (as opposed to being distinctly different across domains of knowledge and facets and dimensions of the child); the aspects of development that are endogenous (basically, part of the genome, ready to unfold when triggered) as opposed to strongly shaped and altered by models in the culture; how much knowledge is innate and how much has to be constructed (and by what means); how flexible is the course of development, particularly after the initial years of life; and which of developmental milestones occur after adolescence.

Both Kuhn and Olson focus attention on the issue of human beliefs—how they are arrived at and how they might change. Reflecting her Piagetian roots, Kuhn focuses on the endogenous nature of beliefs—the ways that they unfold and develop in all children. Reflecting his sociocultural turn, Olson stresses the extent to which the developing child is surrounded by, and ultimately picks up, the beliefs of the ambient community. Reflecting the Janus-view of psychology, I have tried to appreciate both the psychological and the sociological facets of beliefs, and the frequent clashes between then. Indeed, I see education as a continuing effort to fashion and refashion beliefs so that they come to reflect the most sophisticated thinking in various disciplines and domains.

How, more broadly, does developmental psychology translate into educational practice and recommendations? I have always maintained that one cannot go directly from a scientific finding to an educational (or any other kind of) practice. Science represents our best efforts to describe the world as we observe it. Education is quintessentially a realm of values. We need first to establish our educational values. Then, and only then, can we begin to ascertain whether scientific findings—including psychological ones—might be relevant to our educational goals and values; and, if so, in what ways.

An example may be helpful here. Before the publication of the book *The Bell Curve* (1994), I had an opportunity to speak with Richard Herrnstein, its senior author. We discussed the claim that psychometric intelligence is difficult to change. We then agreed that, from this putative fact, two diametrically opposite conclusions could be drawn. Following the argument put forth by Herrnstein and Murray, we could conclude that it is difficult to change intelligence and so it is not worth the effort. However, we could take the opposite course. If intelligence is hard to change, we should devote all of our efforts to do so. Perhaps we will succeed, and, indeed, we may even discover a way to change intelligence easily. Same fact—two opposite educational implications. Or, put different: two value systems. If one valorizes the selection of talent, one focuses on a determination of who is the brightest (on a certain definition). If one valorizes the heightening of opportunity, then one focuses on the optimization of talent in all children.

Reply to Deanna Kuhn

Kuhn focusses on two classical developmental issues: what does it mean for something to be developed, and how does development actually occur? She correctly identifies 'thinking in a disciplined way' and 'understanding the disciplines' as my key educational goals. I believe that the major intellectual justification of school—once essential literacies have been mastered—is the acquisition of the capacities to think mathematically, scientifically, historically, and artistically. And I amass considerable evidence that most students fail to acquire these disciplinary capacities. They assimilate vast amount of information that they learn to spout back, under appropriate stimulation; but they cannot make use of their acquired knowledge to elucidate unfamiliar problems and phenomena. Hence the knowledge remains inert—it cannot be activated under appropriate circumstances. Only deep immersion in select topics can yield two important dividends: 1. the experience of genuine understanding of a topic; 2. the skills to think in a disciplined way about such a topic.

Averting the discussion of specific disciplines, Kuhn invokes the familiar education goal of 'thinking well' or 'thinking critically'. In her recently published *Education for Thinking* (2005) she provides an extended brief in favor of two specific forms of thought: inquiry and argument. She amasses evidence that most students are not able to display these forms of thought but that the proper educational milieu can cultivate skills of inquiry and argument.

Now, of course, I would be delighted if students can learn to inquire and argue well; and I suspect that Kuhn is completely in favor of the acquisition of disciplinary knowledge and skill. We could simply stipulate these goals and both declare victory. The tension between our positions, as we both realize, lies in the extent to which inquiring, arguing, and other intellectual virtues are truly general. If these skills are, or can be, acquired in a universal way, then Kuhn's educational regimen suggests itself.

My own work over the years has made me skeptical of this position. Like Kuhn, I began as a committed Piagetian, one who believed in general intellectual operations. The operations that Piaget uncovered are genuine ones and they exhibit a degree of generality. But fundamentally, they apply in mathematics, logic, science, and fields that build directly upon them. There are critical thinking skills across the range of domains—from law and history to art and music—but the nature of these thinking skills differs significantly, depending on whether one is arguing (or inquiring) about how a phrase of music should be played, a historical event should be interpreted, a scientific experiment should be replicated or altered.

Within psychology, this issue is termed 'transfer'. All educators, all psychologists, hope for transfer—the acquisition of skill in one arena and its ready migration to other arenas where it is appropriate. After a century of research, nearly all educators and psychologists agree that transfer is difficult to attain. As with the Herrnstein example above, this conclusion leads some practitioners to abandon the hope for transfer, while it stimulates others to work harder or be more imaginative in their training regimens.

No doubt, the truth about transfer lies somewhere in the middle. To the extent that Kuhn is correct, it will make sense to look for and to nurture the most general skills of inquiry, argument, and the like. To the extent that skeptics like me are correct, it makes more sense to attempt to develop the relevant skills in each discipline separately. In the latter case, transfer is less elusive and more likely. And even if it does not occur, one will ultimately have individuals who can think critically in the set of disciplines that they have studied.

Which leaves the second issue: 'what develops'? When one takes a Piaget-Kuhn perspective, the assumptions is that development is a general and generic phenomenon. The neat sequence described by Kuhn—facts to opinions to justified beliefs (judgments)—certainly has the air of a general trend in children's developing thought capacities. And the sequence also has an endogenous feel to it: one infers that the sequence would occur, across a range of populations.

Once one posits multiple intelligences, a number of options present themselves. It could be that the intelligences develop in lockstep with one another: all at stage 1, then all at stage 2, etc. I am quite sure that is not true. It could be that the intelligences develop—or unfold—at their own rate but that they each still reflect the same general stages: this is the perspective taken by neo-Piagetians, like Robbie Case (1991) and Kurt Fischer (Fischer and Bidell 1998). On this reading, the fact-opinion-belief sequence would recur, but not necessarily at the same time, across intelligences.

My own position, however, is quite different; and here I find myself closer to David Olson than to Deanna Kuhn. Only in the very earliest stages of development does one find any kind of endogenous development in an intelligence: perhaps, in the initial parsing of one's native language, or the initial efforts to orient oneself in space—what developmentalists of a nativist strip call "core knowledge." (In the early chapters of my books *The Unschooled Mind* and *The Disciplined Mind*, I lay out just such a set of paths.) Once one enters into a community, complete with its respective disciplines, crafts, and roles, the intelligences no longer develop on their own. Rather, a far more intricate and dynamic interaction occurs: bio-psychological tendencies interact constantly with the particular symbolic systems and social roles that are available.

Take, as an example, early language use. Strong endogenous principles may well be at work when one learns the initial phonology and syntax of one's native language. But the uses to which language are put become quite different by the time the child enters school (Heath 1983). In one family (or society), the child is expected to express herself regularly; in another she is expected to listen and to speak only when spoken to. In one setting, the child is expected to be factual and accurate. In another, tall tales or pure fantasies are the norm. In yet another, the child is expected to raise existential questions ("What is going to happen to Grandpa after he dies?") and to listen assiduously to the answers. By this point, we cannot speak of 'intelligences' developing on their own. The answer clearly resides in a dialectic between endogenous capacities and operations, on the one hand, and the particular demands and options afforded by the society, on the other.

Kuhn raises the interesting question of whether I am calling for all children to develop along their unique paths, or for a greater uniformity in terms of mastery of the same small set of disciplines. My answer here is that I believe that nearly all youngsters should strive to achieve the major disciplinary competences; in that sense, I am a traditionalist. Where I become a progressive is in the *means* toward mastery. I believe that any topic can be taught in numerous ways; and, correlatively, that students should have many ways to show their understanding.

In a similar vein, Kuhn asks whether youngsters should focus on the development of their stronger intelligences, or instead adopt a compensatory strategy. The answer here reflects my view on policy matters. Like education, policy inevitably entails a positing of values. There is value in focussing on your strengths—you are more likely to become chess champion that way. There is value in being rounded—you are more likely to become a Rhodes scholar. (Note that the odds against both are prohibitive!). Once an individual—more likely a family—makes a decision about where to focus energies, then experts on 'individual differences' can make recommendations about how best to achieve that goal.

Kuhn is correct in saying that I do not devote much time to an explication of how development occurs. In my earlier writings, I said that I would allow the experts in the respective spheres to draw the fine details of development in musical, linguistic, spatial competence, and the like. I adhere to that general viewpoint today. Where I'd differ from my earlier writings is in my skepticism about the possibility of portraying later phases of development of an intelligence *per se*. Instead of investigating the development of spatial intelligence, I would instead focus on far more specific applications of that intelligence, in such skills as map-reading, chess play, or sculpting. In other words, I would prefer to think of development of skill in specific domains and disciplines—an idea that was first put forth thirty-five years ago by David Olson.

Reply to David Olson

Olson issues a sharp challenge to the whole enterprise of multiple intelligences. While he recognizes the differences between traditional theories of intelligence, and my slant on multiple intelligences, he asserts that both approaches are anachronistic within contemporary cognitive psychology. According to his account, current workers do not focus their attention on the dispositions and capacities that young persons bring to their culture and to their classroom. To the extent that capacities are examined, the interest falls in how these capacities work—not, who is gifted in music, but rather, what does it mean to be competent in music? How can this competence be modelled in some kind of a formal, computational system? And, in many cases, the 'capacity issue' is bypassed altogether. The focus is on a particular community—say, the community of competent musicians—and the investigator seeks to understand what it takes for a person to master the rules and procedures that allow one to participate in that community, what are the mental states and beliefs that he constructs and can, if he so chooses, alter in some way.

Now, I assume that Olson would not deny the claim that individuals differ in talent, in what they bring to the table from their biological membership and their biological parentage. I suppose his claim is that we can't do anything about this, and so it falls properly outside the realm of psychology, and certainly outside the realm of education. I disagree.

Let me take, as an example, the controversial claim put forth, in January 2005, by Harvard University President Lawrence H. Summers. Seeking to understand the paucity of women in the hard sciences, particularly physics, Summers considered a number of alternatives. He ended up suggesting that perhaps women had less 'innate aptitude' than men for success in scientific work at the highest levels. Many people, including me, objected to this formulation. We did so, both because the phrase 'competence in science' is far too broad; and because there are many non-biological factors (ranging from the absence of role models to the pressures on women to bear and nurture children and take care of the home) that might suffice to explain the lesser incidence of women in the hard sciences.

Let us assume, however, that the aforementioned sociological and psychological obstacles to success in science were magically removed. It would then become possible to investigate whether women are, indeed, less good at certain cognitive skills that are deemed important for success in science. Just to pick three candidates: it might be possible that, on the average, women are less capable of complex spatial manipulations 'in their head'; or of handling a large number of mathematical variables at one time; or of concentrating for hours at a stretch on a scientific puzzle. I want to stress that all of these suppositions might well be false; and that many aspects of science do not depend particularly on any of these three factors or could be ameliorated by technological aids. Yet, to consider the practice of science without taking into account factors like those cited above would be to limit one's understanding artificially.

I submit that the Summers problem, if I may so dub it, is a problem to which psychology has contributions to make; but that Olson's view, as I understand it, would rule such an investigation as off limits. Because such an inquiry deals with human capacities or dispositions, it is a given and cannot be changed. Hence, in considering the practice of science, one needs to focus on beliefs and practices that are under conscious control and for which the rules can, at least in principle, be delineated. I believe this to be a highly constrained and artificial view of the scientific enterprise, and of many other enterprises as well.

Viewed more generally, I believe that the issue of individual differences—whether found in the area of prodigiousness, in remarkable disorders like autism, or in more garden-variety profiles of learning disabilities—is a vital one in psychology, human development, and education. We need to understand these profiles, since they represent a point of departure for any educational intervention. Moreover, just because a condition is genetic or congenital by no means indicates that it can't be ameliorated. Presumably I owe my near-sightedness to my parents' genetic profiles but glasses have rectified the situation. I may owe my spatial limitations to them as well; but through a combination of high motivation, good teachers, ample resources (including maps) and new technological adjuncts, I can perform as well as the next guy or gal.

As he moves into his discussion of rules and normative behavior, Olson makes an interesting point about the relation between disposition and character. If I understand him correctly, he says that aspects of personality and temperament are present at the beginning—in his terms, they are dispositional. But the decision about what kind of a person to be, and how one actually behaves, fall strictly within the purview of psychology in an Olson socio-cultural sense. As he puts it, dispositions become normative when they are subject to a moral standard. In our GoodWork project, we encounter these issues perennially. I would add that the decision about which profession to enter—and which role to assume within that profession—clearly rests in part on the intellectual dispositions that the person possesses. It may even be that the potential for carrying out good work depends in part on the snugness of fit between the person's capacities and what the performances called for in a given work role. I fully agree that any judgments about goodness depend on the implicit or explicit moral standards that are held by agents and by the surrounding community, most especially those gatekeepers who determine access to positions of significance.

I believe that Olson has done the field of psychology a service by stressing those domains and beliefs that reflect communal achievements and that are open to conscious reflection and decision. In this sense, a psychology based on rats and infants will be notoriously incomplete. But I see no reason to reject that part of psychology which is rooted in our biological heritage; and I feel that our understanding of many problems—both scholarly and practical—is enhanced if we seek to understand the capacities and dispositions possessed by individuals. The danger is that this knowledge could blind parents and teachers to alternative roads to mastery; and so it is up to us to be vigilant that capacities be seen as positive building blocks rather than as immovable obstacles.

As Olson puts it, "The central task of education and socialization generally [is] to help children transform such habits and dispositions into intentional actions for which they can take responsibility." Here Olson crosses the Rubicon that he has constructed. For once he talks about the transformation of dispositions, we can join hands as educators.

Multiple Intelligences
Introduction

The work for which I am best known is the theory of multiple intelligences. I began this work in the middle 1970s, as I was attempting to synthesize my own findings about human symbol-using capacities obtained in developmental and neuropsychological research. Thanks to support from the Bernard Van Leer Foundation, the pace and breadth of the work grew. I was able to broaden the synthesis to include material from several disciplines, including genetics, brain science, anthropology, psychometrics, and the study of special populations, such as prodigies, savants, and others who displayed 'jagged' cognitive profiles. My original book-length statement of the theory was found in *Frames of Mind* (1983). I reported alterations in the theory, as well as various educational experiments based on the theory, in *Multiple Intelligences: The Theory in Practice* (1993), *Intelligence Reframed* (1999), and, most recently in *Multiple Intelligences: New Horizons* (2006), as well as dozens of articles. Of course, it is not reasonable to expect any critic to have read of all of these materials, and none would have had access to my 2006 book. At the same time, it seems only sensible to reply to critics in light of my current understandings.

New theories evoke a number of responses ranging from 'This is crazy' to 'What's new is wrong, and what's correct was already known'; over time, the new theories are either forgotten or absorbed—with more or less precision and revision—into the conventional wisdom. Critics range from those who defend the old (traditional) perspective, to those who question the rationale of the new perspective, to those who are concerned with quite specific points. This range of responses and foci is captured well here. As the target of the critiques, more than once I had the feeling that I should just get out of the way, just remove myself from the line of fire, and let the critics take shots at one another.

In what follows, I begin with those who pose the most general critiques: John White is uncomfortable with just about every aspect of the theory, while Nathan Brody questions the need for it, as he defends the traditional psychometric approach to intelligence. Susan Barnett, Stephen Ceci, and Wendy Williams see some merit in the overall enterprise, but wish for greater precision in the claims and for greater contact with the mainstream psychological literature. Tanya Luhrmann directs her attention to a particular candidate intelligence, but in the process raises more general questions about the enterprise.

Before addressing their several concerns, it is important for me to make a few points that apparently need clarification. First of all, the methods and criteria for selecting the intelligences occupied a great deal of my attention. I was determined to go beyond standard psychometrics (testing) and to draw upon the major disciplines that might illuminate the nature of human intellect. A significant step occurred in my own thinking when I came to realize that intelligences were not intertwined with sensory systems; the intelligences are the operations performed by the brain *once input has been received*, irrespective of the channel of reception. Linguistic intelligence operates, whether the language was perceived through eye, ear, or tip of a finger; spatial intelligence operates even in the blind; large aspects of musical intelligence can be apprehended non-auditorally, and those that depend on the ear can at least be analogized through color (or some other comparable signal). Various candidate intelligences were considered and rejected, because they did not meet the criteria sufficiently well—for example, humor intelligence, cooking intelligence, sexual intelligence. And the delineation within the specific list—is logical-mathematical intelligence one or two intelligences? What of the relation between the two personal intelligences?—continues to concern me.

I have always acknowledged that the intelligences represent not basic essences but my best effort to make sense of a complex terrain. I stated quite explicitly in my first book that each intelligence is composed of sub-intelligences (music, for example, contains rhythmic, melodic, harmonic, timbre aspects); and that a full list of intelligences or subintelligences would add up to several dozen. The decisions to list a manageable handful is just that—an effort to introduce people comfortably to a terrain that would be unwieldy if one had to absorb it in fullest detail. Who could sensibly talk of forty, let alone four hundred, intelligences?

The crucial question has been well expressed by philosophers. Have I cut nature at its proper joints? Unpacking this metaphor, the assumption is that there are better and worse ways of delineating human intellectual potentials. One could take the view that there is but a single intelligence, and that, accordingly, all intellectual work is of a piece. One could take an alternative view—that humans are composed of huge numbers of quite specific capacities, ranging from face recognition to preparing a bacon sandwich. I am trying to steer a middle ground that reflects something about the organization of mind and brain, on the one hand, and that proves useful for both theoretical and applied purposes, on the other.

On another issue, I must shoulder the blame. In my earliest writings, I tended to conflate intelligences and domains. But by the early 1990s, it had become clear to me that intelligences were biopsychological potentials, that we all possess by virtue of being humans. Domains, in contrast, are social constructions; they are areas of knowledge or practice that have evolved cumulatively within one or more cultural settings. (They constitute the focus for David Olson's work, as described in the previous section).

The line between intelligences and domains can be confusing, because they may have the same name. However, the capacity to play an instrument does not depend only on musical intelligence; the domain of musical performance can involved bodily intelligence, spatial intelligence, personal intelligences, and no doubt others as well. By the same token, strength in spatial intelligence does not predict that a person will become an expert in space exploration. Indeed, that intellectual strength only means that a person might find it easier to excel at roles that call on skills in spatial manipulation, and those roles can range from architect to surgeon to airplane pilot.

Speaking more generally, the positing, defense of, and expansion of MI theory is a balancing act. I need to respect earlier work in the psychology of intelligence without being overwhelmed by it; I need to take into account both the universal biological bases of intellect and its varied manifestations across culture. I need to remain a developer and creator of a new theory while monitoring—and, when I deem it appropriate, speaking up about—various experiments and implementations that are performed in its name. It does not feel pleasurable be attacked from all sides;

but to the extent that the attacks are mounted by roughly equivalent critics and counter-critics, I infer that perhaps I am on to something.

Reply to John White

As already noted, John White has problems with MI theory from top to bottom. I shall respond to his specific points, but it is important first to speak to his overall characterization.

While I do not consider myself an 'essentialist' in any deep sense, I feel that I have been engaged in a journey of discovery. Drawing on the various tools and disciplines available, I seek the best delineation available of human intellectual competences and potentials. John White could be taking two different positions. He might be saying that the quest is perfectly reasonable, but he would go about it differently and come up with perhaps dramatically different answers. Fair enough. However, I hear him saying something more damning. Taking on a perspective which has its origins in Wittgenstein and has reverberation in more recent writings such as those of D.W. Hamlyn (1978), Rom Harré (1983), and Richard Rorty (1979), White questions my whole effort: it is hopeless, in his view, to try to place on a scientific basis distinctions and categories that essentially grow out of our language, our ways of talking and conceptualizing. If I am right in my characterization of White, there is no way that I could satisfy him. In the phrase made famous by Thomas Kuhn (1970), we are proceeding from "incommensurate paradigms."

Though concluding that there is no bridge between us, I will nonetheless attempt to find enough common ground so that we can have a conversation. (This is, of course, the move that Rorty favors.) I do so by focussing on four topics:

1. *End state.* As a developmentalist, I believe that one cannot study an area without having some sense of what it is like in its full-blown form. Whether you are studying moral development, scientific development, or artistic development, you need to bear in mind what it means to be a scientist, artist, or a moral person. However, this delineation of an end state need not at all be fixed or frozen. Piaget delineated the mental capacities of the scientist but in no way did he constrain the varieties of sciences or scientists that might exhibit these capacities; and his student Howard Gruber (1981) showed what advanced, creative scientific thinking was like in individuals like Darwin and Piaget. End-states are markers, they need not be booby traps.

2. *Criteria for criteria.* White asks, with reference to my criteria for an intelligence, from what source do they emanate? As I explained above, they represent my effort to incorporate the principal disciplinary strands that are relevant to any examination of human cognition. My response to White: The search for criteria for an investigation opens up the possibility of an infinite regress. If he puts forth criteria, I can simply respond by asking him for the criteria for those criteria. I see my list as an entirely reasonable first pass; the proper response would be to suggest an alternative set of criteria, and to show that they are better motivated or less problematic for the task at hand.

The issue of criteria also arises in White's discussion of the specific intelligences. He declares, for example, that "mathematical abilities are, to a large extent, a specialized kind of linguistic ability." Perhaps, but perhaps not. This statement is not one that can be established by authority; it is an empirical issue. My work, and that of many other researchers, points up the ways in which numerical and linguistic abilities are not co-terminous; and hence the rationale for positing two separate intelligences which can, of course, interact for specific purposes (Dehaene 1997). Again: With reference to the criteria for an intelligence, White questions the reliance on evidence from exceptional individuals. He simply dismisses the architectural drawing of autistic artist Stephen Wiltshire as "subnormal mental facility." But the high esteem in which this gift is held by many knowledgeable observers calls into question White's harsh judgment. White does not equal Right.

3. *Domains and intelligences.* White attempts to trace my work on intelligence through an examination of what he knows about my biography (Graeme Sullivan undertakes much the same exercise with reference to my work in arts education). Some of what he says is quite plausible. But he completely misconstrues the distinction that I have recently introduced between intelligences and domains.

I have always held that an approach through symbol analysis allows one to look toward a biological basis, on the one hand, and towards a cultural analysis, on the other. Symbolic capacity originates in the human nervous system but is variously realized in different cultural roles and settings. It turns out that the names of certain specific intelligences are identical to the names of various domains and this homonymy has confused readers: hence the distinction introduced between intelligences and domains. But an intelligence itself has never been a domain; that is why '*susceptibility* to encoding in a symbol system' is one of the criteria for an intelligence. Far from making my theory 'unintelligible', this terminological shift has clarified what I have always sought to do.

4. *Educational implications.* My original involvement with MI was as a conceptualizer and theorizer. No one was more surprised than I at the enormous interest shown in the theory by educators all over the world, including Britain. I have tried hard not to be prescriptive, preferring to encourage a variety of practices that are catalyzed—the proper word—by the idea of multiple intelligences. Only when the practices seem particularly ill-advised have I assumed the role of a policeman. White is correct when he indicates that many of the practices could have been undertaken in the absence of MI theory—and that, by the way, is true of just about any educational practice; seldom if ever do such practices derive ineluctably from a single scientific finding or technological advance. But I don't take seriously his suggestion that MI-derived practices are necessarily ill-advised. I don't take it seriously because hundreds of practitioners do feel that the theory is helpful; and we have empirical evidence, from the work of Mindy Kornhaber (1996), Mara Krechevsky (1998), Jie-Qi Chen (Chen and Gardner, 2005), and others, that MI-inspired practices can be productive in the classroom. Sometimes, White is simply wrong.

Reply to Nathan Brody

Shifting from John White to Nathan Brody involves a sea change. From an individual who is uncomfortable with any scientific effort to unpack intelligence, I turn my attention to an individual who is remarkably satisfied with the current state of the study of intelligence. As early as 1904, Charles Spearman put forth the notion of 'g' or general intelligence. Now over a century later, Brody seems content to accept 'g' as a necessary and sufficient explanation for the nature of human intellect—or, to be more precise, for the bulk of the variance. Moreover, Brody is scarcely alone; perhaps a majority of psychometricians would agree with him. It is difficult to believe that other sciences like physics or biology or other 'applied areas' like medicine or engineering would be content to adhere unswervingly to such conventional wisdom. Indeed, we would look askance at theorists of biology or physics who were satisfied with the state of knowledge in 1904 or 1952. And we would be likely to sue practitioners for malpractice if they dug their heels in tracks that were created a century ago.

There are those who would question the existence of 'g'. Stephen Jay Gould (1981), for example, felt that it was artifactual; factor-analytic studies can balloon or squash a general factor, depending on the assumptions built into the operating statistical model. Still others may accept 'g' but are upset by the implication that it is largely 'heritable'—a contribution of one's biological parents. Questioning the model of behavioral genetics when it is imported to the study of human beings, they assert that the heritability of 'g' would be minimal (Lewontin, Rose, and Ramin 1984). And they can take sustenance from the recent report by Turkheimer *et al.* (2003) that the heritability of IQ varies significantly across social classes.

So far as I can recall, I have never embraced either of these critiques. I accept 'g' as a reasonable summary of a lot of literature and believe that, like almost all human traits, it has a significant heritable component. I have, however, questioned the provenance of 'g'. I have wondered whether we are taking a measure that was derived chiefly from scholastic (linguistic and logical) environments over the last century and generalizing it to milieus and locales where it is not appropriate or has little explanatory power. In fact, it could be argued that, far from being an objective measure of intellect, 'g' is simply the current common factor in that odd set of tasks that psychologists have assembled over the years, as they attempt to predict success in scholastic settings. Another set of tasks might have yielded a quite different 'g' or even no 'g' at all. Psychologists interested in business acumen or artistic creativity would have surveyed a distinctly different landscape of tasks. Switching to the hat of the policymaker, I have had deep concerns about the wisdom of studying 'g' over and over again, rather than turning our attention to how we can best develop the range of human intellectual capacities across a broad population.

I accept Nathan Brody's summary of the 'positive manifold' across many testing situations. Also, it is instructive to know that 'g' emerges even in situations that reflect presumptively basic information processing capacities, such as reaction time. (However, I reject Brody's claim that 'oddball' tasks do not involve language and logic; I can assure him that when I attempt some of these items, those are just the skills that I employ). I am far less certain than he is, that we know what is being measured here—and I note that Brody himself suggests various possible meanings of 'g'. 'g' could be a lodestone of human intellectual functioning. But even if it is, we don't know which if any of the following possibilities or sets of possibilities might be operative:

1. Speed of response;
2. Flexibility of response;
3. Familiarity with apparently meaningless tasks;
4. Motivation to do well in some kind of artificial task;

5. Capacity to follow instructions;
6. Persistence;
7. Socialization at tasks carried out in school or other kinds of institutions;
8. Self-concept about one's ability to perform in an academic setting.

We need to be humble about the meaning and generality of 'g'. From the studies of Michael Cole (Cole and Means 1981), we know that individuals in remote cultures often appear stupid until the task is recast for them, at which point they do perfectly fine. We know from the studies of Stephen Ceci (1996) that individuals with low IQs can do well at complex mathematical tasks like peri-mutual betting. We know from the studies of Robert Sternberg (1985) that measures of contextual and creative intelligence add significantly to the predictive values of standard intelligence measures like the old SAT. And we know from the work of John Flynn (1988) that psychometric intelligence has gone up a full standard deviation in fifty years—an infinitesimally short period from the perspective of human evolution.

There is also the possibility, as Kanazawa (2004) suggests, that 'g' is itself a domain-specific adaptation. Kanazara describes 'g' as the capacity to adapt to an evolutionarily novel world. I like the idea of 'g' as yet another module—but in my view, it is much more likely to be the capacity to deal with apparently meaningless squiggles in a highly artificial situation. Bearing this hypothesis in mind, I suspect that 'g' will prove much less important in an apprentice-style learning situation—which until recently is how most human beings learned most things and which could once again rise in prominence as the costs of a mentor-free environment are calculated (Fischman, Soloman, Greenspan, and Gardner 2004).

But let's say—for the sake of argument—that we accept 'g' as a significant part of human intellect, with a significant heritability component. Then what?

I believe that the proponents and defenders of 'g' soon reach a scientific and a practical impasse. On the scientific dimension, there is still the need to explain the vast array of human talents, and the amazingly diverse profiles of human beings: why one excels in navigation, a second in mediation, a third in meditation; or why one person has a selective difficult in understanding other persons, a second has difficulty in expressing herself in language, a third cannot find her way around a familiar city. How did these talents arise, how do they come to be expressed, how do they interact with 'g'—whatever 'g' might be? All of these striking individual differences are swept under the rug—and remain there until there is an effort, like MI theory, to explain it. Why should one ability be called "general" or "g" and other abilities "s" of "special abilities"? By what criterion, neurally, or psychometrically?

On the practical level, given a putatively powerful factor like 'g', what are the parents, teachers, and other educators to do? Should we just sit back and wait for intellect to assert itself? Should we place those with low 'g' in separate enclaves, as Herrnstein and Murray (1994) come close to suggesting? Should we try to raise 'g', though it may be difficult, as Herrnstein attempted to do in ten years of research on Project Intelligence? Or does the answer lie instead in an approach like multiple intelligences? From an MI perspective, one looks for areas of human strength. And these areas can be used both to help individuals find a productive niche in society and as entry points for the mastery of important disciplines and skills (Gardner 1991; 1999).

I have to question the motives of individuals who keep studying 'g' and who revel in claims, like the one cited by Brody, that higher IQ people live longer. Now, a researcher can study anything that he or she likes, so long as it is not injurious to others. (Of course, it is far from evident to me that studies of 'g' are innocuous.) But how a researcher elects to devote his time and energy is the most important decision that he makes; and from a "good work" perspective, he should be able to offer a public account of why he has elected to choose that topic. Frankly, I find it difficult to find a publicly-discussable reason why researchers should devote their energies to yet one more study of the role of 'g' in arenas ranging from job preparedness to longevity or yet one more effort to document racial or ethnic differences in intellect.

My work on multiple intelligences was not motivated initially by melioristic tendencies. But in fact, I am pleased that this work has been used to question the importance of any single measure of competence and has stimulated a trend toward the use of more performance-based measures. I am gratified that, in his closing pages, Nathan Brody expresses some sympathy with these policy implications. But then I have to ask: is this the same Nathan Brady, or are we dealing with multiple personae?

Reply to Susan Barnett, Stephen Ceci, and Wendy Williams

"The making of bacon sandwiches' is a cute title, though I have to admit at the outset, I don't actually know about such sandwiches—at our local diner, we speak of "bacon plus . . .", with lettuce and tomato, cheese, egg, or turkey being the favorite additional ingredients.

My definition of intelligences specifies information-processing devices that can help individuals to solve problems or to fashion products. If I had simply limited my focus to 'solve problems', no one would have cared or noticed. Solving problems is what scientists do and what we ask children to do in school. By broadening the purview to include 'fashioning products', I was deliberately making sure that we value individuals who can create a work of art, devise a scientific theory, design and construct a building, and other, more holistic, valued activities.

This point is important to underscore for two reasons. First of all, measures of intellect should connect to things that we care about. You can belong to Mensa, with an IQ approaching 200, and yet never be able to execute anything of significance (except an IQ test!). And you can lose your frontal lobes, through injury, disease, or surgery, and still have an IQ of 150, if your crystallized knowledge remains intact. I believed—and still believe—that there is something seriously deficient in a theory of intellect that allows for such anomalies.

Now, obviously, the making of a sandwich—with or without bacon and other accoutrements—is a rather specific production, though, I might note, that sandwiches were invented only a few centuries ago. (The Earl who invented them was certainly creative, whether or not he was intelligent). This end state is too narrow for my tastes (pardon the pun). But if one were to posit as an end state—"good cook"—and, as a valued product—"the preparation of tasty food"—then one would move into the realm of the intellect, in the broader sense of the term that I favor.

As noted above, some have actually proposed a separate cooking intelligence. The reason I have so far rejected that suggestion reflects my essential conservatism as a theorist. I don't like to add intelligences unless I have to, and I've been extremely measured about doing so. Without being a student of cooking, I would suppose that it requires a lot of naturalist intelligence (distinguishing among ingredients), some bodily intelligence (you don't want to spill ingredients or slice off your fingers), some mathematical intelligence (how much of each ingredient should be included), a smidgeon of logic (if I simmer the sauce in wine, the alcohol will evaporate), linguistic skill (reading a recipe or cookbook) and probably some personal intelligences (what would various tasters like or dislike). I see less of a role for musical, existential, or spatial intelligence—though friendly amendments are welcome.

Barnett and colleagues raise two nagging questions: 1. Who gets to decide what is and is not intelligence or an intelligence? 2. Why should the various abilities that I've identified all be united under the rubric of 'intelligences'? They shrewdly point out that even an effort to find a synonym for intelligence in non-literate culture presupposes some underlying commonality—otherwise translation would not be possible. Their apparent recourse is to move to a much finer degree of analysis of specific tasks and information processing skills, on the one hand, and to an examination of 'transferable skills', on the other. This 'experimental psychology" approach is a valid alternative to the one that I have proposed. Note, however, that it is not a contrary approach. For, in the end, an empirical examination of more specific capacities and the transfer among them might yield the palette of multiple intellectual factors that I have posited.

No theorist has done more than Stephen Ceci to critique the classical view of intelligence (just 'g'), to illuminate the remarkable intellectual feats of those who might be dismissed on the basis of low IQ scores, and to underscore the cultural dimensions in defining and developing intellect across various settings. His writings, more so than anything that I have said, are the ones to which Nathan Brody should respond. At the same time, Ceci recognizes that the study of intellect from a biological and psychological perspective is a valid undertaking, one that cannot be subsumed or rendered irrelevant by studies of discourse or norms. In that way, he proves an apt respondent to White and Olson.

Reply to Tanya Luhrmann

Stimulated in part by conversations that we had in the middle 1990s, Luhrmann has penned a finely argued essay on the mental processes involved in spirituality. Luhrmann is one of the most erudite scholars of religion, mysticism, and spirituality of our time; she is unique in her capacity to analyze spiritual and other related phenomena (like dissociation, hypnosis, hallucination, or trance) in terms of the putative cognitive processes entailed in their operation. I learned a great deal from her essay and I'm sure readers not 'under fire' will be similarly edified.

Earlier I spoke about the effort to 'cut nature at its proper joints'. As noted, there are hundreds of ways in which one could classify and distinguish among human cognitive faculties. In developing the theory of multiple intelligences, I put forth my procedure for the identification and delineation of the several intelligences, as well as my rationale for presenting a small number of capacious intelligences, rather than, say, highly specific (and suspect) ones like 'preparing a bacon sandwich' intelligence.

Luhrmann's essay raises two issues entailed in the identification of intelligences. The first one: "Within MI theory, does it make sense to delineate a spiritual intelligence?" The second one: "Which part of the human psyche ought to fall under the rubric of 'intelligence' or 'intelligences'—and which part falls more properly under another aegis, not felicitously described as intelligence?" We might think of this latter as a 'meta-question'—what are the joints within which we make finer discriminations among widely recognized psychological processes?

In an essay written some years ago (Gardner 1999), one that drew on my earlier interchanges with Luhrmann, I raised the question of whether there is evidence for a spiritual intelligence. I rejected two aspects of spirituality as falling outside the realm of intelligence.

The first was the achievement of a certain state of being. I ruled out phenomenological experience as an element of intelligence, because it depends entirely on self-report and is not open to independent verification or refutation. At the same time, I acknowledged that 'some people are simply more skilled than others at meditating, achieving trance states . . . indeed some physiological and brain states may be correlated predictably with the achievement of such alterations of consciousness" (p. 55). I was acknowledging the genuineness of the phenomena delineated here by Luhrmann, while falling short of incorporating these phenomena under the rubric of intelligence.

The second aspect to be rejected was the capacity of some people to affect others, through their inspirational activities or the sheer charismatic power of their being. Again, while recognizing this phenomenon, I do not see such a charismatic capacity as something that an individual develops, apart from the personal intelligences. Rather, there is an interaction between awe-inspiring qualities of a certain person or persona, on the one hand, and the needs or desires of a relevant audience on the other. Here, spirituality entails a commitment that certain individuals (whom we could call 'followers' or 'disciples') extend to rare, magnetic others.

Trying to preserve a core aspect of spirituality, without violating my criteria or my common sense, I alighted on the possibility of an 'existential intelligence'. As mentioned by Luhrmann, there may be a human intelligence that deals with the most cosmic issues—life, death, immortality, love, and war—so to speak, the intelligence of 'big questions.' This capacity seems to be uniquely human and it realizes the criteria for an intelligence surprisingly well. I hesitated to proclaim a full-blown existential intelligence for two reasons: 1. my intellectual conservatism (don't add to the list of intelligences unless you must); and 2. the lack of convincing evidence that certain parts of the nervous system have evolved particularly to deal with issues that are so grand or infinitesimal that they elude ordinary sensing or perception. And there the matter stands to this day—marked by my whimsical reference to "eight and a half intelligences."

Luhrmann asks me to reconsider my position. She identifies a certain capacity—which (following psychologist Auke Tellegen) she labels 'absorption'. The capacity for notable absorption may characterize a range of individuals who dwell in the spiritual realm: individuals who undergo trances or dissociative or 'out of body experiences'; individuals who are readily hypnotized; individuals who have excessively rich and realistic visual imaginative experiences; individuals who find it easy to pray and to converse with God, hearing His voice in the process. And indeed, she finds an intriguing correlation between a high score on the Tellegen Absorption Scale and distinction in one or more of these spiritual achievements.

I have always felt that the most original part of MI theory was my identification of eight criteria that help me to decide what is, or is not, a candidate intelligence. Yet, the criteria themselves have undergone surprisingly little scrutiny. It is to John White's credit that he reviews the criteria, though I wish he had shown more sympathy for the rationale behind their enunciation. Only a few individuals have actually proposed a new intelligence and then reviewed it in terms of the criteria. For example Battro and Denham (2002) proposed a 'digital intelligence'. While I think that the criteria were persuasively invoked, the authors did not convince me that 'digital intelligence' can be usefully separated from 'logical-mathematical intelligence'. By an analogous line of reasoning, I have concluded that certain other candidate intelligences, like humor intelligence or moral intelligence, can be better explicated in terms of the existing set of intelligences, yoked to the values of the ambient culture (Gardner 2006, Chapters 2–5).

Donning the Luhrmann hat, and reviewing her invocation of the criteria, I have the following reaction. I agree that the Tellegen Scale constitutes psychological evidence in favor of a discrete capacity; and a core set of operations may well be involved in absorption. I am also persuaded that some individuals are precocious in their capacity for absorption, and there may well be others—for example, those with severe attentional deficits—who are especially challenged in this area. The evidence mentioned from neurology is too general to be useful; we would need ways to delineate absorption from other aspects of religiosity or spirituality or concentration or motivation. On a distinct developmental history and on the susceptibility to encoding in a symbol system, it is premature to draw any conclusions. Overall, in terms of the criteria that I have set forth, I would say that Luhrmann makes a plausible but not quite a convincing case for 'absorption intelligence'.

But now I must remove the Luhrmann Spirituality Hat and replace it with the Gardner MI Hat. The deeper question raised by her essay is the question of how intelligence relates to other human psychological states and capacities. While I am widely recognized as someone who has broadened the definition of intelligence, I have always maintained that intelligence is like an elastic band—it can be stretched a certain extent but if stretched too far, it will either collapse or break. And so I have gone to some lengths to draw a line between intelligence and emotions (including emotional intelligence), intelligence and creativity, intelligence and morality, and other tempting pairs. Moreover, I have always maintained that intelligence is not the same thing as will, purpose, motivation, attention, personality, style, temperament, and other well-known topics of psychology. Each of these is important, indeed some could well be argued as being *more* important than intelligence. But they are not the same as intelligence—each deserves its own hour in the day, its own chapter in a psychology textbook. Should our conception of intelligence be expanded so far as to incorporate all of these various other psychological capacities and states, it will cease to be useful.

Alas, no magic formula designates where one of these capacities begins and another ends. No rivers or mountain ranges in the psyche allow easy demarcation of where one psychological nation ends and another begins. One has to proceed by argument, common sense, and empirical data, in the hope that, despite the absence of unambiguous landmarks, proper borders are nonetheless being drawn.

In fact, it would take an entire psychology textbook to fix the borders of the aforementioned eight capacities, let alone many others that could be added to the list. Nor would one have any guarantee that the fixation of borders was necessarily correct; psychological turf wars are as unending as geographical border skirmishes. I feel secure in saying that sluggishness is a "temperament" variable; that introversion is a "personality trait"; that "flow" is a motivational state that results when challenge and skills are in mesh; that "will" determines whether a certain intelligence is actually brought to bear in a situation; that 'purpose' is the end toward which will is directed.

As a psychologist, I see 'absorption' as an aspect of 'attention'—one of the most important and most thoroughly studied human capacities. No less an authority that the founding neurocognitive scientist Michael

Posner (2004) has argued that attention should be considered an intelligence; and like Luhrmann, he actually applies my criteria to the examination of attention as a candidate intelligence. At a superficial level, attention clearly seems to be an example of an intelligence: it is, after all, an information-processing capacity used by individuals to solve problems or create products that are valued in at least one cultural setting.

Why, then, do I continue to harbor hesitations about subsuming attention, and a key component of it, like absorption, under the rubric of intelligence? Fundamentally, it is because I see attention or absorption as capacities that are necessary for intelligences to function, rather than as intelligences *per se*. I have often stressed that the intelligences are not sensory systems: rather they are the computational systems that operate on information once it has been received through one or another sensory system. Nor are the intelligences motivational systems: one must be motivated to use any intelligence, and yet the operation of the intelligence is quite separate from the motivation to utilize it. I continue to see 'attention' as a necessary precondition for the operation of an intelligence, be it linguistic, interpersonal, or naturalistic, rather than an operating intelligence per se.

Let me approach this dilemma from another angle. As I construe the intelligences, they each derive from the existence of a certain kind of *content* or *information* or *object* in the world, which the individual is trying to make sense of. It is relatively easy to see spatial intelligence as a way of making sense of spatial information, and an analogous evolutionary argument can be put forth, more or less convincingly, for each of the remaining of the intelligence. Indeed, as suggested above, existential intelligence may have evolved to deal precisely with that content which, while vital, is *not* readily perceived. Attention or absorption on their own are just free-floating; the question is, are there specific contents for which attention or absorption are activated, or can they be marshaled by any old content? Put differently, it remains an empirical question whether the attentional processes entailed in the operation of one intelligence are identical to those involved in activating other intelligences.

Luhrmann makes the intriguing proposal that the capacity for absorption may have originally evolved to allow people to deal with stress and pain, and that this capacity is now an 'exapted' spandrel, available for other purposes, including spiritual ones. One could as well put forth a more positive argument: perhaps absorption evolved so that individuals could solve more complex problems and engage in longer-term planning, which would increase the likelihood of survival and even of securing a mate. In this sense, absorption is like flow—a highly motivating state that can lead to pleasure and can also bring about enormous accomplishments, be they pro- or anti-social. Absorption can be seen, on the one hand, as self-absorption—of use only to the self. But it can also be seen as magnanimous—one is religious, prayerful, shamanistic, in order to perform important tasks for other individuals or for the broader society.

In the end, just where to draw the line between intelligences, on the one hand, and other essential psychological processes, on the other, will probably remain a judgment, indeed, an aesthetic judgment. For some, like Posner and Luhrmann, attention and absorption may fit comfortably along with other intellectual capacities like linguistic, musical, or interpersonal analysis. For me, this positioning remains an intellectual stretch: I find it easier to align attention/absorption with sensory systems, as a precondition for intellectual work, on the one hand, or with motivation, as providing the energy for sustained work, on the other. However, while cartography is fun, it is not the chief activity for most practitioners. And so, if it proves useful for scholars and educators to think of absorption as a kind of intelligence, I will not be dismayed.

CASE STUDIES

Once I had developed the theory of multiple intelligences, I was asked about the implications of the theory for other key topics in psychology. Probably the most frequently posed question pertained to creativity. If there is more than one intelligence, I was asked, 'are there also multiple forms of creativity?'

Having been interested in creativity for many years, I was open to, even prepared for, this question. Just as I saw intelligence as more than problem-solving, I saw creativity in a multiplicity of forms: formulating theories, solving problems, producing works of art, engaging in a stylized performance were, to my mind, quite separate forms of creativity. But, additionally, I wondered whether creativity in different domains might assume different configurations.

Building on my long-term interest in the modern era, I decided to carry out case studies of seven individuals, each of whom was putatively strong in a specific intelligence. I had always had a strong interest in biography and autobiography, and already knew a fair amount about individuals like Sigmund Freud and Mahatma Gandhi. From my own teacher, the psychoanalyst Erik Erikson (himself an expert on Freud and Gandhi), I had learned something about how to carry out case studies. And so it was a natural move for me to examine 'seven creators of the modern era' and see what I could discover about their intellectual journeys and their modes of processing. I selected seven individuals who were unambiguously considered creative, whose lives and works interested me, and about whom I felt I would have something to say. In retrospect, I can add a personal note: The research and writing of *Creating Minds* (2004) was the most enjoyable that I have carried out for any book.

At first blush, creativity seems a rather different sort of capacity than leadership—though, as it happens, Dean Keith Simonton (1994, p 410) has recognized their similarities with reference to both cognition and personality. From the perspective of psychology, both creators and leaders are distinguished by their capacities to influence others. I was able to draw upon a long time interest in political and historical figures, one fueled both my fondness for biography and by my interest in the daily news. So when I decided to tackle the issue of leadership, I again elected to do so by investigating a sample of leaders of the twentieth century.

In studying creativity, I organized my investigation in terms of exemplars of each of the intelligences. When it came to leadership, my collaborator Emma Laskin and I instead chose to group leaders in terms of the kind of arena in which they worked (scholarship, circumscribed organizations, large-scale national or international entities) and how directly their leadership was manifest. Direct leaders are those who exert influence chiefly through their contact with an audience; indirect leaders fashion some kind of a symbolic product (book, work of art, scientific theory) which, in turn, affects other individuals.

Distinctive in my psychological approach to leadership is my focus on its cognitive dimensions, rather than on the more usual approaches in terms of power or personality. I see leaders as individuals who create narratives. The effectiveness of leaders is determined by the impact of these stories on the audience and the extent to which the narrative is actually and effectively embodied in the life of the leader. Leadership, on this analysis, occurs in exchanges between the minds of the leader and the mind of his or her audiences. In later work, not reviewed in this book, I expanded this study to consider how individuals succeed or fail in changing the minds of others. For those interested in an update of my views on effective leadership, I recommend *Changing Minds*.

Reply to Dean Keith Simonton

I was gratified to receive Dean Keith Simonton's evaluation of my 1993 book *Creating Minds*. I have long been an admirer of Simonton's pathbreaking historiometric work in the study of creativity, leadership, genius and other forms of extraordinary influence. Simonton delineates a manageable problem, determines the empirical evidence that is relevant, and regularly comes up with findings that enhance our understanding of the phenomenon in question.

I maintain that the relationship between detailed case studies, on the one hand, and large-scale quantitative historiometric studies, on the other, should be complementary and symbiotic. To be sure, some questions can only be approached through large scale studies—for example, a determination of the ages at which leading practitioners in different domains do their most acclaimed works. Other questions demand individual case studies: we can learn little about the particular discoveries of Darwin, or the painting oeuvre of Picasso, in the absence of intensive studies of their respective working lives. Yet, most of the questions in which Simonton and I are interested benefit from a two-pronged approach.

Where I may depart from Simonton is in the presumed order of these approaches. It is too facile to say that case studies raise issues and hypotheses, and that quantitative studies test them. I see the relation as more flexible and more dynamic. In some cases, for example, a historiometric result pushes one back to additional case studies. Suppose, as Simonton has found, that the last works (the 'swan songs') of artists are often more esteemed. At that point we need to study the individual artist and his or her works to see the reason or reasons why: factors could range from the actual nature of the work to the fact that audiences know that this is the last work to the possibility that final works, like beginning works, are—for some reason—more valued by collectors. The explanation might also differ across art forms.

More generally, historiometric studies can yield correlations but not causes. One of Simonton's most intriguing findings is that esteemed creators create more works than do others in their respective fields, and that corpus includes more works that are considered of poor quality. But why are more of Beethoven's works considered of poor quality than those of a lesser composer who created a smaller body of work? Perhaps in some objective sense the lesser Beethoven works were dashed off or written when the composer was feeling depressed or preoccupied. But quite other reasons come to mind. For example, it may not be possible to value more than a certain number of works by a composer and so there is an inevitable consigning of some works to a junk heap. Or, perhaps, there are historical forces at work, where a certain line of the composer's work was initially valued (such as string quartets) and this focus has had a halo effect over the centuries. Such questions require triangulation:

deeper case studies, on the one hand, and experimental interventions on the other.

In *Creating Minds* I self-consciously positioned my work between two extremes: that of psychologist Howard Gruber, who did only single case studies and who was wary of any kind of comparison; and that of historiometricians like Simonton, Colin Martindale (1990), and, more recently, Charles Murray (2003), who take a completely quantitative approach to issues of extraordinariness. Simonton is absolutely on target in ferreting out the various hypotheses that I put forth, and reviewing the historiometric and empirical data that pertain to those hypotheses.

Simonton focuses on the problems of 'selection' when one is dealing with a small number of subjects. He suggests that if I had chosen different persons, I might have come up with different patterns. True enough, but I take strong issue with Simonton's citation of Galenson's work on the putatively different approaches to an artistic oeuvre. Galenson has laid out two alternative approaches—he terms them conceptual and experimental—but he has not proven that they relate to specific artists. Galenson decides on whether someone is an experimentalist or a conceptualizer by whether his most valued works were produced early or late in the career and then locates quotations that support his classification. As Winner (2004) has pointed out, Galenson has no independent way of determining whether an artist is an experimentalist or a conceptualizer. He claims that Picasso was a conceptualizer and yet ample testimonial and empirical evidence document that Picasso proceeded equally as an experimentalist. Galenson differs here from Simonton in that he is not, in that work, a genuine empiricist, but rather a theorist who is posing as an empiricist. It would take an independent judgment of the approaches taken by various artists to determine whether Galenson's claims have empirical support.

In that vein, I would also demur from Simonton's (and Charles Murray's) claim that Cézanne is a twentieth-century painter. While he died in 1906, and exerted influence for many years thereafter, he is clearly a nineteenth-century painter. The appropriate person to pair with Picasso would be Matisse. Note that in making this comparison I did not need to consult an encyclopedia in order to see how many lines were devoted to each. Rather, I rely on a general consensus reached by the field, based on numerous, often unspoken criteria. I reject the notion that one approach is objective and the other subjective. Indeed, for my purposes, the consensus reached over time by a knowledgeable field is far more important than the number of lines in an encyclopedia or the amount of money paid at the last auction. Van Gogh may take up more space in encyclopedias not because of the merit of his work but because of the dramatic sweep of his short life and the romantic manner of his death.

Much can be learned from the kinds of indices that Simonton has developed. I applaud his ingenuity and his thoroughness. Yet we should not automatically assume that the criteria applied are determinative. Take, for example, the study of philosophers cited by Simonton himself. Determining the extent to which a philosopher's views differ from those of contemporaries, or the number of philosophical issues tackled by a philosopher, are anything but straightforward undertakings. Perhaps underscoring a gulf between the two of us, I would be more inclined to accept the verdict of the two historians of philosophy that I most trust than the convergence of several rough-and-ready indices (for exanple, number of entries in the index of a book).

I do agree with Simonton that it would be extremely useful to have control groups, which would allow one to determine those features that truly distinguish E.C.s from those that would characterize any serious practitioner, independent of how creative he or she is judged to be. Biographical information on the 'near misses' might be difficult to obtain. One could compare individuals who had a good deal of fame in their lifetimes, but are not now considered to have been creative, with those who stand out in the long run. My student Seana Moran is engaged in just such a study at the present time.

The centerpiece of Simonton's fine essay is a discussion of how the various specific claims made in *Creating Minds* fare under the klieg lights of historiometric and psychometric analyses. I am pleased—and, to be honest, relieved—to see that my informally arrived at generalizations fare quite well on this measure. There is no need for me to comment on those findings that survive Simonton's scalpel nor on those that remain to be examined empirically. Let me comment briefly on those findings that appear to be disconfirmed.

1. Whereas I underscore the relative ordinariness of the family of origin, Simonton claims that creators come from successful, educated families. In comparison to randomly selected families, Simonton is almost surely correct. That said, I believe that my generalization is more likely to be true for those in the arts, media, or business, while Simonton's claims are more likely to apply to those who in science or the learned professions. With the passage of time, the background of creators is likely to reflect the higher education of the public in general. We would need to see whether, in the future, creators are more likely to come from families with a college degree or families with more advanced training.

2. Simonton questions a rigid application of the ten-year rule. On his account, for the most creative individuals, there may be more break-throughs, and they may involve larger gaps between each breakthrough. Simonton's claim makes sense. For me, the discovery of a set of break-throughs was itself a surprise, since the literature had only examined the years needed for mastery or an initial breakthrough. I see Simonton's reports as providing a more differentiated view of my claims, rather than a refutation.

3. I had claimed that the nature of the domain is an important deter-minant of continuing breakthroughs. Simonton and I agree that other fac-tors may be important as well. Where we disagree is on our assessment of whether continuing breakthroughs are more likely in the arts than in the sciences. I believe that they will continue to be more likely in the arts, because artists are probing spaces that are particular, even idiosyncratic, to them, while scientists are probing spaces which any other scientist in the world can readily explore as well. Moreover, given instantaneous communication, scientists the world over learn almost immediately about new techniques and findings. However, two other factors may also bear on this disagreement. It may be that, with the rise of computer art, it is easier for other artists to probe the space that might earlier have belonged to a single artist. Also the 'field forces' that are always on the lookout for the youngest new artist may militate against the appreciation of break-throughs by older artists, at least in the short run.

What of the general picture of E.C. that has emerged? Having laid out my hypotheses, I have also been on the lookout for patterns that either confirm or disconfirm the prototype. In general, I have been pleased by the extent to which candidate E.C.s conform to the pattern set forth in *Creating Minds*. When exceptions emerge, I always see whether I can reconceptualize the pattern to include this outlier—or whether the pattern itself is thrown into question.

Let me mention two examples. Charles Darwin stands out because he seems to have avoided the tendency to become a prickly person: one who forges a Faustian bargain in which all things—and all other per-sons—are sacrificed to work. Darwin's exception-to-the rule may have stemmed from three factors: 1. He was independently wealthy and so did not have to worry about meeting the needs of his large family; 2. He was fortunate that his controversial theories were defended by Thomas Henry Huxley and so he himself did not have to expend his own ener-gies in that necessary but (for him) unpleasant task; 3. He had excellent defense mechanisms which allowed him to concentrate on his work, rather than becoming involved in time-consuming yet fruitless pursuits.

Nonetheless, it is good to know that one can become a scientific genius without becoming a difficult human being in the process.

Unlike Freud and other modern masters, Ludwig Wittgenstein was not born in a rural area. Rather his family were among the most influential in Vienna and he grew up surrounded by leading personalities in the artistic, scientific, and commercial worlds. Rather than moving to a world-class metropolis, Wittgenstein seems to have been motivated by a desire to escape roots that he, at least, found stifling. He first moved to Cambridge, England, a small, in many ways provincial city but one that was crucial for the philosophical work that he wanted to carry out. Then, after his initial contribution, he abandoned philosophy altogether, moving to Norway and teaching school. Perhaps it is a more robust generalization to say that the aspiring Creator needs to move to a milieu that contrasts very sharply with the one in which he was reared.

In the cyber-age, many of the generalizations about E.C. may be at risk. As noted, for the first time in all of human history, discoveries are transmitted almost instantaneously. Anyone can play, so to speak. It is possible to remain in your home and yet be part of networks that extend around the world. In areas like musical composition, even a child has access to technological aids that qualitatively change what is possible. Perhaps a whole new set of operating factors may be in play in the coming era.

I consider Dean Simonton's contribution to this volume as a model one. He does me the courtesy of taking my overall enterprise seriously, points out areas of disagreement, and suggests ways in which to advance our joint interests. Should I be asked to critique the work of another, I will strive to emulate Simonton's example.

Reply to Mark Runco

Mark Runco begins by acknowledging the legitimacy and power of detailed examinations of individuals who would be considered creative under almost any definition. While he raises a few questions about my methods and conclusions, most of his essay is devoted to the discussion of an alternative approach to creativity, one which (following a practice also invoked by other scholars) he dubs 'personal creativity.'

Now no one doubts that the existence of two discrete phenomena: 1. the 'historical' creativity of a Galileo or a Michelangelo; 2. the 'personal' creativity of a child's spirited drawings or of Howard Gruber attempting to jump rope backwards (to use Runco's whimsical example). The question to be raised—and I believe Runco would concur—is whether it is useful to describe both of these phenomena by the same term 'creativity'—and, if so, whether one can develop a single framework, or specify a continuum, which could account for both of them. Should we decide that the answer is 'no', there would be little further to discuss; Runco and I could simply proceed in our separate, equally legitimate directions. But, taking a position alongside many psychologists—for example David Feldman (1980) and David Perkins (1981)—Runco finds value in a dialogue that at least explores the relationship between our respective enterprises.

While sympathetic to an approach that seeks to understand the creative activities of young children, I find it difficult to determine the precise nature of Runco's claims. One could take the position that all human activity is creative, at least in part, but that robs the term of any utility. One could take the position that the term 'creative' should be preserved for those activities in which the accent falls on 'assimilation' (to use Piaget's term) rather than on accommodation to reality; or on those activities that involve 'interpretation' (to use Runco's term) rather than simply repetition or reaction.

Even in the latter case, however, it seems clear that nearly all human beings engage in assimilatory behavior (like play or dreaming) and no one is purely a repeater or reactor. Perhaps this is what Runco means in contending that we all have creative potential—and I would not want to pour cold water on that noble sentiment. But then, again, if taken literally, Runco would be reverting to what I would term a Bergsonian position—that all use of mind is creative.

Clearly, then, if one wants to do the psychology of creativity, rather than the psychology of all thought or all action, one needs to put some restrictions on the use of that admittedly loaded term. Here is where Runco runs into difficulty.

Runco boldly asserts that he wants to eliminate or minimize the importance of social elements, and focus only on the individual contribution to creativity. But I submit that social elements—or, otherwise put, social considerations—are essential in two ways.

First of all, except for the earliest forms of assimilatory play in the crib, the young child is always engaged in some kind of an activity that depends on social-cultural support. You can't engage in pretend play or tell stories or make drawings or jump rope backwards unless you live in a society that provides the relevant materials, encourages the aforementioned activities, or at a minimum allows you to pursue them without negative sanctions. Thus, any assimilatory or interpretive activity necessarily presupposes the existence of a society, with its attendant rules and symbol systems, domains and disciplines. This is the chief lesson that all social scientists have learned from George Herbert Mead and Lev Vygotsky, and from influential successors like Jerome Bruner and David Olson.

Second of all, once one begins to engage in socially-supported activities, one inevitably runs into the standards of those respective domains. And once one begins to present oneself as a serious contender in that particular domain, one inevitably runs into the field: the persons and social institutions that render judgments of expertise, quality, originality and—yes—creativity. It is true that young persons may not pay much attention to the judgments of the field; and some of us, as Runco notes, may be less intimidated by negative judgments than are others; but in the end no one can escape the cold eye of these social institutions.

And so, I cannot take seriously Runco's claims of varying creative potential, which may or may not merit nurturing, unless he acknowledges the existence of domains with their respective standards. In the absence of such acknowledgement, any claims to judgments about creativity are illusory.

Runco might retort that psychometric tests of divergent thinking or of problem-finding can help us to ascertain creative potential. Fair enough, but each of these measures itself draws from one or another domain (Getzels and Csikszentmihalyi [1976], for example, were studying serious art students) and imposes some kinds of standards (be they measures of novelty or correlations with the subsequent receipt of prizes). And so that 'ole debbil' of socialization pervades even the psychologically-rooted paper and pencil measures.

Let me respond more briefly to other specific points raised in Runco's essay:

1. Runco is right that generalizations based on seven individuals are tenuous. More data are clearly needed. But in the case cited, those data existed. In his study of nearly 100 individuals in later life, Csikszentmihalyi (1996) confirmed my claim that creative individuals typically exemplify opposites—such as a combination of adult maturity and childlike innocence and playfulness. In addition, I suspect that this generalization may not be time-bound. It seems to have characterized Mozart in the eighteenth century as much as Einstein over a century later.

2. Following an argument put forth by Robert Sternberg, Runco suggests that the decision to be creative is a personal one, and that an individual knowingly elects to be creative or not in a specific situation. There is certainly something to this: few creators exercise that 'interpretive muscle' when they are washing their face or putting on their

socks in the morning. Yet I fear that this generalization misses a larger truth. As they develop, creative individuals become certain kinds of persons. And as such they approach their work in ways that differ from experts or novices. I doubt that, when it came to their respective domains of practice, the people whom I studied decided whether and when to be creative—that is just the way that they were, they could not help it. Einstein rarely wore socks—and when asked why he did not use shaving cream he responded 'two soaps—too complicated'. He reduced the interpretations in his mundane life to a minimum, precisely so that he could concentrate on an ever-deeper exploration of the issues to which his mental life was wholly devoted.

3. Runco stresses the importance of assimilative activity in the creative lives of young children, and that is fine. But, in mastering a domain, all individuals must be extremely accommodating in the Piagetian sense. T.S. Eliot copied the writing styles of different poets, the iconoclastic composer Arnold Schoenberg worked through the classical repertoire, and Picasso famously quipped "Once I drew like Raphael, but it has taken me a whole lifetime to learn to draw like children" (quoted in de Meredieu 1974, p 8). Perhaps creators, more than the rest of us, are characterized by heightened assimilatory *and* heightened accommodative capacities, along with the capacity to navigate between or synthesize both.

Despite these critical comments, I applaud the overall enterprise which Runco has helped to chart. No matter what gifts they bring with them for their biological parents, from divine inspiration and from Fate, creators are human beings who must necessarily begin with the basic psychological capacities defined by Bruner, Freud, Piaget, and Vygotsky. The challenge to all students of creativity is to figure out how, building upon these universal capacities, a select few end up in 'transforming the world' (Feldman, Csikszentmihalyi, and Gardner 1994). Runco offers us part of the answer and invites others to join in an effort to build a bridge to the most cherished forms of adult creation.

Reply to Robert Spillane

In the middle 1970s, I agreed to write a textbook on Developmental Psychology. I arrived at a way of organizing the materials that worked for me and that seemed quite original. In a phrase, I decided to cross a topical approach with a chronological approach. The publisher sent my prospectus to a number of leading authorities in the field. Most were open to my synthesis. One person, however—as it happens, an author of one of the best-selling books in the field—recommended against publication. His critique can be readily summarized: 'You simply can't organize the field in this way'.

As it happens, my book was published; it was quite successful; and in due course, the organizational framework of my 'Developmental Psychology' was itself imitated by other authors and publishers. I came to understand why the one authority was so dead set against publishing of my book. It was not, as I had originally thought, because he was afraid of competition. Rather, he was so deeply involved in his own chronological approach to the topic, that he simply could not envision another way of proceeding. His mind was closed to an alternative paradigm.

I was reminded of this incident in reading Robert Spillane's critique. His critique is not, fundamentally, a critique of my work. While he says some kind words about my study—and I appreciate his courtesy—he does not enter sympathetically into what I was trying to do. Instead, much like the author of the best-selling textbook, he uses the critique as an occasion to put forth his own view of leadership. Spillane's critique stands out as the only one in this volume which makes little attempt to engage my own approach, and which operates instead as a tutorial: here is how one needs to approach the issue of leadership. Indeed, by the time that I got to the section where Max Weber was introduced, I had almost forgotten that this contribution was supposed to be an essay about my work.

In responding to Spillane's critique, therefore, I face a dilemma. I can either attempt, again, to explicate what I have been trying to do; or I can provide a critique of his own slant on leadership, as set forth in these pages. Since the present book is not designed to present the views of other persons, I shall decline the opportunity to critique Spillane's approach. Instead I shall respond quite specifically to the points that he raises with respect to my own work.

1. I am well aware of the importance of power in leadership. However, in my project, I explicitly stated that I am interested in how leaders succeed in changing the thoughts, feelings, and behaviors of others. I deliberately focus on 'voluntary leadership'. When a person has absolute power, his or her persuasive powers diminish in importance. Nonetheless, we know from recent history that once a dictatorship disappears, individuals revert very quickly to earlier modes of thought and behavior. By excluding power from my analysis, I avoid the issue of 'conflict of interest' that Spillane raises; I am interested in forms of influence that occur even when power relationships do not obtain.

2. Given my interest in how individuals affect a significant body of persons, I deliberately chose to examine a wide spectrum of leaders. I regret that Spillane cannot appreciate the leadership or influence powers of Robert Maynard Hutchins or Margaret Mead; those who came within their respective spheres certainly did. By my definition, Mead and Hutchins were effective leaders. During their lifetimes, they affected many persons and institutions. Even more impressively, their legacy continues to exert influence years after their death: the ultimate test of changing minds.

3. Spillane speaks of the leaders of the Second War as a 'control group' for my set of eleven leaders. That term is misleading. I cited these individuals as way of 'testing' my notions about leadership, just as I cited figures like Charles Darwin and Ludwig Wittgenstein as ways of testing my notions about creativity. The phrase 'additional case studies' is a better descriptor.

4. Spillane is of course correct that individuals gain a certain amount of credibility because of the positions that they occupy. My leaders stand out because of two facts: 1. Unlike a hereditary figure, none of them was born to the position that they ultimately came to occupy; each achieved his or her position as a result of personal efforts, garlanded no doubt by a generous dollop of luck. 2. I chose two individuals who did not have any organizational authority—Martin Luther King, Jr., and Eleanor Roosevelt—precisely so that I could observe leadership at work in the absence of any status in an established field.

5. Spillane is also correct in stressing the importance, in any consideration of leadership, of the relations between leader and audience. As he notes, I make this point repeatedly in my study of leadership, as well as in my subsequent writings on changing minds. Still, not all interactions, and not all interactors, are equal. There were reasons why I studied Margaret Thatcher and not James Callahan (her predecessor) or John Major (her successor). And the same could be said about each of the figures on whom I chose to focus. Position and interactions are important; but there remain the capacities that distinguish only a few extraordinary figures. It is not an accident that people like President Hutchins, anthropologist Mead, Pope John XXIII, or executive Alfred Sloan are remembered and emulated decades after they disappeared from the limelight.

6. At various points, Spillane speaks of my work as tautologous, circular, or pleonastic. All definitions involve tautology, and so, at a certain point, I have to concede that 'creative people are creative because they are creative' and 'leaders are leaders because they lead'. The same point would apply to any definition that Spillane (or anyone else) develops. I

deliberately have chosen eleven individuals from disparate fields whose capacity to influence others seems beyond argument. And I added ten individuals whose leadership positions were stipulated in the Second World War. For a set of case studies drawn from the twentieth century, it would be difficult to come up with a better list of twenty-one individuals.

In this context, Spillane chides me for a definition of leadership that is broad enough to include factory supervisers, football coaches, business executives, professors. My answer is 'Precisely—but of course, not *all* coaches or CEOs, just those who exert appreciable influence on others'. But his very dismissal gives away the game. He has no more justifiable basis for excluding CEO Alfred P. Sloan or Professor J. Robert Oppenheimer or Coach Vince Lombardi from leadership than I do for including them!

7. In the critique, I am characterized as a pragmatist (in the philosophical sense). While I don't actually think of myself as belong to one or another philosophical school, I am content to accept that descriptor. Spillane rightly notes that I have much less sympathy with behaviorism that he does. But then he criticizes me for not being able to predict who will be a good or effective leader. My view of my enterprise is light years away from predictive science. I have no idea of how to predict who will become a leader or a creator. I *can* point out those patterns that seem to describe individuals who do succeed in having enormous impact.

8. As Spillane notes, I am a psychologist and the particular tack that I chose to take was that of a cognitive psychologist. I never claimed that this was the only approach to leadership. Indeed, at the very beginning of *Leading Minds* I explicitly recognize a number of other approaches. To quote myself "the acquisition and utility of power"; "the role of specific policies"; "an examination of the public or audience" (pp. 16–17). Echoing Spillane's sentiments, I comment that "the successful leader is the one who most keenly senses the wishes of a potential audience. But this act of intuition does not relieve the leader of the need to articulate a message clearly and convincingly, and to combat other contrary themes reverberating in the culture." Moving to psychology, I point out that even within psychology, I do not focus on "the personality of the leader; his or her personal needs, principal psychodynamic traits, early life experiences, and relationships to other individuals" (p. 17). Finally, I state quite straightforwardly: "In this book I say relatively little about how other authorities have approached the issue of leadership. In no way is this limited discussion meant to question the importance of earlier contributions to this much-studied topic. Indeed, as made clear in

the reference notes to this and many other passages, I have learned a great deal from those authorities who have probed the personal traits and personal histories of leaders, different forms of leadership and the crucial roles of the audience . . . The existence of many excellent compendia on leadership, and my own focus on the cognitive dimensions of leadership, relieves me of the need to review critically other scholarly traditions in this field" (pp. 17–18).

In the general introduction to my responses, I point out that I have elected to write books for a trade audience. In such books, the author focuses on the central argument and devotes relatively little time to a consideration of alternative perspectives. A critic should not conclude, therefore, that the writer is ignorant of "all previous knowledge."

9. Which brings me to the core of Spillane's critique. Spillane would really like me to enter the world of sociology and social psychology, to join the discussion of power, roles, rulers, rulership, authority, position, and other sociological concepts. That is not what I was trying to do. Spillane would have preferred that I had written a book about influence; but that would not have brought about the connections between indirect and direct leadership that is central to my argument. Moreover, if I felt that the sociological approach was adequate for explicating leadership, I would not have felt the need to write a book focusing on leading *Minds*. I wanted to explore leadership from the perspective of cognitive psychology/cognitive science and that is what I did.

Good Work

In two crucial ways, the topic of "good work" differs from others reviewed in this collection. First of all, the GoodWork® Project is a long-term collaborative effort. It began in 1994–95 when three psychologists spent a year together at the Center for Advanced Studies in the Behavioral Sciences, a think-tank for psychologists and other social scientists. Out of that residency, there arose a project, now over a decade old, in which Mihaly Csikszentmihalyi, William Damon, and I have been investigating good work—work that is at once excellent, ethical, and engaging for the practitioners. We carry out this research through intensive interviews of leading practitioners of various professions. To this point, we have interviewed over twelve hundred exemplary professionals in nine different professions: medicine, law, journalism, genetics, theater, business, precollegiate education, higher education, and philanthropy. On the basis of these interviews, and various objective measures that are administered, we have sought to answer the following question: How do individuals who want to do good work—work that embodies the three aspects of goodness mentioned above—succeed or fail at a time when things are changing very quickly, markets are very powerful, and there are few, if any, counterforces to these market forces?

Because this is a large-scale empirical research project, its dimensions and scope depend on our capacity to raise funds. Initially, we sought support from a single source to investigate six domains. Had this funding become available, the project would long since have been completed. It would also have been a much less valuable project. Our struggle to survive as a "soft money" research project has resulted in a far less neat investigation but one that has yielded a wealth of insights across a number of professional domains. These conclusions could never have been anticipated when we began in the middle 1990s.

Which leads to the second distinguishing feature. The GoodWork project is ongoing—neither a finished nor a stationary target. Our first major publication was *GoodWork: When Excellence and Ethics Meet* (2001). Since then, we have published several more books and dozens of articles (see, for example, Fischman, Solomon, Greenspan, and Gardner 2004; Gardner and Shulman 2005); we also have an active website (goodworkproject.org) on which are posted dozens of technical reports. I am writing these lines in the summer of 2006, and by the time you read them, the project will have evolved further and perhaps in new directions.

Given such a large-scale project, it is not possible to summarize its findings. It must be stressed here that the project is first and foremost an empirical project. While we obviously had interests and hunches when we began, we had no settled ideas about what would be found. Are there lots of good workers or not very many? Are the challenges to good work the same or different across domains? Across ages? In different kinds of instititutions? To whom do good workers feel responsible? What causes bad work or compromised work? Can it be prevented? What are the best levers for promoting good work, and do they work similarly across domains, ages, cultures, generations, and institutions? We have secured at least preliminary answers to these questions but it is simply erroneous to suggest that this project is an *a priori* undertaking, and that we already know what we are going to find and what sense we are going to make of the findings. Indeed, the greatest pleasures of this project—I would add, of any scholarly project—are the surprises that emerge along the way.

It is important to point out that we have no assurance that all of our subjects are good workers—in fact, subsequent events have called into question the 'goodness' of the work of several of our subjects. We are not investigative reporters and, except in rare instances, we have little first-hand evidence of how our subjects actually behave at the work place. But in each case, our subjects have been nominated because of the recognized excellence of their work and because of their inclination to reflect on their activities. Moreover, in many cases, the explicit criterion of ethical distinction has been put forth as a reason for interviewing a candidate. We can say with confidence that the vast majority of our subjects aspire to do good work. And we would add that, even if they themselves may fall short on one or another criterion, their responses may still illuminate the ways in which good work *can* be carried out under present circumstances and pressures.

Our project is a research project and is properly judged on the basis of the quality of that research—a judgment on which the two critics disagree. Ultimately, however, we do have a broader social aim. We want to increase the incidence of good work. And so we have embarked on a number of applied interventions, where we work directly with new or established personnel in different domains. Readers may learn about the travelling curriculum, the Toolkit, and other interventions by visiting our website.

These points serve as a point of departure for any response to critiques. As a collaborative project, the writings reflect a consensus among the authors, and not simply my own point of view. As a still ongoing project, and one that is dependent on external support, the actual scope of the project is not completely under our control. We can only carry out research on issues for which we have funding. As new questions and challenges arise, we try—sometimes successfully, sometimes not—to secure funding to answer these questions.

The two critics here have very different stances toward the project. Carlos Vasco is extremely critical of the whole project; he suggests that the work undertaken under its banner is both aprioristic and second rate. Anna Craft, on the other hand, is quite sympathetic to the overall endeavor. In fact, her opening paragraphs suggest that the project is helpful in precisely the ways that Vasco denies. The issues she raises are more corrective and supplementary than fundamental, but are no less important—and they will be easier to deal with in our subsequent work.

Reply to Carlos Vasco

Vasco begins his critique by praising the previous work in psychology undertaken by the three researchers; he then questions why we have turned our attention to issues that are murkier and with respect to which our disciplinary tools are not as relevant. Certainly, it is easier to continue to do paradigmatic research—whether in one's own paradigm or that of others—than to shift course. Yet, studies of creative individuals suggest that just such a change-in-course often takes place in midlife. At least the three investigators are attempting something new—and opinions of 'the field' will necessarily differ on the extent of our initial and our ultimate success.

It is worth mentioning two impetuses for our project. First of all, as long time citizens of the United States, we have observed trends in our society that we find deeply troubling. While we happily accept aspects of the market, we do not believe that a society can endure successfully when all of its realms are governed by, and only by, market forces. And so we are necessarily interested in those individuals and institutions that have somehow succeeded in coping with, or not succumbing to, the powerful 'bottom line' mentality. Second, as regards our own earlier work, we have had opportunity to observe the misuses of our ideas. In my own case, I have witnessed applications of multiple intelligence theory that are unproductive and perhaps even destructive—for example, the labelling of certain racial and ethnic groups as possessing some intelligences but not others. In Csikszentmihalyi's case, his well-known concept of 'flow' has been hijacked by individuals who do not understand its theoretical or empirical connotations—for example, conflating it with happiness. And so there was a personal motivation as well—whether we can be good workers in our own chosen fields of social scientific research.

Vasco wonders whether we have abandoned psychology. In a word, we have not. While our work might be more accurately described as social science than as pure psychology (no experiments, no physiological measures, no control group), our way of conceptualizing is psychological to the core. We are working with individuals. We are trying to understand their ideas and their thought processes. We are devising models of how individuals operate in a complex problem space, which goals they have, which obstacles they confront, which strategies they devise to negotiate their way. Contrary to Vasco, we have not in the least assumed significant differences between good workers and not-so-good workers; this is a one hundred percent empirical question that we are pursuing. Indeed, it would probably be more accurate to critique us as being *too* psychological; as not paying sufficient attention to the broader institutional, cultural, and economic forces that impinge on good work. In our basic model, growing out of earlier work by

Csikszentmihalyi, we do in fact lay out the complex interaction among these forces; but our particular entry point remains the classical one for psychologists—the testimony and the responses to interventions of the individual subject.

The Four Components of Good Work

Note: The four components can interact with each other

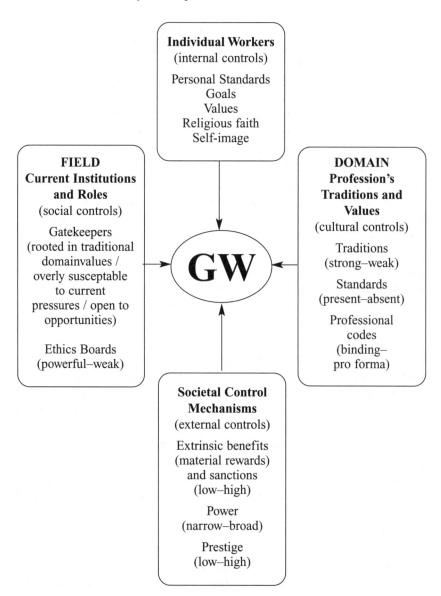

Individual Workers
(internal controls)

Personal Standards
Goals
Values
Religious faith
Self-image

**FIELD
Current Institutions
and Roles**
(social controls)

Gatekeepers
(rooted in traditional
domainvalues /
overly susceptable
to current
pressures / open to
opportunities)

Ethics Boards
(powerful–weak)

GW

**DOMAIN
Profession's
Traditions and
Values**
(cultural controls)

Traditions
(strong–weak)

Standards
(present–absent)

Professional
codes
(binding–
pro forma)

**Societal Control
Mechanisms**
(external controls)

Extrinsic benefits
(material rewards)
and sanctions
(low–high)

Power
(narrow–broad)

Prestige
(low–high)

The study of Good Work—and, less happily, of compromised or bad work—has yielded many surprising and provocative findings. One powerful organizing concept that has arisen from our work is the concept of *alignment*. As depicted in the Figure, good work is most likely to emerge when all four of the just-introduced components are pointing in the same direction; that is, the goals of the workers, the norms of the professions, the current institutions and roles, and the overall reward system of the society are aligned with one another. Conversely, to the extent that these forces are misaligned, GoodWork is difficult to achieve and sustain.

As to the charge that we are sociologists: this is true only in the sense that we are paying attention to factors that impinge on the individuals. As to the quip that we have taken the linguistic turn: not at all, in the sense that we feel that scholarly issues come down to matters of language (as might be claimed by Wittgenstenians like John White), but affirmative in the sense that we are deeply immersed in the reading and coding of transcripts that we have assembled.

Carlos Vasco is certainly correct that this is difficult work, and that at present it is almost completely U.S.A.-centric. To some extent, the focus of the work in the U.S.A. was our decision; we wanted to begin at a place where the threats to good work were patent and where we could carry out research personally. But we have always been open to the extension of the work elsewhere: and I am happy to report that interest in our work has arisen in many parts of the world—ranging from Scandinavia, where our colleague Hans Henrik Knoop has been engaged in studies of Good Work for several years to the Philippines where awards are now given annually to good workers in the areas of each of the intelligences. Anna Craft is hoping to do a study of good work among artists and educators in the United Kingdom. Our book *Good Work* was chosen as one of the ten most important books to appear in Hong Kong in 2003. And so the parochialness of our work need not—and will not, with any luck—be a permanent condition.

Vasco suggests that we are doing ethical or moral philosophy—engaged in analyzing what should count for good work and what not. Certainly this is true, though we see it as more of an inductive process than does he. We have not hesitated to stipulate the features that lead us to term work that is good within a profession. Such work needs to be based upon the deep, enduring values of the profession (as captured, for example, in the Hippocratic oath in medicine); it needs to respond to current conditions and opportunities without abandoning the fundamental, long standing values of the vocation; it involves responsibility to various spheres beyond one's own personal benefit, constant reflection on one's activities, consistency across situations, and above all a recognition of the lines that one will not cross, even though one could probably get away with it. Empirical work confirms that these ideals are widely held, even cross-culturally (Kidder, 2004).

Vasco raises the question of whether we are confusing description—how the world is—with prescription—how the world should be. Certainly, in our own mind, these are separate realms and deserve to remain so. I would add that we also make a clear distinction between the 'emic' view—how their work appears to practitioners, and the 'etic' view—the sense that we make of their testimony. As investigators, our job is to keep these separate realms clearly in mind, to indicate when we are reporting 'emic' findings and when we are assuming an 'etic' pose; when we are describing what we find and when we are indicating what we would like to be the case.

An example may be appropriate. To our surprise, we discovered that grant givers do not, on the whole, identify with the field of philanthropy. Rather, they see their role as 'philanthropoid' as temporary; they think of themselves chiefly as representatives of the area that they are funding—be it the arts, or the environment, or education. The lack of identification with philanthropy is an important discovery—it distinguishes philanthropy from every other profession that we studied. So far, purely description. Should we move to recommendations, however, we will have entered the realm of prescription. The prescriptions that we make will depend on the value system that we embrace. Should we believe that philanthropists ought to be professionals, in the same way as lawyers or doctors, then we need to figure out ways in which to create a profession and help individuals become part of it (etic) and feel part of it (emic). On the other hand, we might think that the 'non-identification' with philanthropy is actually positive; in which case, we would resist efforts to professionalize the domain and point out the advantages of easy entry to and exit from grant-giving and of maintaining a primary identification with the home domain. One could even envision a bifocal system, with some grantsmaker becoming part of an ongoing profession, while other choose to cherish their amateur status. I fail to see a flaw in this approach.

Similarly, with respect to 'emic' (personal) as opposed to 'etic' (distanced) view of testimony: We listen carefully to our subjects and take their reflections seriously—our analyses always begin there. But we do not check our skepticism at the door. Before conducting an interview, we have done a great deal of background research. Should a subject give a response that seems inauthentic or false, we will politely but insistently challenge the response and note how the subject reacts to the challenge. We also do a great deal of triangulation, thus integrating the interview with what other individuals say about the person in question and with how the person is portrayed in the media. These additional sources of information nuance what we have found and how we report it. While we cannot know whether we have been fooled in a particular case, we are quite confident that, with approximately one hundred interviews in each domain, we have arrived at a story that is essentially correct—at least for the historical moment when the interviews were conducted.

Vasco suggests that only those who agree with our ethical philosophy will accept our findings, recommendations, and conclusions. That itself is an empirical question. I think Vasco is wrong and the 'test' that I suggest is the hypocrisy test. To the extent that an individual disagrees with our ethical philosophy, he or she is welcome to state the rival ethical philosophy, look at our results, and make sense of them.

The renowned sociologist Samuel Stouffer used to begin his 'first course' in sociology by giving his students a list of findings from sociology. The students were asked to explain each finding as best they could; being dutiful students, they did so. Stouffer then revealed to the students that none of the findings was in fact true; that indeed, empirical work had demonstrated the exact opposite. I mention this because Vasco intimates that our findings were established *a priori*. Not only is this false; but I defy him to predict what we would find in a new domain that we have not yet investigated, or if the studies were to be carried out in his own country of Colombia. It is trivially easy to justify a finding after the fact—just as one can justify the opposite finding with facility. We do empirical work precisely because we won't know which is the case—A, not A, or an unexpected blend of A, not A—until the work has actually been carried out and analyzed.

Vasco makes the surprising suggestion that the person most truthful about his work is Matt Drudge, the Internet gossip columnist. I am certain that Vasco is wrong about this—many of our subjects made painstaking efforts to be as candid as possible, often at the cost of considerable anguish, even tears. But Vasco is wrong for two additional reasons. First of all, Drudge says that he does not care about telling the truth—and so what he himself says that he should not be believed. More important, the perspective of Drudge cuts to the very heart of journalism—where individuals attempt (admittedly not always with success), to get the story correct one hundred percent of the time and to admit promptly when the story contains error. Drudge is not a journalist at all, precisely because he does not abide by this value. And so, while what he offers may in fact be aligned with the kind of titillation or aggravation that his audience happens to want, it has nothing to do with the desire of a populace to know what is actually happening in issues of domestic or foreign moment.

And here I come to the heart of my clash with my long time friend Carlos Vasco. Taken literally, Vasco emerges as a complete cynic. There is no such thing as good work, it can't be discovered, the only persons to be believed are those that challenge the notion of good work. As an individual who himself strives to carry out good work, Carlos knows the difference in his own life. Indeed, he epitomizes Oscar Wilde's characterization of the cynic as a disillusioned idealist. The purpose of the GoodWork project is to direct attention to the idea of Good Work: that even if we cannot find any individual who meets all facets of good work perfectly, we can learn from those who at least attempt to carry out good work and to reveal to us their struggles and their successes. I do agree with Vasco that the quality of work globally is crucially affected by how work is carried out in the United States at the present time; all the more reason, I say, to pursue this work further but also to broaden it to other societies as well.

Perhaps Vasco is wise enough to have anticipated our recommendations before the fact. We were not, which is why we carried out this large-scale empirical project. But even if we had anticipated the results—and remember Stouffer's caution here—I don't think that they would have been credible without the appreciable database that we have accumulated. When you seek changes—and ultimately, that is what we hope to achieve—you need to be convincing. And, as Anna Craft points out, that requires data as well as reasons.

A few smaller points. Vasco questions whether the 'individual' is a category different from 'the field'. Most assuredly. The individual is simply the solo practitioner, who has to decide, based on conscience and other factors, how to behave and explain her behavior. The field consists of roles and institutions that exist quite apart from individuals. The role of Pulitzer Prize judge, the institution of *The New York Times*, indeed the order of the Jesuits, are all instances of the field; of course, they are composed of individuals but the norms and constraints of the field persist despite the regular appearance and disappearance of specific individuals. Vasco also wonders about how judgments of alignment are made. To some extent they are made by individuals themselves, to some extent by analysts, like us. But these measurements are not made lightly. If people are attracted to a profession in droves, that is a sign of alignment; if they leave rapidly, of nonalignment. Efforts to bring about better alignment can also be measured; do individuals attempt to change their home institution and, if they fail, do they set up new ones that better capture their values or the values of the domain? (Hirshman 1970). On neither account is good work guaranteed; nonetheless the tests of hypocrisy and transparency are valuable in distinguishing instances of genuine good work from those that merely claim to march under that banner.

Reply to Anna Craft

Writing from a different vantage point, and with a far more sympathetic view of the overall undertaking, Craft raises a number of intriguing queries. Questioning our emphasis on the work place, she poses the question of the origins of good work, and the factors that enable it to emerge or to be thwarted in the current, pressured environment.

In our own studies, we have not examined good work in young children. The youngest persons with whom we have worked systematically have been secondary school students; the evidence that we have concerning the childhood of good workers has been almost entirely retrospective. At early ages, of course, young people do not think of themselves as being gainfully employed in some kind of profession. Very few think seriously about experiences at the workplace, that still lie one or two decades in the future. To the extent that they think about work at all, it is likely to be in one of several ways: the work that their parents do; the work that they are expected to carry out at school, (and, at least sometimes, at home or at a part- time job); or their 'work' on some kind of a hobby, like playing an instrument or pursuing an athletic activity. No doubt the origins of good work, or work that is not so good, lie (at least in part) in these early occupations and preoccupations. Studies focused on young individuals could be quite illuminating. Even more important are longitudinal studies of changing attitudes toward work. Fortunately, my colleague Mihaly Csikszentimihaly has been involved in just such as study and its findings will inform our own work with older subjects (Csikzentmihalyi and Schneider 2000).

If there is one finding that has emerged across all of our studies, it has been the high degree of stress involved in work today. To be sure, we have no metric to determine whether stress was as acute in times past, particularly for the high level professionals who constitute the centerpiece of our study. But I am confident in suggesting that concerns about stress and balance emerge at an earlier age than ever before; and that the lack of permanence in most jobs is an aggravating factor. (Only judges and professors still have tenure). These stresses are likely to be even more acute for women, and, perhaps, for minorities, than for mainstream men. As a result, such 'at risk' individuals will need to develop compensatory mechanisms and strategies.

As one looks toward the home, the role of women in good work indeed comes to the fore. In the few analyses that we have done so far, the stance of women toward good work is rather similar to that of men, though the nuances may differ. For example, women feel more conflicted than men about the devotion of energies to home and family versus work, and somewhat less agentive in their role—perhaps because they are less likely than men to be completely in command at the workplace. But more analyses are in the works, and interested readers can follow our progress at the aforementioned website. As women find excellent role models, and as the quantity and quality of help at home increases, I expect that gender differences will attenuate.

Craft also questions our focus on 'high end' achievement and 'middle' or 'big C' creativity. Clearly, we could carry out studies of ordinary workers and we would like to do so. However, good work is likely to be a different enterprise among professionals. Professionals belong to a guild that has been licensed, and members of that guild are accorded a fair amount of autonomy and prestige in return for the performance of services in a disinterested way. Once we (or other researchers) direct our attention to those outside the professional classes, different motivations and rewards are likely to emerge.

Like Vasco, Craft notes the Americentric quality of our study. She raises the intriguing possibility that good work might look different in societies that are less individualistic, and more collectivistic. That may well be true—again, this is an empirical issue. I find it curious in this regard that she notes the willingness, on the part of Asian families, to be separated from children at an early age. While this voluntary separation may reflect confidence that proper values can be inculcated by others, it may also culminate in an abandonment of personal responsibility—a gigantic threat to good work. And, as she notes, creativity may be less likely to develop in the absence of the confident and supportive home environment from which "creating minds" have traditionally benefited (Gardner 1993).

Finally, Craft wonders why we do not have an explicit developmental model of ethical engagement. This question looms especially relevant since William Damon is perhaps the world's leading expert in moral development and has written extensively on the topic (1988, 1994). I could quip that we know too much to have introduced the model; but in truth, for the reasons stated above, we actually know too little about ethical development with respect to the workplace to be able to answer this question. In recent collaborative work with Seana Moran, I have examined developmental trajectories in four spheres: science, art, political leadership, and moral leadership. The latter summary represents our effort to make sense of the disparate findings in that arena and to place them in the context of other developmental trajectories. The Kohlberg and Gilligan models both focus on subjects' intrepretations of moral dilemmas. In our view, ethical engagement involves the actual activities of individuals, and so we have focussed on studies of those young persons who 'vote with their feet'. One intriguing finding is that such young persons often are raised by single mothers (Moran and Gardner 2006; Michaelson 2001).

In an allusion to my most recent work, Anna Craft reviews her own arguments and questions whether—using the seven 'Re' levers that I have identified—she has succeeded in 'changing my mind' (Gardner 2004). I applaud her use of this scheme and, as noted above, I consider her recommendations to be important. Alas, there is one ingredient that is still missing—that of resources to carry out the research. Help from any quarter is welcome!

Arts Education

The psychology of the arts is the area of research in which I have been involved for the longest period of time. In the late 1960s, as a budding developmental psychologist, I was struck by the fact that few developmentalists gave thought to the arts; as far as they were concerned, the terminus of intellectual development was the mind and the *persona* of the scientist. This perspective struck me as incredibly myopic. I determined to elucidate the characteristic skills, thought processes, and creative approaches of artists.

This orientation toward artistic development might have blossomed even if I had not met Nelson Goodman; after all, I had been involved with the arts since childhood. But my encountering of this major philosopher, and his decision to found Project Zero in 1967, had enormous influence on my subsequent career. I began to work at Project Zero as one of the first assistants and have remained there ever since. I studied and began to absorb Goodman's (1976) perspective on artistry. I commenced a research program on the development of artistic skills and capacities. And I moved into management positions, ultimately directing the research of other investigators.

The reasoning behind my initial research was as follows. As the most important thinker in the field, Piaget (1983) has provided a convincing portrait of the development of scientific thinking. Suppose that Piaget had had an analogous interest in artistic thinking. What end-states of artistry would he have investigated? With what methods? What portrait of artistic development would ensue? In one line of research, my colleagues (notably Ellen Winner) and I investigated the origin and development of specific artistic skills—for example, sensitivity to artistic style, sensitivity to artistic expression, the development of metaphoric thinking, the emergence of narrative capacity. In this line of work, we were strongly influenced by the descriptions of artistic competences put forth by leading scholars, such as Rudolf Arnheim (1954) and E.H. Gombrich (1960) in the visual arts, I.A. Richards (1929) in literature, and Leonard Meyer (1956) in music. In another line of research (notably with Dennie Wolf) my colleagues and I monitored the development in a small group of young children of the emergence of capacities in seven different symbolic realms (music, bodily-expression, two dimensional depiction, three-dimensional depiction, symbolic play, narrative, and numerical competence).

Project Zero has been a large-scale collaborative effort—one much looser than the GoodWork Project. For many years, David Perkins headed the Cognitive Skills Group, which explored artistic and other kinds of thinking chiefly in adult practitioners. I directed the Development Group, which examined budding artistic competences through the lens of developmental psychology. As Graeme Sullivan points out, our enterprise expanded and changed over the years. Our focus on artistry broadened to a consideration of the range of disciplines. And our research focus—initially, philosophical, then primarily psychological—was complemented by involvement in various educational interventions, including several notable efforts in the arts.

Project Zero has emerged as one of the few research centers in the world with a long-term interest and focus on the range of the arts (see pzweb.harvard.edu). We have connected with other leading scholars and universities and have over the years hosted many individuals and events of note. We have been centrally involved in discussions and debates about arts education. Our focus on the arts as primarily cognitive was originally seen as controversial; now that perspective is widely accepted. We have also been critical of the efforts to construe the arts instrumentally—as means of enhancing performance in 'real' or 'basic' or 'core' school subjects. This perspective, too, has engendered controversy. Nelson Goodman gave our Project the name 'zero' as a taunting suggestion that nothing systematic was known about artistic processes and education. We hope and trust that, over the past forty years, we have moved toward 'plus one'.

The two critics of this work have both had long term associations with Project Zero, dating back to the time of their respective doctoral dissertations. They know our work well, which includes knowledge of its limitations. Both focus on the visual arts, Graeme Sullivan more from the vantage point of the practicing artist, David Pariser chiefly as an arts educator. Sullivan presents a broad, synoptic view of my own efforts over a forty-year period; Pariser focuses on a specific, controversial claim put forth twenty years ago by Ellen Winner and me, and recently defended with great vigor by another long-term Project Zero associate, Jessica Davis.

Reply to Graeme Sullivan

I appreciate Sullivan's account of the development of my work in artistic development and education; I found it instructive. For the most part, I find his construal sensible. He rightly perceives me as someone who strove to bring a more rigorous and more scientific perspective to the study of the arts. My chosen disciplinary lenses, of course, were developmental, cognitive, and neuro-psychology. In exploring a new terrain, uncertain steps are to be expected. At times, this aim annoyed scientists, who either did not appreciate a focus on the arts or who felt that their science was being stretched; at times, this mission annoyed artists and arts educators, who feared that the arts were being distorted in the service of a particular psychological tool or concept.

Because of personal interests and funding opportunities, we had the luxury of looking at artistry directly, as psychologists, without the need for practical 'deliverables'. When the *Zeitgeist* changed, in the early 1980s, investigators at Project Zero were in a favorable position to direct attention to educational issues and problems. Again, some of our specific slants were controversial. In Arts PROPEL, we offered a critique of the then-dominant view of 'discipline based arts education'. In our view, DBAE assumed too scholastic a view of arts education, and risked relegating the making of the arts into a marginal activity. In a collaborative project with the Lincoln Center Institute, we pushed toward the identification of specific learning achievements, thereby placing under scrutiny the putatively ineffable 'aesthetic experience'.

As in other areas of work described in earlier sections, I see the Project Zero approach to the arts and arts education as opening salvos in a conversation, rather than as definitive demonstrations or answers to questions. If we can elevate the debate, and move it in productive directions, then our major mission has been fulfilled. As I read his essay, Graeme Sullivan construes us in this spirit. He does not confuse the trees with the woods.

Against that opening context, let me move to specific comments. Sullivan correctly identifies me as a scientist, but then focuses on two more specific aspects of my work: the cognitive emphasis and the computational metaphor. As noted, the cognitive emphasis was initially controversial. We saw this focus as a counterweight to earlier views of the arts as ineffable, emotional, or magical. We have never seen the cognitive tack as a full description of the arts; we have never sought to deny the social, cultural, and emotional aspects of the arts. But once one dons a cognitive hat, then computational models of production and perception follow ineluctably—cognitivists nowadays think in computational terms.

Computation, however, has always been a metaphor. To be sure, the analogy put forth by Warren McCulloch in the early 1940s between logical operators and neuronal circuits was a brilliant one. But we do not have electronic computers in our heads; and silicon does not work in the same manner as neural tissue. Importantly, and Sullivan adverts to this, the regnant models of computation have changed enormously during the time of the cognitive revolution. Twenty-five years ago, the dominant model of the computer was the von Neumann serial computer. Today, the vast majority of investigators are examining the operation of neural networks of various sorts. The assumptions and procedures of these two classes of computers are totally different from one another. It is probably the case that some aspects of human cognition—for example, the perception of painting styles—are better modeled through artificial neural networks; while other aspects of human cognition—for example, syntactic operations in language—are more appropriately modeled through the traditional serial computer.

Underlying Sullivan's critique, I believe, is the implication that he is an artist, not a scientist, and that the elucidation of the arts is better tackled by card-carrying artists than by card-carrying scientists. He sees science as too rational, too neat, to embrace the essential messiness and unpredictability of the arts.

In this assertion Sullivan is supported by the rapid changes that have taken place in the arts in the past forty years. When I began writing, abstract expressionism—a prototypical form of modernism—was at its height. We had scarcely heard of pop art, op art, conceptual art, computer art, performance art, and all sorts of mixed media and new media. Sullivan rightly wonders whether the scheme developed some decades ago can handle the potpourri of artistic forms that exist today and the many new ones (including computer-generated forms) that will doubtless emerge in the years to come.

It is useful to tease out two issues. First of all, in my work, did I use too narrow a set of examples of art? For example, would studies of style perception have been different, had I drawn on the arts of 2000, rather than the arts of 1900? Second of all, would the studies have benefited if I had been willing to use methods that are more artistic, less scientific, in the textbook senses of those terms?

On these questions, I tend to be latitudinarian with respect to the first, and conservative as regards the second. That is, I believe Sullivan is right in critiquing the definition of art that has underwritten most of our studies. It should be broadened and such a broadening might lead to different results. As just one example, I am perfectly happy to construe artistic involvement today as entailing the assumptions of several roles by one person. Indeed, I am inclined to rethink my central metaphor for the arts. In the 1970s I saw the arts as forms of communication from artist to audience using a circumscribed set of symbol system. Nowadays, I am inclined to think of the arts more broadly. I would consider as artistic any activity that stimulates new thought or new experiences in its participants. What distinguishes artistic from other cognitive realms is the fact that, in the arts, the form—the mode of presentation—of the activity contributes to its effectiveness and imprints itself on the psyche of the artistic participant.

As for methods of investigation, I believe that Project Zero is well advised to be conservative in the methods that we use, so long as we do not distort the arts in the process. Graeme Sullivan is right to raise the question of whether we should have used play-doh rather than modelling clay in our studies. However it is an empirical question whether the results of our studies would actually have been different across these instantiations of three-dimensional media. More generally, I love good, complex, messy questions; but unlike most post-modernists, I don't want to end with questions, I want to come up with the best answers that I can, conceding that they may be imperfect and partial.

Let me point out, however, that my view of the relevant sciences has not remained unchanged. At a theoretical level, I began as an unreconstructed Piagetian but evolved into a critic of Piaget, and one who has since assumed a far more modular view of the mind. Domain-specificity has become an ever larger consideration in our studies. I began as a standard experimentalist but moved soon to studies that were observational, ethnographic, even phenomenological in nature. And while Sullivan does not mention them, my studies of arts education in China were an effort to pay far greater attention to cultural influences in arts—see *To Open Minds: Chinese Clues to the Dilemma of American Education* (1989). The picture of arts and arts education presented in *Arts Education and Human Development* (1990) is quite different from that presented in *The Arts and Human Development* (1973).

In his concluding remarks, Sullivan laments the apparent sidelining of arts education in my personal agenda and in that of Project Zero. It is true that I have not contributed actively to arts research in recent years. However, that biographical datum need not document a trend; in fact, in both the Good Work Project and in my studies of interdisciplinary education, I have returned to artistic issues. And my current membership on the board of the Museum of Modern Art has thrust me directly into questions about how to educate an audience with respect to contemporary as well as modern (1875–1975) art, and to art forms that are less readily assimilated than Impressionist painting. As for Project Zero, I am happy to reassure Sullivan that the arts are alive and well in our research atelier. Current work ranges from studies of what is actually learned in arts classes to studies of how the brains of young persons are affected by musical training to studies of how commitment is manifest in the lives of creative writers (Hetland *et al.* in press; Moran 2006). I am confident that debates in arts and arts education will continue to be informed by the work of Project Zero, and the researchers who have been trained there or influenced by ideas first developed by its researchers (Davis 2005; Efland 2002).

Reply to David Pariser

In my observations of my own children during the preschool years, and in my early efforts as a teacher of young children, I was struck by an intriguing phenomenon: While the products and the processes of children involved in the arts would rarely be confused with those of mature artists, there were clear connections or resonances between these two groups. On the process side, children would become fascinated by a pattern and would explore it for hours on end, seemingly oblivious to diversions or sheer fatigue. This immersion could happen with words, melodies, blocks, or lines on a page. Moreover, the freedom and flexibility with which children approach these materials were notable. On the product side, at least some of the art works of the young children evoked associations to those fashioned by mature artists: they shared aspects of originality, flavorfulness, expression—to use three descriptors that often leapt to mind. I wrote about the parallels between child and adult art in a 1980 book *Artful Scribbles: The Significance of Children's Art.*

As an empirical investigator, I wondered whether one could find objective support for this apparent affinity between the child as artist and the adult artist. Ellen Winner, other colleagues, and I undertook a set of studies of children's art work in language, visual arts, and music. These investigations pointed to intriguing parallels across symbolic domains. Once children had gained an initial mastery of the basic elements of a symbol system, they began to experiment with the arrangement of these elements. In our society, by the age of five or so, at least some children regularly created picaresque stories, apt metaphors, tunes, drawings, and three-dimensional constructions that exhibited originality, balance, a sense of completion (Chukovsky 1968; Gardner 1982; Milbrath 1998). And nearly all children at least occasionally fashioned symbolic products that were notable for such properties.

Speed forward a few years and one finds a very different picture. Whatever the symbolic domain, the eight-, nine-, or ten-year old is determined to figure out the rules of that domain and to follow those rules scrupulously. From the point of view of the observer, this trend gives rise to a mentality that we named the 'literal stage'. Spurning flights of fancy or symbolic adventuring, the 'middle-aged' child now wants to fashion drawings that are realistic; use language in ways that are precise; sing and perform musical compositions in the specified rhythmic and tonal manner. In all probability, this tendency is exacerbated by school, where a premium is placed on accuracy. Yet the trend would probably exist even in the absence of formal schooling; indeed the timing of formal school may be tied to the child's growing proclivity to 'get it right'.

In his essay, David Pariser takes a critical look at the U-shaped phenomenon, as it is manifest (or not manifest) in the visual arts. Essentially, he makes two points—one art-critical, the other empirical. First of all, he points out that the graphic work of young children resonates particularly—and perhaps exclusively—with those who partake of a modernist sensibility. Put specifically, the art work of four- or five-year-olds in a Western context takes on additional meaning if one is immersed in the paintings of Miro, Klee, Picasso, as well as works of abstract expressionists. He goes on to argue, along with Fineberg (1998), that these modern artists spent time studying the works of young children. Perhaps it is more accurate to say that the adults resemble the children, rather than that the children resemble the adults.

Pariser's point is well taken. It is as plausible to claim that artists are attempting to emulate—or capture something of—young children, as it is to say that young children are aspiring to be artists, or that both are reflecting the same underlying processes. Moreover, the testamentary evidence supports Pariser's claims. If I had been writing in the early nineteenth century, I probably would not have discerned the same value in the works of young children. Of course, that could also have been my limitation. It might be that young children are sensitive to, or capable of feats, that have simply been invisible to prejudiced older observers. And, indeed, the history of developmental psychology over the last fifty years is a sustained documentation of ever greater capacities in ever younger children. And it is hardly a secret that, if you want to learn a new language, or win in the card game *Concentration*, you should trade in your brain for that of a randomly-chosen five year old.

Note, moreover, that, from the first, I have been fully aware of the point that Pariser makes. Here, unedited, are the opening sentences of my 1980 book *Artful Scribbles*:

> A century or two ago few individuals could have conceived of, let alone taken seriously, a book on children's drawings. The mere suggestion that these youthful productions should be pondered, or considered as works of art, would have seemed ludicrous. At that time childhood itself was not considered an important period of life, and so the activities in which young children engaged were hardly considered a topic suitable for scholarly inquiry. Further, any thought of children's drawings as beautiful or intriguing could not have held currency. A society that valued the realistic drawings of an Ingres, a Millet, or a Constable would find little reason to cherish the seemingly careless scribbles of its children. (p. 3)

Pariser's other point is empirical. In a series of studies, he and colleagues have shown that U-shaped curves reflect the knowledge and sensibility of the judges, as much as the objective properties of the art work. Put simply, the more the judge is immersed in Western modernist sensibility, and the more that he or she focuses on expressive properties of the child's work, the more likely a 'U' will emerge. Conversely, those who are younger, not artists, not immersed in the modernist sensibility, will pay little attention to, and find little merit in, the graphic experts of the young. They are like the pre-1900 audience described in the preceding parargraph.

Faced with Pariser's results, one may offer two kinds of ripostes. Jessica Davis (1997) has taken issue with Pariser's instructions and paradigm; she insists that under the appropriate experimental conditions U-shaped curves will continue to be manifest. Davis points out that Pariser's judges receives less precise instructions, used much less refined categorical distinctions, and attained lower degrees of reliability. I suspect that experimentalists will continue to explore the conditions under which U's do or do not emerge.

I see no reason to question Pariser's more recent results, which contextualize his findings properly. The U-shaped curve becomes not the universal, univocal story of children's artistic development, but rather one of a number of possible patterns. Science proceeds by differentiation, and Pariser has made a significant differentiation. It is important to underscore that non-U curves are not the 'natural' picture either. When I studied artistic development in young children in China twenty years ago, I saw that children were systematically discouraged—even forbidden—from making abstract patterns: all drawings had to represent something. Abstract patterns by four-year-olds were renamed 'wallpaper' by their nervous teachers. It is hardly surprising that U's do not emerge under such conditions. I would speculate—indeed, I would wager—that as China becomes increasingly influenced by a Western sensibility, U's may begin to emerge at the very schools where they would have been anathema a quarter century ago.

As I have repeatedly stressed, one cannot and should not ever go directly from a scientific finding to an educational recommendation. Pariser is entirely correct to caution against any direct educational implications of a U-shaped curve in artistic development. Needless to say, to the extent that the "U" claim is flawed, educational implications should be approached with even greater caution. But we should not toss out the baby with the bath water here. Teachers should be encouraged to look carefully at, and not dismiss, the works of the young. To the extent that these early works contain the seeds of future artistry, that fact should be cherished. Most important, teachers ought to be open to the plurality of routes to artistry, and to the multitude of intentions and meanings that may be embedded in any work. They should not rush to inculcate any particular artistic route—be it premodern, modernist, or postmodern. I suspect that David Pariser would agree with these sentiments.

By his very focus on a specific line of study, Pariser leaves unexamined a set of larger questions, the sorts that Sullivan and I explore. It may be, for example, that many young students are simply sloppy or undirected, but what about those with special talents? Milbrath (1998) has shown that in early childhood, a small set of children are already very sensitive to contours, placement, line, and texture; these 'perception-oriented' children are likely to exhibit an artistic trajectory that is distinct from the 'cognitive-oriented' mainstream. Pariser himself has studied the juvenilia of world-class artists, including Klee, Picasso, and Toulouse-Lautrec, and has noted striking facets of expression, technical expertise, and composition in their early works. It is important to know at what time, and in what ways, future artistic creators initially signal their distinctiveness. The advent of computer-aids to depiction make available to children all sorts of moves which would have been inconceivable some decades ago. And we should not forget the amazing depictions by the occasional autistic individuals who—as early as five or six—can produce works that appear to have emerged from a Renaissance atelier (Selfe 1977).

In the years since the controversy about U's was first joined, developmental psychology has undergone a number of revolutions. We now recognize that young children, even infants, already posses a vast amount of knowledge about the world. This knowledge, which many consider innate, is called 'core knowledge' and, upon it, more specific and culturally-nuanced forms of knowledge must be constructed. We also know that there are early intimations of advanced knowledge across many domains: four years olds have theories of psychology, biology, and physics; seven-year-olds have 'common-sense' understanding of phenomena that won't coalesce for a decade; fundamental intuitions about fairness exist not only in preschoolers but even in primates. Moreover, almost no domain features a single trajectory toward mastery; rather, one finds complex networks, webs, trajectories—including quite idiosyncratic ones. Even as we differentiate the claims of U/non-U into its component parts, we should remain alert to the possibility that young children may anticipate adult artistry in a myriad of ways that we cannot yet conceive with precision. A first draft knowledge is an initial knowledge, a draft knowledge; but it also may harbor prescient intimations of lies ahead.

A final point. In other writings, Pariser has noted that the innocence which we associate with early childhood may be 'at risk'. In a postmodern global world, young children may already have access to information and methods that integrate them more readily into the adult world. Pariser has mixed feelings about these trends, as do I. Childhood is not—or at least should not be—simply preparation of the adult years and what happens thereafter. The fresh vision of the young child, and her earliest, untutored efforts to use media of expression should not be readily dismissed. The rules and conventions of society are powerful but they can also be powerfully constraining. The artists of the twentieth century—and scientific counterparts ranging from Albert Einstein to Jean

Piaget—were not deluding themselves when they sought to capture and to recreate the special conditions of early childhood. Whatever the ultimate shape of the trajectory of artistic development, a deeper understanding of its initial phases may have profound scientific and educational implications.

REFERENCES

Arnheim, R. 1954. *Art and Visual Perception*. Berkeley: University of California Press.

Battro, A., and P. Denham. 2002. *Hacia una Inteligencia Digital*. Buenos Aires.

Case, R. 1991. *The Mind's Staircase*. Hillsdale: Erlbaum.

Ceci, S. 1996. *On Intelligence*. Expanded edition. Cambridge, Massachusetts: Harvard University Press.

Chen, J., and H. Gardner. 2005. Assessment Based on Multiple Intelligences Theory. In D. Flanagan and P. Harrison, eds., *Contemporary Intellectual Assessment: Theories, Tests, and Issues*. Second edition (New York: Guilford), pp. 77–102.

Chukovsky, K. 1968. *From Two to Five*. Berkeley: University of California Press.

Cole, M., and B. Means. 1981. *Comparative Studies of How People Think*. Cambridge, Massachusetts: Harvard University Press.

Csikszentmihalyi, M. 1996. *Creativity*. New York: HarperCollins.

Csikszentmihalyi, M., and B. Schneider. 2000. *Becoming Adult*. New York: Basic Books.

Damon, W. 1988. *The Moral Child*. New York: Free Press.

———. 1994. *Greater Expectations*. New York: Free Press.

Davis, J. 1997. *Does the U in the U-Curve Also Stand for Universals? Reflections on Provisional Doubts*. Studies in Art Education 39:3, pp. 179–185.

———. 2005. *Framing Education as Art: The Octopus Has a Good Day*. New York: Teachers College Press.

De Meredieu, F. 1974. *Le dessin de l'enfant*. Paris: Editions universitaires Jean-Pierre de Large.

Dehaene, S. 1997. *The Number Sense*. New York: Oxford University Press.

Efland, A. 2002. *Art and Cognition: Integrating the Visual Arts in the Curriculum*. New York: Teachers College Press.

Feldman, D.H. 1980. *Beyond Universals in Cognitive Development*. Norwood: Ablex.

Feldman, D., M. Csikszentmihalyi, and H. Gardner. 1994. *Changing the World. A Framework for the Study of Creativity*. Westport: Praeger.

Fineberg, J. 1998. *Discovering Child Art*. Princeton: Princeton University Press.

Fischer, K. and T. Bidell. 1998. Dynamic Development of Psychological Structures in Action and Thought, In W. Damon, ed., *Handbook of Child Psychology* (New York: Wiley), Volume 1, pp. 467–562.

Fischman, W., B. Solomon, D. Greenspan, and H. Gardner. 2004. *Making Good: How Young People Cope with Moral Dilemmas at Work*. Cambridge, Massachusetts: Harvard University Press.

Flynn, J.R. 1988. The Ontology of Intelligence. In J. Forge, ed., *Measurement, Realism, and Objectivity* (Dordrecht: Reidel), pp. 1–40.

Galenson, D. 2001. *Painting Outside the Lines: Patterns of Creativity in Modern Art*. Cambridge, Massachusetts: Harvard University Press.

Gardner, H. 1980. *Artful Scribbles*. New York: Basic Books.

———. 1982. *Art, Mind, and Brain*. New York: Basic Books.

———. 1999. Are There Additional Intelligences? The Case for Natural, Spiritual, and Existential Intelligences. In J. Kane, ed., *Education, Information, and Transformation* (Saddle River: Prentice Hall), pp. 111–131.

———. 2004. Changing Minds. Boston: Harvard Business chool Press.

———. 2006. *Multiple Intelligences: New Horizons*. New York: Basic Books.

Gardner, H. and L. Shulman, eds. 2005. On Professions and Professionals. *Daedalus* 134, p. 3.

Gardner, H., J.S. Benjamin, and L. Pettingill. 2006. An Examination of Trust in Contemporary American Society. Available at goodworkproject.org.

Getzels, J. and M. Csikszentmihalyi. 1976. *The Creative Vision*. New York: Wiley.

Gilligan, C. 1982. *In a Different Voice*. Cambridge, Massachusetts: Harvard University Press.

Gombrich, E.H. 1960. *Art and Illusion*. Princeton: Princeton University Press.

Goodman, N. 1976. *Languages of Art*. Second edition. Indianapolis: Bobbs-Merrill.

Gould, S.J. 1981. *The Mismeasure of Man*. New York: Norton.

Gruber, H., and P. Barrett. 1981. *Darwin on Man*. Second edition. Chicago: University of Chicago Press.

Hamlyn, D. 1978. *Experience and the Growth of Understanding*. London: Routledge.

Harré, R. 1983. *Personal Being: A Theory for Individual Psychology*. Oxford: Blackwell.

Heath, S.B. 1983. *Ways with Words: Language, Life, and Work in Communities and Classroom*. New York: Cambridge University Press.

Herrnstein, R. and C. Murray. 1994. *The Bell Curve*. New York: Free Press.

Hetland, L., S. Veenema, P. Palmer, K. Sheridan, and E. Winner. In press. *Studio Thinking: How Visual Arts Teaching Can Promote Disciplined Habits of Mind*. New York: Teachers College Press.

Hirschman, A.O. 1970. *Exit, Voice, and Loyalty*. Cambridge, Massachusetts: Harvard University Press.

Kanazawa, S. 2004. General Intelligence as a Domain-specific Adaptation. *Psychological Review* 11, pp. 512–523.

Kidder, R. 2004. *Moral Courage*. New York: Morrow.

Kohlberg, L. 1981. *The Philosophy of Moral Development, Volume l*. New York: HarperCollins.

Kornhaber, M.. E. Fierros, and S. Veenema. 2004. *Multiple Intelligences: Best Ideas from Research and Practice*. Boston: Allyn and Bacon.

Krechevsky, M. 1998. *Project Spectrum Preschool Assessment Handbook*. New York: Teachers College Press.

Kuhn, D. 2005. *Education for Thinking*. Cambridge, Massachusetts: Harvard University Press.

Kuhn, T.S. 1970. *The Structure of Scientific Revolutions*. Second edition. Chicago: University of Chicago Press.

Lewontin, R., S. Rose, and L. Kamin. 1984. *Not in Our Genes*. New York: Pantheon.

Martindale, C. 1990. *The Clockwork Muse*. New York: Basic Books.

Meyer, L. 1956. *Emotion and Meaning in Music*. Chicago: University of Chicago Press.

Michaelson, M. 2002. *Poised to Act: Profiles of Fifteen Young Activists*. Unpublished doctoral dissertation. Harvard Graduate School of Education.

Milbrath, C. 1998. *Patterns of Artistic Development in Children*. New York: Cambridge University Press.

Moran, S. and H. Gardner. 2006. The Development of Extraordinary Achievements. In W. Damon, ed., *Handbook of Child Psychology*. Sixth edition (New York: Wiley), Volume 2.

Moran, S. 2006. *A Study of Literary Commitment*. Unpublished doctoral dissertation, Harvard Graduate School of Education.

Murray, C. 2003. *Human Accomplishment*. New York: HarperCollins.

Olson, D. 2003. *Psychological Theory and Educational Reform*. New York: Cambridge University Press.

Perkins, D. 1981. *The Mind's Best Work*. Cambridge, Massachusetts: Harvard University Press.

Piaget, J. 1983. Piaget's Theory. In P. Mussen, ed., *Handbook of Child Psychology* (New York Wiley), Volume 1.

Posner, M. 2004. Neural Systems and Individual Differences. *Teachers College Record* 106: 1, pp. 24–30.

Richards, I.A. 1929. *Practical Criticism*. New York: Harcourt, Brace.

Rorty, R. 1979. *Philosophy and the Mirror of Nature*. Princeton: Princeton University Press.

Selfe, L. 1977. *Nadia: A Case of Extraordinary Drawing Ability in an Autistic Child*. New York: Academic Press.

Simonton, D.K. 1994. *Greatness: Who Makes History and Why*. New York: Guilford.

Sternberg, R. 1985. *Beyond IQ*. New York: Cambridge University Press.

———. 2005. The Triarchic Theory of Successful Intelligence. In D. Flanagan and P Harrison, eds., *Contemporary Intellectual Assessment: Theories, Tests, and Issues*. Second edition (New York: Guilford), pp. 103–119.

Turkheimer, E., A. Haley, M. Waldron, B. D'Onofrio, and I. Gottesman. 2003. Socioeconomic Status Modifies Heritability of IQ in Young Children. *Psychological Science* 14:6 (November), p. 623-628.

Winner, E. 2004. Art History Can Trade Insights with the Sciences. *Chronicle of Higher Education* (2nd July), pp. B10–12.

Wittgenstein, L. 1953. *Philosophical Investigations*. Oxford: Blackwell.

Bibliography of
Howard Gardner

COMPILED BY
Jeffrey A. Schaler

Bibliography of
HOWARD GARDNER

1965.   Gerontopia: The Retirement Community in America. Undergraduate thesis, Harvard College, Harvard University.

1970a.   With M. Grossack. *Man and Men: Social Psychology as Social Science.* Scranton: International Textbook.

1970b.   Children's Sensitivity to Painting Styles. *Child Development* 41, 813–821. See also *Harvard Project Zero Technical Report #4.*

1970c.   From Mode to Symbol: Thoughts on the Genesis of the Arts. *British Journal of Aesthetics* 10, 359–375.

1970d.   Piaget and Lévi-Strauss: The Quest for Mind. *Social Research* 37, 348–365. Translated into German.

1970e.   With J. Gardner. Development Trends in Sensitivity to Painting Style and Subject Matter. *Studies in Art Education* 12, 11–16.

1970f.   With J. Gardner. A Note on Selective Imitation in a Six-Week Old Infant. *Child Development* 41, 911–16.

1971a.   The Development of Sensitivity to Figural and Stylistic Aspects of Works of Art. Ph.D. dissertation, Harvard University. Published as *Harvard Project Zero Technical Report #3.*

1971b.   Problem-Solving in the Arts. *Journal of Aesthetic Education* 5, 93–114.

1971c.   With J. Gardner. Children's Literary Skills. *Journal of Experimental Education* 39, 42–46. See also *Harvard Project Zero Technical Report #4.*

1971d.   Children's Duplication of Rhythmic Patterns. *Journal of Research in Music Education* 19, 355–360.

1971e.   The Development of Sensitivity to Artistic Styles. *Journal of Aesthetics and Art Criticism* 29, 515–527.

1971f.   Children's Sensitivity to Musical Styles. In *Harvard Project Zero Technical Report #4.* See also *Merrill-Palmer Quarterly* 19 (1973), 67–77.

1971g.   Two Artists in One. Review of *The Duality of Vision,* by W. Sorrell. *Contemporary Psychology* 16: 6, 354–56.

1972a.   With J. Kagan. *Infancy, Language, Cognition: Three Films on Child Development.* New York: Harper and Row. Film. Winner of Cine Golden Eagle, Cine Statuette, American Film Festival Screening Award. Translated for Italian National Television.

1972b.   The Structural Analysis of Protocols and Myths. *Semiotica* 5, 31–57.

1972c.   On Figure and Texture in Aesthetic Perception. *British Journal of Aesthetics* 12, 40–59.

1972d.   The Development of Sensitivity to Figural and Stylistic Aspects of Paintings. *British Journal of Psychology* 63, 605–615. See also *Harvard Project Zero Technical Report #3.*

1972e.   Style Sensitivity in Children. *Human Development* 15, 325–338.

1972   With N. Goodman and D. Perkins. Summary Report. *Harvard Project Zero.*

1973a.   *The Quest for Mind: Jean Piaget, Claude Lévi-Strauss, and the Structuralist Movement.* New York: Knopf. Vintage Paperback (1974); Coventure Publication in England (1975). Translated into Italian and Japanese. Second Edition (1981) University of Chicago Press.

1973b.   *The Arts and Human Development.* New York: Wiley. Translated into Chinese and Portuguese. Second edition (1994) New York: Basic Books.

1973c.   With J. Gardner. *Classics in Psychology* (42 Volume Series). New York: Arno Press.

1973d.   Structure and Development. *The Human Context* 5, 50–67. Published simultaneously in *Le Domain Humain.*

1973e.   With J. Gardner. Developmental Trends in Sensitivity to Form and Subject Matter in Paintings. *Studies in Art Education* 14, 52–56.

1973f.   Some Notes on the Finale of Levi-Strauss's *L'homme nu. The Human Context* 5, 222–27.

1973g.   With M. Albert, A. Yamadori, and D. Howes. Comprehension in Alexia. *Brain* 96, 317–328.

1973h.   With F. Boller, J. Moreines, and N. Butters. Retrieving Information from Korsakoff Patients: Effects of Categorical Cues and Reference to the Task. *Cortex* 9, 165–175.

1973i.   The Contribution of Operativity to Naming in Aphasic Patients. *Neuropsychologia* 11, 213–220.

1973j.   With G. Denes. Connotative Judgments by Aphasic Patients on a Pictorial Adaptation of the Semantic Differential. *Cortex* 9, 183–196.

1973k.   France and the Modern Mind. *Psychology Today* 58 (June).

1973l. Developmental Dyslexia: The Forgotten Case of Monsieur C. *Psychology Today* (August), 63–67. Also Published in *Psychologie* (January 1974), 7.

1973m. Review of *Artistry of the Mentally Ill* by H. Prinzhorn. *Journal of Aesthetics and Art Criticism* 32, 285–87.

1974a. With V. Howard and D. Perkins. Symbol Systems: A Philosophical, Psychological, and Educational Investigation. In D. Olson. *Media and Symbols: The Forms of Expression, Communication, and Education*, 27–56. Chicago: University of Chicago Press.

1974b. The Naming and Recognition of Written Symbols in Aphasic and Alexic Patients. *Journal of Communication Disorders* 7, 141–153.

1974c. A Psychological Examination of Nelson Goodman's Theory of Symbols. *The Monist* 58, 319–326.

1974d. Metaphors and Modalities: How Children Project Polar Adjectives onto Diverse Domains. *Child Development* 45, 84–91.

1974e. The Naming of Objects and Symbols by Children and Aphasic Patients. *Journal of Psycholinguistic Research* 3, 133–149.

1974f. The Contribution of Colors and Texture to the Detection of Painting Styles. *Studies in Art Education* 15, 57–62.

1974g. With R. Strub. The Repetition Defect in Conduction Aphasia: Linguistic or Mnestic? *Brain and Language* 1, 241–256.

1974h. Review of *Aesthetics and Psychobiology*, by D.E. Berlyne. *Curriculum Theory Network* 4, Nos. 2 and 3, 205–213.

1975a. *The Shattered Mind.* New York: Knopf. Main Selection, *Psychology Today* Book Club, January 1974; Vintage Paperback, 1976. Quality Paperback Book Club Selection. Routledge and Kegan Paul, British Edition. Translated into Japanese.

1975b. With J. Gardner. *Classics in Child Psychology* (32 volume series). New York: Arno Press.

1975c. With M. Albert and S. Weintraub. Comprehending a Word. *Cortex* 11, 155–162. Reprinted in *Readings in Early Childhood Music Education,* Music Educators National Conference (1992).

1975d. With R. Strub and M. Albert. A Unimodal Deficit in Operational Thinking. *Brain and Language* 2, 333–344.

1975e. With E.B. Zurif. *Bee* but not *Be*: Oral Reading of Single Words in Aphasia and Alexia. *Neuropsychologia* 13, 181–190.

1975f. With E. Winner and M. Kircher. Children's Conceptions of the Arts. *Journal of Aesthetic Education* 9, 60–77. Translated into Italian.

1975g. With M. Kircher, E. Winner, and D. Perkins. Children's Metaphoric Productions and Preferences. *Journal of Child Language* 2, 125–141.

1975h. With G. Denes and E.B. Zurif. Critical Writing at the Sentence Level in Aphasia. *Cortex* 11, 60–72.

1975i. With D. Wolf and A. Smith. Artistic Symbols in Early Childhood. *New York Education Quarterly* 6, 13–21.

1975j. With E. Baker, T. Berry, E.B. Zurif, L. Davis, and A. Veroff. Can Linguistic Competence be Dissociated from Natural Language Functions? *Nature* 254, 609–610.

1975k. With K. Ling, L. Flamm, and J. Silverman. Comprehension and Appreciation of Humor in Brain-Damaged Patients. *Brain* 98, 399–412.

1975l. With J. Silverman, E. Winner, and A. Rosentiel. On Training Sensitivity to Painting Styles. *Perception* 4, 373–384.

1975m. Brain Damage: A Window on the Mind. *Saturday Review* (August 9), 26–29. Also in *Centerscope* 8 (1976), 31–34. Reprinted in *Mind and Supermind* (1977). In A. Rosenfield. New York: Holt, Rinehart.

1975n. With W. Lohman. Children's Sensitivity to Literary Styles. *Merrill-Palmer Quarterly* 21, 113–126.

1976a. Vico's Theory of Knowledge in the Light of Contemporary Social Science. In G. Tagliacozzo and D. Verene, eds., *Giambattista Vico's Science of Humanity* (Baltimore: Johns Hopkins Press), 351–364.

1976b. Unfolding or Teaching: On the Optimal Training of Artistic Skills. In E. Eisner, ed., *The Arts, Human Development, and Education* (Berkeley: McCutchan), 100–110. See also You, Your Child, and Art, *Child Study Association* 1975.

1976c. With E.B. Zurif, T. Berry, and E. Baker. Visual Communication in Aphasia. *Neuropsychologia* 14, 275–292.

1976d. With E.B. Zurif. Critical Reading of Words and Phrases in Aphasia. *Brain and Language* 3, 173–190.

1976e. With D.F. Benson and J. Meadows. Reduplicative Paramnesia. *Neurology* 26, 47–51.

1976f. On the Acquisition of First Symbol Systems. *Studies in the Anthropology of Visual Communication* 3, 22–37.

1976g. With L. Davis. Strategies of Mastering a Visual Communication System in Aphasia. *Annals of the New York Academy of Sciences* 280, 885–897.

1976h. Challenges for a Psychology of Art. *Scientific Aesthetics* 1, 19–33.

1976i. With E. Winner and A. Rosenstiel. The Development of Metaphoric Understanding. *Developmental Psychology* 12, 289–297. Reprinted in M.B. Franklin and S.S. Barten, eds., *Child Language* (New York: Oxford University Press, 1988).

1976j. Promising Paths to Knowledge. *Journal of Aesthetic Education* 10, 201–07.

1976k. With J. Silverman and E. Winner. On Going Beyond the Literal: The Development of Sensitivity to Artistic Symbols. *Semiotica* 18, 291–312.

1976l. Illuminating Comparisons. In M. Henle, ed., *Vision and Artifact* (New York: Springer), 105–114.

1976m. With E. Winner. How Children Learn: Three Stages of Understanding Art. *Psychology Today* 42 (March). Translated into French, Italian, and Spanish.

1976n. Review of *The Grasp of Consciousness*, by J. Piaget. *New York Times Book Review* (August 1st), 1–2.

1977a. Senses, Symbols, Operations: An Organization of Artistry. In D. Perkins and B. Leondar, eds., *The Arts and Cognition* (Baltimore: Johns Hopkins Press), 88–117.

1977b. With E. Winner. The Clinical Method as a Key to Children's Understanding: A Reply to José Rosario. *Journal of Aesthetic Education* 11, 101–02.

1977c. With J. Silverman, G. Denes, C. Semenza, and A. Rosenstiel. Sensitivity to Musical Denotation and Connotation in Organic Patients. *Cortex* 13, 242–256. See also *Archivo di Psychologia Neurologia e Psichiatria* 39 (1978), 346–362.

1977d. With A. Rosenstiel. The Effect of Critical Comparisons upon Children's Drawings. *Studies in Art Education* 19, 36–44.

1977e. With E. Winner. The Comprehension of Metaphor in Brain–Damaged Patients. *Brain* 100, 719–727.

1977f. With B. Mercer, W. Wapner, and D.F. Benson. A Study in Confabulation. *Archives of Neurology* 34, 429–433.

1977g. Sifting the Special from the Shared: Notes Toward an Agenda for Research in Arts Education. In S. Madeja, ed., *Arts and Aesthetics: An Agenda for the Future* (St. Louis: Cemrel), 267–278. See also *Journal of Aesthetic Education* 11 (1977), 31–44.

1977h. The Embattled Prophet. Review of Erick H. Erikson, *The Power and Limits of a Vision,* by Paul Roazen. *Saturday Review* 1: 8 (January 8th), 46–47.

1977i. Review of *Progress in Art*, by S. Gablik. *Times Literary Supplement* (January 28th).

1977j. Light from Darkness. Review of *Insights from the Blind,* by S. Fraiberg. *New York Times Book Review* 9 (April 17th), 48–50.

1977k. Beastly Behavior. Review of *Behind the Mirror,* by K. Lorenz. *New York Times Book Review* (August 21st), 12, 26, 28.

1977l. Review of *The Uses of Enchantment: The Meaning and Importance of Fairy Tales,* by B. Bettelheim. *Semiotica* 21, 363–380. Reprinted in *Phaedrus* 5 (1978), 14–23.

1977m. Review of *Body, Mind, and Behavior,* by M. Scarf. *New York Times Book Review* (February 2nd).

1978a. The Development and Breakdown of Symbolic Capacities: A Search for General Principles. In A. Carramazza and E.B. Zurif, eds., *Language Acquisition and Language Breakdown: Parallels and Divergencies* (Baltimore: John Hopkins Press), 291–98.

1978b. With E. Winner, R. Bechhofer, and D. Wolf. The Development of Figurative Language. In K. Nelson, ed., *Children's Language* (New York: Gardner Press), 1–38.

1978c. With A.K. Rosenstiel, P. Morison, and J. Silverman. Critical Judgment: A Developmental Study. *Journal of Aesthetic Education* 12, 95–107.

1978d. With W. Wapner and T. Judd. Visual Agnosia in an Artist. *Cortex* 14, 343–364.

1978e. With P. Morison. Dragons and Dinosaurs: How the Child Distinguishes Reality and Fantasy. *Child Development* 49, 642–48.

1978f. With L. Davis, N. Foldi, and E.B. Zurif. Repetition in the Transcortical Aphasias. *Brain and Language* 6, 226–238.

1978g. With E. Winner. A Study of Repetition in Aphasic Patients. *Brain and Language* 14, 343–364.

1978h. With A. Caramazza and E.B. Zurif. Sentence Memory in Aphasia. *Neuropsychologia* 16, 661–670.

1978i. From Melvin to Melville: On the Relevance to Aesthetics of Recent Research on Story Comprehension. In S. Madeja, ed., *The Arts, Cognition, and Basic Skills* (St. Louis: Cemrel), 250–56.

1978j. With J. Silverman and W. Wapner. The Appreciation of Antonymic Contrasts in Aphasia. *Brain and Language* 6, 301–317.

1978k. With E. Winner. The Development of Metaphoric Competence. *Critical Inquiry* 5, 123–141.

1978l. A Social Synthesis. *The Behavioral and Brain Sciences* 1: 4, 572–73.

1978m. What We Do and Don't Know About the Two Halves of the Brain. *The Harvard Magazine* (March–April), 24–27. Also in *Journal of Aesthetic Education* 12 (1978), 113–119; *International Neuropsychology Society Bulletin* (December 1978).

1978n. The Loss of Language. *Human Nature*, 76–84. Reprinted in *Psychology,* Annual edition, 1986–87.

1978o. Philosophy in a New Key: A Study in the Symbolism of Reason, Rite and Art. *Human Nature* 1: 11, 92–96.

1978p. A Psychologist without Peer. A Review of *Jean Piaget: Psychologist of the Real,* by B. Rotman. *Chronicle of Higher Education* 21 (16th January).

1978q. Review of *The Essential Piaget,* by H. Gruber and J. Vonéche. *Chronicle of Higher Education* 21 (16th January).

1978r. Achieving Artistry. A Review of *Ways of the Hand,* by D. Sudnow. *Chronicle of Higher Education* 23 (10th April).

1979a. *Developmental Psychology: An Introduction.* Boston: Little Brown, International Edition. Second edition, 1982.

1979b. With E. Winner. Fact, Fiction, and Fantasy in Childhood. *New Directions for Child Development* 6.

1979c.   With D. Wolf. Style and Sequence in Early Symbolic Play. In N.R. Smith and M.B. Franklin, ed., *Symbolic Functioning in Children* (Hillside: Erlbaum), 117–138.

1979d.   With E.B. Zurif, A. Caramazza, and N. Foldi. Lexical Semantics and Memory for Works in Aphasia. *Journal of Speech and Hearing Research* 22, 456–467.

1979e.   On Preserving and Extending Piaget's Contributions. *Behavioral and Brain Sciences* 2: 1, 141.

1979f.   With W. Wapner. A Study of Spelling in Aphasia. *Brain and Language* 7, 363–374.

1979g.   With J. Shotwell and D. Wolf. Exploring Early Symbolization: Styles of Achievement. In B.Sutton–Smith, *Playing and Learning* (New York: Gardner Press), 127–156.

1979h.   J. Shotwell and D. Wolf. Styles of Achievement in Early Symbolization. In M. Foster and S. Brandes, eds., *Symbol as Sense: New Approaches to the Analysis of Meaning* (New York: Academic Press), 175–199.

1979i.   With D. Wolf. First Drawings: Notes on the Relationships Between Perception and Production in the Visual Arts. In C. Nodine and D. Fisher, eds., *Perception and Pictorial Representation* (New York: Praeger), 361–387.

1979j.   Developmental Psychology after Piaget: An Approach in Terms of Symbolization. *Human Development* 22, 73–88.

1979k.   With J.T. Carothers. When Children's Drawings Become Art: The Emergence of Aesthetic Production and Perception. *Developmental Psychology* 15, 570–580.

1979l.   With W. Wapner. A Note on Patterns of Comprehension and Recovery in Global Aphasia. *Journal of Speech and Hearing Research* 29, 765–771.

1979m.   With E. Winner, M. McCarthy, and S. Kleinman. First Metaphors. *New Directions in Child Development* 3, 29–42.

1979n.   With D. Wolf. Dimensions of Early Symbol Use. *New Directions for Child Development* 3, vii–xi.

1979o.   With D. Delis, N. Foldi, S. Hamby, and E.B. Zurif. A Note on Temporal Relations Between Language and Gesture. *Brain and Language* 8, 350–54.

1979p.   With M. Cicone, W. Wapner, N. Foldi, and E.B. Zurif. The Relation Between Gesture and Language in Aphasic Communication. *Brain and Language* 8, 324–349.

1979q.   With P. Morison and M. McCarthy. Exploring the Realities of Television. *Journal of Broadcasting* 23, 453–464.

1979r.   With E. Winner and W. Wapner. Measures of Metaphor. *New Directions for Child Development* 6, 67–75.

1979s. Entering the World of the Arts: The Child as Artist. *Journal of Communication* (Autumn), 146–156.

1979t. Computational Neurolinguistics: Promises, Promises. *The Behavioral and Brain Sciences* 2, 464–65.

1979u. Getting Acquainted with Jean Piaget. *New York Times* (3rd January), C1.

1979v. With E. Winner. The Child is Father to the Metaphor. *Psychology Today* (May), 81–91.

1979w. Exploring the Mystery of Creativity. *New York Times* (March 1979), C1.

1979x. Encounter at Royaumont. *Psychology Today* (July), 14–16.

1979y. Children's Art: Nadia's Challenge. *Psychology Today* (September).

1979z. Toys with a Mind of Their Own. *Psychology Today* (November).

1979aa. U-Shaped Behavior Challenges Basic Concept of Development. *New York Times* (25th September), C3.

1979ab. Review of *The Last Frontier,* by R. Restak. *Psychology Today* (May), 131–34.

1979ac. Foreword. In *Interaction of Media, Cognition, and Learning,* by G. Salomon. San Francisco: Jossey-Bass.

1980a. *Artful Scribbles: The Significance of Children's Drawings.* New York: Basic Books. *Behavioral Sciences* book service selection. English edition: Jill Norman. Basic Books Paperback (1982). Translated into Japanese, French, Spanish, and Chinese.

1980b. With D. Wolf. Beyond Playing or Polishing: The Development of Artistry. In J. Hausman, ed., *The Arts and the Schools* (New York: McGraw Hill).

1980c. Children's Literary Development. In P.E. McGhee and A.J. Chapman, eds., *Children's Humour* (London: Wiley), 191–218.

1980d. With E. Winner and M. McCarthy. The Ontogenesis of Metaphor. In R. Honeck and R. Hoffman, eds., *Cognition and Figurative Language* (Hillsdale: Erlbaum).

1980e. With E. Winner and M. Engel. Misunderstanding Metaphor: What's the Problem? *Journal of Experimental Child Psychology* 30, 22–32.

1980f. With M. Cicone and W. Wapner. Sensitivity to Emotional Expressions and Situations in Organic Patients. *Cortex* 16, 145–158.

1980g. Comments on R. Downs, *et al.* On Education and Geographers: The Role of Cognitive Developmental Theory in Geographic Education. *Annals of the Association of American Geographers* 80: 1, 123–135.

1980h. Reprogramming the Media Researchers. *Psychology Today* (January).

1980i. Strange Loops of the Mind. *Psychology Today* (March).

1980j. Composing Symphonies and Dinner Parties. *Psychology Today* (April).

1980k. Children's Art: The Age of Creativity. *Psychology Today* (May).

1980l. The Lives of Alexander Luria: History's Impact on a Scientist. *Psychology Today* (June).

1980m. China's Born-Again Psychology. *Psychology Today* (August).

1980n. Gifted World Makers. *Psychology Today* (September). Reprinted in W.T. Anderson, ed., *The Truth About the Truth* (1995), 182–88.

1980o. Jean Piaget: The Psychologist as Renaissance Man. *New York Times* (September 21st), Section 4.

1980p. On Becoming a Dictator. *Psychology Today* (December). Also in *Writer* (October 1981), 7–8.

1980q. The Piaget-Chomsky Debate: What Future for the Cognitive Sciences? *New Boston Review* 5 (November–December), 6–7.

1980r. Cognition Comes of Age. Foreword to M. Piatelli-Palmarini, ed., *On Language and Learning* (Cambridge, Massachusetts: Harvard University Press). Translated into Polish.

1980s. Review of *The Art of Psychotherapy,* by A. Storr. *New York Times Book Review* (5th October).

1981a. With H. Kelly. Viewing Children through Television. *New Directions for Child Development* 13.

1981b. With D. Wolf. On the Structure of Early Symbolization. In R. Schiefelbush and D. Bricker, eds., *Early Language: Acquisition and Intervention* (Baltimore: University Park Press).

1981c. With M. Cicone and E. Winner. Understanding the Psychology in Psychological Metaphors. *Journal of Child Language* 8, 213–16.

1981d. Children's Perceptions of Works of Art: A Developmental Portrait. In D. O'Hare. *Psychology and the Arts.* Brighton: Harvester.

1981e. With L. Davidson and McKernon. The Acquisition of Song: A Developmental Approach. *Documentary Report of the Ann Arbor Symposium: Allocation of Psychology to the Teaching and Learning of Music.* Reston: Music Educators National Conference.

1981f. With W. Wapner. Profiles of Symbol Reading Skills in Organic Patients. *Brain and Language* 12, 303–312.

1981g. With W. Wapner and S. Hamby. The Role of the Right Hemisphere in the Apprehension of Complex Linguistic Materials. *Brain and Language* 14, 15–33.

1981h. With B.E. Shapiro and M. Grossman. Selective Musical Processing Deficits in Brain Damaged Populations. *Neuropsychologia* 19, 161–69.

1981i. With M. Grossman and B.E. Shapiro. Dissociable Musical Processing Strategies after Localized Brain Damage. *Neuropsychologia* 19, 425–434.

1981j. With L. Jaglom. Decoding the Worlds of Television. *Studies in Visual Communication* 7, 33–47.

1981k. With E. Winner. Artistry and Aphasia. In M.T. Sarno, ed., *Acquired Aphasia.* New York: Academic Press.

1981l. With S. Wagner, E. Winner, and D. Cicchetti. Metaphorical Meaning in Human Infants. *Child Development* 52, 728–731.

1981m. With B.E. Shapiro, M. Alexander, and B. Mercer. Mechanisms of Confabulation. *Neurology* 31, 1070–76.

1981n. With H. Brownell. Hemispheric Specialization: Definitions, not Incantations. *The Behavioral and Brain Sciences* 4, 64–65.

1981o. With W.A. Postlethwaite, H. Brownwell, E.B. Mendelsohn, and W. Wapner. Finding It: The Effects of Visual Searching on Object Identification by Aphasic Patients. *Harvard Project Zero Technical Report #29.* Cambridge, Massachusetts: Harvard University Graduate School of Education.

1981p. With H. Kelly. Tackling Television on Its Own Terms. *New Directions in Child Development* 13, 1–8.

1981q. With S.W. Ives, J. Silverman, and H. Kelly. Artistic Development in the Early School Years: A Crossmedia Study of Storytelling, Drawing, and Clay Modeling. *Journal of Research and Development in Education* 14, 91–105. See also *Harvard Project Zero Technical Report #8.*

1981r. With E. Winner. The Art in Children's Drawings. *Review of Research in Visual Arts Education* 14, 18–31.

1981s. With L. Jaglom. The Preschool Television Viewer as Anthropologist. *New Directions in Child Development* 13 (September), 9–30.

1981t. With P. Morison and H. Kelly. Reasoning about the Realities on Television: Developmental Study. *Journal of Broadcasting* 25, 229–242. See also *Harvard Project Zero Technical Report #18.*

1981u. With L. Jaglom. The Child as an Anthropologist: Solving Television. *The Dial* (August).

1981v. How the Split Brain Gets a Joke. *Psychology Today* (February).

1981w. The Prodigies' Progress. *Psychology Today* (May).

1981x. Breakaway Minds: Howard Gruber Interviewed by Howard Gardner. *Psychology Today* (July), 64–73.

1981y. Author of Authors: Endeavors in Psychology: Selections from the Personology of Henry A. Murray. *The New Republic* (August 22nd and 29th).

1981z. Do Babies Sing a Universal Song? *Psychology Today* (December), 70–77. Translated into Hebrew for *Hachina Hameshutuf* 108 (April 1983), 23–35. Reprinted in B. Andress and K.M. Walker, eds., *Readings in Early Childhood Music Education* (Reston: Music Educators National Conference, 1992), 32–38.

1982a. *Art, Mind, and Brain: A Cognitive Approach to Creativity.* New York: Basic Books. Basic Books Paperback (1984). Translated into Spanish, Hebrew, Japanese, Italian, Chinese, and Portuguese.

1982b. With E. Winner. First Intimations of Artistry. In S. Strauss, ed., *U–Shaped Behavioral Growth* (New York: Academic Press), 147–168.

1982c. Artistry Following Damage to the Human Brain. In A. Ellis, ed., *Normality and Pathology in Cognitive Functions* (London: Academic Press), 299–323.

1982d. With M.O. Landry and H. Kelly. Reality-Fantasy Discriminations in Literature: A Developmental Study. *Research in the Teaching of English* 16, 39–52.

1982e. Response to Comment on Project Zero, by Jessie Lovano-Kerr and Jean Rush. *Review of Research in Visual Arts Education* 15, 82–84.

1982f. With L. Silberstein and E. Winner. Autumn Leaves and Old Photographs: The Development of Metaphoric Preferences. *Journal of Experimental Child Psychology* 34, 135–150. See also *Harvard Project Zero Technical Report #14.*

1982g. Giftedness: Speculations from a Biological Perspective. In D. Feldman, ed., *Developmental Approaches to Giftedness and Creativity. New Directions for Child Development* 17, 47–60.

1982h. The Making of a Story-Teller. *Psychology Today* (March), 48–53, 61.

1982i. The Music of the Hemispheres. *Psychology Today* (June).

1982j. People who Don't Think Alike. Review of *Comparative Studies of How People Think,* by M. Cole and B. Means. *Psychology Today* (January), 84–89.

1982k. The New Science of Cognition. Review of *The Mind's I,* In D. Hofstadter and D. Dennett. *The New Republic* (February 24th), 32–34.

1982l. Review of *The Play of Musement,* by T. Sebeok. *Semiotica* 38: 3–4, 347–356.

1982m. Reading and Misreading. Review of *On Learning to Read,* by B. Bettelheim. *New York Times Book Review* 11 (31st January), 26.

1983a. *Frames of Mind: The Theory of Multiple Intelligences.* New York: Basic Books. Selected by five book clubs. British Edition, W. Heinemann. Translated into Spanish, Japanese, Italian, Hebrew, Chinese, French, and German. Basic Books Paperback, 1985. Tenth Anniversary Edition with new introduction, New York: Basic Books, 1993. Translated into Swedish, German, Portuguese, Spanish, Italian, Chinese (Taiwan), French, Norwegian, Hebrew, Slovenian, Korean, and Czech. Selected by three book clubs. Selected by the Museum of Education for *Books of the Century* exhibit, Columbia, SC, 1999. Tenth Anniversary British Edition, London: HarperCollins (Fontana), 1993. Twentieth Anniversary Edition with new introduction, New York: Basic Books.

1983b. With N. Foldi and M. Cicone. Pragmatic Aspects of Communication in Brain Damaged Patients. In S. Segalowitz, ed., *Language Functions and Brain Organization.* New York: Academic Press.

1983c. With H.H. Brownell, W. Wapner, and D. Michelow. Missing the Point: The Role of the Right Hemisphere in the Processing of Complex Linguistic Materials. In E. Perceman, ed., *Cognitive Processing in the*

Right Hemisphere. New York: Academic Press. Reprinted in A. Kasher, ed., *Pragmatics: Critical Concepts* 6 (London: Routledge, 1998), 170–192

1983d. L.K. Meringoff, M.M. Vibbert, C.A. Char, D.E. Fernie, and G.S. Banker. How Is Children's Learning from Television Distinctive? Exploiting the Medium Methodologically. In J. Bryant and D.R. Anderson, eds., *Watching TV, Understanding TV: Research on Children's Attention and Comprehension* (New York: Academic Press).

1983e. With D. Wolf. Waves and Streams of Symbolization. In D.R. Rogers and J.A. Sloboda, eds., *The Acquisition of Symbolic Skills.* London: Plenum.

1983f. With D. Delis, W. Wapner, and J. Moses. The Contribution of the Right Hemisphere to the Organization of Paragraphs. *Cortex* 19, 43–50.

1983g. With H. Brownell, D. Michel, and J. Powelson. Surprise and Coherence: Sensitivity to Verbal Humor in Right Hemisphere Patients. *Brain and Language* 18, 20–27.

1983h. Artistic Intelligences. *Art Education* 36, 47–49. Reprinted in S. Dobbs, ed., *Research Readings for Discipline Based Art Education: A Journey Beyond Creation.* (Reston: National Art Education Association, 1988).

1983i. With T. Judd and N. Geschwind. Alexia Without Agraphia in a Composer. *Brain* 106, 435–457. See also *Harvard Project Zero Technical Report #15.*

1983j. With A. Demorest, L. Silberstein, and E. Winner. Telling It as It Isn't: Children's Understanding of Figurative Language. *British Journal of Developmental Psychology* 1, 121–134.

1983k. With E. Winner and C. Massey. Children's Sensitivity to Aesthetic Properties of Line Drawings. In D.R. Rogers and J.A. Sloboda, eds., *The Acquisition of Symbolic Skills* (London: Plenum), 97–104.

1983l. Some Differences Between Chinese and American Art Education. Report prepared for the Rockefeller Brothers Fund, New York.

1983m. With E. Winner. Graphic Skills: Introduction. In D.R. Rogers and J.A. Sloboda, eds., *The Acquisition of Symbolic Skills* (London: Plenum), 43–45.

1983n. With D. Michelow, H. Brownell, L. Masson, and W. Wapner. On the Sequencing of Emotional and Non–Emotional Verbal Materials. *Harvard Project Zero Technical Report #30.* Cambridge, Massachusetts: Harvard University Graduate School of Education.

1983o. Can Piaget and Lévi-Strauss Be Reconciled? *New Ideas in Psychology* 1, 187–190.

1983p. With C. Massey, H. Blank, and E. Winner. Children's Sensitivity to Stylistic Features in Literature. *Leonardo* 16, 204–07.

1983q. Does Television Stimulate or Stultify? *TV Guide Canada* (7th May), 30.

1983r.   Science Grapples with the Creative Puzzle. *New York Times* (13th May).

1983s.   When Television Marries Computer. Review of *Pilgrim in the Microworld*, by D. Sudnow. *New York Times Book Review* (March 27th), 12.

1983t.   He Came, He Saw, He Cognized. Review of *In Search of Mind*, by J.S. Bruner. *The New Republic* (December 26th), 31–33.

1983u.   Review of *Language and Learning: The Debate Between Jean Piaget and Noam Chomsky*. In M. Piatelli-Palmarini, ed., *New Vico Studies*, 112–13.

1984a.   With S.W. Ives. Cultural Influences on Children's Drawings: A Developmental Perspective. In R. Ott and A. Hurwitz, eds., *Art Education: An International Perspective* (University Park: Penn State University Press).

1984b.   The Development of Competence in Culturally-Defined Domains. In R. Shweder and R. Levine, eds., *Culture Theory: Essays on Mind, Self, and Emotion* (New York: Cambridge University Press).

1984c.   With E. Mendelsohn, S. Robinson, and E. Winner. Are Preschoolers' Renamings Intentional Category Violations? *Developmental Psychology* 20, 187–192.

1984d.   With A. Demorest, C. Meyer, E. Phelps, and E. Winner. Words Speak Louder than Actions: Understanding Deliberately False Remarks. *Child Development* 55, 1527–534.

1984e.   With H.H. Brownell, H.H. Potter, and B. Michelow. Sensitivity to Lexical Denotation and Connotation in Brain-Damaged Patients: A Double Dissociation? *Brain and Language* 22, 253–265.

1984f.   Assessing Intelligences: A Comment on Testing Intelligence without IQ Tests, by Robert Sternberg. *Phi Delta Kappa*, 699–700.

1984g.   With L.K. Brown. Symbolic Capabilities and Children's Television. In J. Murray, *Children and Television* (Boy's Town, NB).

1984h.   With C. Massey and E. Winner. Perceiving What Paintings Express. In W.R. Crozier and A.J. Chapman, eds., *Cognitive Processes in the Perception of Art* (Amsterdam: North Holland).

1984i.   From the Cradle to the Mainframe. Review of *The Second Self*, by S. Turkle. *New York Times Book Review* 3 (22nd July), 27.

1985a.   *The Mind's New Science: A History of the Cognitive Revolution*. New York: Basic Books. Translated into Spanish, Japanese, French, German, Italian, Chinese, and Portuguese. Adopted by six book clubs. Basic Books Paperback with new Epilogue, 1987.

1985b.   With S. Rubin. Once Upon a Time: The Development of Sensitivity to Story Structure. In C. Cooper, ed., *Researching Response to Literature and the Teaching of Literature: Points of Departure* (Ablex).

1985c. Towards a Theory of Dramatic Intelligence. In J. Kase-Polisini, ed., *Creative Drama in a Developmental Context* (University Press of America).

1985d. The Centrality of Modules. A Comment on J.A. Fodor, *The Modularity of Mind. Behavioral and Brain Sciences* 8, 12–14.

1985e. The Development of Symbolic Competencies in Children. In C. Thomson, ed., *The Phylogeny and Ontogeny of Communication Systems* 1. Working Papers of the Toronto Semiotics Circle.

1985f. With J. Walters. The Development and Education of Intelligences. In F. Link, ed., *Essays on the Intellect* (Washington, D.C.: Curriculum Development Associates). Reprinted in part: If Teaching Had Looked Beyond the Classroom: The Development and Education of Intelligences. *Innotech Journal* 16: 1 (1992), 18–36.

1985g. Arts Education in the People's Republic of China: A Second Look. A Report prepared for the Rockefeller Brothers Fund, New York (May).

1985h. The Scientistic Fallacy: A Reply to Ellen Handler Spitz. *New Ideas in Psychology* 3, 87–92.

1985i. On Discerning New Ideas in Psychology. *New Ideas in Psychology* 3, 101–04.

1985j. With Y. Dudai. Biology and Giftedness. *Items* 39, 1–6.

1985k. With J. Walters and M. Krechevsky. Development of Musical, Mathematical, and Scientific Talents in Normal and Gifted Children. *Harvard Project Zero Technical Report # 31.* Cambridge, Massachusetts: Harvard University Graduate School of Education.

1985l. Reintroducing Frames of Mind. New introduction for paperback edition of *Frames of Mind* (New York: Basic Books).

1985m. With H. Weinrich-Haste. The Varieties of Intelligence: An Interview with Howard Gardner. *New Ideas in Psychology* 3: 1, 47–65.

1986a. With G. Windmueller, C. Massey, and E. Winner. Unpacking Metaphors and Allegories. *Human Development* 29, 236–240.

1986b. With J. Walters. The Crystallizing Experience: Discovery of an Intellectual Gift. In R. Sternberg and J. Davidson, eds., *Conceptions of Giftedness* (New York: Cambridge University Press). Reprinted in *College Board, Measures in the College Admissions Process: A College Board Colloquium*, 130–32. New York: College Entrance Examination Board. Reprinted in R.S. Albert, ed., *Genius and Eminence* (Oxford: Pergamon, 1992).

1986c. With G. Salomon. The Computer as Educator: Lessons from Television Research. *Educational Researcher* 1, 13–19. See also *Harvard Project Zero Technical Report #21.*

1986d. With J. Walters. The Theory of Multiple Intelligences: Some Issues and Answers. In R. Sternberg and R. Wagner. *Practical Intelligences* (New York: Cambridge University Press).

1986e. With H. Brownell, H. Potter, and A. Bihrle. Inference Deficits in Right Brain-Damaged Patients. *Brain and Language* 27, 310–332.

1986f. The Waning of Intelligence Tests. In R. Sternberg and D. Detterman, eds., *What Is Intelligence?* (Hillsdale: Erlbaum).

1986g. With A.M. Bihrle, H.H. Brownell, and J. Powelson. Comprehension of Humorous and Non-Humorous Materials by Left and Right Brain-Damaged Patients. *Brain and Cognition* 5, 399–411.

1986h. With T. Hatch. From Testing Intelligence to Assessing Competencies: A Pluralistic View of Intellect. *The Roeper Review* 8, 147–150.

1986i. With E. Winner, E. Rosenblatt, G. Windmueller, and L. Davidson. Children's Perception of Aesthetic Properties of the Arts: Domain-Specific or Pan-Artistic? *British Journal of Developmental Psychology* 4, 149–160.

1986j. Aesthetic Education: The Long Haul. *Journal of Aesthetic Education* 20: 4 (Winter), 53–56.

1986k. Freud in Three Frames: A Cognitive Scientific Approach to Creative Lives and Creative Products. *Daedalus* (Summer), 105–134.

1986l. Notes on Educational Implications of the Theory of Multiple Intelligences. *College Board Colloquium on Measures in the College Admissions Process.*

1986m. With J. Andrews, E. Rosenblatt, U. Malkus, and E. Winner. Children's Abilities to Distinguish Metaphoric and Ironic Utterances from Mistakes and Lies. *Communication and Cognition* 19, 281–297.

1986n. An Undergraduate at Midlife. *Commencement Issue of the Harvard Gazette* (June 6th).

1986o. Comments on Karen Davidson: The Case Against Formal Identification. *The Gifted Child* 11 (November–December).

1986p. Notes on Cognitive Development: Recent Trends, New Directions. In S. Friedman, K. Klivington, and R. Peterson, eds., *The Brain, Cognition, and Education* (New York: Academic Press, 259–285).

1986q. The Development of Symbolic Literacy. In M. Wrolstad and D. Fisher, eds., *Toward a Greater Understanding of Literacy* (New York: Praeger). See also R. Posner, ed., *Zeitschrift fuer Semiotik* 4 (1985), 319–333.

1986r. Foreword to *Taking Advantage of Media,* by L.K. Brown. Boston: Routledge.

1986s. The Bilingual Blur. Review of *The Mirror of Language,* by K. Hakuta. *New York Review of Books* 36 (October 23rd), 43–46

1987a. With E. Winner. Attitudes and Attributes: Children's Understanding of Metaphor and Sarcasm. In M. Perlmutter, ed., *Minnesota Symposia on Child Psychology* (Hillsdale: Erlbaum), 131–152.

1987b. The Assessment of Intelligences: A Neuropsychological Perspective. In M. Meier, A. Benton, and L. Diller. *Neuropsychological Rehabilitation* (London: Churchill).

1987c. With M. Roman, H.H. Brownell, H.H. Potter, and M.S. Seibold. Script Knowledge in Right Hemisphere Damaged and in Normal Elderly Adults. *Brain and Language* 31, 51–70.

1987d. With H.H. Brownell, A. Letourneau, and A. Bihrle. The Effects of Normal Aging on Narrative Comprehension: A Test of the Right Hemisphere Hypothesis. *Harvard Project Zero Technical Report #32.* Cambridge, Massachusetts: Harvard Graduate School of Education.

1987e. An Individual-Centered Curriculum. *The Schools We've Got, the Schools We Need.* Washington, D.C.: Council of Chief State School Officers and the American Association of Colleges of Teacher Education.

1987f. Beyond the IQ: Education and Human Development, Developing the Spectrum of Human Intelligences. *Harvard Educational Review* 57, 187–193. Reprinted in *National Forum:* 1–4 (Spring 1988); In C. Hedley, ed., *Cognition, Curriculum, and Literacy* (Norwood: Ablex, 1990); In D. Hamacheck, ed., *Educational Psychology Reader* (New York: Macmillan, 1990); *Canadian Children* 15: 1 (1990), 9–18; and in *Sun Foundation Journal* 6: 5 (Summer 1991).

1987g. The Theory of Multiple Intelligences. *Annals of Dyslexia* 37, 19–35.

1987h. Symposium on the Theory of Multiple Intelligences. In D.N. Perkins, J. Lochhead, and J.C. Bishop. *Thinking: The Second International Conference* (Hillside: Erlbaum), 77–101.

1987i. With J. Wolfe, H.H. Brownell, A. Bihrle, and S. Weylman. Verbal Abstraction Abilities in Unipolar and Bipolar Depression Patients. *Harvard Project Zero Technical Report #34.* Cambridge, Massachusetts: Harvard University Graduate School of Education.

1987j. With D.L. McDougall, H.H. Brownell, and A.L. Letourneau. Comprehension of Proverbs by Right Brain Damaged Patients. *Harvard Project Zero Technical Report #35.* Cambridge, Massachusetts: Harvard University Graduate School of Education.

1987k. With E. Winner, J. Dion, and E. Rosenblatt. Do Lateral or Vertical Reversals Affect Balance in Paintings? *Visual Arts Education* 13, 1–3.

1987l. With E. Winner, G. Windmueller, E. Rosenblatt, L. Bosco, and E. Best. Making Sense of Literal and Nonliteral Falsehood. *Metaphor and Symbolic Activity* 2: 1, 13–32.

1987m. On Assessment in the Arts: A Conversation with Howard Gardner. *Educational Leadership* (December–January, 1987–88), 30–34. Reprinted in *Conversations with Leading Educators* (Washington, D.C.: Association for Supervision and Curriculum Development, 1989).

1987n. With D. Wolf. The Symbolic Products of Early Childhood. In D. Gorlitz and J. Wohlwill, eds., *Play, Curiosity, and Exploration* (Hillsdale: Erlbaum).

1987o. Foreword to L.K. Obler and D. Fein, eds., *Neuropsychology of Talent and Special Abilities* (New York: Guilford).

1987p. Introduction to Japanese Edition of *The Mind's New Science*.

1987q. Introduction to Chinese Edition of *The Arts and Human Development*.

1987r. Cognitive Science after 1984. Epilogue to the paperback edition of *The Mind's New Science* (New York: Basic Books).

1987s. With J. Grunbaum. The Assessment of Artistic Thinking: Comments on the National Assessment of Educational Progress in the Arts. Essay commissioned by the Commission on the National Assessment of Educational Progress. Available on microfiche.

1988a. With E. Winner. Creating a World with Words. In F. Kessel, ed., *The Development of Language and Language Researchers: Essays in Honor of Roger Brown* (Hillsdale: Erlbaum), 353–372.

1988b. With A.M. Bihrle and H.H. Brownell. Humor and the Right Hemisphere: A Narrative Perspective. In H. Whitaker, ed., *Neuropsychological Studies* (New York: Springer).

1988c. With U. Malkus and D.H. Feldman. Dimensions of Mind in Early Childhood. In A.D. Pelligrini, ed., *The Psychological Bases of Early Education* (Chichester: Wiley), 25–38.

1988d. The Need for More Specificity: A Comment on S. Findlay and C. Lumsden, The Creative Mind. *Journal of Social and Biological Structures* 11, 89–92.

1988e. Creative Lives and Creative Works: A Synthetic-Scientific Approach. In R. Sternberg, ed., *The Nature of Creativity* (New York: Cambridge University Press).

1988f. With S.T. Weylman and H.H. Brownell. It's What You Mean, Not What You Say: Pragmatic Language Use in Brain Damaged Patients. In F. Plum, ed., *Language Communication and the Brain* (New York: Raven Press).

1988g. Mobilizing Resources for Individual-Centered Education. In R.S. Nickerson and P.P. Zodhiates, eds., *Technology in Education: Looking Toward 2020* (Hillsdale: Erlbaum).

1988h. With C. Wolf. The Fruits of Asynchrony: A Psychological Examination of Creativity. *Adolescent Psychiatry* 15, 106–123.

1988i. Creativity: An Interdisciplinary Perspective. *Creativity Research Journal* 1, 8–26.

1988j. With J. Walters. Managing Intelligences. *Harvard Project Zero Technical Report #33*. Cambridge, Massachusetts: Harvard University Graduate School of Education.

1988k. With J. Goldman, M. Krechevsky, and J. Meyaard. A Developmental Study of Children's Practical Intelligence for School: A Brief Report. Cambridge, Massachusetts: Harvard University Graduate School of Education, Project Zero.

1988l. Towards More Effective Arts Education. *Journal of Aesthetic Education* 22. Reprinted in R. Smith and A. Simpson, eds., *Aesthetics and Arts Education* (Urbana: University of Illinois Press), 18–19.

1988m. Beyond a Modular View of Mind. In W. Damon, ed., *Child Development Today and Tomorrow* (San Francisco: Jossey-Bass), 222–239. Also in W. Damon, ed., *New Directions in Child Development* (Tenth anniversary edition, 1987).

1988n. With C. Wexler-Sherman and D. Feldman. A Pluralistic View of Early Assessment: The Project Spectrum Approach. *Theory into Practice* 27, 77–83.

1988o. Achieving Critical Balances in Neuropsychology: A Tribute to Harold Goodglass. In S. Blumstein and E.B. Zurif,eds., *Festschrift for Harold Goodglass, Aphasiology,* 2: 3–4, 433–36.

1988p. The Theory of Multiple Intelligences: Educational Implications. *Language and the World of Work in the 21st Century*. Massachusetts Bureau of Transitional Bilingual Education.

1988q. With H. Brownell. Neurological Insights into Humor. In J. Durant and J. Miller, eds., *Laughing Matters* (London: Longman).

1988r. Projects, Prejudices, and the Domain of Developmental Psychology: A Comment on Rick Robinson's Project and Prejudice. *Human Development* 31: 3, 173–75.

1988s. With R. Zessoules and D. Wolf. A Better Balance: Arts PROPEL as an Alternative to Discipline-Based Art Education. In J. Burton, A. Lederman, and P. London, eds., *Beyond DBAE: The Case for Multiple Visions of Art Education* (University Council of Art Education).

1988t. Multiple Intelligences in Today's Schools. *Human Intelligence Newsletter* 9: 2, 1–2.

1988u. With J. Goldman. Multiple Paths to Educational Effectiveness. In D.K. Lipsky and A. Gartner, eds., *Beyond Separate Education: Quality Education for All Students* (Baltimore: Brookes), 121–140.

1988v. Challenges for Museums: Howard Gardner's Theory of Multiple Intelligences. *Hand to Hand* 2: 4 (Fall), 1–7. Salt Lake City: Children's Museum Network.

1988w. With T. Hatch. How Kids Learn: What Scientists Say. *Learning* (December), 36–39.

1988x. With V. Ramos-Ford and D.H. Feldman. A New Look at Intelligence through Project Spectrum. *New Horizons in Learning* 6 (Spring), 7–15.

1988y. At Issue in the Schools: Are We Prepared to Pay the Price of Comprehensive Arts Programs? *Vantage Point in Horizon* (May), 4.

1988z. With E. Winner. Review of *How We Understand Art,* by Michael Parsons. *Human Development* 31: 4 (April 22nd), 256–260.

1989a. *To Open Minds: Chinese Clues to the Dilemma of Contemporary Education*. New York: Basic Books. Translated into Italian. Basic Books Paperback with new introduction, 1991.

1989b.   With D.N. Perkins. *Art, Mind, and Education.* Urbana: University of Illinois Press.

1989c.   With C. Wolf. Arts Education in China. *Journal of Aesthetic Education* 23: 1 (Spring).

1989d.   With J. Kaplan. Artistry after Unilateral Brain Disease. In F. Boller and J. Grafman, eds., *Handbook of Neuropsychology* (Amsterdam: Elsevier).

1989e.   Balancing Specialized and Comprehensive Knowledge: The Growing Education Challenge. In T. Sergiovanni, ed., *Schooling for Tomorrow: Directing Reforms to Issues that Count.* Boston: Allyn and Bacon. Paper originally presented at the Breckenridge Forum, San Antonio, August 1987.

1989f.   With E.B. Zurif and H. Brownell. The Case Against the Case Against Group Studies. *Brain and Cognition* 10, 237–255.

1989g.   The Key in the Slot: Creativity in a Chinese Key. *Journal of Aesthetic Education* 23 (Spring), 141–158.

1989h.   With P. Prather and H.H. Brownell. Providing an Anchor for Neurolinguistic Processing: Should the Right Hemisphere Step Forward? *New Ideas in Psychology* 7, 19–25.

1989i.   Zero-Based Arts Education: An Introduction to Arts PROPEL. *Studies in Art Education* 30: 2, 71–83. Reprinted in *Journal of Art and Design Education* 8 (1989), 167–182.

1989j.   With T. Hatch. Multiple Intelligences Go to School. *Educational Researcher* 18, 4–10.

1989k.   With S.T. Weylman, H.H. Brownell, and M. Roman. Appreciation of Indirect Requests by Left- and Right-Brain Damaged Patients: The Effects of Verbal Context and Conventionality of Wording. *Brain and Language* 36, 580–591.

1989l.   Intelligences. In K. Jervis and A. Tobler, eds., *Education for Democracy: Proceedings from the Cambridge School Conference on Progressive Education* (Weston: The Cambridge School). Reprinted in *Putney Post* (Winter 1992), 16–20, 30.

1989m. With R. Nemirovsky. From Private Institutions to Public Symbol Systems: An Examination of Creative Process in Georg Cantor and Sigmund Freud. Paper presented at the Conference on Creativity and Discovery in the Medical Sciences, the Royal Society of Medicine (October). See also *Creativity Research Journal* 4: 1 (1991), 1–21.

1989n.   The Vision of Social Relations Endures: Comments on the Symposium on Cognitive Development. *Society for Research in Child Development.*

1989o.   The Academic Community Must Not Shun the Debate Over How to Set National Educational Goals. *The Chronicle of Higher Education* (November 8th, 1989), A 52. Republished in Japanese in *Trends.* Reprinted in *Education Digest* (1990), 41–43.

1989p. Learning Chinese Style. *Psychology Today,* 54–56. Reprinted In K. Paciorek and J. Munro, eds., *Early Childhood* (Guilford: Dushkin, 1991–92), 219–221.

1989q. Introduction to the Chinese edition of *The Mind's New Science.*

1989r. Foreword to *Without Reason: A Family Copes with Two Generations of Autism,* by C. Hart. New York: Harper and Row.

1989s. Preface to *Discourse Ability and Brain Damage: Theoretical and Empirical Perspectives,* edited by Y. Joanette and H. Brownell. New York: Springer.

1989t. Symbolic Development. In E. Barnouw, ed., *International Encyclopedia of Communication* (New York: Oxford University Press).

1990a. *Art Education and Human Development.* Los Angeles: Getty Center for Education in the Arts. Translated into Italian and Spanish.

1990b. With E. Phelps and D. Wolf. The Roots of Creativity in Children's Symbolic Products. In C. Alexander and E. Langer, eds., *Higher Stages of Human Development* (New York: Oxford University Press).

1990c. Cognitive Neuroscience and Developmental Psychology: Who Needs Whom? *The Genetic Epistemologist* 18: 2, 7–16.

1990d. With M. Krechevsky. Multiple Intelligences, Multiple Chances. In D. Inbar, ed., *Second Chance in Education: An Interdisciplinary and International Perspective* (London: The Falmer Press), 69–88.

1990e. With H.H. Brownell, T.L. Simpson, A.M. Bihrle, and H. Potter. Appreciation of Metaphoric Alternative Word Meaning by Left and Right Hemisphere Brain Damaged Patients. *Neuropsychologia* 28: 4, 375–383.

1990f. With J.A. Kaplan, H.H. Brownell, and J.R. Jacobs. The Effects of Right Hemisphere Damage on the Pragmatic Interpretation of Conversational Remarks. *Brain and Language* 38, 315–333.

1990g. With R. Molloy and H.H. Brownell. Discourse Comprehension by Right Hemisphere Damaged Patients: Deficits of Prediction and Revision. In Y. Joanette and H.H. Brownell, eds., *Discourse Ability and Brain Damaged: Theoretical and Empirical Perspectives* (New York: Springer).

1990h. With M. Krechevsky. The Emergence and Nurturance of Multiple Intelligences. In M.J.A. Howe, ed., *Encouraging the Development of Exceptional Abilities and Talents* (Leicester: British Psychological Society).

1990i. The Difficulties of School: Probable Causes, Possible Cures. *Daedalus* 119: 2, 85–113. Reprinted in S. Graubard, ed., *Literacy* (New York: Hill and Wang), 85–113.

1990j. With M. Krechevsky. Approaching School Intelligently: An Infusion Approach. In D. Kuhn, ed., *Developmental Perspectives on Teaching and Learning Thinking Skills* (Basel: Karger), 79–94.

1990k. Building on the Range of Human Strengths. *The Churchill Forum* 12: 1, 1–7.

1990l. Four Factors in Educational Reform. *In Context* 27, 15.

1990n. With J.M. Ostrove and T. Simpson. Beyond Scripts: A Note on the Capacity of Right-Hemisphere-Damaged Patients to Process Social and Emotional Content. *Brain and Cognition* 12, 144–154.

1990o. With T. Hatch. If Binet had Looked Beyond the Classroom: The Assessment of Multiple Intelligences. *International Journal of Educational Research,* 415–429. Reprinted (abridged) in *Innotech Journal* 16: 1 (1992), 18–36; *NAMTA Journal* 21: 2 (1996), 5–28; and B. Torff, ed., *Multiple Intelligences and Assessment* (Arlington Heights: IRI Skylight, 1997).

1990p. Multiple Intelligences: Implications for Education. In W. Moody, ed., *Artistic Intelligences: Implications for Education in a Democracy* (New York: Teachers College Press), 11–27. Reprinted in D. Keane, ed., *National College of Ireland Learning and Teaching Journal* 1: 1 (April 2004).

1990q. With T. Blythe. A School for All Intelligences. *Educational Leadership,* 33–37.

1990r. With M. Kornhaber and M. Krechevsky. Engaging Intelligence. *Educational Psychologist* 25: 3–4, 177–199.

1990s. With J. Walters. Domain Projects as Assessment Vehicles in a Computer-Rich Environment. *Technical Report* (New York: Bank Street College, Center for Technology in Education). Reprinted in B. Torff, ed., *Multiple Intelligences and Assessment* (Arlington Heights: IRI Skylight, 1997).

1990t. With J. Viens. Multiple Intelligences and Styles: Partners in Effective Education. *The Clearinghouse Bulletin: Learning/Teaching Styles and Brain Behavior* 4, 2, 4–5. Seattle: Association for Supervision and Curriculum Development.

1990u. Teach them to Write. In A. Ornstein, ed., *Strategies for Effective Teaching* (New York: Harper and Row), 197.

1990v. Introducing *Lift–Off.* Australian Children's Television Foundation, Annual Report (1990–1991), 8–12.

1990w. Preface to *Varieties of Thinking,* by V. Howard and I. Scheffler. New York: Routledge.

1991a. *The Unschooled Mind: How Children Think and How Schools Should Teach.* New York: Basic Books. Translated into Spanish, Italian, German, Swedish, Norwegian, Chinese (R.C.), Chinese (Taiwan), Portuguese, Croatian, French, and Danish. Adopted by the Reader's Subscription Book Club. British Edition, London: HarperCollins (Fontana, 1993). Second edition with new preface, 2004.

1991b. Assessment in Context: The Alternative to Standardized Testing. In B.R. Gifford and M.C. O'Connor, eds., *Changing Assessments:*

Alternative Views of Aptitude, Achievement, and Instruction (Boston: Kluwer), 77–120.

1991c. The School of the Future. In J. Brockman. *Ways of Knowing: The Reality Club 3* (Englewood Cliffs: Prentice Hall), 199–217.

1991d. With E. Winner. The Course of Creative Growth: A Tribute to Joachim Wohlwill. In R.M. Downs, L.S. Liben, and D.S. Palermo, eds., *Visions of Aesthetics, the Environment, and Development: The Legacy of Joachim F. Wohlwill* (Hillsdale: Erlbaum), 23–43.

1991e. With C. Von Karolyi and V. Ramos-Ford. Giftedness from a Multiple Intelligences Perspective. In N. Colangelo and G. Davis, eds., *Handbook of Gifted Education, Second edition* (Boston: Allyn and Bacon), 55–65.

1991f. With M. Kornhaber. Critical Thinking Across Multiple Intelligences. Paper presented at the O.C.E.D. Conference, Learning to Think, Thinking to Learn (Paris, July 1989). In S. Maclure and Davies, eds., *Learning to Think: Thinking to Learn: The Proceedings of the 1989 OECD Conference* (Oxford: Pergamon, 1991), 147–168.

1991g. With D. Wolf, J. Bixby, and J. Glenn. To Use Their Minds Well: Investigating New Forms of Student Assessment. In Gerald Grant, ed., *Review of Research in Education:* (Washington, D.C.: AERA), 31–74.

1991h. With R. Zessoules. Authentic Assessment: Beyond the Buzzword and into the Classroom. In V. Perrone, ed., *Expanding Student Assessment*, 47–71. Yearbook of the Association for Supervision and Curriculum Development.

1991i. Intelligence in Seven Phases. Paper presented at the Centennial of Education at Harvard. Précis published in the *Harvard Graduate School Alumni Bulletin* 36: 1 (Fall), 18–19.

1991j. The Tensions Between Education and Development. *Journal of Moral Education* 20: 2, 113–125.

1991k. With E. Winner and A. Rehak. Artistry and Aphasia. In M.T. Sarno, ed., *Acquired Aphasia Second Edition* (New York: Academic Press), 373–404.

1991l. Multiple Intelligences and the Arts. Paper delivered at a Meeting of Music Education at the University of Southern Florida (Tampa, March). Published in Proceedings.

1991m. Cognition: A Western Perspective. In D. Goleman and R.A.F. Thurman, eds., *MindScience: An East-West Dialogue* (Boston: Wisdom Publications), 75–87. Based on a paper delivered at *Symposium on Mind Science: The Dialogue Between East and West*. Symposium conducted at the Massachusetts Institute of Technology.

1991n. Making Schools More like Museums. *Education Week* 40 (October 9th). Reprinted in *Atlanta Journal* (November 17th).

1991o. The Nature of Intelligence. In A. Lewin, ed., *How We Think and Learn* (Washington, D.C.: National Learning Center), 41–46.

1991p. A Voucher Plan to Enrich Education. *Boston Sunday Globe* (September 15th), A26.

1991q. Foreword to *Seven Ways of Knowing: Teaching for Multiple Intelligences,* by D. Lazear. Palatine: Skylight.

1991r. Mind Explorers Merge Their Maps. Review of *In the Palaces of Memory,* by G. Johnson. *New York Times* (February 8th).

1991s. Intelligence in Seven Steps. In D. Dickinson, ed., *Creating the Future: Perspectives on Educational Change* (Birmingham: Accelerated Learning Systems), 68–75. Also in *Intelligent Connections* 1 (Fall 1991), 1–8; *Harvard Graduate School of Education Alumni Bulletin* 36: 1 (Fall 1991), 17–19. Reprinted in *Provoking Thoughts* 4: 2.

1992a. Scientific Psychology: Should We Bury It or Praise It? William James Award Address. *New Ideas in Psychology* 10: 2, 179–190.

1992b. With P. Prather. Developmental Neuropsychology: Lessons from Cognitive Development. In S. Segalowitz and I. Rapin, eds., *Handbook of Neuropsychology* 6 (Amsterdam: Elsevier), 419–438.

1992c. With A. Rehak and J.A. Kaplan. Sensitivity to Conversational Deviance in Right Hemisphere Damaged Patients. *Brain and Language* 42, 203–217.

1992d. With A. Rehak, J.A. Kaplan, S. Weylman, B. Kelly, and H.H. Brownell. Story Processing in Right Hemisphere Brain Damaged Patients. *Brain and Language* 42, 320–336.

1992e. With J. Davis. The Cognitive Revolution: Its Consequences for the Understanding and Education of the Child as Artist. In B. Reimer and R.A. Smith, eds., *1992 Yearbook of the National Society for the Study of Education* (Chicago: University of Chicago Press), 92–123

1992f. Psychological Studies, Maybe—Scientific Psychology, No: A Response to Five Constructive Critics. *New Ideas in Psychology* 10: 2, 229–231.

1992g. With N. White and T. Blythe. Multiple Intelligence Theory: Creating the Thoughtful Classroom. In A. Costa, J. Bellanca, and R. Fogarty, eds., *If Mind Matters: A Foreword to the Future* 2 (Palatine: Skylight), 127–134.

1992h. Reflecting on Project Zero. Theoretical Perspectives: Research into Children's Cognition and Knowledge in the Visual Arts. Proceedings from *Third Occasional Seminar in Art Education.* Sydney: University of New South Wales, College of Fine Arts.

1992i Response to Kieran Egan's Review of *The Unschooled Mind. Teachers College Record* 94: 2 (Winter), 407–413.

1992j. On Psychology and Youth Museums: Toward an Education for Understanding. *Hand to Hand* 6: 3 (Fall), 1–6. Salt Lake City: Children's Museum Network.

1992k. From Intelligence to Intelligences and Beyond. *Synapsia: The International Brain Club Journal* 3: 3 (Autumn), 5–8. Paper presented at Young Presidents' Organization, 1991.

1992l. With J. Walters and T. Hatch. If Teaching had Looked Beyond the Classroom: The Development and Education of Intelligences. *Innotech Journal* 16: 1, 18–36.

1992m. The Unschooled Mind. Presentation to The Cambridge Forum (4th March, 1992).

1992n. The Two Rhetorics of School Reform: Complex Theories versus the Quick Fix. *Chronicle of Higher Education* 38: 35 (6th May), B1–2.

1992o. Constraints and Opportunities in Life. Commencement Address, Curry College, Milton, Massachusetts (May 17th).

1992p. Combining Two Conversations. *Education Week/Special Report* (June 17th), S20.

1992q. Beyond the Walls of School. *Newsweek* (September 21st), A4.

1992r. A New Edition of Frames of Mind. Developing Human Intelligence. *Publication of New Horizons for Learning* 13: 1 (Fall 1992), 10–11.

1992s. The Activist Library: A Symposium. *The Nation* 300 (September 21st).

1992t. Foreword to *Parenting our Schools,* by J. Bloom. Boston: Little Brown.

1993a. *Multiple Intelligences: The Theory in Practice.* New York: Basic Books. Translated into Spanish, Portuguese, Italian, French, Chinese (Taiwan), Hebrew, Korean, Polish, Chinese (R.C.), Danish, Ukranian, and Japanese. Selected by three book clubs. Excerpted in the magazine *Behinderte in Familie, Schule und Gesellschaft* 2 (1997). Abridged Danish translation, 1997, Copenhagen: Glydendal Undervisning

1993b. *Creating Minds: An Anatomy of Creativity Seen Through the Lives of Freud, Einstein, Picasso, Stravinsky, Eliot, Graham, and Gandhi.* New York: Basic Books. Quality Paperback Book Club. Translated into Swedish, German, Spanish, Chinese (Taiwan), Portuguese, Italian, Slovenian, Korean, Polish, and French.

1993c. With J.M. Ostrove, J. Kaplan, and H.H. Brownell. The Components of Linguistic Discourse: Lessons from Neuropsychology. In P. Gryzbyk. *Psychosemiotics-Neurosemiotics* (Bochum: Universitatsverlag Dr. Norbert Brockmeyer), 111–132.

1993d. With E. Winner. Metaphor and Irony: Two Levels of Understanding. In A. Ortony,ed., *Metaphor and Thought.* Second edition (New York: Cambridge University Press), 425–443.

1993e. With J. Davis. The Arts and Early Childhood Education: A Cognitive Developmental Portrait of the Young Child as Artist. In B. Spodek, ed., *Handbook of Research in Early Childhood Education* (New York: Macmillan), 191–206.

1993f. With M. Kornhaber. Varieties of Excellence and Conditions for Their Achievement. Paper prepared for *Commission on Varieties of Excellence in the Schools,* New York State. New York: The National Center for Restructuring Education, Schools, and Teaching (March).

1993g. With T. Hatch. Finding Cognition in the Classroom: An Expanded View of Human Intelligence. In G. Salomon, ed., *Distributed Cognitions* (New York: Cambridge University Press), 164–187.

1993h. With J. Li. How Domains Constrain Creativity: The Case of Traditional Chinese and Western Painting. *American Behavioral Scientist* 37: 11, 94–101.

1993i. The Intelligence-Giftedness Complex. In H. Rosselli and G. MacLauchlan, eds., *Blueprinting for the Future.* Proceedings of the Edyth Bush Symposium on Intelligence, Tampa.

1993j. Mahatma Gandhi: A Hold Upon Others. *Creativity Research Journal* 6: 2, 29–44.

1993k. Seven Creators of the Modern Era. In J. Brockman, ed., *Creativity* (New York: Simon and Schuster), 28–47.

1993l. The Relationship Between Early Giftedness and Later Achievement. *Ciba Conference* 178, 175–186. Chichester: Wiley. Paper presented at *The Origins and Development of High Ability,* CIBA, London.

1993m. From Conflict to Clarification: A Comment on Kieran Egan's Narrative and Learning: A Voyage of Implication. *Linguistics and Education* 5: 2, 181–85.

1993n. The School and the Work Place of the Future. *Synapsia: The International Brain Club Journal* (Winter), 22–26.

1993o. Progressivism in a New Key. Paper delivered at the *Conference on Education and Democracy.* Jerusalem (June 1993).

1993p. Intelligence and Intelligences: Universal Principles and Individual Differences. *Archives de Psychologie* 61, 238, 169–172. Prepared for a Festschrift in honor of the 80th birthday of Professor Bärbel Inhelder.

1993q. With J. Davis. Open Windows, Open Doors. *Museum News* (February), 34–37, 57, 58.

1993r. Music as Intelligence. *Kodaly Envoy* 20: 1 (Fall), 14–21.

1993s. Educating the Unschooled Mind. Capital Hill Presentation sponsored by the Federation of Behavioral, Psychological, and Cognitive Sciences, Association of Science-Technology Centers.

1993t. The Unschooled Mind: Why Even the Best Students in the Best Schools do not Understand. *International Schools Journal* 26 (Autumn), 29–33. Originally presented as the Alec Peterson Lecture to the International Baccalaureate Conference, Geneva (December 1992). See also *IB World Magazine.*

1993u. With L.A. Baker, J. Asendorpf, D.Bishop, D.I. Boomsma, T.J. Bouchard, C.R. Brand, D.W. Fulker, and M. Kinsbourne. Intelligence and its Inheritance: A Diversity of Views. In T.J. Bouchard and P. Propping, eds., *Twins as a Tool of Behavioral Genetics* (Chichester: Wiley), 85–108.

1993v. Educating for Understanding. *American School Board Journal* 180: 7 (July), 20–24.

1993w. Les Dimensions de l'intelligence spatiale. *Mscope Revue* 6, 45–53.

1993x. Choice Points as Multiple Intelligences Enter the School. *Intelligence Connections* 3: 1 (Fall).

1993y. Halting the Spread of Educational Fraud and Deception. *Chronicle of Higher Education* (January 13th), B3.

1993z. Tackling the Two Crises of Music. Commencement Address, New England Conservatory of Music (May 23rd).

1993aa. With L. Mammen. Interview with Howard Gardner. *Think* (April), 2–5.

1993ab. A Discussion with Jacqueline Anglin. *Midwestern Educational Supplement* 6: 1 (Winter), 18–20.

1993ac. Comments on K. Howard's Portfolio Culture in Pittsburgh. In R. Jennings. *Fire in the Eyes of Youth: The Humanities in American Education* (St. Paul: Occasional Press), 99–102.

1993ad. Lost Youth. *The Guardian* (London, October 12th) Education Section.

1993ae. Opening Minds. *Demos* 1, 1–5. Reprinted in G. Mulgan, ed., *Life After Politics: New Thinking for the Twenty–First Century* (London: Fontana, 1997), 101–110.

1993af. Foreword to C. Edwards, L. Gandini, and G. Forman, eds., *The Hundred Languages of Children* (Norwood: Ablex). Translated into Italian.

1993ag. Preface to K.A. Heller, F.J. Monks, and A.H. Passow, eds., *International Handbook of Research and Development of Giftedness and Talent* (London: Pergamon).

1993ah. With H.H. Brownell, J.R. Jacobs, and D. Gianoulis. Conditions for Sarcasm. Unpublished paper from the Boston University Aphasia Research Center and Harvard Project Zero.

1993ai. With H.H. Brownell, J.M. Ostrove, W.A. Postelthwaite, M.S. Seibold, M. Roman, and D.L. McDougall. Senstivity to Tonal Goodness and Pitch Height in Unilaterally Left- and Right-Hemisphere Brain Damaged Patients.

1994a. With D. Feldman and M. Csikzentmihalyi. *Changing the World: A Framework for the Study of Creativity.* Westport: Praeger.

1994b. With M. Krechevsky. Multiple Intelligences in Multiple Contexts. In D.K. Detterman. *Current Topics in Human Intelligence: Volume 4. Theories of Intelligence* (Norwood: Ablex), 285–305.

1994c. How Extraordinary was Mozart? Paper presented at the *Woodrow Wilson Center Symposium on the 200th Anniversary of the Death of Mozart,* Washington, D.C. In J.M. Morris, ed., *On Mozart* (Washington, D.C.: Woodrow Wilson Center Press), 36–51.

1994d. With N. Granott. When Minds Meet: Interactions, Coincidence, and Development in Domains of Ability. In R.J. Sternberg and R.K.

Wagner, eds., *Mind in Context: Interactionist Perspectives on Human Intelligence* (New York: Cambridge University Press), 171–201.

1994e. With S. Simmons. Thinking in the Arts. Paper prepared for NEA and DOE Conference, *Arts in American Schools: Setting a Research Agenda for the 90s.*

1994f. On Intelligence. In R.H. Ettinger, R.L. Crooks, and J. Stein, eds., *Psychology: Science, Behavior, and Life* (Fort Worth: Harcourt Brace), 515–521.

1994g. The Stories of the Right Hemisphere. In W.D. Spaulding, ed., *Integrative Views of Motivation, Cognition, and Emotion, Volume 41 of The Nebraska Symposium on Motivation* (Lincoln: University of Nebraska Press), 57–69. First Delivered as a paper at the Nebraska Symposium on Motivation (October 1992).

1994h. With M. Krecehvsky, R. Sternberg, and L. Okagaki. Intelligence in Context: Enhancing Students' Practical Intelligences for School. In K. McGilly, ed., *Classroom Lessons: Integrating Cognitive Theory and Classroom Practice* (Cambridge, Massachusetts: MIT Press), 105–127.

1994i. The Creators' Patterns. In M. Boden. *Dimensions of Creativity* (Cambridge, Massachusetts: MIT Press), 143–158.

1994j. With J. Walters and S. Seidel. Children as Reflective Practitioners: Bringing Metacognition to the Classroom. In J. Mangieri and C. Collins Block, eds., *Creating Powerful Thinking in Teachers and Students: Diverse Perspectives* (Orlando: Holt, Rinehart), 288–303.

1994k. With V. Boix-Mansilla. Teaching for Understanding within and Across the Disciplines. *Educational Leadership* 51: 5 (February), 14–18.

1994l. With V. Boix-Mansilla. Teaching for Understanding in the Disciplines—and Beyond. *Teachers College Record* 96: 2 (Winter), 198–218. Paper prepared for the Conference on Teachers' Conceptions of Knowledge, Tel Aviv, June 1993.

1994m. Five Forms of Creative Activity: A Developmental Perspective. In N. Colangelo, S. Assouline, and D.L. Ambroson, eds., *Talent Development, Volume 2: Proceedings from the 1993 Henry B. and Jocelyn Wallace National Research Symposium on Talent Development* (Dayton: Ohio Psychology Press), 3–17. Presented at a Conference on Giftedness, University of Iowa (May 1993).

1994n. Intelligences in Theory and Practice: A Response to Elliot W. Eisner, Robert J. Sternberg, and Henry M. Levin. *Teachers College Record* 95: 4 (Summer), 1–8.

1994o. The Patterns of Creation. *Helix* 3: 2, 36–43.

1994p. Multiple Intelligences: A View from the Arts. *Issues 1994*, 5–22. Based on a talk delivered to a conference of the Art Educators of New Jersey, October 1993.

1994q. More on Private Institutions and Public School Systems. *Creativity Research Journal* 7: 3–4, 265–275.

1994r. With J. Gray and B. Torff. Learning and Teaching in the Behavioral Sciences: Intuitive Conceptions, Scholastic Knowledge, and Disciplinary Expertise. Unpublished paper prepared for the Faculty Research and Innovation Fund at HGSE.

1994s. Entry on Multiple Intelligences Theory. In R. Sternberg, ed., *Encyclopedia of Human Intelligence* 2 (New York: Macmillan), 740–42.

1994t. Multiple Intelligences. *Quest* (January). Kumon Institute of Education.

1994u. Are Intelligence Tests Intelligent? In R.H. Ettinger, R.L. Crooks, and J. Stein, eds., *Psychology: Science, Behavior, and Life*. Third edition (Fort Worth: Harcourt Brace), 214–221.

1994v. The Need for Anti-Babel Standards. *Education Week* 56 (September 7th).

1994w. With D. Perkins. The Mark of Zero: Project Zero's Identity Revealed. *HGSE Alumni Bulletin* 39: 1 (December), 2–6.

1994x. Foreword to T. Marks–Tarlow, *Creativity Inside Out: Learning through Multiple Intelligences* (New York: Addison Wesley).

1994y. Review of *The Protean Self*, by R.J. Lifton. *Boston Book Review* 1: 2, 19–20.

1994z. Preface to *Multiple Intelligences in the Classroom*, by T. Armstrong. Alexandria: Association for Supervision and Curriculum Development.

1995a. With the collaboration of E. Laskin. *Leading Minds: An Anatomy of Leadership*. New York: Basic Books. Translated into German, Italian, Swedish, Portuguese, Chinese (Taiwan), Greek, Korean, Spanish, and Japanese. British Edition: HarperCollins, 1996. Basic Books Paperback.

1995b. Perennial Antinomies and Perpetual Redrawings: Is There Progress in the Study of Mind? In R. Solso and D. Massaro, eds., *Science of the Mind: 2001 and Beyond* (New York: Oxford University Press), 65–78.

1995c. With H. Brownell, P. Prather, and G. Martino. Language, Communication, and the Right Hemisphere. In H. Kirschner, ed., *Handbook for Neurological Speech and Language Disorders* (New York: Marcel Dekker), 325–350.

1995d. With M. Krechevsky and T. Hoerr. Complementary Energies: Implementing MI Theory from the Laboratory and from the Field. In J. Oakes and K.H. Quartz, eds., *Creating New Educational Communities*. 94th Yearbook of the National Society for the Study of Education, Part I (Chicago: University of Chicago Press), 166–186.

1995e. With M.L. Kornhaber. Solving for *g* and Beyond. In *Triumph of Discovery: A Chronicle of Great Adventures in Science* (New York:

Holt), 121–23. Selected by Quality Paperback Book Club and Book of the Month Club.

1995f. With E. Policastro. Naive Judgment and Expert Assessment: A Critique of the Attributional Perspective. *Creativity Research Journal* 8: 4, 391–95.

1995g. Reflections on Multiple Intelligences: Myths and Messages. *Phi Delta Kappan* 77: 3 (November), 200–09. Reprinted in: *International Schools Journal* 15: 2, 8–22. K.G. Duffy, ed., *Annual Editions: Psychology 97/98* (Guilford: Dushkin, 1997), 101–05. K.M. Cauley, F. Linder, and J.H. McMillan, eds., *Annual Editions: Educational Psychology 97/98* (Guildford: Dushkin, 1997, 108–112. Translated in E. Beck, *et al.*, *Lernkultur im Wandel* (St. Gallen: UVK, Fachverl. für Wiss. und Studium, 1997), 45–60. K.G. Duffy, ed., *Annual Editions: Psychology 99/00* (Guilford: Dushkin, 1999), 89–93. *Books of the Century* (Catalogue of the University of South Carolina, Museum of Education, 2000), 126–127. With response by Klein in L. Abbeduto, ed., *Taking Sides: Clashing Views on Controversial Issues in Educational Psychology.* Second edition (Guilford: Dushkin, 1999), 78–203. Translated, in M. Baldacci, R. Gaspari, A. Giallongo, C. Marini, and R. Travaglini, eds., *Educazione e Civilta: Studi in Onore di Nando Filograsso* (Rome: Anicia, 2004).

1995h. Limited Visions, Limited Means: Two Obstacles to Meaningful Educational Reform. *Daedalus* 124: 4 (Fall), 101–05.

1995i. Why Would Anyone Become an Expert? Critique of A. Ericsson and N. Charness, *Expert Performance: Its Structure and Acquistion. American Psychologist* 50: 9 (September), 802–04.

1995j. A Response on Four Fronts. Comments on D. Lubinski and C. Benbow, "An Opportunity for Empiricism" (Review of H. Gardner, *Multiple Intelligences*). With rejoinder. *Contemporary Psychology* 40: 10 (October), 938–39.

1995k. Creativity: New Views from Psychology and Education. Talk Delivered to the Royal Society for the Encouragement of Arts, Manufactures, and Commerce. *RSA Journal* 143: 5459 (January), 33–42.

1995l. Multiple Intelligences and the Learning Society. Address delivered to the North of England Education Conference, York (5th January, 1995). *Record of Proceedings* (York: University of York and North Yorkshire County Council), 22–28.

1995m. Individual Learning Differences: The Quest for New Perspectives. Address delivered at the New York Historical Society (3rd December, 1993). Proceedings published by Winston Preparatory School, New York.

1995n. Multiple Intelligences as a Catalyst. *English Journal* 84: 8, 16–18.

1995o. With T. Blythe and N. White. Teaching Practical Intelligence. *What*

Research Tells Us. Series of booklets (West Lafayette: Kappa Delta Pi).

1995p. With M. Csikszentmihalyi, W. Damon, and E. Winner. Forging Links between Creativity and Morality. Extracts from a Symposium Moderated by Raphi Amram. Jerusalem: The Israel Arts and Science Academy (30th August).

1995q. Creating Creativity. *Times Educational Supplement* 1 (6th January).

1995r. When Leaders Set Out to Conquer the Word. *Independent* (London, 23rd January).

1995s. Loners Who Shape Our Destiny. *The Times* (London, 2nd January), 4.

1995t. Essays about Programming Themes: Education. *Programming that Defines the Power and Promise of Public Television.* 1995 Statement of Programming Objectives for Public Television (Corporation for Public Broadcasting), 9–10.

1995u. Self–Raising Power. *Times Higher Education Supplement* (28th July), 15–16. Reprinted: A Cognitive View of Leadership. *Education Week* (13th September, 1995), 34–35. Reprinted: Leading Minds. *Harvard Graduate School of Education Bulletin* 40: 1 (December 1995), 24–25. Reprinted: The Intelligence of Leadership. *Interactive Teacher* 1: 1 (February–March 1996), 26–28.

1995v. ECT Interview of the Month. *Early Childhood Today* 10: 1 (August–September), 30–32.

1995w. Interview with Phil Harris. *Technos* 4 (Summer), 2, 4–7.

1995x. Yet. In L.B. Frumkes, ed., *The Logophile's Orgy* (New York: Delacorte), 62–63.

1995y. Information Is Not the Same Thing as Knowledge. Based on presentation to the Milken Family Foundation Conference (5th May, 1995). Reprinted: Teaching for Understanding. *Teacher-to-Teacher* 4: 2 (1996), 2–3.

1995z. The Meaning of Multiple Intelligence. *Post-Dispatch* (St. Louis, 26th December), 15B.

1995aa. With E.F. Shores. Interview. Howard Gardner on the Eighth Intelligence: Seeing the Natural World. *Dimensions of Early Childhood* (Summer), 5–7.

1995ab. Cracking Open the IQ Box. Review of *The Bell Curve: Intelligence and Class Structure in American Life,* by R. Hernstein and C. Murray. *The American Prospect* 20 (Winter), 71–80. Reprinted in *Rethinking Schools* 9: 2 (1994), 15–16. Reprinted in S. Fraser, ed., *The Bell Curve Wars* (New York: Basic Books, 1995), 23–25. Reprinted in R. Jacoby and N. Glauberman, eds., *The Bell Curve Debate* (New York: Times Books of Random House, 1995), 61–72. Reprinted (abridged) in T.L. Roleff, ed., *Genetics and Intelligence* (San Diego: Greenhaven, 1996), 115–19.

1995ac. Green Ideas Sleeping Furiously. Review of *The Language Instinct: How the Mind Creates Language,* by S. Pinker; *Beyond Modularity: A Developmental Perspective on Cognitive Science,* by A. Karmiloff–Smith; *Acts of Meaning,* by J. Bruner. *New York Review of Books* 42: 5 (23rd March), 32–38.

1995ad. Foreword to *Integrating Curricula with Multiple Intelligences: Teams, Themes, and Threads,* by R. Fogarty and J. Stoehr (Palatine: Skylight).

1995ae. The Man Without a Past. Review of *Memory's Ghost,* by J. Hilts. *New York Times Book Review* (13th August), 13.

1995af. Anatomy of Melancholy. Review of *An Unquiet Mind: A Memoir of Moods and Madness,* by K.R. Jamison. *Nature* 377 (19th October 19), 587.

1996a. With M. Kornhaber and W. Wake. *Intelligence: Multiple Perspectives.* Fort Worth: Harcourt Brace. Translated into Croation, Korean, Portuguese, and Polish.

1996b. With W. Williams, T. Blythe, N. White, J. Li, and R. Sternberg. *Practical Intelligence for School.* New York: Harper Collins.

1996c. With R. DiNozzi, producer. *MI: Intelligence, Understanding, and the Mind.* Los Angeles: Into the Classroom Media. Related material: *Howard Gardner: Answers.*

1996d. The Assessment of Student Learning in the Arts. In D. Boughton, E. Eisner, and J. Ligtvoet, eds., *Evaluating and Assessing the Visual Arts in Education* (New York: Teachers College Press), 131–155. Based on a paper presented in Bosschenhooft, The Netherlands, December 1990. Response by J. Steers and rejoinder by H. Gardner.

1996e. With J. Davis. Creativity: Who, What, When, Where? In A. Montuori, ed., *Unusual Associates: A Festschrift for Frank Barron* (Cresskill: Hampton Press), 138–147.

1996f. The Years Before College. In N.H. Farnham and A. Yarmolinsky, eds., *Rethinking Liberal Education* (New York: Oxford University Press), 91–107. Based on a paper prepared for the Conference on Educational Leadership, Christian A. Johnson Endeavor Foundation, Cambridge, Massachusetts, 1994.

1996g. With B. Torff and T. Hatch. The Age of Innocence Reconsidered: Preserving the Best of the Progressive Traditions in Psychology and Education. In D.R. Olson and N. Torrance, eds., *The Handbook of Education and Human Development: New Models of Learning, Teaching, and Schooling* (Cambridge, Massachusetts: Blackwell), 28–55. Translated into French in *Revue Française de Pédagogie* 111 (Spring 1995), 35–36.

1996h. With S. Veenema. Multimedia and Multiple Intelligences. *The American Prospect* (November–December), 69–75. Based on a presentation, 4th June, 1996.

1996i. La Sensibilità Stilistica nel Campo delle Arti. In J. Tafuri, ed., *La Comprensione degli stili musicali: Problemi teorici e aspetti evloutivi* 6: 10, 37–49. Bologna: Società Italiana per L'educazione Musicale.

1996j. Zur Entwicklung des Spektrums der Menschlichen Intelligenzen. *Beiträge zur Lehrerbildung* 14: 2, 198–209.

1996k. Viewpoints: Should Novels Count as Dissertations in Education? *Research in the Teaching of English* 30: 4 (December), 403–427. Based on a transcript of the AERA presentation, Yes, But Is It Research? (April 1996).

1996l. Probing More Deeply into the Theory of Multiple Intelligences. *NASSP Bulletin:* (November) 1–7.

1996m. Leadership: A Cognitive Perspective. *SAIS Review* 16: 2 (Summer–Autumn), 109–122.

1996n. Working at Harvard: My First Thirty-Five Years. *GSD News* (Fall), 40–41.

1996o. Issues in Arts Education: Toward the 21st Century. Based on commencement address, Cleveland Institute of Music (May). Available online www.cwru.edu/cim/prep/issues.htm.

1996p. The Darwinian Family. Review of *Born to Rebel,* by F.J. Sulloway. *Nature* 384 (14th November), 125–26. Reprinted in *High Ability Studies* 8: 1 (1997).

1996q. Foreword to T. Hoerr, *et al., Succeeding with M.I.* St. Louis: New City School.

1997a. *Extraordinary Minds: Portraits of Exceptional Individuals and an Examination of Our Extraordinariness.* New York: Basic Books. British edition, London: Weidenfeld and Nicolson, 1997. Translated into French, Portuguese, Chinese (Taiwan), Chinese (PRC), Polish, Hungarian, Czech, Spanish, Korean, and German.

1997b. *De Mange Intelligensers Paedagogik.* Copenhagen: Glydendal Undervisning.

1997c. With M. Levine. *Reaching Minds.* Chapel Hill: All Kinds of Minds (Audiocassette series).

1997d. With T. Hatch and B. Torff. A Third Perspective: The Symbol Systems Approach. In R. Sternberg and E. Grigerenko, eds., *Intelligence, Heredity, and Environment* (New York: Cambridge University Press), 243–268.

1997e. Creative Genius. In S. Schachter and O. Devinsky, eds., *Behavioral Neurology and the Legacy of Norman Geschwind* (New York: Lippincott-Raven), 47–51.

1997f. With J. Chen. Alternative Assessment from a Multiple Intelligences Theoretical Perspective. In D. Flanagan, J. Genshaft, and Harrison, eds., *Contemporary Intellectual Assessment: Theories, Tests, and Issues* (New York: Guilford), 105–121. Reprinted in B. Torff, ed., *Multiple Intelligences and Assessment* (Arlington Heights: IRI Skylight, 1997).

1997g. Six Afterthoughts: Comments on Varieties of Intellectual Talent. *Journal of Creative Behavior* 31: 2, 120–24. Based on a presentation with Julian Stanley at AERA (1995).

1997h. With V. Boix-Mansilla. Of Kinds of Disciplines and Kinds of Understanding. *Phi Delta Kappan* 78: 5 (January), 381–86.

1997i. Fostering Diversity through Personalized Education: Implications of a New Understanding of Human Intelligence. *Prospects* [Journal of UNESCO's International Bureau of Education] 27: 3, 347–363. Translated and Reprinted in French in *Perspectives* 27: 3, 369–387; in Spanish in *Perspectivas* 27: 3, 371–389; in Russian, Chinese, and Arabic.

1997j. With J. Viens and J-Q. Chen. Theories of Intelligence and Critiques. In J.L. Paul *et al.*, *Foundations of Special Education* (Pacific Grove: Brooks-Cole), 122–141.

1997k. Is Musical Intelligence Special? In V. Brummett, ed., *Ithaca Conference '96: Music as Intelligence, a Sourcebook* (Ithaca: Ithaca College). Based on a conference keynote, September 1996. Reprinted in *Choral Journal* (March 1998), 23–24.

1997l. With M. Csikzentmihalyi and W. Damon. Reporting the News in an Age of Accelerating Power and Pressure: The Private Quest to Preserve the Public Trust. Unpublished paper from the Project on Human Creativity.

1997m. Creativity over the Lifespan. *HILR 20th Anniversary* (April), 37–44. Based on presentation of the Robert C. Cobb, Sr., Memorial Lecture to the Harvard Institute on Learning in Retirement (September 1996).

1997n. Developmental Views of Multiple Intelligence. In G.O. Mazur, ed., *Twenty Year Commemoration to the Life of A.R. Luria (1902–1977)* (New York: Semenenko Foundation), 61–79.

1997o. Learning and the Imagination. *The Touchstone Center Journal*, 71–89. Based on remarks at the Touchstone Center, New York (April 1996).

1997p. Unpublished remarks based on an address at a professional development conference of the Massachusetts Teachers Association (MTA) (Boston, March).

1997q. That Jewish Thing. *New Statesman* 53, (11th July).

1997r. Why Study Extraordinary Minds? Unpublished remarks at the Commencement of Macalester College, St. Paul (25th May).

1997s. Multiple Intelligences as a Partner in School Improvement. *Educational Leadership* 55: 1 (September), 20–21.

1997t. With K. Checkley. The First Seven . . . and the Eighth: A Conversation with Howard Gardner. *Educational Leadership* 55: 1 (September), 8–13.

1997u. Our Many Intelligences: Kinds of Minds. In Betty Debnam, ed., *The Mini Page*. A Children's supplement to local newspapers. Universal Press Syndicate (1st March).

1997v. Truth, Beauty, and Goodness: Education for all Human Beings.
        Interview with John Brockman. www.edge.org (September). Reprinted
        in B. Presseisen, ed., *Teaching for Intelligence I: A Collection of Articles*
        (Arlington Heights: SkyLight, 1999), 27–38.

1997w. The Confidence Man. Review of *The Creation of Dr. B.: A Biography
        of Bruno Bettelheim,* by R. Pollak. *Los Angeles Times Book Review* 3
        (19th January).

1997x. Introduction to B. Powell, *Two Cases of Understanding* (Providence:
        Annenberg Institute). Prepared for the Annenberg Institute/Coalition
        of Essential Schools.

1997y. Thinking about Thinking. Review of *The Prehistory of the Mind: The
        Cognitive Origins of Art, Religion, and Science,* by S. Mithen. *New
        York Review of Books* 44: 15 (9th October), 23–27. An exchange of let-
        ters published May 14th, 1998.

1998a. With D.H. Feldman and M. Krechevsky, general eds. *Project Zero
        Frameworks for Early Childhood Education: Volume 1, Building on
        Children's Strengths: The Experience of Project Spectrum,* by J-Q
        Chen, M. Krechevsky, J. Viens, and E. Isberg. New York: Teachers
        College Press. Translated into Chinese, Italian, Spanish, and
        Portuguese.

1998b. With D.H. Feldman and M. Krechevsky, general eds. *Project Zero
        Frameworks for Early Childhood Education: Volume 2, Project
        Spectrum Early Learning Activities,* by J-Q Chen, E. Isberg, and M.
        Krechevsky. New York: Teachers College Press. Translated into
        Chinese, Italian, Spanish, and Portuguese.

1998c. With D.H. Feldman, and M. Krechevsky, eds. *Project Zero
        Frameworks for Early Childhood Education, Volume 3, Project
        Spectrum Preschool Assessment Handbook,* by M. Krechevsky. New
        York: Teachers College Press. Translated into Chinese, Italian,
        Spanish, and Portuguese.

1998d. With R. DiNozzi, producer. *Creativity and Leadership: Making the
        Mind Extraordinary.* Los Angeles: Into the Classroom Media.

1998e. Extraordinary Cognitive Achievements: A Symbols Systems
        Approach. In W. Damon, ed., *Handbook of Child Psychology, 5th
        Edition, Volume 1: Theoretical Models of Human Development* (New
        York: Wiley), 415–466.

1998f. Melding Progressive and Traditional Perspectives. In M.S. Wiske, ed.,
        Teaching for Understanding (San Francisco: Jossey-Bass), 345–350.

1998g. With V. Boix-Mansilla. What Are the Qualities of Understanding? In
        M.S. Wiske, ed., *Teaching for Understanding* (San Francisco: Jossey-
        Bass), 161–196.

1998h. Response to Perry Klein's "Multiplying the Problems of Intelligence
        by Eight." *Canadian Journal of Education* 23: 1, 96–102.

1998i.   Leadership 1. *K–12 Education: Perspectives on the Future*, 5–24. Based on a presentation to the Van Andel Educators Institute, August 1997, Grand Rapids: Van Andel Education Institution.

1998j.   Gifts and Responsibilities: A Tribute to Raphi Amram. Tribute delivered at the Israel Arts and Science Academy, Jerusalem (19th May).

1998k.   With A. Gregory, M. Csikszentmihalyi, and W. Damon. The Empirical Basis of Good Work: Methodological Considerations. *Good Work Project Occasional Paper #3* (revised in 2001). Available at *goodworkproject.org*.

1998l.   With M. Michaelson and B. Solomon. The Origins of Good Work. Unpublished paper from the *Project on Humane Creativity.*

1998m.   With D. Cavanaugh, J. Fallows, R. Gilmartin, M. Gearan, L. Nash, and W. Isaacson. The New Leadership: Visions for the 21st Century. Panel discussion presented by *Harvard Magazine* and *The Conference Board.* New York.

1998n.   Keynote address delivered to the Evaluation and Pedagogy Conference. Lisbon, 10th October. Published in the Proceedings.

1998o.   The Intelligences of Leaders. *International Journal of Leadership in Education* 1: 2 (April–June), 203–06.

1998p.   Dreams, Nightmares, and the Unknown. *New Statesman* 29 (6th February).

1998q.   Inside the Minds of a Creator: Comments on an Interview with the British Painter Emma Sergeant. *The Sunday Times* (Spring 1998).

1998r.   An Interview with Howard Gardner. *The High School Magazine* 5: 3 (January–February), 50–53. Reprinted in *Intelligence Connections* 6: 3 (February 1998), 2–7.

1998s.   A Multiplicity of Intelligences. *Scientific American Presents: Exploring Intelligence* (A Special Issue of *Scientific American*), 19–23.

1998t.   Low Test Scores Are No Disgrace. *New York Times* (2nd March), A21.

1998u.   Les Sept Chances. *Le Monde de L'Èducation* (January), 53.

1998v.   An Intelligent Way to Progress. *The Independent.* Education section (London, 19th March), 4, 5. A reply to John White, London University.

1998w. Writing Different Kinds of Books, Non-Fiction Style. Unpublished paper based on remarks made at Wesleyan University (April).

1998x.   Navigating toward Good Work. Unpublished remarks at the Pennsylvania State University commencement (8th August).

1998y.   Howard Gardner's Alternative to the Educational Wars. Letter to the Editor, *Education Week* (5th August).

1998z.   The TIMSS, the *Times,* and the Times. *Harvard Education Letter* 7 (September–October). Cambridge, Massachusetts: Harvard Graduate School of Education.

1998aa. What do Tests Test? *New York Times* (4th December), op ed. Reprinted in *School Board News,* publication of the National School Boards Association, Alexandria, Virginia.

1998ab. Does IQ Matter? *Commentary*. Response to "IQ Since the Bell Curve," by C. Chabris. *Commentary* (August 1998), 13–14.

1998ac. Preface to D. Allen, *Assessing Student Learning* (New York: Teachers College Press).

1998ad. Foreword to Korean Edition of *Multiple Intelligences: The Theory in Practice*.

1998ae. Do Parents Count? Review of *The Nurture Assumption,* by J.R. Harris. *New York Review of Books* 45: 17 (5th November), 19–22. Translated and reprinted in *Das Magazine* 50: 98, 24–32.

1999a. *The Disciplined Mind: What All Students Should Understand.* New York: Simon and Schuster. Translated into Portuguese, German, Spanish, Chinese (Taiwan), Italian, Swedish, Korean, Hebrew, Danish, Turkish, Romanian, and Croatian. Excerpted in *The Futurist* 34: 2 (March–April 2000), 30–32. Paperback edition with new afterword, "A Tale of Two Barns" (New York: Penguin Putnam, 2000).

1999b. *Intelligence Reframed: Multiple Intelligences for the 21st Century.* New York: Basic Books. Translated into German, Spanish, Korean, Hebrew, Chinese, Swedish, Portuguese, Japanese, Italian, Bulgarian, Polish, Turkish, Dutch and Croatian.

1999c. *Çoklu Zekâ: Görüşmeler ve Makaleler* [Multiple Intelligences: Interviews and Essays], edited by C. Vickers. Istanbul: Enka Okullari.

1999d. Are there Additional Intelligences? The Case for Naturalist, Spiritual, and Existential Intelligences. In J. Kane, ed., *Education, Information, and Transformation* (Upper Saddle River: Prentice Hall), 111–131. Reprinted in *Gifted Education Press Quarterly* 11: 2 (Spring 1997), 2–5. Translated into Italian in R. Vianello and C. Cornoldi, eds., *Intelligenze Multiple in una Società Multiculturale* (Bergamo: Edizioni Junior, 1999), 7–26.

1999e. With E. Policastro. From Case Studies to Robust Generalizations: An Approach to the Study of Creativity. In R. Sternberg, ed., *Handbook of Creativity* (New York: Cambridge University Press), 213–225.

1999f. With B. Torff. The Vertical Mind: The Case for Multiple Intelligences. In M. Anderson, ed., *The Development of Intelligence* (East Sussex: Psychology Press), 139–159.

1999g. Multiple Approaches to Understanding. In C.M. Reigeluth, ed., *Instructional-Design Theories and Models: A New Paradigm of Instructional Theory*, Volume 2 (Mahwah: Erlbaum), 69–89.

1999h. With B. Solomon and K. Powell. Multiple Intelligences. In M. Runco and S. Pritzker, eds., *Encyclopedia of Creativity*, Volume 2 (San Diego: Academic Press), 273–283.

1999i. With V. Boix-Mansilla. On Disciplinary Lenses and Interdisciplinary Work. In S.S. Wineburg and P.L. Grossman, eds., *Interdisciplinary Curriculum: Challenges to Implementation* (New York: Teachers College Press), 17–38.

1999j. The Vehicle and the Vehicles of Leadership. *American Behavioral Scientist* 42: 6, 849–863. Based on a presentation to the Center for Advanced Study in the Behavioral Sciences, Stanford University (April 1998).

1999k. De la Responsabilité du chercheur au XXIe siècle [The Responsibility of the Scientific Researcher in the 21st Century]. *Dialogues* 52, 19–22.

1999l. A Disciplined Approach to School Reform. *Peabody Journal of Education* 74: 1, 166–173.

1999m. Howard Gardner Debates James Traub on Multiple Intelligences. *Cerebrum: The Dana Forum on Brain Science* 1: 2 (October), 13–36.

1999n. The Ethical Responsibilities of Professionals. In L. Hetland and S. Veenema, eds., *The Project Zero Classroom: Views on Understanding* (Cambridge, Massachusetts: Harvard Project Zero), 169–176.

1999o. Alexander Calder: The Circus. In *Frames of Reference: Looking at American Art, 1900–1950* (New York: Whitney Museum of American Art), 169–171.

1999p. Intelligence. Entry in the *Fontana/Norton Dictionary of Modern Thought*.

1999q. Who Owns Intelligence? *Atlantic Monthly* (February), 67–76. Excerpted in *Gifted Education Press Quarterly* 13: 3 (Summer 1999), 2–4. Translated and reprinted in *Pluri Verso* (Spring 2001), 6–16. Reprinted in *Annual Editions Psychology, 31st Edition*, 88–95. Translated into Chinese, *Peking University Education Review* (2004).

1999r. A Prescription for Peace. *Time* (25th January), 62–63. Reprinted in *r.w.t.* (November 1999), 16–18.

1999s. The Wonder of it All. *Hartford Courant* (31st January), C1, 5.

1999t. Thought Leader: Howard Gardner, Interview with Joel Kurtzman. *Strategy and Business*, 90–99.

1999u. Rethinking Education. *World Link, Magazine of the World Economic Forum* (May–June), 16–20.

1999v. With M. Kimmelman. Keeping the Arts in Mind and the Mind on the Arts, Interview with Michael Kimmelman. *New York Times* (14th February), Section 2, 38, 40.

1999w. Was Darwin's Creativity Darwinian? *Psychological Inquiry* 10: 4, 338–340. Commentary on D.K. Simonton's "Creativity as Blind Variation and Selection/Retention."

1999x. Embodying the Story. *Across the Board* 23 (April). Based on a presentation at the Metropolitan Club in New York City, 20th October, 1998.

1999y. Harvard's Howard Gardner Teaches Parents to Nurture Children's Natural Gifts for Learning. *Bottom Line/Personal* 11 (1st September).

1999z. The Disciplined Mind (Debate with E.D. Hirsch). *New York Times,* (1st September), A1, A14. Reprinted as Getting the Discussion Started:

Two Views on how to Get Johnny to Read and Think. *Jewish Education Leadership* 2 (Winter 2004), 56–59.

1999aa. The Hay Meeting of Multiple Intelligences and the Arts. *Harvard Education Letter* 15: 6 (November–December), 5.

1999ab. Keynote address to Conference on Cognitive Processes of Children Engaged in Musical Activity. Urbana, June 3rd–5th. Published in *Bulletin of the Council for Research in Music Education* 142 (Fall 1999), 9–21.

1999ac. (1) African Civil Wars; (2) Evolutionary Theory Is Not Intuitive, Creationism Is. Response to What Is Today's Most Important Unreported Story? www.edge.org/3rd_culture.

1999ad. Getting Smart about Intelligence. *The Philadelphia Inquirer* (5th December), D7. Reprinted as Rethinking the Concept of Intelligence. *Boston Globe* (1st January, 2000), A23.

1999ae. With M. Scherer. The Understanding Pathway: A Conversation with Howard Gardner. *Educational Leadership* 57: 3 (November), 12–16.

1999af. With S. Hayes. Interview. *Creative Classroom* (November– December). Reprinted as "Making the Most of Young Minds," *The Education Digest* 65: 6 (February 2000), 4–6.

1999ag. With A.J. Vogl. The True, the Good, and the Beautiful. Interview in *Across the Board* 36: 9 (October), 27–32.

1999ah. Foreword to J. Cohen, *Educating Minds and Hearts: Social Emotional Learning and the Passage into Adolescence* (New York: Teachers College Press), ix–xi.

1999ai. Foreword to Chinese Edition of *Multiple Intelligences: The Theory in Practice.*

1999aj. The Enigma of Erik Erikson. Review of *Identity's Architect,* by L.J. Friedman. *New York Review of Books* 46: 11, 51–56.

1999ak. With Pencils Sharpened. *The Big Test: The Secret History of the American Meritocracy,* by N. Lemann. *Harvard Magazine* 29 (November–December), 31–35.

1999al. With B. Torff. Conceptual and Experiential Cognition in Music. *Journal of Aesthetic Education* 33: 4 (Winter), 93–106. Also in *Musings: Art Education Essays in Honor of Bennett Reimer.* In J. Richmond and Webster, eds., unpublished festschrift presented to Bennett Reimer at Northwestern University, Evanston, on 6th June, 1997.

2000a. The Giftedness Matrix: A Developmental Perspective. In R. Friedman and B. Shore, eds., *Talents Unfolding: Cognition and Development* (Washington, D.C.: American Psychological Association), 77–88. Based on a paper presented at the Symposium on Giftedness, University of Kansas, Lawrence (February 1992).

2000b. With J. Davis. Symbolic Literacies: The Developmental Portrait Research Has Provided. In R. Smith, ed., *Readings in Discipline-*

Based Art Education (Reston: National Art Education Association), 257–263.

2000c. The Case Against Spiritual Intelligence. *International Journal for the Psychology of Religion* 10: 1, 27–34. Response to "The Psychology of Ultimate Concern: Personality, Spirituality, and Intelligence," by R. Emmons.

2000d. Project Zero: Nelson Goodman's Legacy in Arts Education. *Journal of Aesthetics and Art Criticism* 58: 3, 245–49.

2000e. With M. Connell. Response to "The Theory of Multiple Intelligences: A Case of Missing Cognitive Matter," by Nicholas Allix. *Australian Journal of Education*, 288–293.

2000f. Now that the Battle's Over. Informal remarks on the occasion of receipt of the Samuel T. Orton Award by the International Dyslexia Association, Chicago (November 1999). In *Annals of Dyslexia* 50, 9–16.

2000g. The Complete Tutor. *Technos* 9: 3, 10–13.

2000h. Dissolving Repression: A Half–Century Report. In N. Blackmun and M. Tymoczko, eds., *Born into a World at War* (Manchester: St. Jerome), 201–06.

2000i. Jerome Bruner as Educator: Personal Reflections, a Postscript. In D. Bakhurst and S. Shanker, eds., *Culture, Language, Self: Essays in Honor of Jerome Bruner* (New York: Sage).

2000j. In Dedication to Edgar Basil Zurif. In Y. Grodzinsky, L. Shapiro, and D. Swinney, eds., *Language and the Brain: Representation and Processing* (San Diego: Academic Press), xix–xxi.

2000k. Can Technology Exploit Our Many Ways of Knowing? In D.T. Gordon, ed., *The Digital Classroom: How Technology Is Changing the Way We Teach and Learn* (Cambridge, Massachusetts: President and Fellows of Harvard College), 32–35. A special publication of the *Harvard Education Letter.* Reprinted in J. Ohler, ed., *Future Courses* (Bloomington: Technos, 2001), 92–96.

2000l. Response to "Why the Future Doesn't Need Us," by B. Joy. *Wired,* www.wired.com/wired/archives/8.04/joy.html (May–June). In *World Link: Magazine of the World Economic Forum* 17.

2000m. An Education for the Future. Unpublished keynote address delivered to the Tsuzuki International Scholarship Fund's Symposium, Tokyo (21st May).

2000n. With M. Csikszentmihalyi and W. Damon. The Project on Good Work: A Description. Unpublished description of ongoing research projection (April 2000).

2000o. With A.M. Paul. Future Smart: An Interview with Howard Gardner. *Salon.com,* www.salon.com (5th January).

2000p. With P.M. Senge. The Context of Reframing Learning: A Conversation. In P.M. Senge, *et al.*, *Schools that Learn: A Fifth*

Discipline Fieldbook for Educators, Parents, and Everyone who cares about Education (New York: Doubleday), 555–566.

2000q. Extraordinary Deviations. In K. Kay, ed., *Uniquely Gifted: Identifying and Meeting the Needs of the Twice-Exceptional Student* (Gilsum: Avocus).

2000r. Vygotsky to the Rescue! *Boston Review* 25: 6, 11–12. Response to "The Future of Affirmative Action," by S. Sturm and L. Guinier, *Boston Review* 25: 6, 4–10. Reprinted. in Guinier and Sturm, eds., *Who's Qualified?* (Boston: Beacon Press), 49–54.

2000s. With B. Solomon. The Origins of Good Work: Getting Kids, Parents, and Coaches on the Same Page. *CYD Journal* 1: 3 (Summer), 37–41.

2000t. With R. Weiss. Howard Gardner Talks about Technology. *Training and Development* (September), 52–56.

2000u. Using Multiple Intelligences to Improve Negotiation Theory and Practice. *Negotiation Journal* 16: 4 (October), 321–24. Based on remarks on March 10th, 2000, at Harvard University Law School.

2000v. With E. Cicerone. Tanti individui, tante intelligenze. Interview in *Le Scienze* 386 (October), 12–13.

2000w. With C. Delacampagne. Howard Gardner: l'intelligence au pluriel. *La Recherche* 337 (December), 109–111.

2000x. The Testing Obsession. *Los Angeles Times* (31st December), M1, M6.

2000y. Let's Get Past the Bell Curve. *Cerebrum* 2: 4 (Fall), 7–9. Letter to the editor in response to L. Gottfredson, "Pretending that Intelligence Doesn't Matter." *Cerebrum* (Summer 2000).

2000z. Howard Gardner, Unfiltered. *Policy Review* 99 (February–March), 89–92. Letter to the Editor in response to "The Schools They Deserve," by M. Eberstadt, *Policy Review* (October–November 1999).

2000aa. An Education Based on Science and Values. Introduction to Korean edition of *Intelligence Reframed.*

2000ab. A Tale of Two Barns. Afterword to the paperback edition of *The Disciplined Mind* (New York: Penguin Putnam).

2000ac. Paroxysms of Choice. Review of *Charter Schools in Action: Renewing Public Education,* by C. Finn, Jr., B. Manno, and G. Vanourek; *When Schools Compete: A Cautionary Tale,* by E. Fiske and H. Ladd; *Inside Charter Schools: The Paradox of Radical Decentralization,* edited by B. Fuller; *A Legacy of Learning: Your Stake in Standards and New Kinds of Public Schools,* by D. Kearns and J. Harvey; and *The Market Approach to Education: An Analysis of America's First Voucher Program,* by J. Witte. *New York Review of Books* 47, 44–49.

2000ad. Introduction to S. Kallenbach and J. Viens, eds., *MI Grows Up: Multiple Intelligences in Adult Education* (New York: Teachers College Press).

2000ae. With M. Csikszentmihalyi. Science and Art, in Extremis: The Writings of George Klein. *Boston Book Review.*

2001a. With M. Csikszentmihalyi and W. Damon. *Good Work: When Excellence and Ethics Meet.* New York: Basic Books. Paperback edition with Afterword, 2002. Translated into Korean, Spanish, German, Portuguese, Swedish, Chinese and Romanian. Selected as one of ten most important books in Hong Kong, 2003. Chosen as a Book of Distinction by the Templeton Foundation.

2001b. Minds and Understanding. Tape 3. *Harvard Project Zero Educating for Understanding,* video set. Port Chester: National Professional Resources.

2001c. Jerome S. Bruner as Educator. In J.A. Palmer and D.E. Cooper, eds., *100 Great Thinkers on Education* (London: Routledge).

2001d. Creators: Multiple Intelligences. In K. Pfenninger and V. Shubik, eds., *The Origins of Creativity* (New York: Oxford University Press), 117–143. Based on a presentation to the Given Biomedical Conference, Aspen, 1993.

2001e. The Philosophy-Science Continuum. *The Chronicle of Higher Education* (9th March), B7–B10.

2001f. Combining Rationality with Responsibility. Remarks on receiving the Medal of the Presidency of the Italian Republic, Pio Manzù (October). Published in *Il Fuoco nel Cristallo* 2, 97–105.

2001g. With P. Sims. An interview with Howard Gardner: Arts Education in the Museum Environment. *MoMA: Magazine of the Museum of Modern Art,* 12–13.

2001h. An Education for the Future: The Foundation of Science and Values. Paper presented to symposium of The Royal Palace Foundation, Amsterdam, 14th March. Available at http://pzweb.harvard.edu. Italian: Un educatiozione per il futuro. *Nuovo Antologia (Rivista di lettere, science, et arti)* 2002 (January–March). Translated into Spanish.

2001i. Too Soon for a Requiem. *World Link, Magazine of the World Economic Forum* (March–April), 4–5

2001j. Stick to Testing Basics. *New York Times* (21st April), A25.

2001k. With W. Amanna. What Leaders Have in Common. *PS for Business Communicators.* Newsletter of the Executive Communications Group (Spring), 1, 3.

2001l. Navigating toward Good Work. Remarks at University of Toronto, 21st June.

2001m. Carrying Out Good Work in Turbulent Times. *Boston Globe* (27th August), A9.

2001n. Looking at the World through Cognitive Glasses. *Newsday* (20th September), A51.

2001o. Remarks upon receipt of the Children's Arts Medal from Young Audiences. New York (23rd April).

2001p. Graduation Address. The Ross School, Southampton, New York (16th June).

2001q. Leadership talk delivered to Lions Leadership Program, Young, and Rubicam. Prague, May.

2001r. What Human Beings Become. *Harvard Graduate School of Education's Alumni Bulletin* 14: 1, 19.

2001s. Le conception standard de l'intelligence est fausse. Interview. In Jean-Claude Ruano-Borbalan, ed., *Éduquer et Former* (Paris: Editions Sciences Humaines), 165–172.

2001t. Good Work at Harvard. *Harvard Book Store* (September).

2001u. With W. Fischman. Lessons in Homework. *Newark Star-Ledger* (7th January).

2001v. Foreword to J.S. Renzulli, *Enriching Curriculum for all Students* (Arlington Heights: Skylight).

2001w. Introduction to new edition of M. Mead, *Growing Up in New Guinea* (New York: Harper Collins), xv–xxiv,

2001x. Foreword to Japanese edition of *Intelligence Reframed.*

2001y. Introduction and conclusion to Reggio Children and Project Zero, *Making Learning Visible: Children as Individual and Group Learners* (Reggio Emilia: Reggio Children).

2001z. The Death of Copyediting and Fact Checking . . . and the Costs Thereof. Unpublished article.

2002a. *Howard Gardner in Hong Kong.* Edited by L. Lo. Hong Kong: Hong Kong Institute of Educational Research.

2002b. With R. DiNozzi, producer. *M.I. Millennium: Multiple Intelligences for the New Millennium.* Los Angeles: Into the Classroom Media.

2002c. With K. Barberich. Good Work in Business. In M. Goldsmith, *et al.*, *Leading for Innovation* (New York: Drucker Foundation), 57–69.

2002d. With W. Williams, T. Blythe, N. White, Li, Jin, and R. Sternberg. Practical Intelligence for School: Developing Metacognitive Sources of Achievement in Adolescence. *Developmental Review* 22: 2, 162–210.

2002e. Mente e cervello: nuove prospettive in educazione. In E. Frauenfelder and F. Santoianni, eds., *Le Scienze Bioeducative* (Naples: Liguori), 177–187.

2002f. With M. Suarez-Orozco. Education for Globalization. Paper prepared for the Conference on Globalization and Education, 11th–13th April.

2002g. Good Work: Where Excellence and Ethics Meet. Paper presented at the International Network on Personal Meaning Conference, British Columbia. Published in Proceedings.

2002h. It's Time for Bush to Say, God Bless Us, Every One. *Newsday* (23rd January), A30.

2002i. A Job Well Done. *Worldlink: The Magazine of the World Economic Forum* (January–February), 88–90.

2002j. The Three Faces of Intelligence. *Daedalus* (Winter), 139–142. Translated into German in *Gluck* (Stuttgart: Klett Cotta), 391–99. Translated into Castilian and Catalan in *Web of Music.*

2002k. In a World of Work's Realignment, Good Careers Move to the Forefront. *Boston Globe* (24th February), E1.

2002l. Tests of Good Work. *Executive Excellence* (February), 12.

2002m. Coping with Fragility: A Psychologist's View. World Economic Forum Special Publication (January).

2002n. Interview with Steen Larsen. *Education and Humanism* (Spring). Denmarks Padaogiske Universitet.

2002o. The Tipping Point Between Success and Failure. *NEXOS*. Mexico.

2002p. Contemporary Consciousness and the Study of the Humanities. Comments on Diane Ravitch's "Education After the Culture Wars." *Daedalus* 131, 22–25.

2002q. Good Work Well Done. *Chronicle of Higher Education* (22nd February). Reprinted in *The Daily Telegraph.*

2002r. Test for Aptitude, Not Speed. *New York Times.*

2002s. The Quality and Qualities of Educational Research. *Education Week* 72 (4th September), 49.

2002t. Good Work: An Interview with Howard Gardner, by Randy Seevers and Michael Shaughnessy. *North American Journal of Psychology* 5, 1.

2002u. In the World of Work's Realignment, Good Careers Move to the Forefront. *Boston Globe* (24th February), E1, 2.

2002v. You Can't Test Lessons the Way You Do Meds. *Newsday* (30th December).

2002w. Too Many Choices? Review of *The Other Boston Busing Story: What's Won and Lost Across the Boundary Line,* by S. Eaton and *Kingdom of Choice: Culture and Controversy in the Home Schooling Movement,* by M. Stevens. *New York Review of Books* 49: 6, 51–54.

2002x. Rhapsody in Bloom. Review of *Genius,* by Harold Bloom. *Boston Globe* (20th October), D6, D9.

2002y. Learning from Extraordinary Minds. In M. Ferrari, ed., *The Pursuit of Excellence through Education* (Mahwah: Erlbaum), 1–20.

2003a. Csikszentmihalyi, M. and R. DiNozzi, (producer). *Flow: Interview by Howard Gardner* (Los Angeles: Into the Classroom Media).

2003b. Three Distinct Meanings of Intelligence. In R. Sternberg, J. Lautrey, and T. Lubart, eds., *Models of Intelligence: International Perspectives* (Washington, D.C.: American Psychological Association), 43–54.

2003c. My Way. In R. Sternberg, ed., *Psychologists Defying the Crowd* (Washington, D.C.: APA Books), 78–88.

2003d. With C. von Károlyi and V. Ramos-Ford. Multiple Intelligences: A Perspective on Giftedness. In N. Colangelo and G. Davis, eds., *Handbook of Gifted Education,* third edition (Boston: Allyn and Bacon), 100–112.

2003e. How to Teach for Understanding. Challenges and Opportunities. In C. Coreil, ed., *Multiple Intelligences, Howard Gardner, and New*

Methods in College Teaching: Papers from the Fifth Annual Urban Conference: Pedagogical Innovations in Higher Education. (Jersey City: New Jersey City University).

2003f. The Ethical Responsibilities of Scientists. In J. Scheler, S. Marshall, and M. Palmisano, eds., *Science Literacy for the 21st Century: Essays in Honor of Leon Lederman* (Aurora: Illinois Mathematics and Science Academy).

2003g. Multiple Intelligences after Twenty Years. Paper presented at the American Educational Research Association, Chicago 21st April 21. To appear in revised form as introduction to the 21st year edition of *Frames of Mind.* Reprinted in *Kognition and Paedagogik,* Denmark (2004). Translated into Chinese and French.

2003h. Higher Education for the Era of Globalisation. *The Psychologist* 16: 10, 520–22.

2003i. Afterword for *Opening Doors to the Arts, the Mind and Beyond: Readings About Learning in Museums and Schools.* Mexico City: Consejo Nacional Para la Cultura y el Arte.

2003j. With L. Abarbanell. Teaching our Children Well. *CIO* (Fall–Spring), 40–41.

2003k. Can Technology Exploit our Many Ways of Knowing? In J. Ohler, ed., *Future Courses* (Bloomington: Technos), 92–96.

2003l. My Life as a Teacher. Remarks at the Klingenstein Award Ceremony, 28th February.

2003m. Make Teaching a True Profession. *Newsday* (23rd April), A31.

2003n. The *Real* Head Start. *Boston Sunday Globe* (7th September), D1, 4.

2003o. With M. Suarez-Orozco. Educating Billy Wang for the World of Tomorrow. *Education Week* 44 (22nd October), 34.

2003p. Howard Gardner in American Education. In R. Hefner, ed., *A Conversational History of Modern America* (New York: Carroll and Graf), 537–38.

2003q. Higher Education for the Era of Globalisation. *The Psychologist* 16: 10 (October), 520–22.

2003r. Gunnar Myrdal's *An American Dilemma*: Do Whites Still Wish that Blacks Would Simply Go Away? *The Journal of Blacks in Higher Education* 42 (Winter 2003–2004).

2003s. With V. Boix-Mansilla. Assessing Interdisciplinary Work at the Frontier: An Empirical Exploration of Symptoms of Quality. Available at www.Interdisciplines.org. (Paris: CNRS and Institut Nicod).

2003t. With M.W. Connell and K. Sheridan. Abilities and Domains. In R.J. Sternberg and E.L. Grigorenko, eds., *The Psychology of Abilities, Comptencies, and Expertise* (New York: Cambridge University Press), 126–155.

2003u. Confusion of Phenotype with Genotype: The Case of Jayson Blair. Remarks at the workshop on Greatest Hits in Positive Psychology at the University of Pennsylvania, 27th May.

2004a. With W. Fischman, B. Solomon, and D. Greenspan. *Making Good: How Young People Cope with Moral Dilemmas at Work.* Cambridge: Harvard University Press. Translated into Spanish, Korean, and Chinese.

2004b. With D. Schutte and B. Solomon. Influences on the Development of Young Talent. In M. Ferrari and L. Shavinina, eds., *Beyond Knowledge: Extracognitive Facets in Developing High Ability* (Mahwah: Erlbaum), 120–135.

2004c. With M. Keinanen. Vertical and Horizontal Mentoring for Creativity. In R.J. Sternberg, E.L. Grigorenko, and J.L. Singer, eds., *Creativity: From Potential to Realization.* (Washington, D.C.: American Psychological Association).

2004d. Scientific Psychology: Should We Bury It or Praise It? In R.J. Sternberg, ed., *Unity in Psychology: Possibility or Pipedream?* (Washington, D.C.: American Psychological Association).

2004e. How Education Changes: Considerations of History, Science, and Values. In M. Suarez-Orozco and D. Qin–Hilliard, eds., *Globalization: Culture and Education in the New Millennium* (Berkeley: University of California Press).

2004f. Audiences for the Theory of Multiple Intelligences. *Teachers College Record* 106, 111, 212–19.

2004g. What We Do and Don't Know about Learning. *Daedalus* (Winter), 5–12.

2004h. One Way of Making a Social Scientist. In J. Brockman, ed., *Curious Minds: How a Child Becomes a Scientist* (New York: Pantheon).

2004i. With M. Farah, J. Illes, R. Cook-Deegan, E. Kandel, P. King, E. Parens, B. Shakian, and P.R. Wolpe. Neurocognitive Enhancement: What Can We Do and What Should We Do? *Nature Reviews Neuroscience* 5 (May), 421–25.

2004j. Elliot Eisner as Educator. In B. Uhrmacher and J. Matthews, eds., *Intricate Palette: Working the Ideas of Elliot Eisner* (Upper Saddle River: Pearson).

2004k. The Hundred Languages of Successful Educational Reform: Comments in Honor of Loris Malaguzzi for the Reggio Schools in *Children in Europe.*

2004l. Discipline, Understanding, and Community. *Journal of Curriculum Studies* 36: 2 (March–April), 233–36.

2004m. With Ellie McGrath. The Many Faces of Power Learning (an interview with Howard Gardner). *NRTA Live and Learn* (Winter).

2004n. Taking the Next Steps for Exploring Intelligences in the Future. An interview with Howard Gardner. *Southern Journal of Teaching and Education* (Spring).

2004o. What We Know about Human Creativity. *Think On: The Magazine of Atlanta AG* 4, 10–15.

2004p. 9/11 Report Reveals a Hunger for Trustees. *Boston Sunday Globe* (15th August), D11. Reprinted in *Sacramento Bee.*

2004q. Introduction to *The Unschooled Mind,* second edition (New York: Basic Books).

2004r. Foreword to M. Kornhaber, E. Fierros, and S. Veenema, eds., *Multiple Intelligences: Best Ideas from Research and Practice* (Boston: Pearson Education).

2004s. O Brother, Who Art Thou? Review of *The Pecking Order,* by D. Conley. *Boston Sunday Globe,* Books, D6.

2004t. Turning Away from the Spotlight. Review of *When the Music Stopped: Discovering My Mother,* by T. Cottle. *Boston Sunday Globe*, Books, E7.

2004u. Foreword to Korean edition of *Flow,* by M. Czikszentmihalyi.

2004v. Review of *Cult of Personality: How Personality Tests are Leading Us to Miseducate our Children, Mismanage Our Companies, and Misunderstand Ourselves,* by Annie Murphy Paul. *Boston Sunday Globe*, Books, D6.

2004w. *Changing Minds: The Art and Science of Changing Our Own and Other People's Minds.* Boston: Harvard Business School Press. Translated into French, Spanish, Japanese, Italian, Korean, Portuguese, Greek, Polish, Russian, Norwegian, Dutch, Chinese, Danish, Romanian, and Turkish. Awarded Strategy + Business's Best Business Books of the Year (2004).

2004x. With L. Barendsen. Is the Social Entrepreneur a New Type of Leader? *Leader to Leader* 34, 43–50.

2004y. An Education Grounded in Biology: Interdisciplinary and Ethical Considerations. To be published in Proceedings. Paper presented at the conference on Usable Knowledge in Mind, Brain, and Education.

2004z. Academic Integrity Begins with Professors. *The Appian* (18th October).http://gseacademic.harvard.edu/~theappian/articles/fall04/gardner1004.htm.

2004aa. Can There Be Societal Trustees in America Today? Presented at the Forum for the Future of Higher Education's Aspen Symposium (August).

2004ab. The Brain Basis of Talent. *EDGE: The World Question Center.* http://www.edge.org/q2005/q05_print.html.

2004ac. Project Zero and the Arts in Education Program: Passion Tempered by Discipline (October).

2004ad. With A. Battro. A Dialogue with Antonio Battro (December).

2004ae. A Multiplicity of Intelligences: In Tribute to Professor Luigi Vignolo. *Neuropsychology and Neurolinguistics in Progress: A Tribute to Luigi A Vignolo.*

2005a. Scientific Psychology: Should We Bury It or Praise It? In R. Sternberg, ed., *Unity in Psychology: Possibility or Pipe Dream* (Washington, D.C.: American Psychological Association), 77–90.

2005b. With J. Solomon and P. Marshall. Crossing Boundaries to Generative Wisdom: An Analysis of Professional Work. In R.J. Sternberg and J. Jordan, eds., *A Handbook of Wisdom* (New York: Cambridge University Press).

2005c. Beyond Markets and Individuals: A Focus on Educational Goals. In R. Hersh and J. Merrow, eds., *Degrees of Mediocrity: Higher Education at Risk* (New York: Palgrave-Macmillan).

2005d. With K. Sheridan and E. Zinchenko. Neuroethics in Education (in press). In J. Illes, ed., *Neuroethics: Defining the Issues in Research, Practice, and Policy* (New York: Oxford University Press), 265–275.

2005e. With V. Boix-Mansilla. Teaching for Global Consciousness, Conceptualizations, and Practical Tales. Presented at the Stockholm-Ross Project's Globalization and Learning Conference, Stockholm (17th–18th March).

2005f. With S. Verducci. Good Work: Its Nature, Its Nurture. In F. Huppert, ed., *The Science of Well-being* (New York: Oxford University Press), 343–360.

2005g. With J. Chen. Assessment Based on Multiple Intelligences Theory. In D. Flanagan and P. Harrison, eds., *Contemporary Intellectual Assessment: Theories, Tests, and Issues*, second edition (New York: Guilford).

2005h. Mentes Cambiantes. *Revista International Magisterio: Educacion y Pedagogia* 14, 7–9.

2005i. Multiple Lenses on the Mind. Paper delivered at Expo-Gestion, Bogota, May 2005. www.howardgardner.com.

2005j. With L. Shulman. The Professions in America Today: Crucial but Fragile. *Daedalus*, 13–15.

2005k. Compromised Work. *Daedalus*, 42–51.

2005l. With L. Barendsen. The Three Elements of Good Leadership in Rapidly Changing Times. In F. Hesselbein and M. Goldsmith, eds., *The New Leader of the Future* (San Francisco: Jossey-Bass). Also in J. Knapp, ed., *Festschrift for Betty Siegel*.

2005m. With P. Marshall. Response to Simone Reagor. *Daedalus*, 2–3.

2005n. The Synthesizing Mind: Making Sense of the Deluge of Information. Paper presented at the Joint Workshop of the Pontifical Academies of Sciences and Social Sciences: Education and Globalization, Rome, 16th November.

2005o. The Loss of Trust. *Boston Globe* (18th June), A13.

2005p. A Missed Connection. *Boston Globe* (20th July), A13.

2005q. With W. Fischman. Inspiring Good Work. *Greater Good* II: I, 10–13.

2005r. Beyond the Herd Mentality. *Education Week* 44.

2005s. Cronies Mispochoh, and Trustees. Presented at the opening of the Steinhart Social Research Institute (2nd November).

2005t.   Review of *Blink,* by Malcolm Gladwell. *Washington Post Book World,*
         3 (15th January).

2005u.   Introduction to Ann Lewin Benham, *Possible Schools* (New York:
         Teachers College Press).

2005v.   Foreword to S. Baum, J. Viens, and B. Slatin, *Multiple Intelligences in
         the Elementary Classroom: A Teacher's Toolkit* (New York: Teachers
         College Press).

2005w.   Las Cincos Mentes del Futuro: Un Ensayo Educativo. Paidos Asterico.

2005x.   Service Learning and GoodWork®. Presented at National Conference
         on Service Learning, Long Beach. To be published in *Proceedings.*

2006a.   *The Development and Education of the Mind: The Collected Works of
         Howard Gardner* (London: Routledge). Translated into Italian.

2006b.   *Multiple Intelligences: New Horizons.* New York: Basic Books.
         Translated inti Italian, Spanish.

2006c.   With M. Keinänen and K. Sheridan. Opening up Creativity: The
         Lenses of Axis and Focus. In J. Kaufman and J. Baer, eds., *The
         Relationship between Creativity, Knowledge, and Reason* (New York:
         Cambridge University Press).

2006d.   With S. Moran. The Development of Extraordinary Achievements. In
         W. Damon, ed., *Handbook of Child Psychology,* sixth edition. Volume
         2, *Cognition, Perception, and Language* (New York: Wiley).

2006e.   With S. Moran. Multiple Intelligences: Do We Need a Central
         Intelligence Agency? In L. Meltzer, ed., *Understanding Executive
         Function: Implications and Opportunities for the Classroom* (New
         York: Guilford).

2006f.   Las Inteligencias Múltiples: ¿Mito o Realidad? Sister Montserrat of
         Collegio Montserrat, Barcelona.

2006g.   With W. Fischman and J. DiBara. Creating Good Education Against
         the Odds. *Cambridge Journal of Education.*

2006h.   The Synthesizing Leader. *Harvard Business Review.*

2006i.   Howard Gardner. In J. Brockman, ed., *What We Believe but Cannot
         Prove: Today's Leading Thinkers on Science in the Age of Creativity*
         (London: Free Press), 163–65.

2006j.   With J. Jacobs and H.H. Brownell. Interpreting Sarcasm: The
         Influence of Speaker Motivation. Submitted for Publication.

2006k.   The Domains of Play and Art: A Developmental Perspective. A
         Comment on Brian Sutton–Smith's Divorce of Play from Art.
         Submitted to *New Ideas Psychology.*

2006l.   Is There Moral Intelligence? In M. Runco, ed., *Perspective on
         Creativity Series* (Creskill: Hampton Press).

2006m.   With M. Kornhaber . Multiple Intelligences: Developments in
         Implementation and Theory. In M.A. Constas and R.J. Sternberg, eds.,
         Translating Theory and Research into Educational Practice (Mahwah:
         Erlbaum).

2006n. Seeing Earlier and Seeing Farther: In Tribute to Howard E. Gruber. In forthcoming Festschrift for Howard Gruber.

2006o. Keyboards. In S. Turkle, ed., *Evocative Objects: Things We Think With*.

2006p. A Copernican Shift in Philanthropy. Tribute to Claude Rosenberg, Jr.

2006q. Foreword to T. Hoerr, *Becoming a Multiple Intelligences School* (Alexandria: Association for Supervision and Curriculum Development).

2006r. Letter to Young People. On the website of Breakthrough Organization, Hong Kong, www.breakthrough.org.hk.

2006s. Afterword to V. Boix-Mansilla, *Opening Doors to the Arts*.

2006t. With L. Barendsen. On Social Entrepreneurship. *Leader to Leader*

2006v. Review of E Kandel, *In Search of Memory*. *Washington Post Book World* (April).

2006w. With S.Moran and M. Kornhaber. Orchestrating Multiple Intelligences. *Educational Leadership* (September).

2006x. Foreword to the paperback edition of *Changing Minds*.

2006y. On Failing to Grasp the Core of MI Theory: A Response to Visser *et al*. *Intelligence*.

2006z. With J. Benjamin and L. Pettingill. An Examination of Trust in Contemporary American Society. In B. Kellerman, ed., *Center for Public Leadership Working Papers*, Harvard University (Spring).

2006aa. With S. Moran. The Science in Multiple Intelligence Theory: A Response to Lynn Waterhouse. *Educational Psychologist*.

2006ab. Leaders Who Listen. *Harvard Crimson* (23rd February).

2006ac. Obituary, Howard Gruber 1992–2005. *American Psychologist*.

2006ad. In Memoriam: James O. Freedman, 1935–2006. Dartmouth College (15th May).

2006ae. Getting the Fundamentals Right and Opening to the Possibilities of the Human Spirit. In *Crossing Boundaries* (Reggio Emilia: Edizioni Junior).

2007a. *Five Minds for the Future*. Boston: Harvard Business School Press..

Index

absorption, as state, 124, 126
  core of, 138
  proclivity to, as trainable, 137
accelerated programs, as earned
  privilege, 43
Ackerman, P.L., 87
Albert, R.S., 175
Alexander the Great, 189
Alland, Alexander, 239
anthropologists, on belief in magic,
  116–17
Aristotle, 153
Arnheim, Rudolf, 12, 260, 332
artistic creativity, conceptual-experimental
  distinction in, 150
"Art of Hearing God" (conference), 128
Arts PROPEL, 333
Ashcroft, John, 213
assessment center methods, critique of,
  79
Atkinson, G., 124
Atlantic Philanthropies, 22
Augustine, St., 128
Austin, J.L., 204

Bamberger, Jeanne, 17
Barber, Theodore X., 122
Baritz, Loren, 201
Barnett, Susan, 293
Bate, Walter Jackson, 10
Battro, Antonio M., 304
Baudelaire, Charles, 256
Bauman, Patricia, 22
Beauchamp, C.M., 75

Beethoven, Ludwig van, 309
  Ninth Symphony, 1
Beier, M.E., 87
Bernard van Leer Foundation, 19, 62
Bernstein, Basil, 204
Binet, A., 107
Bloemaert, Hendrik, 153
Boden, Margaret A.
  Dimensions of Creativity, 143
Boix-Mansilla, Veronica, 21
Bonaparte, Napoleon, 189
Bourguignon, Erika, 120
Brockman, John
  Creativity: The Reality Club IV, 143
Brody, Nathan, 293, 297–300
Bromer, Lisa, 26
Brown, A.L., 105
Brown, Laurie Krasny, 18, 21
Brown, Roger, 11
Brownell, Hiram, 18
Bruner, Jerome, 2, 3, 11, 12, 13, 14, 24,
  30, 176, 283, 285, 315, 316
Bryant, John, 22
Burt, Cyril, 52
Butler, Lisa, 123

Caesar, Julius, 189
Callahan, James, 318
Caretta, T.R., 82
Carra, Carlo, 154
Carroll, J.B., 74
Caruso, D.R., 82, 83
Case, Robbie, 288
Cassirer, Ernst, 13, 61

397